The Search for Normality

THE SEARCH FOR NORMALITY

*National Identity and Historical Consciousness
in Germany Since 1800*

Stefan Berger

Berghahn Books
Providence • Oxford

First published in 1997 by

Berghahn Books

© 1997 Stefan Berger

Library of Congress Cataloging-in-Publication Data

Berger, Stefan.
    The search for normality : national identity and historical
consciousness in Germany since 1800 / Stefan Berger.
        p.   cm.
    Includes bibliographical references and index.
    ISBN 1-57181-863-4 (alk. paper)
    1. Conservatism--Germany--History--19th century. 2. Germany-
-Historiography. 3. Nationalism--Germany. 4. Conservatism-
-Germany--History--20th century. 5. Political culture--Germany.
I. Title.
DD204.B475   1996
907'.2043--dc21   96-53355
                                                          CIP

British Library Cataloguing in Publication Data

A catalogue record for this book is available from the
British Library.

Printed in the United States on acid-free paper.

Cover Illustration: 'Die Gerippe Spielen zum Tanz' 1944 (detail) by
Felix Nussbaum c DACS 1997

For Jutta

'For more than 150 years German historians have been writing in favour of a German nation ... They have wanted to revive or strengthen the German nation state, but only few have aimed at taming it.'

Hans-Ulrich Wehler, 'Einleitung', in: Theodor Schieder, *Das deutsche Kaiserreich von 1871 als Nationalstaat*

'There is no close relationship between "securing identity" and "German national history" or "European history", as is sometimes alleged ... If the task is to mediate between "life history" and "universal history", then there is no need at all for "national history".'

Bodo von Borries, *Geschichtsbewußtsein als Identitätsgewinn? Fachdidaktische Programmatik und Tatsachenforschung*

'The future has become more open, one waits expectantly and has the feeling of treading on thin ice.'

Jürgen Kocka, 'Die alte Bundesrepublik wird Geschichte', in *Frankfurter Rundschau*

CONTENTS

ACKNOWLEDGEMENTS

'Historians are dangerous. They have to be watched carefully.' These words, attributed to Nikita Kruschev, certainly give undue importance to the work of a small number of people engaged upon, what surely seems to most others, a wholly impractical task: to find answers to the questions, what happened in the past and why it happened the way it did. Yet, there is some truth in the late Soviet leader's comment, as historians have participated and intervened in public political debates for at least the last two centuries, routinely pointing to their position as privileged knowledge-holders of the past to legitimate their advice, both sought and unsought, for the present and future.

This study is based on close observation of the political-historical debates about nation-building in Germany which have unfolded over the past seven years or so, and relating these observations to the historical profession's history. Being a historian myself, I have a 'natural' interest in this profession. However, it has been impossible to do justice to the whole spectrum of its members and their work. By concentrating on the intervention of historians in public political debates, I have tended to overemphasise the importance of the 'big names' in the profession. This is certainly not out of disregard for the many hundreds of historians who produce extremely valuable and good work and who might not find themselves represented one way or another in the following pages. I have not attempted to demolish the many accomplishments of German historiography and its representatives. Almost all those historians whom I have criticised in the following have proven their talents as historians many times over. My criticisms do not, therefore, mean to challenge their reputation or the value of their historical work, for which I often have the highest regard. Yet I do believe that the trends and tendencies outlined here may well mark a new direction in which certain aspects of German historiography are moving.

As someone who grew up in the old Federal Republic but received most of his training as a historian in Britain, I felt enough of an outsider to watch and comment freely on the way the profession has been developing since reunification. However, being an outsider, of course, also means that one does not have access to much privileged and private information which historians closer to German academia will have – especially in a profession which is as gossipy and rumour-laden as the historical one. Hence, and not for this reason alone, this volume no doubt has many shortcomings which are entirely my own.

I should like to add that Wolfgang Wippermann's recent book *Wessen Schuld? Vom Historikerstreit zur Goldhagen-Kontroverse*, Berlin 1997, which – in an extremely lucid manner – also discusses aspects of the development of German historiography after 1989/90, only came to my attention after the manuscript had been typeset and was ready to be submitted to the printer.

Nevertheless, I would like to thank a number of people for their support and help in writing this book. My colleagues at the University of Wales, Cardiff have provided a stimulating and lively atmosphere for intellectual debate. David Hanley, as head of department, ensured that I had the time and financial means to carry out the necessary research. In particular I would like to thank David Jackson and Helmut Peitsch for reading and commenting on the whole manuscript. Kevin Passmore, Andy Croll, Mark Donovan, Chris Ealham and Jonathan Osmond read parts of it, and I have valued their suggestions greatly.

Furthermore I am indebted to Karen Schönwälder for reading the whole manuscript. Much more accomplished as a historiographer than myself, her critical comments have improved the volume in several ways. I am grateful to the organisers of the conference on 'German Historiography at Era's End' at Tel Aviv University (April 1995), the German history research seminar at the Institute of Historical Research, London (November 1995), and of the workshop on 'German History Since 1800' at UCL (January 1996) for inviting me to present part of this book's argument. On all three occasions I received many valuable comments. To put the German historiographical tradition into a comparative context and test the validity of some of my arguments in this book, I organised the conference 'Apologias for the Nation State. Historiography and Nation-Building in Italy, France and Germany since 1800', held at Cardiff between 9 and 11 April 1996. The papers and the discussions helped me to clarify a whole range of questions and issues, and I would like to thank all conference delegates from Britain, Germany, Italy, the United

States and Israel. I feel particularly indebted to Georg Iggers who addressed the conference and, during his stay in Cardiff, kindly discussed key aspects of this book with me. Finally I am grateful to all archivists and staff at the newspaper archives and libraries, listed in the bibliography, who had to put up with me. My greatest debt, however, is, as always, to Jutta and Kristina. No acknowledgment can reflect my gratitude to them adequately.

Stefan Berger
Cardiff 1997

ABBREVIATIONS

1999	1999. Zeitschrift für Sozialpolitik und -geschichte
AfS	Archiv für Sozialgeschichte
BDO	Bund deutscher Offiziere (German officers' organisation who, as prisoners of war in the Soviet Union, declared against Nazism)
Blätter	Blätter für deutsche und internationale Politik
BZG	Beiträge zur Geschichte der Arbeiterbewegung
CDU	Christlich Demokratische Union
CEH	Central European History
CSCE	Conference on Security and Cooperation in Europe
EU	European Union
FAZ	Frankfurter Allgemeine Zeitung
FR	Frankfurter Rundschau
GG	Geschichte und Gesellschaft
GWU	Geschichte in Wissenschaft und Unterricht
HZ	Historische Zeitschrift
IRSH	International Review of Social History
IWK	Internationale Wissenschaftliche Korrespondenz
MFG	Militärgeschichtliches Forschungsamt (Research Institute for Military History)
ND	Neues Deutschland
NKFD	Nationalkommittee Freies Deutschland (German Communist organisation in the Soviet Union opposing Nazism)
NLR	New Left Review
PDS	Partei des demokratischen Sozialismus (Party of Democratic Socialism, successor party to the SED)
SED	Sozialistische Einheitspartei Deutschlands
SPD	Sozialdemokratische Partei Deutschlands
SZ	Süddeutsche Zeitung
TAJB	Tel Aviver Jahrbuch für deutsche Geschichte
VfZ	Vierteljahreshefte für Zeitgeschichte
ZfG	Zeitschrift für Geschichtswissenschaft
ZfP	Zeitschrift für Politikwissenschaft

Chapter 1

HISTORIOGRAPHY AND
NATION-BUILDING
Some Preliminary Remarks

The nation has returned to Germany with a vengeance. A 'new right' has emerged in the reunified country with the resurrection of 'a self-confident nation' as the focal point of its programme.[1] Of course, nationalism always survived within the plethora of extreme right-wing organisations that accompanied the history of the old Federal Republic. It scored spectacular successes at the ballot box in the early 1950s, the late 1960s and the mid-1980s. However, what is worrying about the post-reunification renaissance of the national idea is that 'new right' thinking had some impact on the centre-right and even on some sections of the left in Germany.[2] An 'extremism of the centre'[3] has surfaced in the reunified country, and public discourse has steadily shifted to the right for the past seven years. Changes to the liberal asylum laws, discussions about the fight against organised crime and the remilitarisation of foreign policy all testify to the changing *Zeitgeist*. The repercussions amongst Germany's intellectuals are unmistakable. Some of its most prominent writers such as Hans-Magnus Enzensberger, Botho Strauß and Martin Walser have, in their different ways, all put forward ideas for a renationalisation of German identity.[4] Philosophers such as Dieter Henrich and Karl Heinz Bohrer,[5] film-makers like Hans Jürgen Syberberg,[6] and theatre directors like Frank Castorf[7] have all contributed to what is one of the most hotly debated public issues in Germany today. This

---

national debate has been rekindled not only by extreme right-wing
newspapers like *Junge Freiheit* (weekly circulation by March 17, 1997:
36,000) or *MUT*, but also by the more mainstream papers such as
Die Welt, Rheinischer Merkur and *Frankfurter Allgemeine Zeitung*.[8] The
Ullstein publishing house and publishers like Herbert Fleißner provided the neo-nationalists with an important outlet for their 'new
right' agenda.[9]

Historians have been prominent participants in this debate. After
1989 the alleged 'normality' of the nation-state found its enthusiastic
propagators amongst German historians, both inside and outside of
the university sector. It is mostly historians of the old Federal Republic who are at the very heart of the current debate. Therefore this
book largely concentrates on developments in West Germany. However, former East German historians should not be further marginalised than they already have been (if that is possible). Ignoring East
German historiography altogether would, in a perverse way, contribute to the post-1990 'national turn'. Hence, I have included brief
surveys of the GDR historians and their views on the national question in chapters two, three, four and seven.

This study's focus on the role of historians as nation-builders further demands close attention to the politics of historians and its
impact on their research agendas and historical interpretations.
Unlike Thomas Nipperdey, for example, I do not believe in the
autonomy of history as an academic subject from politics. Yet I do
recognise that my emphasis on historical consciousness and national
identity has to leave aside a number of methodological debates and
key concepts which have been crucial for the development of the
discipline over the past two centuries. This current study does not
pretend to be a total history of German historiography. Its aim is
more modest. It seeks to highlight one particular tradition and its
renaissance in contemporary historical discourses – that of the historians' commitment to nation-building. The shaping of historical
consciousness and culture[10] is not only, not even predominantly
done in scholarly tomes written by university professors. However,
the increased public media presence of academic historians in and
after the events of 1989/90 is in itself testimony to efforts to recreate
the nineteenth-century role of history as the leading subject for political orientation. Nevertheless, prominent participants in the debates
on national identity have been political scientists, often with a strong
interest in contemporary history, like Karl Dietrich Bracher, Kurt
Sontheimer, Hans-Peter Schwarz, Eckhard Jesse or Bernard Willms.
Others have been historically trained journalists and/or publishers
such as Joachim Fest or Wolf-Jobst Siedler. I have therefore adopted

a broad definiton of who can actually lay some claim to being a historian, so as not to exclude significant opinions from the debate.

The commitment of historians to nation-building can look back on a long tradition in German historiography,[11] its major function being to uphold national honour and glory and create national identity. The self-perception of German historians as promulgators of the national idea has had a lot to do with their high social status and the very strength of historism. Historism is a confusing term. Historicism, the far more common term in English, is even more confusing, because the one word refers to two quite separate set of ideas. On the one hand it describes a notion, criticised and rejected by Karl Popper, that history develops towards a particular end according to predetermined laws. On the other hand it refers to a concept, represented most prominently by Leopold von Ranke, which understands all political order within its own historical context. Hence, I propose to use historicism only for Popper's concept and to introduce the term 'historism' for the German *Historismus* (in contrast to the German *Historizismus*).

Yet even if we distinguish between Popper's notion of historicism and historism, the latter still remains a multi-faceted phenomenon which often is defined in very different forms. In our context of nation-building historism became important in three different ways. At a basic level the assumption underlying historism that any given society can only be understood on the basis of its historical development, meant in effect, that historians were given the automatic right to interpret the present given that they supposedly held the key to the past. Secondly, the historist's insistence that an emphatic 'understanding' *(Verstehen)* forms the only basis from which to grasp both the 'individuality' and the 'development' of historical phenomena has been interpreted by Friedrich Meinecke as specifically German.[12] Historism's methodology was explicitly pitted against the allegedly more facile methods of 'Western' positivism. Meinecke's hugely influential emphasis on different cultural traditions with reference to German historism served the purpose of underpinning the widespread belief in German superiority over the West and thus strengthened the nationalist mood amongst German historians. Thirdly, the individualising concept of *Verstehen* suffered from a value relativism which did not allow for any normative assessment of historical events. Together with the Rankean belief in an evolutionary process inherent in history, historism tended to write the history of the victors and condemn the losers to the garbage heap. Hence the small-German Prussian historiography, equipped with the instruments of historism, teleologically wrote the history of the nineteenth century as one great movement towards 1870. Historians became, in Nipperdey's words, the 'main speakers for the nation' (*Festredner der Nation*).[13]

The dominance of historism over German historiography only came to an end after 1945. In East Germany it was replaced by a Marxist-Leninist perspective highly critical of historism's methodological and political legacy. In West Germany a delayed break with historism occurred in the 1960s. A heterogeneous group of historians, sometimes referred to as 'critical historians', aimed at ending the close relationship between defence of the nation and historiography. Much of critical historiography was Social Democratic or, more broadly speaking, left-liberal in its political orientation. Yet it would be misleading to speak of a school of 'critical historians' in the Federal Republic. With reference to methodological innovation, it would be more correct to speak of the emergence of 'historical social science' in the 1960s.[14] Often the supporters of 'historical social science' were also to the fore in criticising the national tradition of German historiography. Yet, more traditional scholars like Karl-Dietrich Bracher or Eberhard Jäckel could also be found amongst the critics of that national tradition. Hence critics of the national paradigm were not synonymous with practitioners of 'historical social science'. The politics of historiography often cut across the methodological debates.

At times the politics of German historians has been linked to generational experience which in turn is often linked to political ruptures epitomised in German history by such dates as 1815, 1848, 1871, 1918, 1933, 1945, 1968 and 1989.[15] For many of the early nineteenth-century historians the restoration period following the Napoleonic era became, according to generational theory, the paramount reference point for their historical work. The shockwaves produced by the French Revolution made them focus on questions of how a political order could be stabilised and immunised against revolutionary threats. For those historians who came of age in the middle years of the nineteenth century, the struggle for national unity came to be their guiding light, whilst those who matured in Imperial Germany sought to defend the united nation against its perceived internal and external enemies. The generation of the First World War allegedly transformed the 'experience of the trenches' into *Volksgeschichte* and fought to revise the Treaty of Versailles so as to allow the national reawakening. Many saw in National Socialism the promise of such national revival. The generation of the 'founding fathers' of the Federal Republic still had a largely unproblematic relation to the nation-state as they knew it before 1945. The 'Yalta generation', by contrast, born in the late 1920s, socialised under National Socialism and matured in the Europe divided at Yalta, came to accept the division of Germany more easily. The 1968 generation's concern with the fascist past led to a critical re-assessment of national history. The 1989 generation's concern with nation-building has led to an attempt to save the national idea from the alleged denigration of its predecessors. Whilst there is clearly some mileage in generational interpretations of historiographical change, such explanations remain at the same time both limited and limiting. Some founding fathers of the FRG, such as Bracher or Golo Mann, for example, were among the first to question the merit of clinging to the idea of a unified nation state in the 1960s. Members of the Yalta generation, such as Bernard Willms, always remained rabid nationalists tirelessly stressing the 'national imperative'. Old 1968ers, like Imanuel Geiss, have returned to more conservative positions in the 1980s and 1990s. Although I should belong to the 1989 generation, I cannot find much sympathy for efforts to renationalise German identity. A generational approach to the politics of historiography in Germany might therefore well obscure more than it reveals. I shall restrict myself to referring occasionally to generational impacts, where it seems appropriate, whilst generally confining myself to discussing the various ruptures and continuities in German historiography within their respective political contexts. In this way I hope to have avoided any unnecessary homogenisation of generational experience.

A wide range of historians have recognised that 1989 marked the latest 'rupture of consciousness' in German history and questions have been asked about its consequence for German historiography. In April 1995 the Institute for German History at Tel Aviv University, in conjunction with the Wiener Library, held a stimulating conference on the subject of historiographical change 'at era's end'.[16] Jürgen Kocka has spent considerable intellectual energy on interpreting the events of 1989, emphasising that 'such radical change will not leave unaffected the way in which we write history'.[17] Peter Bender reached a similar conclusion: 'The years 1989/90 form a caesura for the historian as well. It does not matter what his politics are. He simply cannot ignore the question of what the unexpected unification of Germany means for our concept of the history of past decades.'[18] For neo-nationalists like Karlheinz Weißmann, the changes of 1989 mark a welcome opportunity to start revising the misconceptions about the past.[19] Imanuel Geiss wants to reopen the *Historikerstreit* of the 1980s. The turning point of 1989, according to Geiss, ultimately serves to show up the failures of critical historians and proves Nolte and the revisionists right.[20] Kocka has already argued that the appetite of critical historians for a second round of the *Historikerstreit* may well have been whetted by tendencies to renationalise German historiography.[21] Even so, as will be argued below, the contours of the opposing camps in this latest of the great battles amongst German historians are still largely visible, yet they have also been changing since 1989/90. Commenting generally on the intellectual controversies which have followed reunification, Lothar Probst wrote: 'The process of German unity has in many ways reinforced the decomposition of ideologically rigid blocs and led to an increasing differentiation of the various discourses' on the nation.[22] This is certainly the case in German historiography.

Discourses on national identity and historical consciousness[23] have for a very long time been extraordinarily broad and complex. The topic has attracted considerable attention from historians, sociologists, anthropologists and political scientists who have come up with a bewildering variety of explanations. Some scholars have dismissed national identity as false consciousness. Marxist historians have tended to interpret national identity as a thinly veiled attempt to cloak some specific class interest.[24] Weberians have also been analysing nationalism largely in terms of an ideology which fulfilled and continues to fulfil certain functions in society.[25] Others have stressed the need for national identity. Karl-Rudolf Korte, for example, writes: 'National perceptions of the self and the other are of the utmost importance in structuring both society and politics.'[26] For A.D. Smith 'ethnic identity' lies at the core of 'national identity'. 'The nation and nationalism', according to Smith, ' remain the only realistic basis for a free society of states in the modern world.'[27]

National identity, according to Ernest Gellner, emerges in the process of industrialisation.[28] The latter dissolves traditional ties of kinship and replaces them with shared norms of a national 'high culture'. For Gellner such 'a common idiom' is necessary to allow individuals in any modern society to negotiate their position in society. National identity becomes a major stabilising factor in modern societies, and historical consciousness aims at underpinning it. National identity thus becomes an aspect of modernity. The formation of industrial societies and the modern state in the nineteenth century was necessarily connected to the emergence of national identities.

Whilst such a functionalist explanation of the need for national identity, which is present in many Weberian and Marxist accounts of the phenomenon, goes some way towards explaining the strong hold of the nation on many minds and takes seriously the threat of nationalism, one nevertheless has to ask how functional the nation-state still is. At the end of the twentieth century, faced with the increasing globalisation of markets and communication, a global environmental crisis and the limits of national welfare states in advanced capitalist countries, one might equally want to draw attention to the nation as a contingent, historically limited and limiting condition of humankind. Other constructions might well take its place in the twenty-first century. Indeed the nation-state would seem to be either too small or too big for most things. This fundamental truth has not been changed by the collapse of Communism in Eastern Europe. We cannot and should not take the concept of the nation for granted. There is no 'normality' of the nation-state. It is a concept devised for a particular set of questions, a concept which fits a certain set of beliefs. To do this, it is constructed in a particular way – usually by 'inventing traditions' or 'imagining communities' which then allegedly form the basis for the claim to national identity.[29] The interesting thing about national identity is how it is constructed, by whom and why? Historians clearly play a major role in the processes of constructing national identity. The struggle for cultural hegemony between rival political concepts functionalises the past and selectively perceives the present in the light of a constructed past.

The task of the historian, I would argue, is to guard against such political and ideological misuse of history, to rationalise the politics of national identity by identifying the variety of national, ethnic and political myths underpinning it. After all, as Michel Foucault argued, it cannot be the aim of historiography to offer 'substitute identities' to individuals 'who do not know who they are or what name they carry'.[30] The 'hunger to belong' has often been the result of social disorganisation.[31] Irrational emotive identification with larger collectives is clearly not indispensable. Recent empirical studies have demonstrated that a lack of national pride does not have to coincide with either political destabilisation or psychological illness. It is rather the other way round: a low degree of national or indeed any collective pride can be seen as an indicator of a mature self-confidence of the individual.[32] Therefore, representations of the past should not seek to recreate mythical roots for our national identity. On the contrary, they should aim at dissolving ideas of imagined identities, thus barring any easy fallback positions for individuals in their struggle to give direction and meaning to their lives. The first step, to paraphrase Marx on culture, is to avoid allowing 'fog in the brain' *(Nebelbildung im Gehirn)* to build up. This is all the more necessary as the politics of national identity is often a politics of exclusion. It frequently works on a them versus us opposition, a friend versus foe dichotomy. In our quest for national identity we distance ourselves from others. In inventing our own past we have to invent the past of others who are perceived as our enemies.[33] At the same time, however, we depend

on our enemies for our self-definition which makes the concept of
national identity all the more confusing and disturbing. Sometimes
national programmes gave prominent place to civic rights and democratic reforms yet equally, there are strong links between the national
idea and military aggression. To encourage tolerance and understanding, to make people accept differences, that is a pressing task in
today's multi-cultural Germany. The concept of citizenship, based on
the territorial definition of the *ius soli* is of key importance here. By
contrast, the concept of the nation has little part to play.

If this study starts from the assumption that today's politics in
Germany makes any return to the concept of national identity
unnecessary and potentially harmful, it also seeks to remind the
reader of the long and unhappy relationship between historiography
and the politics of national identity. The fact that most academic historians in Germany have been civil servants surely had a part to
play in the emergence of a strong link between nation-building and
history writing. With a guaranteed job, high social prestige and fixed
salaries, history professors had little incentive to bite the hand that
fed them. By the late nineteenth century the state had become the
major sponsor of jobs and research funds. A historical profession
which concentrated on constructing a collective national identity was
helpful to the state in several ways. It instilled loyalty to the state in
the history taught at schools and universities. It provided an excellent training ground for future civil servants, particularly those serving in the German Foreign Ministry. Furthermore, it enhanced the
state's prestige when it could point to 'scientific' research which confirmed its own claims and pretensions. Hence the criteria of the
Prussian state for the appointment of professors included not only
academic excellence and prominence in scholarly debate, but also
loyalty to the Hohenzollerns and a political standpoint 'above
party'.[34] This in effect excluded Social Democrats, Jews, Catholics,
Democrats and left-wing Liberals. However, German historians'
motives for legitimating the state's actions have roots other than economic ones. It was not only dependence on the state, but also identification with the state which transformed historians into apologists
for the nation-state. Hegel's hypostasis of the state as the incarnation
of historical right and Herder's insistence on the people as the basis
of a distinct historical collective were both to become hugely influential. Reacting against the universalism of Enlightenment principles, historians emphasised the distinct and unique role of the nation.
Nations were increasingly regarded as 'natural'. They were identified
with specific features, for example ethnicity, culture or language,
which allegedly formed the 'national spirit' *(Volksgeist)*. Tracing such

a 'spirit' down the centuries became the central task in constructing the nation. In the German context the concepts of ethnicity and cultural identity constituted the very core of the 'national spirit'. Cultural identity, it was argued, had long been established in the German lands. Political unity, in this view, would be the natural result of cultural identity. Hence, in the early nineteenth century, there was rarely any hard and fast distinction between cultural and political historians. The Germans, according to the early advocates of the national idea, had to build a nation by appealing to the twin forces of culture and history, which in turn became the backbone of German national identity.

Of course, such a relationship between history and politics was not peculiar to Germany. In Eastern Europe historians played prominent roles as nation builders.[35] Frequent political ruptures regularly produced reinterpretations of the past, as can be seen most recently in Russian historiography.[36] All too often historians came to perceive themselves as national pedagogues. They thus contributed to the narrow concentration on national history which has characterised almost every historical profession from the nineteenth century to the present day. In France after 1830 a generation of young liberal intellectuals such as François Guillaume Guizot (1787-1874), Augustin Thierry (1795-1856) and Jules Michelet (1798-1874) all wrote history with a political mission in mind: to interpret the constitutional monarchy as a historic compromise between the principles of tradition and the principles of the Great Revolution. After 1880 French historians were widely perceived as guardians of the national heritage, propagating the myth of the continuous growth of a homogeneous French nation-state and justifying French nationalism and imperialism.[37] Ernest Renan's famous definition of national belonging as a daily plebiscite is often quoted as contrasting with the German insistence on ethnicity as the basis for national togetherness. Certainly, a more political and territorial definition of citizenship took root in France in comparison with its Eastern neighbour. Yet, as in Germany, history became a main ingredient in the creation of French national identity, and this, according to Henry Rousso, is why the German debates on *Vergangenheitsbewältigung* and National Socialism have found a direct parallel in the French debates on Vichy and the collaboration with the German occupants.[38]

The long shadow of Whig historiography and of Thomas Babington Macauley in particular were essential in the making of national identity in Britain. In the middle of the nineteenth century he and his followers provided the nation with a powerful myth of its evolutionary progress: 'The history of our country during the last hundred and sixty years is eminently the history of physical, of moral and of intellectual improvement.'[39] At the very centre of this idea of progress was the notion that the constitution of Britain had evolved through the centuries. In the words of James Joll: 'English history could be seen as a kind of continuous dialogue in which opposites were repeatedly reconciled and even the most painful episodes such as the Civil War and the execution of Charles I could be seen as having turned out for the best.'[40] At least up until the 1930s constitutional history thus formed the prime focus of British historiography.[41] Matthew Arnold's biography-of-nations approach to the writing of history explicitly followed German romanticism in the belief that nations have an organic life cycle. Britain also had its Treitschke in the late nineteenth century. J.R. Seeley, appointed to the Regius Chair of History at the University of Cambridge in 1869, was one of the most effective propagators of British imperialism.[42] The conscious rationale underlying his historical writings was 'to idealise the nation and familiarise it in its unity to the minds of its members'.[43]

Ever since Heinrich von Treitschke and Ferdinand Gregorovius, the Italian nation-building process in the nineteenth century has been seen as the closest parallel case to that of Germany. Culture and history did indeed form the essential background for the construction of both of these nations, and Italian historians have been prominent nation-builders ever since Mazzini. The myths of classical Rome and its imperial civilising mission underpinned Italian nationalism and imperialism long before Mussolini came to power. The idea of the superiority of the Italians over other nations has a long tradition and can even be found in the works of, amongst others, Vincenzo Gioberti and Francesco Crispi. Even so, in the absence of an Italian Herder, the voluntarism of the nation-building process was emphasised by Italian historiography more than by its German counterpart. Mazzini's influence meant that the links between nation-building and political freedom, universalism and humanitarianism were more strongly developed than in Germany. Finally, the strength of anti-modern impulses in German historiography found no real equivalent in Italy.[44]

Equally the parallels with Britain and France should not be overemphasised. Within a highly abstract conceptualisation there is surely an all-European development of historiography, and the major trends are all recognisable in different national historiographies, and yet these national developments do possess specificities which need exploring. In the British and French cases, the emphasis was on the political construction of the nation, via the concept of citizenship and the concept of constitutional development respectively.

The identification was with the republic in France and with the parliamentary system in Britain. The national rhetoric was closely linked to the traditions of 1789 in the French case and of 1688 in the British case. The special emphasis on history, culture and ethnicity which characterised the German case was much weaker in British and French historiography. As Ludwig Dehio rightly observed: 'Historiography has played a far greater role in the development of the immature nations of central Europe ... than in the nation-building process of Western nations which had long reached national maturity.'[45] Seeley was strongly influenced by Ranke and in turn he influenced many of the imperialist neo-Rankean historians in Germany. In Britain, by contrast, his influence remained limited.[46] The liberal individualism underpinning much of British historiography in modern times was weaker in Germany. G.P. Gooch, for example, successfully resisted efforts by the Conservative government in the late 1920s to adapt his work to the national cause.[47] Such explicit refusals to become 'official' historians remained the exception in Germany.

The link between historiography and nation-building was an integral part of the establishment of history as an academic discipline all over Europe. Only more comparative studies of the historiography of different European nation-states will shed further light on the exact nature of that relationship in different European countries.[48] However, in the following I will concentrate on the way German historians have in the past contributed to the construction of their nation and particularly on the way they are doing so at present.

The fact that German historians' civil service jobs were protected from the vagaries of market forces and their corresponding closeness to the state encouraged a tendency amongst them to form a consensus on national matters. An anti-pluralism emerged within the *Zunft* – a term which itself calls to mind a closed circle of priests and knowledge-holders. There were outsiders, but institutionally they were marginalised, professionally they remained isolated.[49] After Quidde had published his critical comments about Wilhelm II in Imperial Germany, he became a social outcast. Even a liberal representative of the profession, like Walter Goetz, wrote in 1894: 'I for one will never again set foot into the house of that cosmopolitan *Demokratenseele* and his Jewish wife. I find them both disgusting.'[50] Academic careers of non-conformists were systematically torpedoed. Political denunciation, as in the case of Veit Valentin, was vicious. After Valentin had defended the historical right of Belgium to exist as a nation in the First World War, Georg von Below ensured that his *venia legendi* (a kind of licence which gives German professors the right to lecture at German universities) was withdrawn in 1917. Like the pacifist Ludwig Quidde, who was also dismissed from his Munich professorship in the First World War,[51] Valentin never got a chair in the Weimar Republic. The hatred of their fellow historians saw to that. Under National Socialism, most of those who did not share in the nationalist consensus were forced to emigrate. The majority never returned, and in West Germany they were, for the most part, duly forgotten. In the early 1960s two major works on historiography, Heinrich von Srbik's two-volume 'History of Historiography' and the 'Fischer Dictionary of History' found it unnecessary to have a single entry on Valentin. To counter the impression that German historians were totally united on their views on national identity and the nation, which might otherwise easily arise from this book, I would at least like to discuss some prominent examples of outsiders who challenged the nation-building efforts of their colleagues.

Maybe the earliest example of such behaviour was Georg Gottfried Gervinus from 1848 onwards. Before the revolution, he, like other Prussian historians, saw the emergence of a German nation-state as a necessity, almost a law of history. In the 1840s he thought of the writing of national history as a patriotic duty. As in the case of Droysen, Sybel and Treitschke, his commitment to the national cause led to an extreme Russophobia. Equally, he more than once demanded political hegemony on the continent for the emergent Germany. Hence, it is not totally without justification that Charles McClelland has interpreted Gervinus as a racist and nationalist.[52] And yet Gervinus was convinced that 'it was Prussia's fate to achieve hegemony in Germany'[53] only if it developed liberal constitutional structures and only if the 'old Teutonism' could be overcome. In the event this proved to be a big 'if'. Unlike most Prussian historians, Gervinus never became a convert to Prussian state idolatry after 1848. Instead he remained true to his liberal democratic ethos, and, if anything, took a left turn in later years. Disillusioned with the potential of the Prussian state to lead the way to unity and freedom, he became one of the most prolific critics of the Prussianisation of Germany.

According to Gervinus, the middle classes were caught in the process of nation-building between an alliance with the reactionary aristocracy and an acceptance of the social emancipation of the working class. As he left no doubt about his preference for the second option, a political scandal erupted. Gervinus was tried for high treason, and his right to teach at the University of Heidelberg withdrawn. As *persona non grata*, he found it almost impossible in the following years to continue his work as a historian as most state archives closed their doors to him.[54] Things were not improved by his hostile reception of the unified Germany when it finally arrived in 1870/71. Gervinus was one of the few historians who, at this early stage, identified lack of political legitimacy as one of the major problems of the German Reich. By deliberately excluding whole sections of the population from the nation-state, this lack of legitimacy would, according to Gervinus, inevitably lead to greater aggressiveness and assertiveness in Germany's foreign policy and ultimately to war.[55] His methodological rejection of historism completed his exclusion from the *Zunft*. Instead of accepting the individualising approach, his works were often comparative, and concerned with establishing typologies of historical events and processes.

Theodor Mommsen, who shared many of the fundamental beliefs of the Prussian historians, ended, towards the end of his life, closer to Social Democracy than to National Liberalism. He began to criticise the 'Germanic servility' of his countrymen, ridiculing the Pan-Germans in particular as 'our national fools'. Targeting Treitschke, Mommsen called anti-Semitism a 'deformation of national sentiment', and in 1900 he even pleaded for the abolition of Sedan day. These views ensured that even a historian with his towering reputation increasingly felt isolated amongst his colleagues.[56] Treitschke's implicit anti-Semitism became popular amongst the academically educated German middle classes, whilst Mommsen was ridiculed as 'Mommsohn' and portrayed as having been in the pay of the Jews.[57]

Eckart Kehr, Arthur Rosenberg, Hans Rosenberg, Veit Valentin, Gustav Mayer and Johannes Ziekursch are prominent examples of historians marginalised by the profession during the Weimar Republic. Ziekursch remained completely isolated in the history department at the University of Cologne. Mayer's *Habilitation* was prevented in 1917 by a *fronde* of Pan-German ultra-nationalists in the Humanities Faculty of the University of Berlin. When, as a result of his growing reputation as one of the pioneers of labour history in Germany, he finally got a chair in 1923, he remained a social outcast amongst fellow professors, was sacked in 1933 and subsequently forced to emigrate. His work on the early labour movement was, in any case, never regarded as 'proper' history by the majority of his colleagues.

Valentin, who as pupil of Erich Marcks had been reared in the dominant imperialism and Prussianism of Wilhelmine Germany, began developing a more critical view of German history during the course of the First World War. His pro-war stance in 1914/15 gave way to a more sceptical evaluation of many of his fellow historians' apologias. He became one of the most fervent supporters of the League of Nations idea in the 1920s, and wrote vigorously against the propagation of historical myths such as the 'stab-in-the-back theory'.[58] He turned the positive view of the German *Sonderweg* on its head in his *Geschichte der deutschen Revolution von 1848/49*. Reminding the public of alternative paths – including alternative paths of defining national identity – which had been blocked by the 'failure' of 1848 and subsequently abandoned by most of their erstwhile champions, Valentin saw the development of illiberal and anti-Western ideas as the major root of Germany's ill-fated history in the twentieth century. In this respect Bismarck in particular received a more sober assessment than he did from all previous and many subsequent historians.

Towards the end of the 1920s Eckart Kehr began explicitly denouncing both the nationalism and the anti-socialism of German historiography. True social history, he argued, could only come about in the German context if the attachment to nation-building was overcome. Subsequently Gerhard Ritter attacked Kehr as a Communist fellow traveller who should go to the Soviet Union for a job rather than try his luck in Germany. Up to and including Fritz Fischer and Imanuel Geiss in the 1960s, the threat of marginalisation, isolation and worse loomed large over any historian who dared to go against the national orthodoxy prevailing in the guild of German historians.

The making, unmaking and potential remaking of this national orthodoxy is the subject of this volume. Chapter two traces the overwhelming commitment to nation-building amongst German historians from the early nineteenth century to the 1950s. Chapter three then assesses the impact of changes in German historiography in the 1960s. Here the Fischer controversy plays a central role. In chapter four, the widespread notion of an 'anti-national' paradigm change in the 1960s and 1970s is challenged by tracing the survival and continued strength of the national position in German historiography. Chapters five to nine then assess the changes in German historiography since reunification in 1990. Finally the reaction of Anglo-American historians to changes in German historiography in the 1990s is discussed. The central argument of this volume is that a minority of German historians are at present setting a new agenda (which is essentially a very old one) for historical studies by trying to legitimate the reunification of Germany. Peter Glotz has written of a 'normalisation nationalism' (*Normalisierungs-Nationalismus*) gaining ground in post-reunification Germany.[59] This study discusses the significance of such new nationalism amongst German historians.

With reunification, the future shape of the German nation-state has become the topic of a hotly contested public debate. In the words of Michael Stürmer: 'The future is open once again. Nothing will be as it was previously.'[60] The present is up for grabs and the past becomes a battlefield for those who want to legitimate their definitions of the new nation-state by referring to the 'lessons of history'.

Jürgen Habermas, who was so instrumental in starting the *Historikerstreit* in the mid-1980s, has recognised that 'since German unification the battle about the meaning of contemporary history has begun in earnest'. Acknowledging the role that historians have previously played in that battle, Habermas sounds the all-clear for the present: 'The connection between historism and nationalism has now dissolved.'[61] The question of whether this optimism is justified in the light of recent developments in German historiography will form a large part of the subsequent analysis.

NOTES

1. A good introduction to the new right thinking is provided by Heimo Schwilk and Ulrich Schacht (eds), *Die selbstbewußte Nation: 'Anschwellender Bocksgesang' und weitere Beiträge zu einer deutschen Debatte*, Frankfurt-on-Main, 1994.
2. Stefan Berger, 'Nationalism and the Left in Germany', *NLR*, no. 206, 1994, pp. 55-70.
3. Hans-Martin Lohmann, *Extremismus der Mitte: vom rechten Verständnis deutscher Nation*, Frankfurt-on-Main, 1994.
4. Hans Magnus Enzensberger, *Die große Wanderung*, Frankfurt-on-Main, 1992; idem, *Civil War*, London, 1994; Botho Strauß, 'Anschwellender Bocksgesang', *Der Spiegel*, 8 Feb. 1993, pp. 202-07; Martin Walser, 'Deutsche Sorgen', *Der Spiegel*, 28 June 1993, pp. 40-7; idem, 'Über freie und unfreie Rede', *Der Spiegel*, 7 Nov. 1994, pp. 130-38.
5. Dieter Henrich, *Nach dem Ende der Teilung: Über Identitäten und Intellektualität in Deutschland*, Frankfurt-on-Main, 1993; Karl Heinz Bohrer, 'Warum wir keine Nation sind. Warum wir eine werden sollten', *FAZ*, 13 Jan. 1990.
6. On Syberberg see Peter Glotz, 'Die Bewaffnung mit Identität: Eine Analyse des deutschen Normalisierungs-Nationalismus am Beispiel Hans Jürgen Syberbergs', *FR*, 22 Jan. 1994.
7. On Castorf see Martin Doerry, 'Wir brauchen Stahlgewitter', *Der Spiegel*, 16 Jan. 1995; Peter Iden, 'Ein Irrer. Frank Castorf bekennt sich', *FR*, 10 Jan. 1995.
8. On the *FAZ* see the scathing article by Lothar Baier, 'Kulturlandschaft mit Giftzwergen', *Freitag*, 10 April 1992, p. 9.
9. Maria Zens, 'Vergangenheit verlegen – Über die Wiederherstellung nationaler Größe im Hause Ullstein', *Blätter*, vol.38, 1993, pp. 1364-75; Hans Sarkowicz, *Rechte Geschäfte. Der unaufhaltsame Aufstieg des deutschen Verlegers Herbert Fleissner*, Frankfurt-on-Main, 1994. However, it should be noted that the removal of Fleißner from Ullstein and the appointment of Wolfram Göbel as new director of Ullstein in March 1996 may well indicate a return of the prominent publishing house to its distinguished liberal roots.
10. For the concept of 'historical culture' (*Geschichtskultur*) see Klaus Füssmann (ed.), *Historische Faszination: Geschichtskultur heute*, Cologne, 1994.
11. There are a number of very useful introductions to German historiography to which I am indebted. They are Georg G. Iggers, *The German Conception of History*.

The National Tradition of Historical Thought from Herder to the Present, 2nd rev. edn,
Middletown/Ct., 1983; Hans-Ulrich Wehler (ed.), Deutsche Historiker, 9 vols., Göt-
tingen, 1971-82; Manfred Asendorf (ed.), Aus der Aufklärung in die permanente
Restauration. Geschichtswissenschaft in Deutschland, Hamburg, 1974; Bernd Faulen-
bach (ed.), Geschichtswissenschaft in Deutschland, Munich, 1974; Wolfgang Weber,
Priester der Klio. Historisch-sozialwissenschaftliche Studien zur Herkunft und Karriere
deutscher Historiker und zur Geschichte der Geschichtswissenschaft 1800-1970, 2nd edn,
Frankfurt-on-Main, 1987; Wolfgang Hardtwig, Geschichtskultur und Wissenschaft,
Munich, 1990; Horst Walter Blanke, Historiographiegeschichte als Historik, Stuttgart,
1991; Friedrich Jaeger and Jörn Rüsen, Geschichte des Historismus. Eine Einführung,
Munich, 1992; on the institutionalisation of the historical sciences in Germany see
Hermann Heimpel, 'Über Organisationsformen historischer Forschung in
Deutschland', HZ, vol. 189, 1959, pp. 139-222. Typical examples of Prussian
apologetics can be found in Heinrich von Srbik, Geist und Geschichte vom deutschen
Humanismus bis zur Gegenwart, 2 vols, Munich, 1950-51. Compare also from a
GDR Marxist perspective Joachim Streisand (ed.), Studien über die deutsche
Geschichtswissenschaft, 2 vols, Berlin 1963-65.

12. Friedrich Meinecke, Die Entstehung des Historismus, Munich, 1936.

13. Thomas Nipperdey's contribution to a panel discussion on German and Italian
historiography in Arnold Esch and Jens Petersen (eds), Geschichte und Geschichtswissenschaft in der Kultur Italiens und Deutschlands, Tübingen, 1989, p. 233.

14. Complimentary terms are 'Bielefeld school' and 'Kehrites'. The first referring to
the fact that two of the doyens of 'historical social science', Hans-Ulrich Wehler
and Jürgen Kocka held chairs at the University of Bielefeld. The second pointing
to the influence of Eckart Kehr on many of the 1960s social historians. Yet the
wider term 'historical social science' is best-suited to describe shared methodological assumptions of a group of West German social historians who came to
prominence in the 1960s.

15. For an excellent discussion of generational theory in the context of German history see Mark Roseman (ed.), Generations in Conflict. Youth Revolt and Generation
Formation in Germany 1770-1968, Cambridge, 1995.

16. See the conference report by Stefan Berger and Karen Schönwälder, 'German
Historiography At Era's End. The Nineteenth and Twentieth Century', German
History, vol. 13, 1995, pp. 379-82.

17. Jürgen Kocka, Vereinigungskrise. Zur Geschichte der Gegenwart, Göttingen, 1995,
p. 60.

18. Peter Bender, 'Ansätze zu einer deutschen Nachkriegsgeschichte', Merkur, vol. 47,
1993, pp. 197-8.

19. Karlheinz Weißmann, Rückruf in die Geschichte. Die deutsche Herausforderung. Alte
Gefahren – Neue Chancen, 2nd rev. edn, Frankfurt-on-Main, 1993, p. 9.

20. Imanuel Geiss, '"Wende" und Ende im "Historikerstreit"', Historische Mitteilungen,
vol. 4, 1991, p. 102.

21. Jürgen Kocka, Die Auswirkungen der deutschen Einigung auf die Geschichts- und
Sozialwissenschaften, Bonn, 1992, p. 18-9.

22. Lothar Probst, 'Deutsche Vergangenheiten – Deutschlands Zukunft', Deutschland-
Archiv, vol. 27, 1994, p. 173.

23. For efforts to define 'historical consciousness' see Karl-Ernst Jeismann, 'Geschichtsbewußtsein', in: Klaus Bergmann (ed.), Handbuch der Geschichtsdidaktik, vol. 1,
Düsseldorf, 1979, pp. 42 ff; Jörn Rüsen, Historische Vernunft. Grundzüge einer Historik, vol. 1: Die Grundlagen der Geschichtswissenschaft, Göttingen, 1983, especially
chapter 2.

24. Eric Hobsbawm, Nations and Nationalism since 1780. Programme, Myth, Reality, 2nd
edn, Cambridge, 1992.

25. For a Weberian interpretation which at the same time serves as a wonderful comparative introduction to the phenomenon of nationalism see John Breuilly, *Nationalism and the State*, 2nd rev. edn, Manchester, 1993.

26. Karl-Rudolf Korte, 'Deutschlandbilder', in: Werner Weidenfeld (ed.), *Politische Kultur und deutsche Frage*. *Materialien zum Staat- und Nationalbewußtsein in der Bundesrepublik*, Cologne, 1989, p. 113.

27. Anthony D. Smith, *Nations and Nationalism in a Global Era*, Oxford, 1995, p. 147. Compare also idem, *The Ethnic Origins of Nations*, London, 1986, and idem, *National Identity*, London, 1991.

28. Ernest Gellner, *Nations and Nationalism*, Oxford, 1983; idem, *Encounters with Nationalism*, Oxford, 1994.

29. Benedict Anderson, *Imagined Communities: Reflections on the Origin and Spread of Nationalism*, rev. edn, London, 1991, Eric Hobsbawm and Terence Ranger (eds), *The Invention of Tradition*, Cambridge, 1983, Christopher Shaw and Malcolm Chase (eds), *The Imagined Past: History and Nostalgia*, Manchester, 1989.

30. Michel Foucault, *Von der Subversion des Wissens*, Munich, 1974, pp. 104 ff.

31. Hobsbawm, *Nation*, p. 177.

32. Borries, *Geschichtsbewußtsein*, p. 91.

33. This link between national identity and xenophobia is also stressed by Reinhart Kosellek, *Hermeneutik und Historik*, Heidelberg, 1987, pp. 14-5.

34. Christian Simon, *Staat und Geschichtswissenschaft in Deutschland und Frankreich 1871-1914. Situation und Werk von Geschichtsprofessoren an den Universitäten Berlin, München und Paris*, 2 vols, Bern, 1988, vol. 1, pp. 128 f.

35. Dennis Deletant and Harry Hanak (eds), *Historians as Nation-Builders: Central and South-East Europe*, London, 1988.

36. Dietrich Geyer (ed.), *Die Umwertung der sowjetischen Geschichte*, GG special vol. 14, Göttingen, 1991.

37. Lutz Raphael, 'Epochen der französischen Geschichtsschreibung', in: Wolfgang Küttler, Jörn Rüsen and Ernst Schulin (eds), *Geschichtsdiskurs*, vol. 1: *Grundlagen und Methoden der Historiographiegeschichte*, Frankfurt-on-Main, 1993, pp. 101-132, Peter Stadler, *Geschichtsschreibung und historisches Denken in Frankreich 1789 – 1871*, Zurich, 1958, William R. Keylor, *Academy and Community. The Foundation of the French Historical Profession*, Cambridge/Mass., 1975.

38. Henry Rousso, *Le Syndrome de Vichy de 1944 à nos Jours*, 2nd edn, Paris, 1990; idem, *Vichy, un Passé qui ne passe pas*, Paris, 1994.

39. Thomas Babington Macauley, *The History of England*, Harmondsworth, 1979, p. 52.

40. James Joll, *National Histories and National Historians: Some German and English Views of the Past*, London, 1985, p. 5-6.

41. On British historiography compare Christopher Parker, *The English Historical Tradition Since 1850*, Edinburgh, 1990; John W. Burrow, *A Liberal Descent: Victorian Historians and the English Past*, Cambridge, 1981; John Kenyon, *The History Men: The Historical Profession in England since the Reformation*, London, 1983.

42. D. Wormell, *Sir John Seeley and the Uses of History*, Cambridge, 1980.

43. Parker, *Tradition*, p. 67.

44. Franz J. Bauer, 'Nation und Moderne im geeinten Italien (1861-1915)', *GWU*, vol. 46, 1995, pp. 16-31.

45. Ludwig Dehio, *Deutschland und die Weltpolitik im 20. Jahrhundert*, Munich, 1955, p. 39.

46. John L. Herkless, 'Seeley and Ranke', *Historian*, vol. 43, 1980, pp. 1-22.

47. F. Eyck, *G.P. Gooch. A Study in History and Politics*, London, 1982.

48. There are already promising examples of a comparative approach. Apart from the comparative literature mentioned above, see in particular Heiner Timmer-

mann (ed.), *Geschichtsschreibung zwischen Wissenschaft und Politik. Deutschland – Frankreich – Polen im 19. und 20. Jahrhundert,* Saarbrücken, 1987, Georg G. Iggers, 'Social History, the Social Sciences and Political Culture, 1890-1914. An International Perspective', *TAJB,* vol. 16, 1987, pp. 117-34; Peter Wagner, *Sozialwissenschaften und Staat. Frankreich, Italien, Deutschland 1870-1980,* Frankfurt-on-Main, 1990; Franziska Wein, *Deutschlands Strom – Frankreichs Grenze. Geschichte und Propaganda am Rhein 1919-1930,* Essen, 1992; Stefan Berger, Mark Donovan and Kevin Passmore (eds), *Writing National Histories. Western Europe Since 1800,* London, (forthcoming).

49. Robert Deutsch und Wolfgang Weber, 'Marginalisierungsprozesse in der deutschen Geschichtswissenschaft im Zeitalter des Historismus', *Schweizerische Zeitschrift für Geschichte,* vol. 35, 1985, pp. 174-97.

50. Cited in Wolf Volker Wiegand, *Walter Wilhelm Goetz 1867-1908. Eine biographische Studie über den Historiker, Politiker und Publizisten,* Boppard am Rhein, 1992, p. 43.

51. On Quidde compare Reinhard Rürup, 'Ludwig Quidde', in: Wehler (ed.), *Historiker,* pp. 358-81. On Valentin see Hans Schleier, *Die bürgerliche deutsche Geschichtsschreibung der Weimarer Republik,* Berlin, 1975.

52. Charles McClelland, 'History in the Service of Politics. A Reassessment of G. G. Gervinus', *CEH,* vol. 4, 1971, p. 386.

53. Cited in Gangolf Hübinger, *Georg Gottfried Gervinus. Historisches Urteil und politische Kritik,* Göttingen, 1984, p. 132.

54. Hübinger, *Gervinus,* pp. 199, 205.

55. Jaeger and Rüsen, *Geschichte,* p. 124.

56. Albert Wucher, *Theodor Mommsen. Geschichtsschreibung und Politik,* Göttingen, 1956, pp. 183, 195-198; Walter L. Böhlich (ed.), *Der Berliner Antisemitismusstreit,* Frankfurt-on-Main, 1965.

57. Christhard Hoffmann, 'Der Berliner Antisemitismusstreit 1879/80', *GWU,* vol. 46, 1995, pp. 167-78.

58. Veit Valentin, 'Das Ende der Dolchstoßlegende', *Die Weltbühne,* vol. 20, 1924, pp. 757 ff.

59. Peter Glotz, 'Die Bewaffnung mit Identität', *FR,* 22 January 1994, p. ZB 2.

60. Michael Stürmer, *Die Grenzen der Macht. Begegnung der Deutschen mit der Geschichte,* Berlin, 1990, p. 7.

61. Jürgen Habermas, 'Die Last der doppelten Vergangenheit', *Die Zeit,* no. 20, 13 May 1994, p. 54.

PART I

NATIONAL IDENTITY AND HISTORICAL CONSCIOUSNESS IN GERMANY 1800-1989

Chapter 2

THE NATIONAL TRADITION
IN GERMAN HISTORIOGRAPHY,
1800-1960

Ever since the nineteenth century much of German historiography has been dominated by professional historians whose main aim was to educate, emancipate, agitate or indoctrinate. German historism's claim to objectivity only thinly veiled its tendency to legitimate the existing political conditions and therefore to write the history of the victors. By the middle of the nineteenth century the so-called Prussian historians were writing history which could ably support the demands for a unified nation-state. Most of them would probably have agreed with Hayden White's remark that only antiquarians or cultural necrophiles studied the past as an end in itself.[1] This chapter traces the importance attached to the concept of the nation and the making of national identity well beyond the Bismarckian solution to the 'German problem'. It is evident in the imperialism of the neo-Rankean school before the First World War, in the anti-parliamentarianism of large parts of academic historians in the Weimar Republic, in the tacit understanding between the majority of professional historians and the National Socialist regime and finally in the national stance taken up by influential historians after 1945. There had been, in particular in the first half of the nineteenth century, a range of alternative discourses which were not primarily oriented towards the national paradigm. These cannot be adequately dealt with here, as this study is only concerned with the national tradition which, it argues, became by far the dominant one from the mid-nineteenth to the mid-twentieth centuries.

'Nationalism is a doctrine invented in Europe at the beginning of the nineteenth century.'[2] In Germany there had been lively public debates surrounding the national question from about 1730 onwards, with a first high point in the so-called German Movement after the Seven Year War. Wolfgang Hardtwig discovered a first attempt at 'organised nationalism' in the German societies, which were founded in university towns across Germany from the 1730s onwards.[3] Even before, humanist historians such as Beatus Rhenanus or Jakob Wimpfeling wrote national history aimed at glorifying the German nation. In direct competition with Italian humanists, the Germans sought to demonstrate that the German nation had much to be proud of.[4] Some of these older ideas about national identity showed a remarkable persistence in the centuries to come. The notion of a 'national character' justified a timeless superiority of one nation over others, as the essence of a nation remained fixed once and for all. The idea of *Kulturnation* (cultural nation), for example, was to serve German nationalists in providing a sense of togetherness in times of political division, but it was also useful for the propagation of an aggressive, expansionist foreign policy, as the cultural nation usually extended far beyond the political nation. The *Reichsgedanke* (Imperial ideal) was equally influential in justifying expansionist foreign policies, since any idea of Empire rested on notions of German hegemony in an ethnically heterogeneous association. Yet much of this emerging nationalism in humanist historiography and later on in the German Movement remained centred on the old Reich with Herder as its leading propagator. It encompassed only cultural elites and lacked any significant popular support.

Nineteenth-century historians, in so far as they perceived the unification of Germany as a Prussian mission, rarely harked back to these older notions of national identity. They, like the Baden historian Karl von Rotteck, perceived the wars of liberation against Napoleon as the starting point when historians explicitly perceived themselves as nation-builders.[5] As Heinrich von Sybel wrote in 1856: 'Like everything great and good which pleases our national existence, our modern historiography goes back to the beginning of the century – to the unique time of our national renaissance and liberation. Bringing together past and present, the idea of nationality perceived as a great and growing personality which encompasses all individuals throughout the ages, was born.'[6] Similarly Wilhelm Giesebrecht emphasised the importance of the 'national awakening' at the beginning of the nineteenth century in the first volume of the

Historische Zeitschrift in 1859.[7] Statements such as those by Rotteck, Sybel and Giesebrecht should not be taken at face value. An explicitly national historiography was certainly not dominant in the early nineteenth century. J. G. Fichte could, after all, lament in 1807/08 precisely the absence of a national history book which was capable of becoming as popular in the German lands as the Bible or the hymn book.[8] Hence, it would be more to the point to say that Prussian historians like Sybel, writing in the mid-nineteenth century, created a backwards-oriented teleological myth of the nation as 'sleeping beauty'. It had been kissed by the prince in the 'wars of liberation'. Yet, one hastens to add, it was rather slow to wake up.

However, the kiss had some effect. Friedrich Christoph Dahlmann, Heinrich von Luden and Georg Barthold Niebuhr were examples of the impact of the 'national awakening' in the first decade of the nineteenth century. Caught up as a young man in the national mood of 1809/10, Dahlmann wrote in 1814/15: 'an inner unity has to develop in divided Germany, or the blood of so many noble men has been spilled in vain.'[9] Like many of the older generation of German liberals Dahlmann could only conceive of this German nation as a constitutional monarchy under Prussian leadership. Niebuhr emerged after the defeat of the Prussian armies at Jena as a symbol of national unity, and his 'Roman History', first published in 1811, told the reader as much about the current state of the German nation as it did about Rome. Like Dahlmann, Niebuhr never lost touch with the liberal political views of the Enlightenment and tried to combine liberalism with nationalism.[10] Heinrich von Luden, professor of history at the University of Jena after 1806, began lecturing on German history in 1808/09 with the explicit aim of contributing towards the liberation of Germany from French rule and towards German unity.[11] His influence was substantial as his lectures were circulated widely amongst German university students. Luden also wrote a twelve volume *Geschichte des teutschen Volkes* between 1825 and 1837 and a three volume *Geschichte der Deutschen* in 1842/43. Both of these works served the explicit purpose of linking the national idea to the course of German history. As he wrote in the introduction to the former work: 'I have always been of the opinion that the historian has to devote his mental powers to the history of his fatherland above everything else.'[12] The urge of German historians – in conjunction with leading politicians, like the Freiherr vom Stein – to link the national idea firmly to the study of history inspired the foundation of the *Monumenta Germaniae Historica* in 1819 and the formation of numerous local historical associations in Germany in the first half of the nineteenth century.

From these earliest examples onwards the idea of national identity was linked to the idea of ethnicity. In particular Johann Gottfried
Herder's ideas of the *Volk* (people) forming a *Blutsgemeinschaft* (community of blood), and the *Volksseele* (national soul) and the *Volksgeist*
(national spirit) forming a specific historical individuality had enormous influence on subsequent generations of historians.[13] According
to Herder, nationalism has little to do with the state, let alone politics
or citizenship. Nations were pre-political, their roots lay in culture,
language and ethnicity; they were organic, not artificially constructed. Whilst Herder developed his ideas within the context of an
enlightened cosmopolitanism and hence cannot be viewed unproblematically as a direct precursor of nineteenth-century German
nationalism, J. G. Fichte took Herder one step further by putting the
German collective identity above everyone else's. A particularly
unique and original nation, it had to be on guard against being con-
taminated by other nations. Salvation lay solely in the vigorous
defence from all foreign influences of its own culture and language
(regarded as the original language of mankind, the *Ursprache*).

Both Herder's and Fichte's work on national identity is far richer
in ambiguities and infinitely more complex than this short paragraph
can even allude to. Herder in particular incorporated a universalist,
cosmopolitan and deeply humanitarian strain in his writings about
the national principle: 'However much we love our nation, such sentiments should never prevent us from recognising that everything
which is good has only been achieved in the course of the evolutionary progress of all peoples over time.'[14] Within the very diverse
codifications of nationalism, formulated in the nineteenth century,[15]
Herder's idea of the nation was open to a variety of different interpretations. Yet, his (and even more so, Fichte's) work was often interpreted by subsequent generations of historians as justification for a
xenophobic idea of a national collective identity based on the *Volk*.
They were used to conveniently marginalise earlier efforts to link
national identity to universally accepted values and ideas. In the
mid-nineteenth century even the liberal Theodor Mommsen argued
that the idea of the nation was firmly linked, not to political traditions and institutions, but to the *Volk*. A people for him had a particular individuality, and it was the task of the historiographer to
discover this collective individuality. Like most nineteenth-century
liberals, Mommsen believed in progress, and this was linked fatally
to the idea of ethnicity in that it allowed Mommsen and others to
create a hierarchy of peoples and nations according to the degree of
progress they had already achieved. There were higher cultures and
higher peoples (to whom Germany, of course, belonged) and there

were primitive nations (like the Slav, and in particular the Russian ones) who were mentally and physically inferior.[16]

Johann Gustav Droysen also aimed at the identity of people and state, thereby excluding everyone whom he regarded as alien to the German *Volk*. According to Droysen, religion, culture and the power of the state shaped the spirit of the *Volk*. These characteristics of a people were 'the holiest' possessions of each nation, and their retention and defence against alien influences was the prime aim of the powerful state. The belief that a state had to be powerful in order to defend the characteristics of a people led him to demand a strong position in Europe for a unified Germany. It had to become an 'invincible barrier' against 'sea despotism' (Britain), as well as 'barbarity' (Russia). In relation to smaller nations like Poland, Droysen even argued for a 'healthy egoism of the German people', i.e., an aggressive expansionist course of German foreign policy.[17]

In Imperial Germany even a relative outsider like Otto Hintze was not immune to the widespread ethnic nationalism. Along with the majority of academic historians, he firmly rejected blatant racism in pseudo-historical narratives *à la* Gobineau, Claß and Chamberlain. Historical change, according to Hintze, had nothing to do with race, but was related to economic and social conditions and political institutions. Yet he talked about the 'German people' who could only survive on the basis of excluding all 'racially inferior', especially Slavic groups. The task of the future for him lay in creating 'a *Volkstum* ... which is anchored not just in the mind but in the blood – the future German race.'[18]

Johannes Haller spoke for many in the Weimar Republic when he explicitly rejected efforts to define the German nation in political rather than ethnic terms. He maintained that nations had a lasting and unchangeable character derived from long centuries of common history and culture: 'A six-hundred-year old past which has left deep marks in the life of a people simply cannot be erased by parliamentary decree.'[19] Under National Socialism Karl Alexander von Müller wrote about 'the conscious struggle against everything *artfremd*'.[20] Representatives of *Volksgeschichte*, like Adolf Helbok, suggested that one should write the history of the *Volk* as the history of 'an organic community of people united by blood and language and tied to a specific soil.'[21]

Even after 1945 numerous efforts to justify continuing national apologias – which, by that time, had almost become second nature to German historiography – were linked to the adoption of a kind of collective ethnic psychology. In the words of Hans Buchheim, it was self-evident 'that a people cannot live on the edge of a precipice ...

As in the life of an individual human being, the courage of a people to move ahead depends vitally on a past with which it can identify with a clear conscience.'[22] National historians routinely contrasted the positive idea of the nation-state with the National Socialist perversion of it. And some, like Gerhard Ritter, could still define one of the tasks of the historian after 1945 as that of identifying 'race peculiarities' *(rassische Eigenart)* within peoples.[23]

Apart from the early and lasting link to ethnicity, national identity merged, in the writings of many historians, with an adoration of the state and a firm rejection of revolutionary change. Dahlmann, for example, argued that the state, as a primordial phenomenon, could not possibly be revolutionised.[24] Sybel's political thought in 1848 was dominated by fear that social revolution could sweep away the edifice of the existing state.[25] For Droysen, the Prussian state was the ideal compromise between the sovereignity of the people declared by the French Revolution and the absolutism of the restoration period after 1815.[26] Even the liberal Mommsen, a republican opposed to all inherited rights and an enemy of Junkerdom par excellence, insisted on the creation of a powerful state with strong authority.[27]

German historiography after 1871 was characterised by an overwhelming consensus: German history was seen as constituting a positive counterpart to French history. The tendency to contrast strong German bonds of ethnicity and culture with shallow French universalism and the dangerous revolutionary tradition was extremely widespread amongst German historians in Imperial Germany and beyond.[28] In 1918, when the democratic revolution swept away the monarchy in Germany, the strength of anti-revolutionary sentiment in the overwhelming majority of German historians was impressively confirmed. Almost to a man, they condemned the German revolution and many refused to accept the republican state which emerged from it.[29] The 'national revolution' of the Nazi *Machtergreifung*, by contrast, was widely perceived as the beginning of a new period of national glory. It was accompanied by the hope that Germany would rise from the ashes of Versailles. In 1933 the parallel most frequently drawn by German historians was with 1870/71. Like Bismarck, Hitler held out the promise of national salvation after a prolonged period of national humiliation. After 1945 Gerhard Ritter's identification with the national paradigm made him an unreconstructed advocate of 'selfless love of the state' which he continued to propagate as central to the post-war education of Germans.

State adoration and anti-revolutionary thinking became anchored in German historiography through the towering influence of Leopold von Ranke. In 1832 Ranke was convinced that 'history ... prepares

the way for a healthy policy'.[30] Between 1832 and 1836, as editor of
the *Historisch-Politische Zeitschrift*, Ranke, in the interest of his Prussian
paymasters, used historical argument to demonstrate, first, that Germany did not necessarily have to go down the French path of revolution, and, secondly, that the individual was subordinate to the will
of the state. In Ranke's political thought, the state was a quasi-myth-
ical category which provided the cement between its contemporary
inhabitants as well as between present and past generations. His rea-
soning, however, was not so much political as religious. The divine
order of things lay at the very heart of each epoch. What had developed historically was sanctioned by God's will. Service to the state
was service to God.[31] This attitude was conservative in the sense that
it seemed to stabilise each existing state with reference to the divine
will. Inherently it was directed against change. Only that which had
evolved through a historical process was deemed to be politically
desirable. Any radical breaks with the past had to be major catastrophies. Hence, both in 1848 and again in 1870/71, Ranke was gripped
by violent fear of revolution, of a weakening of monarchical power
before the forces of rebellion and *sans-culottisme.*

If Ranke paved the way for significant aspects of Prussianism, he
was not himself an early convert to the idea of a unified German
nation: 'Who will be able to grasp in a word or concept what is German? Who will call it by name, the genius of our country, of the past
and of the future? It would only be another phantom to lure us down
one more false road.'[32] Unlike the national-liberal historians Ranke
never assumed an identity of state and nation, let alone people,
which ultimately lay the foundations for an ethnic understanding of
nationality. However, by 1867 he was writing of German historiography as belonging to those elements which make and shape the
national consciousness and thus the essence of the nation-state. He
welcomed Bismarck's unification of Germany in 1871, albeit cautiously at first, and only because he could see the new Empire as an
enlarged Prussia. Ranke, who since 1841 had been official historiographer to the King of Prussia, shared in the propagation of the credo
of Prussianism, that the establishment of the German Empire had
been Prussia's destiny. He wholeheartedly approved of the conservative turn of the late 1870s, when Bismarck ended his tacit alliance
with German liberalism *(zweite Reichsgründung)*. Yet, whilst endorsing
the German nation-state, Ranke's historical concern for the emergence of nation-states in Europe prevented him from turning into a
narrow nationalist singing the glory of the German nation alone. He
did, however, insist that the historical process was characterised by
the rivalries of different, succint national interests. Such rivalries,

emerging from efforts to uphold the unique *Volksgeist* against competing claims of other nations, translated into foreign policy and at
times even military conflict. Those nations with the strongest moral
energies emerged victorious from this competition and thus moved
history inevitably forward towards progress and higher morality. In
linking ethnicity to nations and nations to moral forces, Ranke thus
fostered nationalist tendencies. As soon as the national liberal historians began identifying the superior moral forces in the German
nation, its people became superior to any others.

Although his politics and world view clearly influenced Ranke's historical writings, he had always insisted on objectivity and detachment.
His history wanted to avoid taking sides in the major ideological battles
of the nineteenth century. In this area he found little understanding
with the generation of Prussian historians who paralleled and followed
him. Historians, they argued, had to provide answers to contemporary
problems. Political engagement and historical method should combine
to form the ideal of 'historians of life'. Droysen condemned the 'impo-
tent objectivity' *(eunuchische Objektivität)* of historians.[33] Heinrich von
Treitschke abhorred what he called their 'horrendous unprincipled
pussyfooting'.[34] Historians had to take sides and get involved in the
political controversies of the day, otherwise they were, in the words of
Sybel, 'blood- and lifeless'.[35]

The attitude of national liberal historians to the nation-state was
decisively shaped by the experience of 1848. In the *Vormärz* many
sought to link national identity to the progressive values and ideas of
the Enlightenment and to participatory demands for the educated
middle classes. Their understanding of the nation was anti-absolutist,
even if it was only rarely linked to notions of a democratisation and
parliamentarisation of political rule. Above all, notions of a *Rechtsstaat*,
a state based on the rule of law, inspired the liberal historians of the
Vormärz epoch. Dahlmann and Gervinus belonged to the Göttingen
Seven who were expelled from the University of Göttingen in 1837
for protesting against the suspension of the Hannover constitution,
while Theodor Mommsen edited a radical liberal newspaper in
Schleswig-Holstein. In 1848, Droysen argued that good nations have
to rest on ethical foundations. Many historians served as deputies in
the 'parliament of the professors' in 1848: Dahlmann, Droysen, Max
Duncker, Gervinus, Karl Welcker, Rudolf Haym, Georg Waitz. Sybel
was a member of the Frankfurt pre-parliament, and Ludwig Häusser
was a member of the Baden *Landtag.*

In the eyes of these 'revolutionaries', 1848 was really about preventing a revolution and bringing into one their hopes for a Prussian-
led and liberal unified Germany. Their central dilemma lay in

squaring the anti-liberalism of the Prussian state with their ambitions
for a liberal united Germany. After the Prussian king had rejected the
German crown in 1848 from the hands of these well-meaning revolutionaries, national-liberal historians began to tone down demands
for a liberalisation of Prussia. In the words of Haym: 'A nation is willing to sacrifice some of its domestic liberty if in return it is presented
with an increase in power and prestige abroad.'[36] The Prussian historians had 'turned politics into metaphysics' long before 1848 by
judging every political event according to what was allegedly historically necessary, i.e., the building of a German nation by Prussia.[37]
For Droysen the terms Prussia and Germany became almost indistinguishable.[38] The *Preußische Jahrbücher*, founded in 1857, became an
important mouthpiece for demands for the unification of Germany
under the leadership of Prussia. Sybel, Heinrich von Treitschke and
Hermann Baumgarten all contributed to this effect. War was perceived as legitimate means of nation-building. Sybel confessed to
Duncker in 1860: 'For a long time now I have been wishing Prussia
a healthy, just war, which would be German in an eminent way. This
would have to be a war for healthy, just German purposes ...'.[39] The
Historische Zeitschrift, which Sybel helped to found, the Historical
Commission and the university departments were all dedicated to
the task of assuring a learned public of the historical foundations of
the German nation-state.[40]

After 1866 very few national liberal historians still doubted that
history was on the side of Bismarck. Theodor Mommsen wrote to his
brother Tycho in 1866: 'Germany will have a future and this future
will be determined by Prussia. This is no longer a mere hope, it is a
momentous fact for all time to come.'[41] Although he was to criticise
Bismarck for his conservative turn of the late 1870s and was, ever
after, one of his sharpest critics, Mommsen had nothing but admiration for Bismarck's foreign policies leading to unification. Like Cae-
sar in his Roman history, Bismarck was the one who brought unity
from above and allowed the rebirth of a fallen nation. He was the
necessary genius who fulfilled history's will. It was, of course, also in
the political climate of 1866 that Hermann Baumgarten wrote his
famous self-criticism of liberalism, castigating liberals for having
placed constitutional values before considerations of power politics,
thereby allegedly undermining the *Volk*.[42]

Bismarck's violent unification of Germany had an important
impact on how historians committed to the national paradigm, from
Heinrich von Sybel to Hans-Peter Schwarz, have consistently used
the category of 'success' to legitimise or delegitimise historical developments. A historical action was not justified by its moral credibility

but by its success. Such thinking, in a way, is already present in Ranke and his belief in historical development as God's will. It is also present in Hegel's belief that reason and history are identitical. For Hegel, history has to be rational because rationality itself is historical. There is no other rationality than the one which finds expression in historical personalities and events. All this is the foundation of a historiography of victors, in which losers have no place, as all values and actions are relative to their success. Such delinking of historical judgement from moral criteria anticipates the later value relativism of German historians, which made them defenceless in the face of National Socialism. Most historians greeted the Nazis as the latest victors whose history they, by the very nature of their profession, had to write.

By 1871 German historians had learnt their lesson. In 1871 Sybel, for example, justified 'historically' the annexation of Alsace and Lorraine.[43] The wars of unification led to an idealisation of war in German historiography which predestined historians to become the herolds of war both in 1914 and 1939. For Treitschke war had been the 'school of personality'. In 1914 Erich Marcks, one of the most well known and respected of German historians, wrote about the war which was to engulf Europe: 'We bow our heads before it in pain and smallness, and yet we lift them up to the splendour emanating from its almighty being. It keeps in front of our coy eyes the radiating, threatening and liberating *menschlich Ewige*. The greatness of this human-superhuman power, which alone makes our life worth living, breaks through directly into our poor existence. In human terms there is nothing greater than war, nothing more manly, but also nothing more inspiring for the inner soul.'[44] During the Second World War, a majority of German historians were full of admiration for the German armies in 1940, when enthusiasm for the war reached a high point, but even as late as 1943 some, e.g., Hans Hallmann, could still write of the 'heroic struggle' of the German soldiers at Stalingrad.[45]

It was against the background of the nationalisation of German history after 1871 that Jakob Burckhardt famously remarked that one would only have to wait for a few years 'until the whole of world history beginning with Adam would be coated with German triumphalism' *(siegesdeutsch angestrichen).*[46] The historical consciousness of National Liberals now moved firmly to the right which became evident with the debate surrounding Treitschke's *Deutsche Geschichte* in 1882/83.[47] Nationalist historiography was to find its climax in the Berlin historian Heinrich von Treitschke. In Treitschke's Berlin seminars the future elites of Wilhelmine Germany were indoctrinated with teutomanic, imperialist and anti-Semitic ideas. His popular five-volume *Deutsche Geschichte im Neunzehnten Jahrhundert* magisterially played all the different tunes of the powerful legend of Prussia's German vocation. A series of gigantic Hohenzollern heroes had made German national history. In the dedication of his unfinished *magnum opus* he had expressed his sense of '... the richness and simple greatness of the history of our fatherland. No people has better reason than we to honour the memory of our fathers who fought so hard. And yet no people remembers so rarely how much blood and tears have been spilt to bring the blessings of unity.' Hence it was the historian's task to awaken in the reader 'the joy of having a fatherland.'[48] In April 1874 his appointment in Berlin was already linked with an explicit hope that Treitschke was not so much a brilliant scholar but a pedagogue who would encourage his students to develop national identity.[49] In Social Darwinist fashion Treitschke viewed the relations of nation-states as the battle for the survival of the fittest. Racial overtones intermingled with anglophobe and anti-socialist, anti-democratic sentiments to make Treitschke the most effective apologist of the Wilhelmine period.[50] Treitschke propagated the view that a 'healthy' nation rests on the ethnic homogeneity of its people. Hence he became an intellectual founding father of the Prussian Germanisation policies in Poland, and he referred to Jews as 'an alien people, no doubt hated by the overwhelming majority of the German people.'[51]

Yet, despite Treitschke and despite the strong nationalist tradition in German late-nineteenth century historiography, regional and local ties of historians remained important too. Unification under Prussian leadership was at times immensely unpopular in the non-Prussian regions of Germany, and one should not underestimate the number of historians who were and remained anti-Prussian both before and after 1870/71. Local and regional historical paradigms thus could act as counterbalances to the national paradigm. Furthermore there was a continued strong tradition, deriving from the eighteenth-century Göttingen school, to write the history of the European state system which, by its very nature, went beyond the national paradigm. Jakob Burckhardt and Eberhard Gothein both wrote cultural history which remained sceptical of the national paradigm. Socialist historiography which developed in the Social Democratic sub-culture outside the universities remained hostile to the dominant historiographic nationalism. Its commitment to the nation, as reflected in the works of Eduard Bernstein, Wilhelm Blos, Franz Mehring and Gustav Mayer, far from being absent, was not the Prussianised, authoritarian, undemocratic and monarchical Bismarckian version.[52] Apart from the socialist tradition, Catholic historiography represented for example by Friedrich Emanuel von Hurter, Constantin Höfler, Johannes Janssen, Julius Ficker, Martin Spahn and Ignaz Döllinger overwhelmingly remained anti-Prussian. The very beginnings of the biannual assemblies of German historians *(Historikertag)* in 1892 was a reaction against Prussianism. A number of South German historians raised their voices against a reform of the school curricula along Prussian lines.[53] The Catholic *Historisch-Politische Blätter*, founded in the 1860s, and later on the *Historisches Jahrbuch*, founded in 1880, remained journals in which the Prussian myths were viewed with a great deal of scepticism. Catholics felt excluded by the Protestant definition of Germanness inherent in Prussian historiography. Yet Catholics were not necessarily less nationalist than the Prussians. Attachment to 'greater German' *(großdeutsch)* notions of the national paradigm remained strong in the Catholic camp up to 1945. Similarly, attachment to regional and local history *(Landesgeschichte)* was not necessarily in opposition to nationalist perspectives. Local history could and did merge with the national paradigm. Even the socialists' efforts to delineate a positive democratic patriotism from a negatiave xenophobic nationalism sometimes blurred the extent to which the socialists shared in the dominant national consensus.

Such national consensus was certainly achieved amongst the so-called neo-Rankean school, which, according to many textbook accounts of German historiography, began to replace the Prussian school at some time during the last quarter of the nineteenth century. The neo-Rankeans might have stressed the 'objectivity' of historical study more than the Prussians, but in their justification of German imperialism they continued the earlier trends set by the Prussian historians. It has been rightly observed that there were moderate and conservative neo-Rankeans with very different perceptions on domestic politics. However, there was little disagreement over foreign policy and the question of the nation-state. The function of history remained explicitly to preserve the 'idea of nationality'.[54] For Max Lenz, the superiority of the Europeans over 'other races' lay in the Europeans' capacity to organise themselves in nation-states and develop a national consciousness.[55] Their Social Darwinism, expressed through a diffusion of organic imagery, contributed towards the aggressive nationalist *Zeitgeist* so characteristic of the Wilhelmine period of German history. Ranke's concept of the 'Great Powers' served them well to prop up German *Weltpolitik*.[56] German historians contributed to the emergence and cementation of the Anglo-German rivalry before 1914.[57]

Characteristic representatives of Pan-German historians were Georg von Below, Karl Lamprecht, Otto Hoetzsch and Dietrich

Schäfer. Schäfer, one of the most prominent historians in Imperial Germany, was active in almost all nationalist and imperialist organisations. In his autobiography he defined the task of the historian thus: 'The ultimate aim of both my political and my scholarly work has always been to contribute to the emergence of a strong German nation-state. The German historian can serve the national idea without in the least betraying his duties to truthfulness.'[58] Schäfer's populist histories of Germany secured him a wide readership and considerable influence amongst Germany's middle classes.[59] He defined Germans as the 'Volk der Mitte', arguing that its geographic location made the country particularly vulnerable to aggression. A strong state and a strong military force were thus necessary if Germany was to survive. The theory of *geographische Mittellage* was born out of the almost exclusive concern of the historians of the Wilhelmine period with the politics of the European states. A broad consensus emerged, ranging from the Pan-Germans on the far right to the National Social movement *(Nationalsozialer Verein)* associated with Friedrich Naumann on the centre-left, that the German Reich, threatened by external enemies and internal subversives alike, could not afford to become a constitutional democratic state. Only a monarchic government with a strong civil service and a strong army would be capable of maintaining Germany intact.[60] The neo-Rankeans' support for authoritarian government and their pompous Bismarck cult were once again justified with reference to Ranke's 'great men' theory.[61]

In Imperial Germany historians played a prominent role in what Benedict Anderson has termed 'official nationalism'.[62] As we have seen in the cases of Treitschke and Schäfer, nationalist historiography was officially supported and sanctioned by political elites and the government in Imperial Germany who sought to whip up German national feeling. Another example of such semi-official histories would be Heinrich von Sybel's *Die Begründung des Deutschen Reiches durch Wilhelm I* which was published in seven volumes between 1889 and 1894. Precisely because there was too little popular national identity, because the Reich was created as an alliance of sovereigns rather than a federal state, and because anti-Prussian feelings were far from absent in other German states, the unification process had to be aided by a conscious propagation of national feeling. Nationalism was used as an anti-democratic, anti-socialist force which could prop up the government's authoritarian regime and support its imperialist ambitions of *Weltpolitik*. Particular importance was attached to the teaching of history in schools. The most critical eye of the censor was directed towards history textbooks for schools, especially after a

Prussian royal edict of 1889 ruled that such books had to support the existing social and political order. Whereas most schools and universities before 1871 had laid particular emphasis on the teaching of *Landesgeschichte*, i.e., the history of the individual German states, thereafter it was increasingly the Prussian version of German national history and the Hohenzollern and Bismarck myths which took first place on the curricula.[63]

Some of the most trenchant critics of Imperial Germany never doubted for one moment the superiority of the Prussian-German state. The conservation of Prussian and Protestant traditions in the unified Germany and its position as a major world power came to be unquestioned principles in the world view of, for example, Hans Delbrück, Max Weber and Gustav Schmoller. Thus, whilst distancing himself from the extreme nationalism of the Pan-Germans, Delbrück supported the Wilhelmine quest for 'a place under the sun'. In fact, he went as far as to argue that Germany's status as a world power would justify limiting its citizens' freedom. Criticisms of Wilhelm's inadequacies as monarch went hand-in-hand with Delbrück's rejection of parliamentary government as incompatible with the Prussian tradition.[64] Weber only left the Pan-Germans in 1899 because he thought that they did not represent German ethnic interests efficiently vis-à-vis the Polish population in Eastern Prussia. For him, economics was only 'another form of the struggle of the nations with each other'. His historical judgement depended on whether it fostered or hindered the 'eternal struggle for the preservation and upward selective breeding of our national kind'.[65] Social reform was a means of unifying the nation and strengthening it for the foreign-policy struggles to come. Schmoller's work demonstrates how the whole issue of social reform – in many ways at the very heart of the Naumann circle before the First World War – could co-exist comfortably with Prussianism. As the influential founder of the German school of historical economics, he contributed extensively to the Hohenzollern hagiography by emphasising their importance in creating a sound social welfare state.[66]

Equally, some of the most famous outsiders in the historical profession in Imperial Germany such as Otto Hintze and Karl Lamprecht shared the deeply nationalist outlook of their colleagues. Both Hintze and Lamprecht were on the one hand trying to find a way out of the narrow political confines of German historiography by exploring, social, structural and comparative history. Yet, underpinning Lamprecht's conception of history in particular was the notion of a collective German psyche.[67] He sought to establish the essential soul of the Germans. The ethno-psychological criteria which structure his

Deutsche Geschichte of 1891 were in line with the dominant ethnic definitions of nationhood. Since Lamprecht was close to the Pan-Germans (before turning *volte face* to the peace movement and back to violent nationalism at the beginning of the war), it is hardly surprising that the long-time chairman of the Pan-German League, Heinrich Claß, copied extensively from Lamprecht's *Deutsche Geschichte* in his own writings. Hintze was 'deeply steeped in Prussian traditions'.[68] He shared the Prussian view that a strong and authoritarian nation-state was the precondition for success in foreign policy. Hence, he argued, if Germany wanted to be a world power, it first had to develop into a homogeneous nation. Social Darwinist notions are present in Hintze's work as are notions of Germany's vulnerable geopolitical situation *(Mittellage)* and of Germany's colonial mission. In 1914, Hintze justified German militarism as the highest form of ethics and civilisation. He belonged to the group of most vociferous propagandists of the German war effort, which he perceived as a defence of the equilibrium of power against Britain's perfidious wish for world dominance. A monarchist at heart, he only hesitantly came to support the Weimar Republic in the 1920s. To minimise Hintze's Prussianism in order to emphasise his innovating role as a social and economic historian is clearly unacceptable.[69]

In Imperial Germany, historians committed to the national paradigm were rarely openly racist, but often imperialist, anti-democratic and anti-parliamentary as well as anti-pluralist and anti-socialist. The legacy of nationalist historiography for the Weimar Republic was devastating. Lone calls for a revision of the national tradition in German historiography by some outsiders such as Walter Goetz and Franz Schnabel were ignored. Goetz clearly realised that this tradition would make any rapprochement between the Republic and German historians impossible.[70] Schnabel even went one step further by questioning the validity of the Prussian historians' claim that Prussia's mission had been to unify Germany. For the Catholic Schnabel, Prussia's leading role in a united Germany had few roots in history.[71]

Almost to a man, the German historians chose to uphold the nationalist myths and looked towards the rehabilitation of Germany as a major European power. As 'political historians' they saw one of their major roles in providing subsequent German governments with 'historical' arguments for the revision of the Treaty of Versailles. Several semi-official propaganda organisations, employing and cooperating with some of the most well-known German historians, aimed at influencing public consciousness.[72] Hans Delbrück, Friedrich Thimme, Paul Herre, Hans Rothfels, Hans Herzfeld, Siegfried A. Kaehler, Wilhelm Mommsen, to mention but a few, cooperated with the so-called department for questions relating to German war guilt in the foreign office *(Kriegsschuldreferat)* which was set up with the explicit task of winning the propagandistic fight against the 'treaty of shame'. The major edition of sources entitled 'Great Politics of the European Cabinets 1871-1914', published in forty volumes between 1922 and 1927 remained clouded by these apologetic tendencies to prove the innocence of Germany in the outbreak of the First World War.[73] Towards the end of the 1920s conspiracy theories laying the blame firmly at the door of the Allies had a very wide currency.[74] In the European power struggle for supremacy, Versailles was now interpreted as the combined effort of the Allies to fight off the challenge of the strong German nation. Major works of the period dealing with the question of war guilt were explicitly written to develop a positive national identity of the German people.[75]

Many established historians like Georg von Below, Max Lenz, Erich Marcks and Dietrich Schäfer despised the Weimar Republic which they connected with defeat and revolution. Hans Herzfeld, prominently supported the extreme right-wing stab-in-the-back theory.[76] Nothing gives a better sense of the *Zunft's* continued firm adherence to forms of ethnic nationalism than Georg von Below's overview of the history of German historiography:

> We are unable to imagine culture without declaring our commitment to our *Volkstum*. Unlike Enlightenment thinkers, we do not believe either in natural law or in universal constitutional values. ... historians in Germany have worked hard to exclude such alien French radicalism from German blood. Romanticism gave to us an understanding of the *Volksgeist* and helped us to build the German nation. Now the nation is dejected. We have been robbed of our German freedom. German historiography of the good old kind will once again encourage and support the rebuilding of the nation.[77]

Below contrasted Prussianism positively with the historical writings of 'democrats lacking scholarly profundity'.[78] Opposed to the 'cloud-cuckoo-land of cosmopolitanism',[79] he endorsed the romantics' view that the state – as the product of the people's spirit – had to stand at the very centre of historical investigation. Below was an extreme enemy of the republic. However, even those who came to accept Weimar, like Hermann Oncken, remained under the spell of national myths, for example the necessity for a strong state, the geopolitical notion of *Mittellage*, the primacy of foreign policy, the *Mitteleuropa* idea as basis for a hegemonic position of Germany on the continent and Russian nationalism as the guilty party in the outbreak of the First World War. Oncken re-affirmed Bismarck's role as a *deus ex*

machina who had unified Germany single-handedly and thereby fulfilled the will of the German people.[80]

The strength of anti-republican nationalism in the Weimar Republic may have had something to do with the lack of generational
change in the historical profession. Few chairs became vacant in the
1920s. Yet a more critical stance towards the national myths can be
observed amongst those younger historians whose professional
career began in the 1920s, for instance Karl Dietrich Erdmann,
G.W.F. Hallgarten, Hajo Holborn, Eckart Kehr, Arthur Rosenberg,
Hans Rosenberg and Ernst Simon.[81] Erdmann, as a twenty-two year
old student, took a courageous stance against the Langemarck myth
and against Prussianism's glorification of war.[82] In 1933 Kehr wrote
one of the most powerful indictments of German nationalist historiography.[83] He analysed the development of German historiography
as a continuous move to the political right ever since the early nineteenth century. For him historians were representative of middle-class
liberalism at large, in that they increasingly abandoned their liberal
heritage and turned to authoritarian statism instead.

The major divide amongst German historians, however, was not
generational. It was between those rejecting republicanism outright
and the so-called *Vernunftrepublikaner*, i.e., those who rejected it in
their hearts but saw no credible alternative to it. The handful of
(mostly younger and often Jewish) *Herzensrepublikaner* remained completely marginal to the historical profession. Some pro-republicans,
like Johannes Ziekursch and Hajo Holborn, remained so committed
to the national concept that they willingly contributed to the fight of
German historians against Versailles.[84] The overwhelming anti-
republicanism was underpinned by the theory of a German *Sonderweg*.[85] According to this theory, the German nation-state was
different from and superior to the West European nation-states on
several accounts. In particular, the Prussian idea of the state standing
above society and party politics prevented an endorsement of the
pluralism of parliamentary democracy. The *Sonderweg* paradigm
together with the deep sense of humiliation only served to strengthen
the deeply held belief of many historians in the merits of monarchical government, military prowess, efficient bureaucracy, excellence
of educational system and industrial achievement.

Historians continued to understand political processes primarily
as power politics. Max Lenz underlined the Prussian belief that in
politics only might is right. For him the struggle for power, survival
and supremacy were basic instincts which could and should not be
overcome because they were signs of the vitality of the nation.[86] History was portrayed as the struggle of nation-states for supremacy.

The primacy of foreign policy hence continued to hold sway in German historiography. Any criticism of Bismarck was regarded as a form of negative nationalism, its author quickly treated as someone keen to foul his own nest. Bismarck remained, in the words of Johannes Haller, 'the saviour of the nation'.[87] The same functionalisation of historical writing can be seen in the widespread portrayal of the Freiherr vom Stein in the Weimar Republic as an anti-democratic, monarchic and statist figure.[88] The continued concern of most historians with 'the great men in history' contributed to their vulnerability to the appeal of Adolf Hitler.

Little that can be classed as genuine Nazi historiography emerged between 1933 and 1945.[89] Historians have long prided themselves in retaining much of their institutional autonomy under Nazism.[90] The works of 'race historians', like Günther Woltmann and Bernhardi, were widely regarded as pure speculation and pseudo-history. The universities continued to be dominated by the same national conservative, Prussian professors. The enforced resignation of Meinecke as editor of the prestigious *Historische Zeitschrift* in 1935 and his replacement by Karl Alexander von Müller, or the foundation of the Nazi Reichsinstitut für Geschichte des Neuen Deutschland, headed by Walter Frank, had only a very marginal impact on the *Zunft* as a whole. History as a subject suffered less from direct politicisation and functionalisation than the younger disciplines of political science and sociology.[91] Walter Frank's call to arms for an explicitly partisan Nazi historiography went virtually unheeded. The majority of German historians had long cultivated their own brand of cultural and political nationalism which proved to be largely compatible with the biological nationalism of the Nazis. The study of German *Volkstum*, for example in the German Academy for the Cultivation of Germandom, had been prominent during the Weimar Republic. In the work of Hermann Oncken, for example, it was linked less to biological and racist ideas and more to the idea of the cultural nation. However, when Frank argued that German historians had to go down the path from *Zunft* to *Nation*,[92] he ignored the fact that the two had entered into a lasting marriage from the early nineteenth century onwards. Frank's 'struggle for a new era of German greatness'[93] had been the aim of German historians ever since the declaration of the Treaty of Versailles in 1919. German historians and Nazism shared in a discourse of *Volksgemeinschaft*. The differences between the historians' interpretation of such community and that of the offical Nazi ideologues were substantial, yet the shared language of nationalism was not conducive to the emergence of oppositional views to the Nazi regime amongst members of the historical profession.[94]

Karl Alexander von Müller, who had been amongst the first of the German Rhodes scholars at the University of Oxford, was in many respects a typical product of the national tradition. His boundless admiration for Bismarck's unification of Germany made him an ardent supporter of a strong state and a champion of Germany's role as major world power before 1914. Shocked by defeat and revolution, he never came to terms with the parliamentary republic of Weimar. Instead, as head of the Institute for Research into German Ethnic Minorities in South and South-Eastern Europe he moved closer to *völkisch* ideas. After 1933 his reputation as mentor of many young Nazi historians catapulted him into prominence. Like the majority of his colleagues he always had nothing but disdain for what he regarded as the plebeian side of Nazism. Even so, he willingly lent himself to the Nazis, accepted honours and positions and readily described National Socialism as fulfilling Germany's destiny. His belief in the National Socialist mission of raising Germany from the ashes of Versailles, of bringing unity to the German people in the form of the *Volksgemeinschaft*, of ending the un-German concepts of liberalism and parliamentary democracy and of putting the ideas of power politics and *Mitteleuropa* back into the centre of Germany's foreign policy made Müller 'representative of the overwhelming majority of traditional German historians'.[95]

Individual historians, like Gerhard Ritter (whose early career was shaped by orthodox Lutheran religion, anti-Semitism and nationalism[96]) played a part in the resistance against National Socialism. Had the putsch in 1944 been successful, he would have been a strong candidate for the Ministry of Culture in a post-Hitlerian German government. Ritter retained enough institutional independence throughout the years of Nazism to risk occasional cautious criticism of Nazi policies. Yet Ritter's stance was characterised by a deep ambiguity. In his biography of Frederick the Great, published in 1936, he had, after all, drawn the famous line from Frederick to Hindenburg to Hitler which the Nazis so longed to propagate.[97]

The Nazis' *Drang nach Osten* was ably supported by a number of historians who had long belonged to the most vociferous proponents of a renewed expansion of Germany into Eastern Europe.[98] Adalbert Wahl dreamed of National Socialism rebuilding a strong German empire. For him the German people's racial superiority was at the heart of Germany's historical mission of ruling other people and countries.[99] The Nazi regime thus was clearly capable of integrating the conservative-nationalist historiography which widely legitimised a criminal regime, an unparalleled war of extermination and the brutal conquest on the Eastern front during the Second World War.

Contrary to widespread perceptions after 1945 there was no with-drawal into depoliticised scholarship. The 'scholarly standards' about which German historians showed themselves to be so con-cerned were indeed largely maintained, yet they could also go hand-in-hand with legitimising Nazi policies.[100]

Those on the margins of German historiography in the Weimar Republic like Veit Valentin, Gustav Mayer, Arthur Rosenberg, and Hajo Holborn emigrated after 1933, many to Britain and the United States. Only 21 of the 134 exiled historians returned after 1945. Those who did return were often representatives of the national tradition, like Hans Rothfels and Hans-Joachim Schoeps. Of those who had remained in Germany during the Nazi period, only those who had been irrevocably tainted by the propagation of Nazi racism, like Erwin Hölzle or Adolf Rein, were purged from the profession. This, however, did not prevent them from finding outlets for their publica-tions. Others continued unharmed as long as they were willing to renounce and disown National Socialism together with its racial con-cept of history. Some, like Walther Hubatsch, even were confirmed in their chairs despite their continued justification of Nazi foreign and military policy. In the mid-1960s Hubatsch could still describe Hin-denburg as a Prussian hero, defending in particular his appointment of Hitler as chancellor.[101] Amongst popular non-academic history books the nationalist positions denying Germany's responsibility for the Second World War could still be found.[102] And Müller remained a paradigmatic case beyond 1945. Although deeply embroiled with Nazism, he was only banned from his professorship for a short period. Continuing his career, he received many more official hon-ours, which he could add to those awarded by the Nazis, and died in 1964 – a respected member of the *Zunft*.

Even more important than the continuity of personnel was the continued commitment to the nation-state in the works of leading post-war historians like Ritter, Rothfels, Herzfeld, and Meinecke. If anything, 1945 marked only a limited parting, a kind of delayed break with older national assumptions amongst German historians, although this conflicts with many of their own assessments. Theodor Schieder, for example, argued that 'the bond between national policy and history had been torn apart ever since the noble concepts of the older German historiography, such as nation, state and fatherland, had been plundered and burnt out amidst the general destruction left by the war.'[103] The director of the Max Planck Institute for History in Göttingen, Hermann Heimpel, argued that the nationalist historiog-raphy of the pre-1945 era had died once and for all after the collapse of National Socialism.[104] Hans Herzfeld wrote: 'Because of the dual

catastrophies of 1919 and 1945, Germany, in the course of one generation, saw itself confronted with the task of revising its concept of
history twice.'[105] Leo Kirch, writing from an orthodox Marxist perspective, even spoke of the 'national nihilism' of West German historiography in the 1950s.[106] However, much of the alleged critical
stock-taking was little more than a rhetorical smoke-screen of lament,
behind which the same old national apologias, somewhat toned done
in volume, could and did continue. No national vacuum emerged in
the immediate post-war years, neither in historiography nor in the
public debate at large.[107] This does not mean that there were no
efforts to examine some of the uncritical assumptions of German historiography.[108] Some of those who returned temporarily to visiting
professorships like Hans Rosenberg had major influence on the next
generation of professional historians.[109] Yet in the light of what many
German historians took to be an international conspiracy to blacken
the whole of German history, many rallied to the defence of the
nation. The founding of the Ranke society in 1950 was directly
linked to such aspirations. For Gustav Adolf Rein, its founding father,
the main task of the time was the struggle against the one-sided and
negative falsification of German history. Many respected members of
the *Zunft* belonged to the society including Hermann Aubin, along
with Otto Brunner and Werner Conze.[110] Ranke and his alleged
objectivity were to serve as bulwark against any more sceptical and
critical approach to German national history.

Rothfels had been notorious for the public support he had given
to German expansionism in Eastern Europe both before and after
1933.[111] He probably would have come to an arrangement with the
Nazi dictatorship had it not been for his Jewish ancestry. After 1945,
next to Meinecke and Ritter, he became the most influential representative of German historiography and headed the Historians'
Association from 1958 to 1962. The nation as 'the political *Volksgemeinschaft* which proves itself as the moral community of free
Volksgenossen'[112] formed the focal point of Rothfels's historical studies
right from the 1920s through to the 1950s. Professor of history at the
University of Königsberg between 1926 and 1934, he argued that the
Baltic before 1917 could serve as a model of how autonomous and
federal structures allowed members of different people and nations
to co-exist. Such a view, however, was intrinsically linked to an
underlying assumption of German dominance. After 1945 he saw little reason fundamentally to alter his position. He continued to speak
in rather vague terms of the 'community of fate of Germans and
Western Slavs' in Eastern Europe and evoked the German presence
in Eastern Europe after it had *de facto* ceased to exist.[113]

Convinced that 'national egotism is a prime moving force in modern history',[114] he routinely distinguished between good nationalism and the National Socialist perversion of it. Whereas in 1956 Rothfels could still write approvingly of the 'splendour and authenticity' of the nationalism of the Langemarck volunteers in the First World War,[115] the Nazis, in his view, had not been nationalists but racists. The artificial distinction between Nazi racism and German nationalism served its purpose well. Thus the good nationalism of the men of the 20 July plot could easily be juxtaposed with Hitler's lack of concern for the nation, as demonstrated by his infamous Nero order of 1945. The historiography on the national opposition to Hitler served as an important means of upholding the national tradition in German historiography. For Ritter, it was only on the basis of the values represented by the men of 20 July that 'a healthy national self-confidence' could grow.[116]

Rothfels, like Ritter, saw the roots of Nazism in modern democratic mass society, in the nihilism and cultural destruction of modern industrial society, in the collapse of traditional religious and moral standards.[117] In Ritter's words: 'In essence, National Socialism is not an original German phenomenon, but the German variant of a European manifestation: the one-party and Führer state. It cannot be explained by referring to German traditions. Its roots lie in the specific modern crisis of liberal society and state.'[118] Foreigners, not Germans had been responsible for Hitler: 'neither Frederick the Great, Bismarck nor Wilhelm II [but] the demagogues and Caesars of modern history from Danton to Lenin to Mussolini' were the Nazis' antecedents.[119] If anything, Nazism was an 'Austrian-Bavarian import'.[120] Prussian values and traditions had little in common with Nazi values. And, once again, geo-political explanations proved handy for a tragic portrayal of events: 'a country in the centre, like Germany, is threatened to a far greater degree than others', if it fails to embark upon the difficult *via media* between 'self-assertion' and 'self-denial'.[121]

Ritter saw his task after 1945 not in criticising the German national tradition but in strengthening the Germans' national identity. He warned: 'Today the national self-confidence of the Germans has been deeply shaken – one should not drive them into self-despair.'[122] For Ritter, a people 'which in principle relinquishes "national consciousness" abandons itself. As a consequence it will not improve but decline morally.'[123] He defined the main objective of post-war historiography as 'creating a new national consensus, laying the foundations for a new national self-confidence.'[124] This was also the underlying rationale of his monumental effort to refute the critics of Prussian militarism.[125] Where Ritter led, others soon followed. Siegfried A. Kaehler called upon his students after 1945: 'After pulling through six years of war with all their uplifting and finally destructive vicissitudes, the moral obligation of the disinherited is incumbent upon your generation in particular, not to forget the true greatness and the true spirit of German history ...'.[126] Hermann Heimpel wrote in 1953: 'every active people needs a certain self-confidence about its tradition, without which it will never be able to come to terms with its own past.'[127] Paul Egon Hübinger warned against any 'historical masochism which finds satisfaction in the blackening of one's own people's history whilst portraying others in a favourable light.'[128]

In 1960 Herzfeld essentially confirmed the validity of the Bismarckian definition of the German nation-state: 'throughout all the crises of the twentieth century, the inner development of Germany seems to confirm clearly that the limited union, created by Bismarck, fulfilled the needs and wishes of the modern nation.'[129] After 1945, in contrast to his earlier anti-Western position, Herzfeld put his historical pen behind Adenauer's policy of Western integration. In this regard and not in the wider form of a revision of his Prussian convictions, Gerhard A. Ritter's emphasis on Herzfeld's changed views after 1945 seems correct.[130] For Herzfeld, historians continued to have a national political mission.[131] In the past they had made mistakes, notably in the Weimar Republic, when, led by 'blind tragedy' and 'the necessity of the contemporary situation'[132] they had contributed to the undermining of the republic. The lesson for the present, according to Herzfeld, was to refocus the politics of German historiography: the resurrection of the Bismarckian nation-state had to be sought within the framework of an anti-Communist Western Europe. Hence he called upon fellow historians to support Adenauer's policy of Western integration as the only credible national policy for the present.[133]

Meinecke's reaction to the German catastrophe was different but not, as is sometimes assumed, diametrically opposed to Ritter's or Rothfels's apologetics. Meinecke, the doyen of West German historiography after 1945, shared their admiration for Prussia. As a true pupil of Sybel and Treitschke, he believed in its historical mission. Yet already before 1918 he was committed to genuinely liberal ideas to an extent that was hard to find amongst his fellow historians. His position during the First World War had oscillated between violent condemnation of the Pan-Germans and equally vociferous support for Germany's colonisation of Eastern Europe, including the large-scale deportation of non-Germanic people. In the Weimar Republic

his version of intellectual history *(Geistesgeschichte)*, which attracted
prominent and promising followers in Berlin, stood in marked contrast to the statist and nationalist types of history writing produced
elsewhere. In the early 1930s he took a courageous and decisive
stance against Nazism. Yet at the same time his fascination with the
ideology of *Volksgemeinschaft* and his continued power fixation had
led him to sympathise with German foreign policy under Hitler;
thus he favoured the Austrian *Anschluß*, justified the carve up of
Czechoslovakia, and welcomed the French defeat in 1940 as just
retribution for the Treaty of Versailles. His opposition to Hitler was
never so strong as to override his primary loyalty to the German
nation-state.[134] His analysis of the German catastrophe after 1945, in
stark contrast to Ritter, emphasised that Nazism had its origins in
specific German national traditions. So, for example, he harshly criticised Prussian militarism and the allegedly weak bourgeoisie in
Imperial Germany. Yet he was also quick to add: 'Hitler's National
Socialism ... does not have its roots solely in German developments.
However terrifyingly unique it appears as perversion of our own
character, it has specific analogies and precursors in the authoritarian political systems of our neighbouring countries.'[135] Meinecke
also delivered a geopolitical tragic portrayal of German history. Germany's position in the middle of Europe, he argued, had forced it to
become either a power vacuum or a great and powerful nation-state.
The latter had brought it inevitably in conflict with other major
European nation-states. Finally it remains rather startling to read in
1946, in a section which stresses the positive contribution of Jews to
German culture and economic prosperity, of their 'negative and dis-
integrating influence' on Germany, and about the 'defects of the
Jewish character'.[136]

   Throughout his life Meinecke remained an advocate of a positive
German *Sonderweg.*[137] Western materialism and utilitarianism were
the twin evils of modernity which remained juxtaposed with a positive German Idealist notion of the state providing a political order
free of social and political conflict: 'We do not need any radical re-
education in order to function effectively again in the Western cultural community. Only Nazi megalomania with its non-culture and
rotten culture must vanish completely. However, its place must not
be taken by a weak, abstract cosmopolitanism void of content ...
The German spirit, we hope and believe, after it has come into its
own again, still has to fulfill its special and irreplaceable mission
within the Western community.'[138] Despite such shared assumptions
with the national tradition in German historiography, the tone of
rueful self-accusation also present in Meinecke's book caused an

uproar amongst the more conservative of his colleagues, who immediately accused him of fouling the national nest.

The themes of lectures and seminars at West German universities
between 1946 and 1949 showed little change.[139] The national-conservative view of German history dominated historical didactics after
1945.[140] Any closer look at the Association of German Historians
founded in October 1948 by Ritter, Aubin, Heimpel and Herbert
Grundmann equally reveals a complete lack of methodological or
topical innovation and a marked hesitancy about embarking upon
any revision of German historiography. No effort was made adequately to deal with the historians' role under National Socialism in
the 1950s. The tone was set by Ritter, the Association's first president
from 1949 to 1953, who regarded as superfluous 'efforts at belated
self-accusation or self-justification'.[141] Continuity as far as possible,
revisionism as far as necessary – that was the guiding principle of
post-war German historians.

Apart from the literature on the resistance, the same old topics
were adapted to post-1945 conditions: the Freiherr vom Stein, and
the Prussian reformers were now portrayed as arch-liberals, almost
father figures of West Germany's Basic Law. They, as well as the revolution of 1848, now served as historical forerunners of the Bonn
republic. Bismarck continued to be 'one of the few very great, unfor-
getful personalities of our political history'.[142] The debate about Bismarck in the 1950s brought limited attempts to break with some of
the most blatant legends, but, on the whole, it just confirmed that any
criticism of Bismarck was still widely regarded as a sacrilege against
the nation.[143] By the late 1950s Walter Bußmann confirmed that German historians could still not perceive any alternative to Bismarck's
unification of Germany in 1870/71.[144] As Werner Conze argued in
parliament on 17 June 1955: 'The German people is one nation and
believes in its unity. It does not want several Germanies; it wants
one. This is the heritage of Bismarck's foundation of the Reich.'[145] In
the discussions on both the reasons for the outbreak of the First
World War and of Imperial Germany generally, the 'primacy of foreign policy' was still recognised by the overwhelming majority of
historians. If Ludendorff and Hindenburg had been the heroes of
most German historians after 1918, Bethmann-Hollweg and the
more liberal representatives of the government were presented in
that role after 1945. On the whole, the national mission of nineteenth-century historiography continued in a toned-down version in
the works of major historians of the post-1945 period.

In many respects even the allegedly new European perspectives
after 1945 should best be seen as an adaptation of earlier trends.

After all, the re-organisation of Europe had already been a major idea in the works of historians during the Second World War. In the light of Nazi Germany's apparent success in creating a new European state order, Aubin, in 1940, had demanded that historians should abandon the writing of national history and concentrate instead on European history. For Aubin, the Nazis were about to recreate Charlemagne's empire.[146] After 1945 one only had to delete all references to a German-dominated Europe, and one was left with the idea of the European Community which was to be at the heart of Adenauer's policy of Western integration in the 1950s.[147] Even Bismarck was now transformed from being a great German to being a great European whose first priority had been the maintenance of peace and stability in Europe.[148] The Europeanisation of historiography after 1945 started from an assumption of a Europe of nation states. Far from overcoming national history, it served the process of rebuilding and relegitimating national historiography. In such a European history 'national history will become anything but superfluous'.[149] The German East continued to play an important role within the Europeanisation of Prussianism. The achievements of German colonisation of Eastern Europe were emphasised in view of the *Drang nach Osten* before 1945. After 1945, the same emphasis was linked to the alleged need to keep these achievements before the eye of a German public in view of the wilful destruction of German culture in Eastern Europe.[150] Hans-Joachim Schoeps even demanded a return of Poland's western territories, as 'only the territorial restitution of Prussia will bring about the unity of Germany'.[151]

The European perspective also remained firmly linked to the theory of totalitarianism. As early as 1930 Friedrich Meinecke had argued for the essential identity of Communism and National Socialism.[152] In the late 1930s American political scientists worked out a theory of totalitarianism which had important repercussions on historical scholarship in Germany.[153] In the period of the Cold War, the theory of totalitarianism facilitated the integration of historians into the FRG. Many of their theories and paradigms had been 'falsified' by the Allied victory. However, they found their anti-Communism fully vindicated after 1947. Hitler could still be interpreted as an 'anti-Marxist Europeanist' (Otto Westphal) after the war.[154] Much of the research on National Socialism was carried out within the framework of European totalitarianism.[155] Hence the Europeanisation of historiography did not necessarily constitute an alternative to the still powerful national paradigm.

A more decisive break with the national tradition occurred in the GDR.[156] Initially, between 1945 and 1948, the development of historical studies in the Soviet zone of occupation was comparable to that in the Western zones. De-Nazification ensured that the worst Nazi historians were dismissed, but the personal and institutional continuity remained considerable. The only difference was that the Soviet military authorities ensured that some Marxists returning from exile like Jürgen Kuczynski and Alfred Meusel, received professorships. Yet the emphasis was on cooperation between Marxist and 'bourgeois' historians. Only with the onset of the Cold War in 1947/48 did the SED ensure the almost total dominance of a dogmatic Marxism-Leninism in East German historiography. Over a period of ten years the historical profession changed its personnel, institutions and outlook almost completely. In 1958, when a separate GDR historians' association was founded, this transformation process was complete. Some Marxist historians, like Meusel or Walter Markov, continued to seek contact with their Western colleagues in the 1950s. In rare cases, for example at the University of Leipzig, cooperation between Marxist and 'bourgeois' historians continued until 1956.[157] Ultimately they failed to establish any productive discourse because of the anti-Communism of many of their Western colleagues[158] (Ritter referred to Markov as that 'red terrorist'), and, more importantly, because of the dominant type of Stalinist SED functionary. Although the radical break with tradition was connected to a loss of substance in one way, in another it allowed the quick development of social and economic history in the GDR, where research on classes, revolutions and fascism from early on provided productive challenges to its Western counterpart.

New methods and areas of research did, however, not automatically mean a complete break with the national tradition. Ironically, such a break was greatest at a time when the institutions had not been Stalinised. Immediately after 1945, many Marxists in the GDR subscribed to very critical perspectives on German national history.[159] At a Berlin conference on the reconstitution of the historical sciences in post-war Germany in May 1946, Anton Ackermann, the Communists' chief ideologue at the time, postulated two central aims for any future historiography: first, to write social rather than political history, and secondly, to overcome the dominant nationalism. He ended his paper by calling for a complete break with the traditions of German historiography.[160] From the early 1950s onwards such radical perspectives on German national history, quickly dubbed 'misery theory' *(Miseretheorie)* were replaced by the search for positive progressive traditions in German national history. With the foundation of the GDR in 1949, the second German state began looking for its historical identity. In subsequent years, impressive research results were presented in areas like the Reformation, the peasant wars, the war of liberation, the 1848/49 revolution, the labour movement and the KPD resistance to Nazism. Conversely, such concentration on positive traditions of national history meant neglecting other fields. More importantly, it foreshadowed the commitment of GDR historians to the socialist nation of the GDR in the 1970s. A socialist myth of the nation was, of course, as limiting and dangerous as a 'bourgeois' one.

This brief overview of the development of the national tradition in German historiography has demonstrated how before 1870 German historians' national mission consisted largely in mapping out Germany in the mind. After 1871 they played their part in homogenising what was a very heterogeneous nation-state. In 1914 they justified German aggression and after 1918 fought against Versaillles and the allegedly un-German concept of parliamentary democracy. After co-existing with the National Socialist regime, West German historiography found a new national mission in keeping the national spirit of unity alive in a divided country. In the GDR the search was on for a new socialist national spirit. It was only in the early 1960s that the national tradition in German historiography was seriously undermined in the FRG, and it is therefore to this important decade for the development of German historiography that we shall now turn.

NOTES

1. Hayden White, *Tropics of Discourse. Essays in Cultural Criticism*, London, 1978, p. 41. A similar nineteenth-century criticism of German historiography as antiquated and useless for life was famously made by Friedrich Nietzsche, 'Vom Nutzen und Nachtheil der Historie für das Leben. Unzeitgemäße Betrachtungen. Zweites Stück', in: idem, *Sämtliche Werke*, ed. by Giorgio Colli and Mazzino Montinari, vol. 1, 2nd edn, Munich, 1988, pp. 243 – 334.
2. Elie Kedourie, *Nationalism*, 4th edn, London, 1993, p. 9.
3. Wolfgang Hardtwig, *Nationalismus und Bürgerkultur in Deutschland 1500-1914*, Göttingen, 1994, p. 45. See also C. Prignitz, *Vaterlandsliebe und Freiheit. Deutscher Patriotismus von 1763 – 1850*, Wiesbaden, 1981.
4. Ulrich Muhlack, *Geschichtswissenschaft im Humanismus und in der Aufklärung. Die Vorgeschichte des Historismus*, Munich, 1991, pp. 47, 163, 206 f., 240 f.
5. Karl von Rotteck, 'Betrachtungen über den Gang, Charakter und heutigen Zustand der historischen Studien in Teutschland' (1840), in idem, *Gesammelte und nachgelassene Schriften mit Biographie und Briefwechsel*, ed. by Hermann von Rotteck, vol. 1, 1841, p. 378. See also Otto W. Johnston, *Der deutsche Nationalmythos*.

Ursprung eines politischen Programms, Stuttgart, 1990. For the role of historians see Franz Schnabel, 'Der Ursprung der vaterländischen Studien', *Blätter für deutsche Landesgeschichte,* vol. 88, 1951.

6. Heinrich von Sybel, 'Über den Stand der neueren deutschen Geschichtsschreibung' (1856), in: idem, *Kleinere historische Schriften,* vol. 1, 3rd edn, Stuttgart, 1880, p. 352 f.

7. Wilhelm Giesebrecht, 'Die Entwicklung der modernen deutschen Geschichtswissenschaft', *HZ,* vol. 1, 1859, p. 11.

8. J. G. Fichte, *Reden an die deutsche Nation,* Leipzig, 1944, p. 104.

9. Friedrich Christoph Dahlmann, 'Ein Wort über Verfassung', in: idem, *Kleine Schriften und Reden,* Stuttgart, 1886, pp. 70-1.

10. Hanns Peter Reill, 'Barthold Georg Niebuhr and the Enlightenment Tradition', *German Studies Review,* vol. 3, 1980, pp. 9-26.

11. Heinrich Luden, *Einige Worte über das Studium der vaterländischen Geschichte,* Jena, 1810.

12. Heinrich Luden, *Geschichte des teutschen Volkes,* vol. 1, Gotha, 1825, p. x.

13. Especially influential was J. G. Herder, *Auch eine Philosophie der Geschichte zur Bildung der Menschheit,* 1774, reprint Frankfurt-on-Main, 1967. See Hans Schleier (ed.), *J.G. Herder und progressive bürgerliche Geschichts- und Gesellschaftstheorien zwischen 1720 und 1850,* Berlin, 1979.

14. Johann Gottfried Herder, 'Briefe zur Beförderung der Humanität. Achte Sammlung', in: idem, *Sämtliche Werke,* vol. 18, p. 137.

15. Berhard Giesen, *Die Intellektuellen und die Nation. Eine deutsche Achsenzeit,* Frankfurt-on-Main, 1993 distinguishes in ideal typical fashion between Enlightenment nationalism, Romantic nationalism, democratic nationalism and Reich nationalism.

16. Wucher, *Theodor Mommsen,* pp. 65, 80 ff., 210.

17. Günter Birtsch, *Die Nation als sittliche Idee. Der Nationalstaatsbegriff in Geschichtsschreibung und politischer Gedankenwelt Johann Gustav Droysens,* Cologne, 1964, pp. 30-112, 123-5, 163.

18. Otto Hintze, 'Rasse und Nationalität und ihre Bedeutung für die Geschichte' (1903), in: idem, *Gesammelte Abhandlungen,* vol. 2: *Soziologie und Geschichte,* ed. by G. Oestreich, 2nd edn, Göttingen, 1964, pp. 46-65.

19. Johannes Haller, *Epochen der deutschen Geschichte,* Berlin, 1923, p. 12.

20. Karl Alexander von Müller, 'Probleme des zweiten Reiches im Lichte des Dritten', in: idem, *Vom alten zum neuen Deutschland,* Munich, 1935, p. 298.

21. Adolf Helbok, *Was ist deutsche Volksgeschichte? Ziele, Aufgaben, Wege,* Berlin, 1935, p. 3.

22. Hans Buchheim, 'Die Nationalsozialistische Zeit im Geschichtsbewußtsein der Gegenwart', in: Karl Forster (ed.), *Gibt es ein deutsches Geschichtsbild?,* Würzburg, 1961, p. 44.

23. Gerhard Ritter, *Geschichte als Bildungsmacht. Ein Beitrag zur historisch-politischen Neubesinnung,* Stuttgart, 1946, p. 25.

24. F. C. Dahlmann, *Die Politik auf den Grund und das Maß der gegebenen Zustände zurückgeführt,* ed. by O. Westphal, Berlin, 1924, p. 53.

25. Volker Dotterweich, *Heinrich von Sybel. Geschichtswissenschaft in politischer Absicht (1817-1861),* Göttingen, 1978, p. 192.

26. Jörn Rüsen, *Begriffene Geschichte. Genesis und Begründung der Geschichtstheorie J.G. Droysens,* Paderborn, 1969.

27. Wucher, *Theodor Mommsen,* p. 147.

28. Heinz-Otto Sieburg, 'Aspekte deutscher Historiographie über Frankreich zwischen 1871 und 1914', in: Timmermann (ed.), *Geschichtsschreibung,* pp. 223-42.

29. Kurt Töpner, *Gelehrte Politiker und politisierende Gelehrte. Die Revolution von 1918 im Urteil deutscher Hochschullehrer,* Göttingen, 1970; Karen Thiessenhusen, 'Politische

Kommentare deutscher Historiker zur Revolution und Neuordnung 1918/19', *aus politik und zeitgeschichte*, B45, 1969, pp. 25 ff.

30. Leopold von Ranke, 'Über die Verwandtschaft und den Unterschied der Historie und der Politik' (1832), reprinted in: Wolfgang Hardtwig (ed.), *Über das Studium der Geschichte*, Munich, 1990, p. 519.

31. M. A. Fitzsimons, 'Ranke: History as Worship', *Review of Politics*, vol. 42, 1980, pp. 533-55.

32. Leopold von Ranke, 'Über die Trennung und die Einheit von Deutschland', idem, *Sämtliche Werke*, Leipzig, 1887, vol. 49/50, p. 172.

33. J. G. Droysen, *Historik*, ed. by P. Leyh, Stuttgart, Bad Cannstatt, 1977, p. 236.

34. Heinrich von Treitschke, *Briefe*, vol. 3, Leipzig, 1920, p. 361.

35. von Sybel, 'Über den Stand', p. 355.

36. Rudolf Haym in an editorial to *Preußische Jahrbücher*, vol. XI, 1863, p. 637.

37. Wolfgang Hardtwig, 'Von Preußens Aufgabe in Deutschland zu Deutschlands Aufgabe in der Welt. Liberalismus und borussianisches Geschichtsbild zwischen Revolution und Imperialismus', *HZ*, vol. 231, 1980, p. 321.

38. Johann Gustav Droysen, *Geschichte der preußischen Politik*, 14 vols, Leipzig, 1855-1886.

39. Cited in Dotterweich, *Heinrich von Sybel*, p. 342.

40. On the history of the *HZ* see Theodor Schieder, 'Die deutsche Geschichtswissenschaft im Spiegel der HZ', *HZ*, vol. 189, 1959, pp. 1-104.

41. Cited in Wucher, *Theodor Mommsen*, p. 151.

42. Hermann Baumgarten, 'Der deutsche Liberalismus. Eine Selbstkritik', *Preußische Jahrbücher*, vol. 18, 1866, p. 576 f.

43. Heinrich von Sybel, *Das neue deutsche Reich. Die Rechte Deutschlands auf Elsaß-Lothringen*, Berlin, 1871.

44. Erich Marcks, *Wo stehen wir? Die politischen, sittlichen und kulturellen Zusammenhänge unseres Krieges*, Stuttgart, 1914, pp. 22-3.

45. Cited in Karen Schönwälder, *Historiker und Politik. Geschichtswissenschaft im Nationalsozialismus*, Frankfurt-on-Main, 1992, p. 262.

46. Letter Jakob Burckhardt to Friedrich von Preen, 31 December 1872, in: M. Burckhardt (ed.), *Briefe. Vollständige und kritische Ausgabe*, vol. 5, Basle, 1963, p. 184.

47. Andreas Biefang, 'Der Streit um Treitschkes "Deutsche Geschichte" 1882/3. Zur Spaltung des Nationalliberalismus und der Etablierung eines national-konservativen Geschichtsbildes', *HZ*, vol. 262, 1996, pp. 391-422.

48. Heinrich von Treitschke, 'Widmung an Max Duncker vom 10. Februar 1879', in: idem, *Deutsche Geschichte im 19. Jahrhundert*, vol. 1, Leipzig, 1879, p. ix.

49. Simon, *Staat*, p. 85.

50. On Treitschke see Andreas Dorpalen, *Heinrich von Treitschke*, New Haven, 1957; Hans Schleier, *Sybel und Treitschke. Antidemokratismus und Militarismus im historisch-politischen Denken großbourgeoiser Geschichtsideologen*, Berlin, 1965.

51. Heinrich von Treitschke, *Deutsche Geschichte im 19. Jahrhundert*, vol. 5, Leipzig, 1928, p. 620.

52. The socialist historians' view of the nation would certainly merit closer attention. For the SPD's attitude towards the nation more generally see Dieter Groh and Peter Brandt, *'Vaterlandslose Gesellen'. Sozialdemokratie und Nation 1860-1990*, Munich, 1992.

53. For the origins of the German *Historikertag* see Winfried Schulze, 'Von München über Leipzig nach Berlin? Zur Entstehung des Historikertages vor 100 Jahren', *GWU*, vol. 45, 1994, pp. 551-7.

54. Max Lenz, 'Ein Blick in das 20. Jahrhundert', in: idem, *Kleine historische Schriften*, vol. 1, p. 595.

55. Hans-Heinrich Krill, *Die Ranke-Renaissance. Max Lenz und Erich Marcks. Ein Beitrag zum historisch-politischen Denken in Deutschland 1880 – 1935*, Berlin, 1962, p. 174.

56. Max Lenz, *Die großen Mächte. Ein Rückblick auf unser Jahrhundert*, Berlin, 1900.
57. Willy Schenk, *Die deutsch-englische Rivalität vor dem ersten Weltkrieg in der Sicht deutscher Historiker*, Aarau, 1967; Charles E. McClelland, *The German Historians and England. A Study in Nineteenth Century Views*, Cambridge, 1971.
58. Dietrich Schäfer, *Mein Leben*, Berlin, 1926, p. 101.
59. Dietrich Schäfer, *Deutsche Geschichte*, Berlin, 1910, and idem, *Weltgeschichte der Neuzeit*, Berlin, 1907. Whereas the latter was written after the *Reichsmarineamt* had asked Schäfer whether he would be interested in writing a textbook on world history, the former was conceived after the Pan-German League and the Prussian cultural minister had urged Schäfer to write a German history.
60. For this difficulty of most historians with parliamentary democracy before 1914 and after see especially Gustav Schmidt, *Deutscher Historismus und der Übergang zur parlamentarischen Demokratie*, Lübeck, 1964.
61. On the Bismarck cult compare Lothar Machtan (ed.), *Bismarck und der deutsche National-Mythos*, Bremen, 1994.
62. Anderson, *Communities*, pp. 80 ff.
63. Ernst Weymar, *Das Selbstverständnis der Deutschen. Ein Bericht über den Geist des Geschichtsunterrichts der höheren Schulen im 19. Jahrhundert*, Stuttgart, 1961; Horst Schallenberger, *Untersuchungen zum Geschichtsbild der Wilhelminischen Ära und der Weimarer Zeit*, Ratingen, 1964; Jürgen Mirow, *Das alte Preußen im deutschen Geschichtsbild seit der Reichsgründung*, Berlin, 1981.
64. For Delbrück see Anneliese Thimme, *Hans Delbrück als Kritiker der Wilhelminischen Epoche*, Düsseldorf, 1955, especially pp. 16, 22, 101-16 and 152-4.
65. Cited in Iggers, *Conception*, p. 169.
66. Karl-Heinz Noack, 'Der soziale Aspekt der Hohenzollern-Legende bei Gustav Schmoller', in: *Evolution und Revolution in der Weltgeschichte. Festschrift für Ernst Engelberg*, Berlin, 1976, vol. 1, pp. 327-43.
67. Luise Schorn-Schütte, *Karl Lamprecht. Kulturgeschichte, Wissenschaft und Politik*, Göttingen, 1984; Roger Chickering, *Karl Lamprecht: A German Academic Life (1856-1915)*, Atlantic Highlands, N.Y., 1993. For the consequences of the Lamprecht controversy on German historiography in an international context see also Georg G. Iggers, 'The "Methodenstreit" in International Perspective. The Reorientation of Historical Studies at the Turn from the Nineteenth to the Twentieth Century', in: *Storia della Storiografia*, vol. 6, 1984, pp. 21-32; Lutz Raphael, 'Historikerkontroversen im Spannungsfeld zwischen Berufshabitus, Fächerkonkurrenz und sozialen Deutungsmustern: Lamprecht-Streit und französischer Methodenstreit der Jahrhundertwende in vergleichender Perspektive', *HZ*, vol. 251, 1990, pp. 325-63.
68. Iggers, *Conception*, p. 232. See also Pierangelo Schiera, 'Otto Hintze und die Krise des modernen Staates', in: Notger Hammerstein (ed.), *Deutsche Geschichtswissenschaft um 1900*, Stuttgart, 1988, pp. 341-55.
69. An example of such an apologia for Hintze is provided by Jürgen Kocka, 'Otto Hintze', in: Wehler (ed.), *Historiker*, p. 278.
70. Walter Goetz, 'Die deutsche Geschichtsschreibung der Gegenwart' (1924), in: idem, *Historiker meiner Zeit*, Cologne, 1957, p. 419.
71. Franz Schnabel, *Deutsche Geschichte im neunzehnten Jahrhundert*, vol. 1, Freiburg im Breisgau, 1929, pp. 100 f.
72. For a detailed account see Wolfgang Jäger, *Historische Forschung und politische Kultur in Deutschland. Die Debatte 1914 – 1980 über den Ausbruch des ersten Weltkrieges*, Göttingen, 1984, pp. 14 – 105.
73. For the public debate on Versailles in the Weimar Republic and the efforts to revise the treaty see Ulrich Heinemann, *Die verdrängte Niederlage. Politische Öffentlichkeit und Kriegsschuldfrage in der Weimarer Republik*, Göttingen, 1983.

74. See, for example, Gerhard Ritter, *Die Legende von der verschmähten englischen Freundschaft 1898-1901*, Freiburg, 1929.

75. See, for example, what can be regarded as the high point of the research on the First World War in the Weimar Republic: Hermann Oncken, *Das Deutsche Reich und die Vorgeschichte des Weltkrieges*, 2 vols, Leipzig, 1933.

76. Hans Herzfeld, *Die deutsche Sozialdemokratie und die Auflösung der nationalen Einheitsfront im Weltkrieg*, Leipzig, 1928.

77. Georg von Below, *Die deutsche Geschichtsschreibung von den Befreiungskriegen bis zu unsern Tagen*, 2nd rev. edn, Munich, 1924, p. 159.

78. Ibid., p. 42.

79. Ibid., p. 29.

80. Hermann Oncken, 'Der Sinn der deutschen Geschichte' (1924), in: idem, *Nation und Geschichte. Reden und Aufsätze*, Berlin, 1935, pp. 15-44.

81. Iggers, *Conception*, p. 238.

82. Eberhard Jäckel, 'Karl Dietrich Erdmann', *HZ*, vol. 252, 1991, p. 529 f.

83. Eckart Kehr, 'Neuere deutsche Geschichtsschreibung', in: idem, *Der Primat der Innenpolitik*, Berlin, 1965, pp. 254-68.

84. Jäger, *Historische Forschung*, pp. 70 ff.

85. Bernd Faulenbach, *Ideologie des deutschen Weges. Die deutsche Geschichte in der Historiographie zwischen Kaiserreich und Nationalsozialismus*, Munich, 1980.

86. Max Lenz, *Wille, Macht und Schicksal*, Munich, 1922, especially pp. 96 f, 181; also idem, *Deutschland im Kreis der Großmächte 1870-1914*, Berlin, 1925.

87. Johannes Haller, *Epochen der deutschen Geschichte*, Berlin, 1923, pp. 351 and 371.

88. This conservative reception of Stein is most visible in Gerhard Ritter, *Stein. Eine politische Biographie*, 2 vols, Stuttgart, 1931.

89. See generally for the politics of German historians under Nazism Schönwälder, *Historiker*; Karl Ferdinand Werner, *Das NS-Geschichtsbild und die deutsche Geschichtswissenschaft*, Stuttgart, 1967; H. Heiber, *Walter Frank und sein Reichsinstitut für Geschichte des neuen Deutschlands*, Stuttgart, 1966.

90. Characteristic of such a positive self-evaluation are Gerhard Ritter, 'Deutsche Geschichtswissenschaft im 20. Jahrhundert', *GWU*, vol. 1, 1950, p. 94; Schieder, 'Die deutsche Geschichtswissenschaft', pp. 68-71; Hans Rothfels, 'Die Geschichtswissenschaft in den dreißiger Jahren', in: Andreas Flitner (ed.), *Deutsches Geistesleben und Nationalsozialismus*, Tübingen, 1965, pp. 90-107.

91. Compare Beate Wagner, 'Politikwissenschaft in Deutschland, 1933-1945', in: *1999*, vol. 4, 1989, pp. 27-38; Otthein Rammstedt, *Deutsche Soziologie 1933-1945. Die Normalität einer Anpassung*, Frankfurt-on-Main, 1986.

92. Walter Frank, 'Zunft und Nation', *HZ*, vol. 153, 1936, pp. 6-23.

93. Ibid., p. 23.

94. Peter Lambert, 'German Historians and Nazi Ideology. The Parameters of the *Volksgemeinschaft* and the Problem of Historical Legitimation, 1930-1945', *EHQ*, vol. 25, 1995, pp. 555-82.

95. Heinz Gollwitzer, 'Karl Alexander von Müller', *HZ*, vol. 205, 1967, p. 310.

96. About Gerhard Ritter's early carreer see Michael Matthiesen, *Gerhard Ritter. Studien zu Leben und Werk bis 1933*, 2 vols, Cologne, 1993.

97. Gerhard Ritter, *Friedrich der Große*, Heidelberg, 1936. These deeply embarassing passages were deleted in all post-war editions of the work. Compare, for example, with reprint, Königstein, 1978.

98. Michael Burleigh, *Germany Turns Eastwards. A Study of 'Ostforschung' in the Third Reich*, Cambridge, 1988.

99. Werner, *NS-Geschichtsbild*, p. 96.

100. Thus the convincing conclusion of Schönwälder, *Historiker*.

101. Walther Hubatsch, *Weserübung. Die deutsche Besetzung von Dänemark und Norwegen 1940*, Göttingen, 1960; Erich Marcks and Walther Hubatsch, *Hindenburg*, Göttingen, 1963, and Walther Hubatsch, *Hindenburg und der Staat*, Göttingen, 1966.

102. One famous example is the Bertelsmann Book Club publication by Hellmuth Rössler, *Deutsche Geschichte*. *Schicksal des Volkes in Europas Mitte*, Gütersloh, 1961.

103. Schieder, 'Die deutsche Geschichtswissenschaft', p. 71.

104. Hermann Heimpel, *Kapitulation vor der Geschichte*, Göttingen, 1956, pp. 54 f.

105. Hans Herzfeld, *Gesammelte Aufsätze*, p. 49.

106. Leo Kirch, 'Die klerikal-imperialistische Abendland-Ideologie', in: Streisand (ed.), *Studien*, vol. 2, p. 418.

107. Markus Kiefer, *Auf der Suche nach nationaler Identität und Wegen zur deutschen Einheit. Die deutsche Frage in der überregionalen Tages- und Wochenpresse der Bundesrepublik 1949-1955*, 2nd edn, Frankfurt-on-Main, 1993, p. 660 f.

108. See, for example, the contributions in Hans Kohn, *German History. Some New German Views*, London, 1954.

109. On Hans Rosenberg see Heinrich August Winkler, 'ein Erneuerer der Geschichtswissenschaft. Hans Rosenberg, 1904-1988', *HZ*, vol. 248, 1989, p. 545.

110. Manfred Asendorf, 'Was weiter wirkt. Die "Ranke-Gesellschaft – Vereinigung für Geschichte im öffentlichen Leben', *1999*, vol. 4, 1989, pp. 29-61.

111. Hans Rothfels, 'Bismarck und der deutsche Osten', *HZ*, vol. 147, 1933; idem, *Ostraum, Preussentum und Reichsgedanke*, Leipzig, 1935.

112. Hans Rothfels, *Gesellschaftsform und auswärtige Politik*, Laupheim, 1951, p. 24.

113. Hans Rothfels, 'Grundsätzliches zum Problem der Nationalität', *HZ*, vol. 175, 1952, p. 358.

114. Hans Rothfels, 'Zur Krise des Nationalstaats', *VfZ*, vol. 1, 1953, pp. 138-52.

115. Rothfels, 'Krise', p. 142.

116. Gerhard Ritter, *Carl Goerdeler und die deutsche Widerstandsbewegung*, Munich, 1964, p. 15. Whilst the Prussian resistance to Hitler was held up as exemplary, the Communist resistance was treated as high treason. See Ibid., pp. 108-11. A similarly one-sided treatment of the German resistance can be found in Hans Rothfels, *The German Opposition to Hitler*, Chicago, 1962. The book was first published in German in 1949.

117. Hans Rothfels, *Die deutsche Opposition gegen Hitler*, Krefeld, 1949, Gerhard Ritter, 'The Fault of Mass Democracy', in: John L. Snell (ed.), *The Nazi Revolution. Germany's Guilt or Germany's Fate*, New York, 1959.

118. Gerhard Ritter, *Das deutsche Problem*, Munich, 1962, p. 23.

119. Ritter, 'Mass Democracy', in: Snell (ed.), *Nazi Revolution*, p. 81.

120. Ritter, *Bildungsmacht*, p. 38.

121. Ibid., p. 34.

122. Ibid., p. 71.

123. Gerhard Ritter an Erwin Eckert, 8 July 1946, in: K. Schwabe and R. Reichhardt (eds), *Gerhard Ritter. Ein politischer Historiker in seinen Briefen*, Boppard, 1984, p. 414.

124. Ritter, *Bildungsmacht*, p. 30.

125. Gerhard Ritter, *Staatskunst und Kriegshandwerk. Das Problem des Militarismus in Deutschland*, 4 vols, Munich, 1954 – 1968.

126. Siegfried A. Kaehler, *Studien zur deutschen Geschichte des 19. und 20. Jahrhunderts*, Göttingen, 1961, p. 374 f.

127. Hermann Heimpel, *Der Mensch in seiner Gegenwart*, Göttingen, 1954, p. 185 f.

128. Cited in Schulze, *Geschichtswissenschaft*, p. 214.

129. Hans Herzfeld, 'Deutschland und Europa im Zeitalter beider Weltkriege', in: Hinrichs and Berges (eds), *Die deutsche Einheit*, p. 177.

130. Gerhard A. Ritter, 'Hans Herzfeld – Persönlichkeit und Werk', *Jahrbuch für die Geschichte Mittel- und Ostdeutschlands*, vol. 32, 1983, pp. 13-91.

131. Hans Herzfeld, 'Politik und Geschichte bei Leopold von Ranke im Zeitraum von 1848 bis 1871', in: Richard Nürnberger (ed.), *Festschrift für Gerhard Ritter*, Tübingen, 1950, pp. 322-41.
132. Herzfeld, *Aufsätze*, pp. 58, 62.
133. Herzfeld, 'Deutschland und Europa', p. 214.
134. Imanuel Geiss, 'Kritischer Rückblick auf Friedrich Meinecke', in: idem, *Studien über Geschichte und Geschichtswissenschaft*, Frankfurt-on-Main, 1972, pp. 89-107. See also Stefan Meineke, *Ein Liberaler in postliberaler Zeit. Persönlichkeit und politisches Denken Friedrich Meineckes bis zum Ende des Ersten Weltkrieges*, Berlin, 1995.
135. Friedrich Meinecke, *Die deutsche Katastrophe. Betrachtungen und Erinnerungen*, 6th edn, Wiesbaden, 1965, p. 9.
136. Ibid., p. 29.
137. I find it difficult to follow the far more positive evaluation of Meinecke's book by Winfried Schulze who choses to ignore the less palatable undertone of Meinecke's work, concentrating instead on his call for a revision of the traditional German historiography which he takes to be the central message of *Die deutsche Katastrophe*. See Winfried Schulze, 'Der Neubeginn der deutschen Geschichtswissenschaft nach 1945', in: Ernst Schulin (ed.), *Deutsche Geschichtswissenschaft nach dem Zweiten Weltkrieg: (1945-65)*, Munich, 1989, pp. 5-8.
138. Meinecke, *Die deutsche Katastrophe*, p. 119.
139. Schulze, 'Der Neubeginn', in: Schulin (ed.), *Geschichtswissenschaft*, p. 16 f.
140. Horst Kuss, 'Geschichtsdidaktik und Geschichtsunterricht in der Bundesrepublik Deutschland (1945/49-1990), *GWU*, vol. 45, 1994, p. 740.
141. Gerhard Ritter, 'Gegenwärtige Lage und Zukunftsaufgaben deutscher Geschichtsschreibung', *HZ*, vol. 170, 1950, pp. 1-22.
142. Ritter, *Bildungsmacht*, p. 65.
143. Hans-Ulrich Wehler, *Bismarck und der Imperialismus*, Cologne, 1969, pp. 412-502.
144. Walter Bußmann, 'Zur Geschichte des deutschen Liberalismus im 19. Jahrhundert', *HZ*, vol. 186, 1958.
145. Werner Conze, *Deutsche Einheit – Erbe und Aufgabe*, Munich, 1956, p. 27.
146. Hermann Aubin, 'Der Aufbau des mittelalterlichen Deutschen Reiches', *HZ*, vol. 162, 1940.
147. Ritter once again set the trend with his *Europa und die deutsche Frage*, Munich, 1948. For the change from a narrow national to a more European historiography in Germany after 1945 see also Fritz Fellner, 'Nationales und europäisch-atlantisches Geschichtsbild in der Bundesrepublik und im Westen in den Jahren nach Ende des Zweiten Weltkrieges', in: Schulin (ed.), *Geschichtswissenschaft*, pp. 213-26.
148. Walter Bußmann, 'Europa und das Bismarckreich', in: Hinrichs and Berges (eds), *Die deutsche Einheit*, pp. 156-73.
149. Arnold Bergstraesser, 'Geschichtliches Bewußtsein und politische Entscheidung', in: Waldemar Besson und Friedrich Freiherr Hiller von Gaertringen (eds), *Geschichte und Gegenwartsbewußtsein. Historische Betrachtungen und Untersuchungen. Festschrift für Hans Rothfels*, Göttingen, 1963, p. 18.
150. A good example is *Deutscher Osten und slawischer Westen. Festschrift für Hermann Aubin*, Tübingen, 1955. See also Hermann Aubin, 'An einem neuen Anfang der Ostforschung', *Zeitschrift für Ostforschung*, vol. 1, 1952.
151. Hans-Joachim Schoeps, *Die Ehre Preußens*, Stuttgart, 1951, p. 47.
152. Friedrich Meinecke, *Werke*, vol. 2, Darmstadt, 1958, p. 444.
153. In particular Carl J. Friedrich and K. Brzezinski, *Totalitarian Dictatorship and Autocracy*, Cambridge/Mass., 1956. Hannah Arendt, *The Originis of Totalitarianism*, New York, 1951 with its much greater emphasis on anti-Semitism and imperialism and its far more sophisticated model of totalitarian dictatorship was comparatively less important in the 1950s.

154. Cited in Herzfeld, 'Deutschland und Europa', in: Hinrichs and Berges (eds), *Die deutsche Einheit*, p. 184.
155. Hans Rothfels, 'Zeitgeschichte als Aufgabe', *VfZ*, vol. 1, 1953, pp. 1 – 8 emphasised that locating Nazism within the European phenomenon of totalitarianism also meant avoiding national self-humiliation.
156. On GDR historiography in the early period see especially Werner Berthold, *Marxistisches Geschichtsbild – Volksfront und antifaschistisch-demokratische Revolution. Zur Vorgeschichte der Geschichtswissenschaft der DDR und zur Konzeption der Geschichte des deutschen Volkes*, Berlin, 1970; Alexander Fischer and Günther Heydemann (eds), *Geschichtswissenschaft in der DDR*, 2 vols, Berlin, 1988 and 1990; Andreas Dorpalen, *German History in Marxist Perspective. The East German Approach*, London, 1985.
157. Walter Markov, *Zwiesprache mit dem Jahrhundert*, Berlin, 1989, pp. 179-220.
158. For the traditionalist and conservate climate at West German universities in the 1950s compare Wolfgang Abendroth, *Ein Leben in der Arbeiterbewegung*, Frankfurt-on-Main, 1981, pp. 206-17.
159. Hugely influential and the best example of this concept is Alexander Abusch, *Der Irrweg einer Nation*, Berlin, 1946. See also Georg Lukács, *Die Zerstörung der Vernunft*, Berlin, 1954.
160. Ilko-Sascha Kowalczuk, '"Wo gehobelt wird, da fallen Späne". Zur Entwicklung der DDR-Geschichtswissenschaft bis in die späten fünfziger Jahre', *ZfG*, vol. 42, 1994, p. 307.

Chapter 3

THE IMPACT OF FRITZ FISCHER

A s has been noted in the previous chapter, the survival of Prussianism rested on historical interpretations which portrayed
Nazism as the evil exception to an otherwise proud national history.
It was at this, the very heart of the post-war national tradition, that
Fischer struck with his publications in the late 1950s and early
1960s.[1] Fischer maintained that Europe had not slithered into war in
1914. Instead he pointed the finger at Germany's elites who, he
argued, saw the Serbian crisis as an opportunity to achieve hegemony in Europe. Fischer sought to underline his thesis by demonstrating how widespread expansionist war aims had been amongst
both the military and moderate civilian leaders shortly after the outbreak of the war. In his second book he explicitly linked the First
World War to the Second World War which he now interpreted as
the second attempt by Germany's elites to create a German-dominated *Mitteleuropa*. Hitler could no longer be portrayed as the sad
exception, on the contrary, the twelve years of National Socialist
rule now appeared as the high point of a continuing development of
Germany in the nineteenth and early twentieth century. The German *Sonderweg* had led the country down the road of illiberalism and
expansionism. Fischer's theses on the outbreak of the First World
War had the potential to shatter the most entrenched national myths,
and hence it was to be expected that they ended the 'peacefulness
and poverty in scholarly controversy' so characteristic of the first fifteen years of the FRG's historiography.[2] In the political climate of
the 1960s a new generation of German historians emerged who

Notes for this chapter begin on page 71.

attempted to break with the national tradition and aimed at a histo-riography committed to emancipatory ideals. The ground for such a rebellion had been prepared before the 1960s by a number of schol-ars and institutions who will be discussed in the first part of this chap-ter. In the second part I will consider the extent of the changed conception of German national history in the 1960s.

After 1945 the national tradition had been challenged by a small number of Catholic historians whose public resonance, however, remained limited. They were supported by Catholic journals like *Frankfurter Hefte* and *Neues Abendland.* Yet the only Catholic historian with the stature to stand up to Gerhard Ritter's continued defence of the Bismarckian nation-state, Franz Schnabel, remained hesitant in his commitment to denationalise German history-writing.[3] Schnabel, despite his ardent espousal of historism and a history of ideas approach which owed much to Meinecke, always had been an iso-lated outsider amongst German historians.[4] When he became pro-fessor of history at the Technical University of Karlsruhe in 1922, his Catholicism and his explicit approval of the Weimar Republic as a liberal democracy antagonised many of his colleagues. They remained utterly opposed to his insistence that 'historians have the right to doubt and criticise even national institutions'.[5] Not that Schnabel remained unaffected by national sentiment. Approving of the role of the historian as 'political educator of his people', he argued that historians had to present the German people with the 'evangelism of history' in order to give them 'strength to bless fate that they were born German even in the hour of the deepest humil-iation of their fatherland'.[6] His history of Germany in the nineteenth century, however, was in more than one sense a counter-project to Treitschke's Prussian version. More than Treitschke, Schnabel embed-ded the German development in the European context, emphasised the universal aspects of the European development and never saw in 1870/71 the epitome of Germany's history. Equally critical of histo-rians like Heinrich von Srbik, who espoused a 'greater Germany',[7] Schnabel found himself harassed out of a job by the Nazis, who, in 1941 prevented the publication of the fifth volume of Schnabel's Ger-man history as it allegedly was 'nationally unreliable'.

With credentials such as these, Schnabel might have become the centre of anti-Prussianism after 1945. Indeed, in several contribu-tions dealing with the national question, Schnabel criticised Bis-marck's unification of Germany and instead propagated the idea of a loose confederation of German states. Schnabel's post-war work portrayed the unified Bismarckian nation-state as the exception in a long tradition of a divided national history – a view which was to win

new prominence in the 1960s.[8] Despite such pathbreaking reinterpretations of German national history, he remained a lonely voice.
With regard to his public and academic importance he was not even
faintly comparable to Meinecke, Ritter and Rothfels.

In addition to Schnabel, Alfred von Martin's poignant criticisms
drew a direct line from Prussianism's attachment to power politics to
the success of National Socialism.[9] Martin, Johann Wilhelm Naumann, Emil Franzel and the historians organised in the Arbeitskreis
christlicher Historiker (founded in 1947), argued that the emancipation from a godly world order had caused the disaster of National
Socialism.[10] For them the roots of Hitler lay in the Reformation, the
Enlightenment, the French Revolution, secularisation and the *Kulturkampf*. In the light of the emerging Cold War their efforts to revive
a notion of a united Christian Europe, however, could not be convincing to the majority of post-war Germans, let alone historians.
Furthermore, their criticism of the Enlightenment tradition alienated
them from those historians who criticised the German national tradition from the political left.

A more influential questioning of long-held assumptions about
German national history can be found in Ludwig Dehio's work. As
the first editor of the *Historische Zeitschrift* after 1945, Dehio occupied
an important position in the profession. In his reinterpretation of
German history which he called 'one of the big tasks of the present
time', he explicitly sought to challenge the national tradition: 'Almost
no other history is as ambiguous as ours. Those interpretations, however, which we have been accustomed to and which we took for
granted, have collapsed.'[11] For Dehio, the powerful nation-state was
both the end product of a long process of civilisation and the result
of a truly Faustian pact with the devil. Bismarck had already cast
'eerie shadows'[12] over the foundation of Germany. The *Kulturkampf,*
the Anti-Socialist Law and the war with Austria signaled a moral and
intellectual rottenness in the emerging nation. Dehio portrayed Wilhelm II and Imperial Germany's elites as lacking a clear vision of the
aims and means of *Weltpolitik*. Prussian militarism and Hitler, he
argued, belonged together: '... the "accident" Hitler has to be interpreted at the same time as the acute symptom of a chronic infir-
mity.'[13] Defining Hitler both as 'elective Prussian in his mentality'[14]
and as the result of 'the Prussian line which carved itself into German
fate',[15] he located Nazism squarely within the whole of Germany's
modern history.

In contrast to Ritter, Dehio maintained that Prussian militarism
had had important implications for German civil and public life
which had been steeped in military values. He accused Ritter of

using the term militarism in a far too narrow sense by only taking
into account its impact on foreign relations and disregarding its
domestic impact.[16] Dehio even dared to criticise Ranke for eulogis-
ing the virtues of the nation-states and preparing the ground for the
imperialist propaganda of the neo-Rankeans around the turn of the
century.[17] He called on fellow historians to abandon the continued
one-sided emphasis on German national history and instead argued
for the establishment of a comparative and truly European history.[18]
Where Dehio became too critical of the national tradition, he was
censored. In 1949 the publishers of the *Historische Zeitschrift*, Olden-
bourg and Schröter, prevented the publication of an introductory
note by Dehio. They maintained that Dehio's 'confession of guilt'
about the entanglement of German historiography with National
Socialism was unnecessary. The autonomy of the editor of the most
prestigious historical journal of the profession stopped short of questions concerning the honour of the nation.[19]

Dehio, like a number of other post-war scholars, e.g., Karl Dietrich Bracher, Theodor Eschenburg and Walther Hofer, had become
a firm believer in natural law. Historical judgment, he argued, could
no longer be guided by success or power politics; it had to be guided
by the parameters of a morality which had to be common to all men
because of a common human nature.[20] Fischer, for one, has always
admitted that the impetus to investigate Imperial Germany's drive
for hegemony had come from Dehio.[21] In the Fischer controversy,
however, Dehio attacked Fischer, thereby revealing the limits of his
willingness to revise the national tradition in German historiography.[22] Dehio shared in the anti-Communist, anti-totalitarian consensus of the early Federal Republic. He interpreted National Socialism
as a response to the Communist threat in the 1920s.[23] He enlisted
old Prussian values like 'devotion to duty and courage' in the fight
against Soviet Communism.[24] In the climate of the Cold War, Dehio's
writings were overwhelmingly read as confirmation of the emerging
anti-Communist consensus and of the Western orientation of the
new Federal Republic. It was only in the 1960s that the 'critical
Dehio' was discovered.

A number of other scholars also began questioning the national
tradition after 1945. When, in October 1945, Theodor Eschenburg
reflected on the rebuilding of the German state after the Second
World War, he emphasised the need to turn away from the nationalism of the past and lay 'the foundations of a new political mentality for the Germans'. A new type of 'democratic pedagogue' had to
be enlisted for this task.[25] Eschenburg himself fulfilled this role perfectly. His works on the Weimar Republic and on state and society

in Germany clearly reflected his assumption that Germany exhib-
ited specific democratic deficits due to a peculiar illiberal development of the country in the nineteenth and twentieth centuries.[26] As
early as 1946 Johann Albrecht von Rantzau, a pupil of Meinecke,
criticised both Ranke and Ritter for their cult of the state. This, he
claimed, was responsible for making historiography the servant of
its political paymasters.[27] In his call for a complete thematic and
methodological overhaul of the historical sciences in post-war Germany, he explicitly referred to the absolute necessity of 'going
beyond the nation-state'.[28]

Karl Dietrich Bracher's pioneering study on the dissolution of the
Weimar Republic argued that 30 January 1933 was less a significant
break with a German political tradition and more a logical conclusion to the demise of the Weimar Republic.[29] Hitler could not be
reduced to contingency anymore. Anneliese Thimme, in her study
of Gustav Stresemann, corrected the myth of the good European
Stresemann and instead managed to show that his foreign policy
aimed first and foremost at the revision of Versailles, the restoration
of Germany's status as a major power in Europe and the dominance
of Germany over Eastern Europe.[30] Kurt Sontheimer, who had been
working at the Institut für Zeitgeschichte in Munich between 1957
and 1959, documented for the first time the strength during the
1920s of that anti-democratic thinking of which Hitler and the
National Socialist were a part and from which they benefitted.[31] The
only conclusion to be drawn from his book was that Hitler's success
stood in direct relation to the strength of such illiberalism. The
refusal of the academic council of the institute to publish Sontheimer's study in its prestigious monograph series revealed what a
difficult subject the Nazi past still was in the early 1960s.[32] In the light
of this more critical view of the development and characteristics of
the German nation Christian von Krockow called on fellow historians and political scientists not to prolong their fixation with the
nation-state in the vain search for an untimely homogeneous
national identity. Instead he argued that it was time to move towards
the analysis of society and help to develop a civic rather than a
national consciousness amongst Germans.[33]

Such firm relocation of National Socialism in a peculiar German
tradition was the precondition for a more critical view of the German
nation-state and for the tentative acceptance of the division of the
country after 1945. Franz Borkenau, ex-Communist and a representative of the totalitarianist paradigm in West Germany, wrote that
Germany had never been a truly united nation. He understood Bismarck's creation as a greater Prussia, and the imperialism of Wil-

helmine and National Socialist Germany as efforts to transcend the nation by creating a world empire. The ultimate failure of these efforts in 1945 had, he argued, destroyed once and for all the tentative beginnings of the German nation-state.[34] The delegitimation of the Bismarckian nation-state went hand-in-hand with the search for alternatives. Some historians began to argue that the Holy Roman Empire or the German Federation had been more appropriate than a unified nation-state which was almost certain to upset the balance of power in Europe over and over again.[35] Golo Mann found the aim of reunification unrealistic. Even if it were possible to achieve reunification in the distant future, it was more important, he argued, to aid internal reform in the GDR so as to allow its citizens greater freedom. He regarded the democratisation of the GDR as more important than national unity.[36]

The philosopher Karl Jaspers delivered a shattering blow to the national tradition in 1960 by radically challenging the national orientation of German historiography: 'After all that's happened, the mere fact that this state once existed does not constitute a moral right to its re-erection. On the contrary, in retrospect, a shadow falls on the Bismarckian creation.'[37] National Socialism had eroded the foundations of the Prussian-German national identity, but historians, according to Jaspers, had not even grasped this basic fact: 'The foundations for a German-Prussian national consciousness are gone. The historical idea that the divided Germany developed with inner necessity into the Bismarckian small-German state, is an invention of political historians of the Bismarckian and Wilhelmine periods and their contemporary descendants.'[38]

Some of the post-war critics of the development of the German nation-state had been influenced by the writings of those who had been exiled under Nazism. Bracher, for example, eagerly read Ernst Fraenkel in the post-war years. Many of the earliest works to be critical of Germany's path in the nineteenth and twentieth century and to locate Nazism in the context of a specific German tradition were written abroad.[39] Only rarely were such critical perspectives published prominently in German after 1945.[40] Overall, the impact of these exile writings on West German historiography remained limited in the 1950s.

In the 1949 debate on Bismarck's role in German national history, Eyck's critical biography of the iron chancellor[41] was overwhelmingly rejected. His liberal perspective on Bismarck, it was argued, could not do justice to the great personality of the founder of Germany. Thus the first post-war West German edition of his important biography was only published in 1963. Franz Neumann's analysis of

National Socialism was totally forgotten after 1945.[42] Neumann interpreted National Socialism as resulting from the specific economic, social and political structures of Germany: the dynamism of Germany's capitalism had contributed to the Nazi success. This analysis, informed by a merger of Weberian and Marxist sociology, proved unpopular amongst German historians after the Second World War. His namesake Sigmund Neumann, who was forced to emigrate in 1933, had in 1932, already published a ground-breaking study about the parties of the Weimar Republic. He argued that the specific German characteristics of capitalism and class formation contributed to the demise of the republic. Weimar, according to Sigmund Neumann, lacked the necessary minimum social homogeneity to survive. Characteristically, his study only experienced a renaissance in the 1960s when a second edition was published in West Germany.[43] George Hallgarten's analysis of the socio-economic conditions of Germany's foreign policy only received a wider audience amongst West German historians after the Fischer controversy.[44] Veit Valentin's re-interpretation of German nineteenth-century history suffered a similar fate. In his view, 1848/49 and not 1870/71 appeared as the major turning point. The failure of the revolution, according to Valentin, marked the point when German liberalism gave way to the authoritarianism of power politics. Valentin's monumental history of the German revolution of 1848/49 appreared as early as 1930/31.[45] Yet the first post-war edition of the work had to wait until 1970. Eckart Kehr had become a virtual non-entity until some of his most important writings were edited by Hans-Ulrich Wehler.[46] Other exiled historians, such as Arthur Rosenberg, and Helmuth Plessner[47] remained either unknown or were unfavourably received by the *Zunft* in the first fifteen years after the Second World War. Most of the exiled historians had to be rediscovered by the new critical social history which developed in West Germany in the aftermath of the Fischer controversy.[48]

It was not only individual scholars who played a part in eroding the foundations of the national tradition in the 1950s; new historical institutions also did so. In 1950 the Institute of European History had been founded at the University of Mainz. One of its major briefs was to encourage a Europeanisation of German national history.[49] At the beginning of the 1950s the Commission for the History of Parliamentarianism and Political Parties was established in the Federal Republic. Given the long history of mistrust, and at times downright hostility, of historians to both of these institutions, this marked an important new starting point for West German historiography. Over the next decades the historical foundations and deficits of liberal

democracy in Germany were thoroughly investigated. Most importantly, the newly established Institut für Zeitgeschichte, founded in
1951, and its journal, the *Vierteljahreshefte für Zeitgeschichte*, contributed
to a critical analysis of National Socialism, despite official efforts to
instrumentalise the institute for national apologias.[50]

A third factor which almost certainly contributed to the emergence
of more critical perspectives on German national history was the
increased contact of German historians with their U.S. and British
counterparts – thanks largely to the Allied re-education programmes.
Bracher had been influenced strongly by American political science
approaches. Fritz Fischer himself had spent a considerable time both
in Britain and the United States in the 1950s, where he met many of
the exiled German historians. Here he came into contact with social
and economic history which was still largely absent from German
universities. He also encountered a much more critical view on Imperial Germany than that which existed in Germany itself.

In the light of the quality and quantity of challenges to the
national tradition in the 1950s, Gerhard A. Ritter has argued that the
early 1960s and the Fischer controversy in particular were not a real
turning point in German historiography.[51] Winfried Schulze has also
denied 'the constitution of a separate tradition from about the 1960s
onwards'.[52] Against Ritter and Schulze, it has to be stressed that only
in the political climate of that time and under the impact of Fischer's
theses, did the national tradition actually have to give up its stranglehold on German historiography. Any genuine pluralisation of the
historical sciences occurred only after the watershed of the 1960s.

The controversy itself was long and bitter.[53] Its repercussions
amongst a wider German public were significant. The debate was
not carried out simply in historical journals. It spread to the press,
radio and there was even a television debate on Fischer's theses. The
bitterness is partly explained by the fact that a significant number of
historians like Aubin, Rothfels, Ritter and Egmont Zechlin had seen
active service in the First World War and still perceived this time as
a moment of national glory and of maximum inner unity of the
nation. It had become, in the words of Friedrich Meinecke 'a most
treasured, ever-lasting memory'.[54] Another reason for the violence of
the debate lies in the simple fact that no one had expected it. The
First World War was widely regarded as well researched. Yet Fischer
challenged more than the historiographical consensus on who was to
blame for the First World War. The debate itself quickly moved away
from the First World War and involved the question of what Fischer's
thesis would do to the remarkably successful apologias for German
national history. This became most evident in Ritter's concluding

remarks in his review of Fischer's book: 'So I cannot put this book aside without a deep sense of sadness. Sadness and concern with regard to the coming generation.'[55] History, in Ritter's conception, becomes the cement which unites the generations and provides them with a continuous national identity. Ritter, in response to Fischer, published a major apologia for the German nation-state and its responsibility for the outbreak of the First World War in the monograph series of the Bundeszentrale für politische Bildung with its guaranteed high circulation.[56] Hans Herzfeld's call to avoid 'strife amongst patriots'[57] ignored the very centrality of national sentiment to that debate. With hindsight Wolfgang J. Mommsen interpreted the Fischer controversy as the 'swansong of older forms of a national political historiography'.[58]

Many of the younger generation of historians sided with Fischer. Some of the established historians like Schieder, Erdmann, and Herzfeld incorporated Fischer's findings into their own publications after some time. Thus, in the 1970s, it looked to some supporters of Fischer, e.g., Geiss or Moses, as though Fischer's theses had won the day and would form the new orthodoxy: 'Nothing short of a new totalitarian seizure of power in West Germany could possibly erase the effect, already perceptible, which this new style of history is having upon the younger generation of students.'[59] A far more sober assessment and cautionary note was struck by Volker Berghahn, whose analysis of German school textbooks on the First World War in the late 1970s came to the conclusion that Fischer's theses had not yet reached a wider public.[60] Yet at the universities the Fischer controversy had a marked impact, not least because of the unparalleled expansion of the institutions of higher education which started around 1960. In the fifteen years between 1960 and 1975 the number of full professorships and lecturerships went up by 400 percent whilst the number of assistants went up by 800 percent.[61] The net effect of this expansion was a pluralisation of West German historiography which made it increasingly difficult for the profession to keep its ideological and methodological ranks closed against outsiders. A new interpretation of modern German history took shape in the 1960s, aimed at ending the powerful national myths by reinterpreting the notion of the German *Sonderweg*.

The development of Germany in the nineteenth and early twentieth centuries was portrayed as an abberation from the allegedly normal West European (often meaning British) path. Scrutinising the illiberalism, anti-pluralism and anti-socialism prevalent in German society, emphasising the unfinished nation-building process, the unresolved social question and the incomplete political modernisation of Germany in the *Kaiserreich*,[62] critics of the national tradition concluded that the triple domestic crises of Germany had led the country's elites to seek a solution in war in 1914. Ultimately such specific peculiarities of the Germans had also been the main reason for the rise of Nazism in Germany. The destructiveness of this German *Sonderweg* was highlighted in an attempt to contribute to the emergence of a more liberal and more democratic state.[63]

In this quest the critics of the national tradition employed a number of basic concepts to undermine the national orientation of German historiography, e.g., the 'backwardness' of Prussia's political system, *Sammlungspolitik*, 'social imperialism' and 'organised capitalism'. Many of these concepts had first been formulated by exiled historians, e.g., Kehr's notion of the primacy of domestic over foreign policy, Plessner's concept of the 'belated nation' or Rosenberg's concepts of the 'great depression' and 'Bonapartist rule'. Now they were embedded in an attempt to write the history of society, *Gesellschaftsgeschichte*.[64] An emphasis on structures and processes went hand-in-hand with increasing scepticism about the role of 'great men' in history.[65] The idea of *Verstehen*, so central to historism, was increasingly replaced by calls for more thorough theoretical reflections on the writing of history.[66] Some saw the historical sciences moving 'beyond historism'.[67] The championing of Max Weber's 'ideal types' and of Otto Hintze's 'generalising methods' and their implications for a comparative social history which was to move beyond the nation-state were signs of a vigorous dialogue between the social sciences and history.

Such a dialogue had already been encouraged by historians like Theodor Schieder and Werner Conze in the 1950s. Conze's Study Group for Social History (Arbeitskreis für Sozialgeschichte) at the University of Heidelberg, which held its first meeting in 1957, fostered the emergence of a structural history of industrial society.[68] The methodological renewal of German history and the belated turn to social history had much more to do with Conze and Schieder than with Fischer. More recently the beginnings of German social history have been traced even further back – to the *Volksgeschichte* which emerged in Germany after 1918.[69] However, it has also been pointed out that whilst *Volksgeschichte* never dented the pre-eminence of political history of the state, it was at the same time so flawed with methodological weaknesses and discredited by its espousal of racism and nationalism under the Nazi regime that it remained unattractive and of little influence to the post-war generation of German social historians.[70] Instead, the majority of young social historians in the 1960s turned to the Western Enlightenment tradition, fostering human freedom and emancipation, and juxtaposed it positively with the influence of German Romanticism and its programmatical propping-up of national myths in German historiography.[71] Dieter Groh, indebted like many of his generation to the Frankfurt school, reformulated the task of historians as contributing towards the political emancipation of citizens.[72] Historiography in this view had to reinforce democratic principles and contribute to the 'rational construction of contemporary society and culture'.[73] Normative values of a more universalist appeal had to replace the still predominant national values in German historiography. As Wolfgang Mommsen put it in 1988, the aim of critical historians was to 'rewrite history from the viewpoint of the democratically constituted societies of the West.'[74]

The need for a strong authoritarian state had been justified in the national tradition with reference to Germany's vulnerable geopolitical position in the middle of Europe, i.e., its *Mittellage*. Foreign policy needs, in this view, dictated the internal constitution of Germany. As with the *Sonderweg*, this primacy of foreign policy theory was now reassessed. Germany's aggressive foreign policy before 1914 was linked to economic interests. One consequence of the industrial revolution in Germany was the effort on the part of Germany's elites to achieve economic hegemony in Europe.[75] Following the example of Kehr, German foreign policy was now analysed as a function of domestic policy, most famously in Volker Berghahn's study of the importance of the battle fleet for German domestic politics.[76] The state, which lacked the legitimacy of a democratically elected government responsible to parliament, tried to solve internal friction by attempting to forge the nation together in imperialist ventures, navalism and ultimately war. The country's big business interests and their link to political decision-making came under increasing scrutiny.[77] Those elites were, it was claimed, dominated by the old feudal classes of Prussia whilst the middle classes were portrayed as having failed by and large to win a decisive say in Imperial Germany.[78] Germany's bureaucratic and feudalised capitalism produced peculiar divisions in society, and deepened the gulf between the working classes and the middle classes.[79] The parties and pressure groups in Wilhelmine Germany were more willing to forge an anti-socialist alliance than they were to reform the constitution of Imperial Germany along liberal and democratic lines.[80] Social Democracy was effectively isolated and became 'negatively integrated' into German society, thereby establishing a *Sonderweg* of the German labour movement.[81]

The critical re-appraisal of German history went beyond the history of Imperial Germany. The revolution of 1918/19 was reassessed.

Instead of being viewed in terms of a stab-in-the-back and as an un-German import, the revolution was now seen as yet another failed attempt thoroughly to democratise German society. The half-heartedness of the SPD leadership in particular was made responsible for burdening the republic with handicaps to which it finally succumbed under economic pressure in the early 1930s. The threat of Bolshevisation, on which earlier generations of historians had concentrated, was presented as a myth, and the democratic potential of the revolution rediscovered. In particular the council movement in Germany in 1918/19 and its potential for a democratic re-organisation of Germany was extensively discussed in the late 1960s. Eberhard Kolb published the first empirical study on the council movement, followed quickly by another major work by Peter von Oertzen.[82] At a time when the New Left was demanding a thorough democratisation of the Federal Republic, the missed opportunities of 1918 had a particular attraction for critical historians. After all, therein seemed to lie important lessons for the present. The studies of Bracher and Sontheimer were now celebrated as vital contributions to the scholarship on the downfall of the first German republic, and Martin Broszat pushed the interpretation of National Socialism away from Hitler demonology and anchored it firmly to a structural, social analysis of the state apparatus and the regime.[83]

The danger here is of overemphasising the degree of coherence amongst historians who developed these new perspectives on modern German history. There have always been significant differences and debates between critics of the national tradition. Alf Lüdtke, for example, argued against Wehler in the 1970s that Imperial Germany was not so much crisis-ridden, as extremely stable on the eve of 1914.[84] Dieter Groh has repeatedly criticised the Bielefelders for what he perceived to be their methodological and theoretical weaknesses.[85] Yet what matters here is that Lüdtke, Groh, Wehler and other critics of historiographical nationalism agreed on its methodological poverty, and, in one way or another, attempted to overcome its legacy. Historical identity, they argued, was rooted in social and psychological criteria rather than in the nation-state. The nation-state was no longer the framework for the realisation of an ideal bourgeois lifestyle complete with political participation and cultural autonomy. Notions like these were replaced by concepts of bourgeois society being determined by economic conditions and social developments. Thus 'class' became of central importance in the writings of critical historians. In the 1970s they focussed on exploring the working class[86] and in the 1980s interest shifted to the bourgeoisie[87] and the nobility.[88] The critical approach to the national tradition in

German historiography should thus best be seen as part and parcel of Willy Brandt's 'Mehr Demokratie wagen' ('to venture more democracy') project of the late 1960s.

The re-interpretation of German national history in the nineteenth and twentieth centuries was comprehensive and wide-reaching. Any short summary cannot do adequate justice to its many facets. Over the years critical historians successfully built up solid institutional bases. The University of Bielefeld, founded in 1971, developed into their stronghold. The publisher Vandenhoek and Ruprecht provided outlets for their publications, in particular the monograph series Kritische Studien zur Geschichtswissenschaft, founded in 1972, and the journal *Geschichte und Gesellschaft*, founded in 1975. Journals like *Geschichtsdidaktik* or *Journal für Geschichte* and historical book series like 'Neue wissenschaftliche Bibliothek', 'Arbeitsbücher zur modernen Geschichte' or 'Neue historische Bibliothek' (all published by suhrkamp) were also largely connected with the Bielefelders. However – and it needs to be stressed again – it would be entirely wrong to perceive critical historians as a homogeneous self-contained group with fixed doctrines. Social history, with a marked theoretical orientation, was championed largely by the so-called Bielefelders, especially Jürgen Kocka and Hans-Ulrich Wehler. Soon other groups emerged which shared the Bielefelders' critical stance vis-à-vis the national tradition, but maintained a distance from Kocka and Wehler in questions of methodology and research agendas. Women's history, gender history, oral history, history from below, everyday life history – they all can trace their origins back to the 1970s in German historiography. After the first generation of critical historians had broken up the *juste milieu* of the national tradition, new histories found it much easier to get a foothold in Germany.

The re-interpretation of modern German history and the pluralisation of historiography's methods and topics went hand-in-hand with direct attacks on the traditional link between nationalism and historiography.[89] The historians' national mission was now systematically criticised for boosting the Nazi regime, uncritically defending it or at least accomodating it. In 1963 Waldemar Besson published an article which emphasised the failure of German historians before 1914 to fulfill their necessary critical function in society. For him, their Germano-centric approach and their preoccupation with the greatness of the German nation made them into mere apologists for those political forces in society which propagated an expansionist and imperialist policy. Rather than critically commenting on the political processes, they became mere servants of particular political interests.[90] Christian Meier emphasised in 1968 that the function of historiography was not to legitimate but to criticise.[91] By 1970 Reinhart Koselleck could write that history had 'lost its political function insofar as the duty of a professor of history to make inflammatory speeches on the occasion of commemoration days seemed out of place today.'[92] Critics of historiographic nationalism pointed out that Clio's loss of stature after 1945 (the much-debated 'crisis of history' thesis) was closely related to its adherence to meaningless concepts of national identity. It would, they argued, only be able to compete with newer disciplines such as sociology and politics, once it had abandoned the national apologetics of the past and defined its task as that of the defence and propagation of a democratic civil society.

In the 1960s the period of the 'hot Cold War' was beginning to be replaced by détente. *Neue Ostpolitik* meant a more relaxed relationship to the Communist regimes behind the Iron Curtain. European integration had reached a stage in which it was at least possible to envision the nation-state as a thing of the past, about to vanish into obscurity. In 1962 the young Arnulf Baring began to abandon the concept of the nation. He argued that the division of the German nation-state had to be accepted as a political fact.[93] By 1967 Karl Dietrich Erdmann (president of the German historians' association from 1962 to 1967) contended that it was possible to accept the GDR as a legitimate state once it had guaranteed a minimum of freedom for its citizens.[94]

Geiss' vigorous support for Fischer was rooted in the political assumption that another major war could only be prevented if Germany accepted the status quo as it had emerged after the Second World War. Geiss explicitly rejected any idea that a reconstituted unified Germany would continue to play power politics. For him history had one lesson: a unified Germany with power would re-emerge as a serious danger to European and world peace. In this view a permanent division of the country was more desirable than unity, since survival (in the age of nuclear weapons) was more important than the nation-state.[95] Support for the *Ostpolitik* of the social-liberal coalition was extremely widespread, as was demonstrated by a declaration in support of the policy, written and presented by Hans Mommsen in the spring of 1972 and signed by about 220 fellow historians, sociologists and political scientists. The declaration explicitly stated that it was necessary to abandon 'national fantasies' and to accept, not only the new frontier with Poland, but also the GDR as a legitimate German state. A counter-declaration only mustered seven signatures. On the occasion of the Ostverträge, Golo Mann again reminded his audience that reunification was not on the agenda. National sentiments would, he argued, only hinder the normalisation of relations between the two German states which in the long run would benefit the people in the GDR.[96] This was to be the line on which a tentative and never unchallenged consensus emerged in the 1970s and 1980s which encompassed, conservative, liberal and left historians alike.

The increasing acceptance of the GDR resulting from a more critical view of German national history and the changed political climate of *Neue Ostpolitik* also resulted in a wide-spread reception of GDR historiography in West Germany. Critical historians now began to establish contacts with GDR and East European historians in an effort to begin dialogue across the ideological divide. Marxism-Leninism, however detrimental its effects were in other respects, ensured that GDR historians had interpreted the First World War firmly within the framework of capitalist expansionism. Thus, amongst GDR historians, the discussions on the outbreak of war in 1914 had long moved beyond political history and into the realm of social and economic history.[97] Precisely because they addressed these questions, their work received much praise by critical historians. Jürgen Kocka, for example, wrote in 1972: '… what, in the West, is either done or has been demanded under the banner of social history has already been incorporated in the work of socialist historians … .'[98]

In GDR historiography the events in Hungary (1956) and Czechoslovakia (1968) and the advent of *Neue Ostpolitik* led to a differently focussed emphasis on the national antecedents of the GDR. Whilst ideas of the socialist *Heimat* were widely sustained, GDR historians in the 1960s and early 1970s located the history of the GDR more strongly in the context of the developments in the whole of Eastern Europe after 1945. Particularly after Honecker had replaced Ulbricht at the helm of party and state, the impact of the Soviet occupation on the emergence of the GDR was widely admitted and discussed for the first time. If the GDR was willing to portray itself as part and parcel of the socialist transformation process in Eastern Europe between 1945 and 1948, then this was also one way of distancing itself from a common national history that it shared with the Federal Republic. The sharper ideological demarcation from the FRG that followed *Ostpolitik* meant that the German question was all but dropped in GDR historiography. Historical consciousness, it was now argued, was connected primarily to socialism. If one had to mention the nation, then GDR historiography took great care to carefully define and distinguish the 'socialist nation' from its capitalist sister in the West. German history was divided into a progressive line which allegedly culminated in the GDR and a reactionary line which conversely found its pinnacle in the FRG.

Like their counterparts in the GDR, critical historians in the FRG began to accept the division of the country. Increasingly they argued that the price Germany had to pay for upsetting European and world peace twice in the twentieth century was the end of an, in any case, ill-founded national unity. In their view, it had to be accepted as the best solution to the German problem which had proved to be so destructive. They rejected the idea of a powerful German nation-state which had guided historiographic nationalism. Instead the division of Germany was regarded as the best means of ensuring that Germany would never again be powerful enough to upset stability in Europe: 'A block of eighty million Germans would remain unpredictable for everyone, yet it would take second place in the world economy, and, due to its political options, it would severely change the status quo in Europe and the world.'[99] Therefore it was more sensible, Wehler argued, to work towards peaceful and permanent co-existence of two German states and 'renounce the one-sided concentration on the concept of the nation which has long become outdated.'[100] And in a similar vein Geiss called for a 'final liquidation of all patriotic dreams of a united Reich'.[101] From here it was only a small step towards the ideas of postnationalism and constitutional patriotism which dominated the discourse of critical historians in the 1980s, and which will be discussed in the next chapter.[102]

NOTES

1. Fritz Fischer, 'Deutsche Kriegsziele, Revolutionierung und Separatfrieden im Osten 1914-1918', *HZ*, vol. 188, 1959, pp. 249-65; idem, *Griff nach der Weltmacht: Die Kriegszielpolitik des Kaiserlichen Deutschland 1914-1918*, Düsseldorf, 1961; idem, *Krieg der Illusionen: Die deutsche Politik von 1911 bis 1914*, Düsseldorf, 1969.

2. Ernst Schulin, *Traditionskritik und Rekonstruktionsversuch. Studien zur Entwicklung von Geschichtswissenschaft und historischem Denken*, Göttingen, 1979, p. 139.

3. Schulze, *Geschichtswissenschaft*, p. 212.

4. Thus the conclusion of Friedrich Hermann Schubert, 'Franz Schnabel und die Geschichtswissenschaft des 20. Jahrhunderts', *HZ*, vol. 205, 1967, pp. 324-5.

5. Franz Schnabel, 'Vom Sinn des geschichtlichen Studiums in der Gegenwart' (1923), reprinted in Hardtwig (ed.), *Studium*, p. 252.

6. Ibid., pp. 251, 257-8.

7. The high point of the great German school of historiography was Heinrich von Srbik, *Deutsche Einheit. Idee und Wirklichkeit vom Heiligen Reich bis Königgrätz*, Vienna, 1935.

8. Franz Schnabel, 'Das Problem Bismarck', *Hochland*, vol. 42, 1949.

9. Alfred von Martin, *Geschichte vom Standpunkt der Humanität*, Ulm, 1947; idem, 'Entpreußung der deutschen Geschichtswissenschaft', *Stimmen der Zeit*, vol. 142, 1948, pp. 61-7.

10. For Christian historiography after 1945 see Schulze, *Geschichtswissenschaft*, pp. 266-80.

11. Ludwig Dehio, *Gleichgewicht oder Hegemonie. Betrachtungen über ein Grundproblem der neueren Staatengeschichte*, Krefeld, 1948, p. 10.

12. Ibid., p. 193.

13. Ibid., p. 223.

14. Ludwig Dehio, 'Der Zusammenhang der preußisch-deutschen Geschichte 1640-1945', in: Karl Forster (ed.), *Gibt es ein deutsches Geschichtsbild?*, Würzburg, 1961, p. 83.

15. Ibid., p. 85.

16. Ludwig Dehio, 'Um den deutschen Militarismus. Bemerkungen zu G. Ritters Buch "Staatskunst und Staatsräson – Das Problem des "Militarismus" in Deutschland"', *HZ*, vol. 180, 1955, pp. 43-64.

17. Ludwig Dehio, *Deutschland und die Weltpolitik im 20. Jahrhundert*, Munich, 1955, pp. 37-70.

18. Dehio, *Gleichgewicht*, p. 235.

19. For the full text of Dehio's introductory note see Schulze, *Geschichtswissenschaft*, pp. 101-4.

20. Karl Ludwig Rintelen, 'Historismus und Naturrecht', *GWU*, vol. 12, 1961, pp. 353-81.

21. Fritz Fischer, *Hitler war kein Betriebsunfall*, Munich, 1992, p. 18.

22. For Dehio's position in the Fischer controversy see Geiss, *Studien*, pp. 130-2.

23. Dehio, *Gleichgewicht*, p. 221.

24. Dehio, 'Zusammenhang', in: Forster (ed.), *Gibt*, p. 90.

25. Wolfgang Benz, 'Staatsneubau nach der bedingungslosen Kapitulation. Theodor Eschenburgs "Überlegungen zur künftigen Verfassung und Verwaltung in Deutschland" vom Herbst 1945', *VfZ*, vol. 33, 1985, p. 178.

26. Theodor Eschenburg, *Die improvisierte Demokratie der Weimarer Republik*, Laupheim, 1954; idem, *Staat und Gesellschaft in Deutschland*, Stuttgart, 1960.

27. Johann Albrecht von Rantzau, 'Geschichte und Politik im deutschen Denken', *Die Sammlung*, vol. 1, 1945/46, pp. 544-54; idem, 'Individualitätsprinzip, Staatsverherrlichung und deutsche Geschichtsschreibung', *Die Sammlung*, vol. 5, 1950, pp. 284-99; idem, 'Das deutsche Geschichtsdenken der Gegenwart und die Nachwirkungen Rankes', *GWU*, vol. 1, 1950, pp. 514-24.

28. von Rantzau, 'Individualitätsprinzip', p. 299.

29. Karl Dietrich Bracher, *Die Auflösung der Weimarer Republik. Eine Studie zum Problem des Machtverfalls in der Demokratie*, Villingen, 1955. See also idem, *Die deutsche Diktatur. Entstehung, Struktur, Folgen des Nationalsozialismus*, Cologne, 1969.

30. Anneliese Thimme, *Gustav Stresemann. Eine politische Biographie zur Geschichte der Weimarer Republik*, Hanover, 1957.

31. Kurt Sontheimer, *Antidemokratisches Denken in der Weimarer Republik*, Munich, 1962.

32. The difficulties of thematising the Nazi past in West German universities in the late 1950s is also remembered by Abendroth, *Leben*, p. 237.

33. Christian von Krockow, 'Nationalbewußtsein und Gesellschaftsbewußtsein', *Politische Vierteljahresschrift*, vol. 1, 1960, pp. 141-52.

34. Franz Borkenau, *Drei Abhandlungen zur deutschen Geschichte*, Frankfurt am Main, 1947.

35. Karl Buchheim, 'Das nationalstaatliche Denken im Deutschland des 19. und 20. Jahrhunderts', in: Forster (ed.), *Gibt*, p. 131.

36. Golo Mann, 'Hat Deutschland eine Zukunft?', *Die Zeit*, 7 September 1962; reprinted in Hans-Adolf Jacobsen and Otto Stenzl (eds), *Deutschland und die Welt. Zur Außenpolitik der Bundesrepublik 1949-1963*, Munich, 1964, pp. 197-203.

37. Karl Jaspers, 'Freiheit und Wiedervereinigung' (1960), in: idem, *Hoffnung und Sorge. Schriften zur deutschen Politik, 1945-65*, Munich, 1965, p. 199.

38. Ibid., p. 224 f. The lack of a national perspective for a future German historiography is also notable in Karl Jaspers, *Vom Ursprung und Ziel der Geschichte*, reprint, Munich, 1963.

39. Bernd Faulenbach, 'Der "deutsche Weg" aus der Sicht des Exils. Zum Urteil emigrierter Historiker', *Exilforschung. Ein internationales Jahrbuch*, vol. 3, 1985, pp. 11-30.

40. Two exceptions are Hajo Holborn, 'Irrwege in unserer Geschichte?', *Der Monat*, vol. 2, 1949/50, pp. 531-5; idem, 'Der deutsche Idealismus in sozialgeschichtlicher Beleuchtung', *HZ*, vol. 174, 1952, pp. 359-83.

41. Erich Eyck, *Bismarck*, 3 vols, Erlenbach, 1941-1944.

42. Franz Neumann, *Behemoth. Struktur und Praxis des Nationalsozialismus 1933 bis 1944*, Cologne, 1977 was the first German translation of the work which had first appeared in English in 1942, and in a revised edition in 1944.

43. Siegmund Neumann, *Die Parteien der Weimarer Republik*, Stuttgart, 1965.

44. Joachim Radkau, 'George W.F. Hallgarten', in: Wehler (ed.), *Historiker*, vi, Göttingen, 1980, p. 103.

45. Veit Valentin, *Geschichte der deutschen Revolution von 1848/49*, 2 vols, Berlin, 1930/31.

46. Eckart Kehr, *Der Primat der Innenpolitik*, ed. and introd. by Hans-Ulrich Wehler, Berlin, 1965.

47. Helmuth Plessner, *Das Schicksal des deutschen Geistes im Ausgang seiner bürgerlichen Epoche*, Zurich, 1935.

48. Essential for the rediscovery of several of these historians was Wehler (ed.), *Deutsche Historiker*.

49. Schulze, *Geschichtswissenschaft*, pp. 212-13.

50. For those apologetic tendencies see John Gimbel, 'The Origins of the "Institut für Zeitgeschichte": Scholarship, Politics and American Occupation', *AHR*, vol. 70, 1964/65, pp. 714-31.

51. Gerhard A. Ritter, *The New Social History in the Federal Republic of Germany*, London, 1991, p. 20.

52. Schulze, *Geschichtswissenschaft*, p. 307.

53. Most of the important contributions to the debate are collected in Ernst Wilhelm Graf Lynar (ed.), *Deutsche Kriegsziele 1914-1918. Eine Diskussion*, Frankfurt-on-Main, 1964.

54. Meinecke, *Katastrophe*, p. 43.

55. Gerhard Ritter, 'Eine neue Kriegsschuldthese? Zu Fritz Fischers Buch "Griff nach der Weltmacht"', *HZ*, vol. 194, 1962, p. 668.

56. Gerhard Ritter, *Der Erste Weltkrieg. Studien zum deutschen Geschichtsbild*, Schriftenreihe der Bundeszentrale für politische Bildung, vol. 65, Bonn, 1964.

57. Hans Herzfeld, 'Die deutsche Kriegspolitik im Ersten Weltkrieg', *VfZ*, vol. 11, 1963, p. 225. The article itself is another harsh attack on Fischer's positions.

58. Wolfgang J. Mommsen, 'Gegenwärtige Tendenzen in der Geschichtsschreibung der Bundesrepublik', *GG*, vol. 7, 1981, p. 162.

59. John A. Moses, *The Politics of Illusion. The Fischer Controversy in German Historiography*, London, 1975, p. 123. Geiss, *Studien*, pp. 183-8.

60. Volker Berghahn, 'Die Fischer-Kontroverse: 15 Jahre danach', in: *GG*, vol. 6, 1980, pp. 403-19. Klaus Bruckmann, 'Erster Weltkrieg – Ursachen, Kriegsziele, Kriegsschuld: Fritz Fischers Thesen in deutschen Schulgeschichtsbüchern', *GWU*,

vol. 32, 1981, pp. 600-17, and vol. 33, 1982, pp. 227-46 came to diametrically opposed conclusions. His analysis stressed that school textbooks were slanted unduly in favour of the Fischer thesis.

61. Werner Conze, 'Deutsche Geschichtswissenschaft seit 1945', *HZ*, vol. 225, 1977, p. 18 f.

62. The key text for this new view on German national history was Hans-Ulrich Wehler, *Das deutsche Kaiserreich 1871-1918*, Göttingen, 1973 (English translation, 1985). Very influential for a new interpretative framework of modern German history also Ralf Dahrendorf, *Gesellschaft und Demokratie in Deutschland*, Munich, 1968.

63. Bernd Faulenbach, 'Emanzipation von der deutschen Tradition? Geschichtsbewußtsein in den sechziger Jahren', in: Weidenfeld (ed.), *Politische Kultur*, pp. 73-92.

64. One of the clearest and most concise introductions to the theoretical concept of *Gesellschaftsgeschichte* is provided by Hans-Ulrich Wehler, *Deutsche Gesellschaftsgeschichte*, i, Munich, 1987, pp. 6-34; see also idem, *Historische Sozialwissenschaft und Geschichtsschreibung. Studien zu Aufgaben und Traditionen deutscher Geschichtswissenschaft*, Göttingen, 1980;Helmut Böhme, *Prolegomena zu einer Sozial- und Wirtschaftsgeschichte Deutschlands im 19. und 20. Jahrhundert*, Frankfurt-on-Main, 1968.

65. Hans-Ulrich Wehler, *Bismarck und der Imperialismus*, Cologne, 1968; Jürgen Kocka, *Klassengesellschaft im Krieg*, Göttingen, 1973.

66. Reinhard Koselleck, 'Über die Theoriebedürftigkeit der Geschichtswissenschaft', in: Theodor Schieder and Kurt Gräubig (eds), *Theorieprobleme in der Geschichtswissenschaft*, Darmstadt, 1977, pp. 37-59.

67. Wolfgang J. Mommsen, *Die Geschichtswissenschaft jenseits des Historismus*, 2nd edn, Düsseldorf, 1972, p. 41.

68. On Conze's view of structural history compare Werner Conze, *Die Strukturgeschichte des technisch-industriellen Zeitalters*, Cologne, 1957; for Schieder compare Theodor Schieder, 'Strukturen und Persönlichkeit in der Geschichte', *HZ*, vol. 193, 1962, pp. 265-96. On the continuities of Conze's and Schieder's historical thinking beyond the alleged watershed of 1945 see Götz Aly, *Macht, Geist, Wahn. Kontinuitäten deutschen Denkens*, Berlin, 1997.

69. Willi Oberkrome, *Volksgeschichte. Methodische Innovation und völkische Ideologisierung in der deutschen Geschichtswissenschaft 1918-1945*, Göttingen, 1993, and Schulze, *Geschichtswissenschaft*, pp. 281 ff.

70. Jürgen Kocka, 'Ideological Regression and Methodological Innovation: Historiography and the Social Sciences in the 1930s and 1940s', *History and Memory*, vol. 2, 1990, pp. 130-8.

71. M. Riedel, *Verstehen oder erklären? Zur Theorie und Geschichte der hermeneutischen Wissenschaften*, Stuttgart, 1978.

72. Dieter Groh, *Geschichtswissenschaft in emanzipatorischer Absicht*, Stuttgart, 1973.

73. Mommsen, *Geschichtswissenschaft*, p. 29.

74. Wolfgang J. Mommsen, *Nation und Geschichte. Über die Deutschen und die deutsche Frage*, Munich, 1990, p. 194.

75. Helmut Böhme, *Deutschlands Weg zur Großmacht. Zum Verhältnis von Wirtschaft und Staat während der Reichsgründungszeit 1848-1881*, Cologne, 1966.

76. Volker Berhahn, *Der Tirpitz Plan*, Düsseldorf, 1971.

77. Hans Jaegers, *Unternehmer in der deutschen Politik 1890-1918*, Bonn, 1967; Hartmut Kaelble, *Industrielle Interessenpolitik in der Wilhelminischen Gesellschaft. Der Centralverband Deutscher Industrieller 1895-1914*, Berlin, 1967.

78. The importance of agrarian interests in Imperial Germany was stressed by Hans-Jürgen Puhle, *Agrarische Interessenpolitik und preußischer Konservatismus im Wilhelminischen Reich 1893-1916*, Hannover, 1966. The weakness of the middle classes has been emphasised by Heinrich August Winkler, 'Der rückversicherte Mittelstand. Die Interessenverbände von Handwerk und Kleinhandel im deutschen

Kaiserreich', in: Walter Ruegg and Otto Neuloh (eds), *Zur sozialen Theorie und Analyse des 19. Jahrhunderts*, Göttingen, 1971.

79. For the peculiarities of Germany's industrialization process see Jürgen Kocka, *Unternehmensverwaltung und Angestelltenschaft am Beispiel Siemens 1847-1914. Zum Verhältnis von Kapitalismus und Bürokratie in der deutschen Industrialisierung*, Stuttgart, 1969.

80. Dirk Stegmann, *Die Erben Bismarcks. Parteien und Verbände in der Spätphase des Wilhelminischen Deutschland. Sammlungspolitik 1897-1918*, Cologne, 1970.

81. Dieter Groh, *Negative Integration und revolutionärer Attentismus. Die deutsche Sozialdemokratie am Vorabend des Ersten Weltkrieges 1909-1914*, Berlin, 1972.

82. Eberhard Kolb, *Arbeiterräte in der deutschen Innenpolitik 1918-1919*, Bonn, 1962, Peter von Oertzen, *Betriebsräte in der Novemberrevolution*, Bonn, 1963.

83. Martin Broszat, *Der Nationalsozialismus. Weltanschauung, Programm und Wirklichkeit*, Hanover, 1960; Hans Mommsen, *Beamtentum im Dritten Reich. Mit ausgewählten Quellen zur nationalsozialistischen Beamtenpolitik*, Stuttgart, 1966.

84. Alf Lüdtke, 'Zur Kontinuitätsfrage. Schwierigkeiten mit Konzeption und Methode', *Das Argument*, no. 70, 1972, p. 108.

85. Dieter Groh, 'Base-Processes and the Problem of Organisation: Outline of a Social History Research Project', *Social History*, vol. 4, 1979, pp. 265-83; idem, 'Le "Sonderweg" de l'histoire allemande: mythe or réalité?', *Annales*, vol. 38, 1983, pp. 1,166-87.

86. A very impressive synthesis of the mass of detailed research on the working class and the labour movement is provided by the multi-volume *Geschichte der Arbeiter und Arbeiterbewegung in Deutschland seit dem Ende des 18. Jahrhunderts*, published by the Dietz publishing house under the general editorship of Gerhard. A. Ritter.

87. Jürgen Kocka (ed.), *Bürger und Bürgerlichkeit im 19. Jahrhundert*, Göttingen, 1987. Lutz Niethammer (ed.), *Bürgerliche Gesellschaft in Deutschland*, Munich, 1990; Hans-Jürgen Puhle (ed.), *Bürger in der Gesellschaft der Neuzeit*, Göttingen, 1991; Klaus Tenfelde and Hans-Ulrich Wehler (eds), *Wege zur Geschichte des Bürgertums*, Göttingen, 1994.

88. Hans-Ulrich Wehler (ed.), *Europäischer Adel 1750-1950*, Göttingen, 1990.

89. Hans Mommsen, 'Historical Scholarship in Transition: The Situation in the Federal Republic of Germany', *Daedalus*, vol. 100, 1971, pp. 485-508; Reinhard Kühnl, 'Anmerkungen zur politischen Funktion der deutschen Geschichtswissenschaft seit der Reichsgründung', in: *Das Argument*, no. 70, 1972, pp. 5-21; Imanuel Geiss, 'Die westdeutsche Geschichtsschreibung seit 1945', *TAJB*, vol. 3, 1974.

90. Waldemar Besson, 'Geschichte als politische Wissenschaft', in: idem and F. Hiller von Gaertringen (eds), *Geschichte und Gegenwartsbewußtsein. Festschrift für Hans Rothfels*, Göttingen, 1963, pp. 75 f.

91. Christian Meier, 'Die Wissenschaft des Historikers und die Verantwortung des Zeitgenossen', in: idem, *Die Entstehung des Begriffs 'Demokratie'. Vier Prolegomena zu einer historischen Theorie*, Frankfurt-on-Main 1970, pp. 182-221. First delivered as his inaugural lecture at the University of Basle in 1968.

92. Reinhart Kosellek, 'Wozu noch Historie?', *HZ*, vol. 212, 1970, p. 3.

93. Arnulf Baring, 'Patriotische Fragezeichen', *Der Monat*, vol. 14, 1962, pp. 7-13.

94. Karl Dietrich Erdmann, 'Die falsche Alternative', *GWU*, vol. 23, 1972, pp. 357-60.

95. Geiss, *Studien*, pp. 45-66.

96. Golo Mann, 'Gedanken zum Grundvertrag', *Neue Rundschau*, vol. 84, 1973, pp. 1-8.

97. Host Handtke, 'Zur sozialgeschichtlichen Forschung in der DDR: Gedanken zu ihrer Entwicklung', *ZfG*, vol. 34, 1986, pp. 291-302; Willibald Gutsche, 'Die DDR-Geschichtsschreibung der siebziger und achtziger Jahre zu den Ursachen des ersten Weltkrieges. Ausgangspunkte, Methoden, Argumente', *Revue Internationale d'Histoire Militaire*, vol. 71, 1989, pp. 56-66.

98. Jürgen Kocka, 'Zur jüngeren marxistischen Sozialgeschichte. Eine kritische Analyse unter besonderer Berücksichtigung sozialgeschichtlicher Ansätze in der DDR' [1972], in: Fischer and Heydemann (eds), *Geschichtswissenschaft*, vol. 1, p. 400.
99. Hans-Ulrich Wehler, *Preußen ist wieder chic. Politik und Polemik in zwanzig Essays*, Frankfurt-on-Main, 1983, p. 75.
100. Ibid., p. 76.
101. Geiss, *Studien*, p. 196.
102. A good summary of the postnational anti-Prussian understanding of critical historiography is provided by Jürgen Habermas, *Eine Art Schadensabwicklung*, Frankfurt-on-Main, 1987, pp. 159-79.

Chapter 4

DECADES OF
POSTNATIONALISM?

*German Historiography from the
1960s to the 1980s*

In the last chapter I argued that the Fischer controversy had a significant impact on West German historiography in that it contributed to ending the stifling consensus on the national tradition. Some historians were quick to announce a fundamental change of paradigm.[1] The writing of history, Rüsen argued, was moving 'from *verstehende Geisteswissenschaft* to historical social science'.[2] Kocka argued that the paradigm change in historiography was in line with a general move from nation to society in the post-war era.[3] For Wehler the old paradigms of a political history of states and their foreign policies were gradually superseded by new paradigms such as 'industrial society', 'class' and the 'primacy of domestic over foreign policy'.[4] In 1972 Kühnl had confidently predicted victory: 'The spell has been broken. Historians of the younger generation find themselves increasingly at odds with the reactionary historical legends of their profession.'[5]

The enthusiasm of the early days has become more muted over the years. Whilst maintaining that the 1960s marked more than mere 'theatrical thunder' *(Theaterdonner)*[6], Kocka has argued that the term 'paradigm change' overestimates the influence and spread of historical social science in German historiography.[7] Wehler also has become more cautious: 'Presumably the new historical consciousness was never fully dominant ...'[8] Volker Berghahn argued that the conservative establishment amongst the historical profession had been remarkably successful in countering the development of a genuine pluralism.[9] Occasionally, however, the old triumphalism still shines through, as, for example, when the editors of a recent book on *Gesellschaftsgeschichte* write: 'the paradigm change' announced in the late 1960s has 'to a very large extent been realised'.[10] It is precisely on this trumped-up issue of dominance that critical historiography finds itself under attack in the 1990s. For Karlheinz Weißmann, Wehler's *Kaiserreich* was 'to a remarkable extent the foundation of a historical school' which 'became to a very large degree the orthodoxy'.[11] Michael Stürmer has argued that only historical social science promised 'both salvation and a career' in West Germany in the 1970s and 1980s,[12] and Gustav Seibt has written of the establishment of a 'social history orthodoxy' after 1968.[13] In order to test the validity of such claims, the first part of this chapter will deal with the challenges to historical social science in the 1970s and 1980s whilst the second part will trace the continuity of the national tradition throughout these two decades.

The historist tradition of West German historiography was vigorously defended by a number of prominent historians, amongst them Andreas Hillgruber, Klaus Hildebrand, Golo Mann, Konrad Repgen, Hermann Lübbe and Thomas Nipperdey.[14] In their view, critical historians acted like great inquisitors, ruthlessly imposing their paradigm onto the profession and threatening the freedom of historians to decide on their own topics of research. The high politics of states and classic diplomatic history had, it was argued, to retain their proper place in German historiography. As the decision of great individuals was ultimately regarded as more important in history than processes and structures, historists continued to emphasise the importance of studying 'great men'. The popularity of biographies throughout the 1970s and 1980s underlines such preoccupations.[15] Scepticism about the use of theory went hand-in-hand with upholding a clear demarcation line between the social sciences and history. Klaus Hildebrand and Golo Mann rejected the influence of Marxism on the writing of history. They contested the concept of the primacy of domestic policy and instead argued for a wide-reaching autonomy of the foreign policy of great states.[16] They considered 'industrial revolution' and 'class' alien concepts imposed upon the writing of history from outside, and retained the old historist illusion of a division of historical scholarship and political opinions of the historian: 'It remains the noble dream of every historian to reconstruct the past out of its possibilities, not out of our own possibilities and perspectives.'[17] The historian had to follow his 'ethos of an unerring search for truth'.[18] The neohistorist 'camp' can hardly be described as homogeneous. Whilst some, like Hildebrand or Hillgruber were fairly traditional diplomatic and political historians, others like Nipperdey stand out as social historians of the highest reputation. As a critic of historical social science, Nipperdey was seminal, because he was prepared to meet Wehler and others in their own domain of social history.[19] Yet virtually all defenders of the historist tradition produced awe-inspiring, important historical works. Institutionally, they had the advantage of being the establishment. Hence, the historist tradition was put on the defensive for a while, but it survived the challenge of historical social science largely intact.

For the historists the history of the German nation-state remained the centre of historical writing. According to Hillgruber 'the great topic for a modern political history will be the history of the German superpower between 1866/71 and 1945'.[20] Hildebrand argued that it was 'impossible to overemphasise the importance of the nation-state' for any modern historiography,[21] while Nipperdey wrote social history with the intention of allowing the current generation of Germans to identify with former generations of Germans.[22] Michael Stürmer found that only the nation-state had the power to replace religion and magic as the major focus of identity for people: 'The German nation as norm and idea ... has been part of a permanent identity for more than two hundred years.'[23] Not without justification, Gall has even cited Wehler as an example of the achievements of German 'modern national history'.[24] A look at the lectures and seminars delivered at German universities in the 1970s and 1980s, at the bibliographies of dissertations and habilitations, and at the established chairs and those occupying them, shows just how strong is the profession's concern for the history of the German nation-state even today.

Even the regionalisation and Europeanisation of German historiography does not necessarily transgress national history if we consider that German national consciousness was often consistent with and strengthened by the ideas of regional *Heimat* and a common European home.[25] Yet, the picture is not wholly bleak, a regional historical approach has emerged which is able to challenge the homogenising national approach.[26] Regional and local themes, often connected to everyday life, environmental history and gender questions, have begun to enter the school curricula in the 1980s.[27] A very effective challenge to the national tradition has come from historians of everyday life, historical anthropologists and poststructuralist historians. They have demonstrated a mode of history writing which looks at the social and cultural without reference to national political identification. Standing apart from both historical social science and neohistorism, these new approaches have opened another discourse on the writing of history which has, over recent years, won more and more converts. The comparative perspectives which have increased throughout the 1980s are also a hopeful sign that in future national blinkers can be overcome.[28]

Historians of everyday life were particularly scathing about historical social science's alleged concentration on processes of nation-building.[29] Instead they aimed at developing methodologies which would enable historians to reconstruct the subjective views and actions of individuals within wider historical processes. By giving people power over their own history and spurring them on to investigate their own past, historiography, they claimed, ultimately fulfilled a truly emancipatory strategy. This could only be done, they argued, by putting human agency back into the centre of history.[30] Thus 'a morphology of the ordinariness of everyday life' *(Alltäglichkeiten)* could be established.[31] The perspectives of histories of everyday life have involved analysing a 'multi-layered social field' within a local and regional context.[32] Historians of everyday life have shown a particular interest in social structures and social conflict, whereas the nation-state has largely ceased to preoccupy them. Thus it was the doyen of everyday life history in West Germany, Lutz Niethammer, who was one of the first historians in the early 1970s to demand an end to debates about reunification and to accept the end of the Bismarckian nation-state. If the critical historians theoretically demanded a move away from the traditional focus on national history without actually practising it, the historians of everyday life practised it without theorising much about it.

Given the very real differences in theoretical approach and underlying values, it cannot be surprising that there have been fierce battles between representatives of historical social science and the history of everyday life. The former have accused the latter of antiquarianism, conservative neo-historism, neo-romanticism and pseudo-realism. Wehler located it somewhere between 'a green soap bubble' and 'conventional millet gruel'.[33] However, there has also been the basic recognition of the value of microhistorical studies of everyday life.[34] Historical social science has signalled its willingness to include anthropological and gender perspectives into its repertoire.[35] However much the different schools of social history might disagree over methodological and/or theoretical assumptions, they have shared common ground which should not be overlooked in their opposition to historiographic nationalism and their commitment to emancipatory forms of history writing.[36]

Representatives of historical social science did not only find themselves criticised by neohistorists and other social history approaches outlined above. More recently poststructuralist historiography has very effectively challenged the underlying sense of a rational evolution in the historical process and indeed the very nature of historiography as a scholarly discipline.[37] Master narratives such as emancipation, civilisation, modernisation, humanism, progress and nation, encounter increased suspicion and are severely criticised for what they have marginalised and excluded. Instead of trying to synthesise multi-layered, fractured and dissonant historical developments into particular interpretative frameworks which by their very nature have to be exclusive, poststructuralist historians have denied the validity of any one history. They dissolve the concept of a single history into an unending mulitplicity of stories. The analysis of texts, of language and symbols, has moved into the foreground of the historical interest. Historiography, in a poststructuralist sense, does not produce synthesis or interpret texts; instead it creates new texts which construct stories according to certain rhetorical strategies. Historiography moves from an attempt to achieve systematic knowledge about the past *(Wissenschaft)* to becoming once again a literary genre. In the German context poststructuralist historiography has very few practitioners or theoreticians so far.[38] Representatives of historical social science dislike it because they feel the very nature of their rational discourse threatened by a historiography which denies that one can establish 'true' statements about the past by such rationality. Historists do not like it because it decentres historical writing from the nation-state and denies the value-free, objective practice of history writing which allegedly lies at the heart of historism. Yet the essential poststructuralist recognition that homogeneity means suppression and exclusion can serve as a starting point for the continuing emancipatory project of the Enlightenment. Although many poststructuralists have come to perceive the Enlightenment itself as burdened with universalist claims which developed an oppressive force, the key project of allowing people to develop critical faculties in order to win increasing power over their own lives is similar in the Enlightenment as in the more sensible theories of poststructuralism.[39] It would certainly serve as a powerful antidote to the renationalisation of collective identities. Any renewed focus on the nation as the central interpretative framework of history would immediately be shown to be what it is: ideology. Its false homogenising tendencies would be powerfully deconstructed by revealing the processes of constant redefinition of identities in any larger 'community'. A historiography which constantly dissolves and questions our notions of collective identity would be most welcome in the present climate.

On the whole, then, this brief survey of the challenges to historical social science in the 1970s and 1980s suggests that it would indeed be misleading to speak of either paradigm changes or hegemony. More correctly, it should be pointed out that the crushing dominance of traditional historism was broken in the 1960s, allowing a variety of different histories and methodologies to emerge. Ever since, historical social science has been fighting a three-cornered contest with neo-conservatism, history of everyday life and – more recently – poststructuralism. In these debates representatives of historical social science have shown an admirable willingness to admit to weaknesses and self-critically re-examine their positions.[40] Kocka specifically endorsed the plurality of approaches and opinions in West German historiography, when in 1989 he talked of German historiography as 'a house with many mansions'.[41] If, in the light of such pluralisation, it is entirely misleading to talk of historical social science as of a 'new orthodoxy', the remainder of this chapter will be devoted to demonstrating the continued existence of the national tradition in the 1970s and 1980s.

No doubt historiographic nationalism was severely shaken by ideas of binationalism and separate West and East German identities which spread amongst historians in the 1970s and 1980s. Eberhard Schulz was one of the very earliest to call for an acceptance of the GDR rather than a continued clinging to the alleged illusion of reunification.[42] In the late 1960s Niethammer and Borsdorf described the Federal Republic as a 'crypto-nation'.[43] Kurt Sontheimer called on his fellow Germans to abandon demands for German unity and instead concentrate on what was probably more relevant: increased freedom for the Germans in the GDR.[44] Hans-Günter Zmarzlik argued in 1970 that the division of Germany after 1945 should not be one-sidely viewed as a loss: 'This [division] increases the richness of opportunities in which Germans can fulfill their socio-political ideas.'[45]

In 1971, in a much-discussed study, Gebhard Schweigler came to the conclusion that Germany as one nation-state had ceased to exist in the consciousness of young Germans in both the Federal Republic and the GDR. Research of the GDR in the FRG took a new direction. Its practitioners ceased to understand their subject as a contribution towards reunification. Totalitarianist theory was increasingly rejected. The GDR was perceived as an authoritarian regime which should be analysed in its own terms and not by using Western political standards. Only by ending the purely negative demonisation of the GDR it would be possible to come to a proper understanding of its functioning and its successes.[46]

Even conservatives like Dolf Sternberger developed concepts of 'constitutional patriotism' which, they argued, reflected the reality in the FRG much more than the outdated concept of the nation. Yet Sternberger is a good example of how, amongst conservatives, the national perspective was never actually abandoned. His deep 'sorrow over the division of the country' and his hope that it would one day be overcome were compatible with his warning that it would be impossible to 'abandon the constitution for the sake of the nation and its unity'.[47] Sternberger's views are already an indicator that, contrary to some of the statements made after 1989, ideas of binationalism, postnationalism and even constitutional patriotism never became *communis opinio* amongst German historians. In fact they were challenged from very early on. Bernd Faulenbach's assessment that in this period 'national history has to a considerable degree been pushed to the sidelines'[48] needs to be questioned just as much as Christoph Kleßmann's thesis that 'German national history or all-German history was cleary not on the agenda ... .'[49] In my view this was true only for some. There were in fact considerable efforts to retain a collective national identity. One should not try to paper over such continued important differences amongst historians in a vain attempt to appeal to some sort of illusory consensus that historiography allegedly had either achieved or abandoned at some point or other.

The resilience of the national tradition had already become evident in the Fischer controversy. 'Official nationalism' supported the historians' indignant reaction to Fischer. The German foreign office withdrew funding for a lecture tour by Fischer through the United States. The parliamentary president, Eugen Gerstenmaier, spoke of Fischer as a representative of that 'German community of flagellators'.[50] F.J. Strauß, alleging that Fischer was a Communist fellow-traveller, argued: 'A people, which has performed an economic miracle has a right not to want to be bothered with Auschwitz anymore.'[51] Fischer's critics seized upon that old and well-tested strategy of nationalists of portraying critics of the nation as clinically ill anti-nationalists. Erwin Hölzle, one of the foremost Nazi propagandists between 1933 and 1945, saw in Fischer's theses little else than the culmination of the 'popular self-accusation' amongst Germans after 1945.[52] Ritter saw Fischer's book as representative of a 'current political-historical fashion', namely the 'increasingly one-sided self-deprecation ... in German historical consciousness.'[53] The far right-wing Armin Mohler, a Swiss citizen who had volunteered for the Waffen-SS in Nazi Germany and, for a long time, was head of the Siemens-foundation in the FRG, wrote of the 'national masochism' of German historians.[54]

German historians flocked to the defence of the nation. In 1965 Hans Rothfels, in a panegyric article on Bismack's historical achievements, confirmed the Prussian myth that there had been no alternative to Bismarcks's solution of the German problem.[55] Karl Bosl could still write in 1970 that 'Bismarck fulfilled the will of the people from above',[56] and in 1971 Peter Graf Kielmannsegg added that it was impossible for Germans to go back on the experience of national unity: 'The empire of 1871 ... was much more than a mere episode because the experience of Germany's unity ... has left a lasting mark on the way Germans perceive themselves. We cannot go back on this experience. Therefore the caesura of 1871 remains valid for us today.'[57] Historians were readily available whenever politicians wanted solemnly to remind the public of the great German past.[58]

In 1966 Nolte saw 'writing national history as one of the most important tasks of the historian'.[59] The nation as a concept, he argued, had ultimately not been discredited by National Socialism because the Nazis despised the nation and replaced it by concepts of race and an expansionist Greater German Empire *(Großdeutsches Reich)*. National history, he argued, should be written in such a way that 'one day in the distant future it will once again become our property'.[60] How this could be done had been demonstrated a few years earlier by Werner Conze. In typically tragic emplotment, German history was presented as a series of missed opportunities (1848), fatal enmities (1871), simple faith (1914), and insecure instinct (1918-1933).[61] Between 1933 and 1945 the Nazis had been 'in a minority' amongst the Germans.[62] Naïvely Conze paid tribute to the German soldiers in the Second World War claiming that 'the level of their readiness to be sacrificed was one not often or easily shown by human beings of their own free will'. He hailed the war's 'power to overcome naked egoism ... in the form of bravery in the face of the enemy'.[63] Expressing his hopes for a reconstitution of the Bismarckian nation-state, he confirmed the centrality of the German question for German historians and the wider German public.[64] 'Despite its loss of unity the divided Germany', he maintained even in the late 1970s, continued to rest on 'the foundation of the Reich of 1871'.[65]

Maybe the most widely acclaimed expert on nations and nationalism in the Federal Republic was Theodor Schieder.[66] Initially deeply influenced by the *völkisch* nationalism of the Nazis,[67] he never became enamoured of concepts of postnationalism. In contrast, for him, the purpose of the new Western Europe which he vigorously supported after 1945, was 'to relearn German history in its characteristic traits'.[68] He did so by explaining German imperialism as a normal variant of a European phenomenon, whilst he put fascism safely outside the continuity of German national history. After all, Nazism started in southern Germany, not in the Prussian heartland, and, what is more, the Nazi party was led by an Austrian. National Socialism, in his view, had little to do with Prussian traditions whilst it had a lot in common with Communism.[69] Many of the old Ritter arguments can be traced in Schieder's writings on the questions of nation and nationalism in Germany. Schieder remained a strong admirer of Treitschke. He never left any doubt that he saw no alternative to the Bismarckian 'small-German' solution to the German problem in the nineteenth century.

Only for a brief period, in the context of the Social Democratic euphoria for new departures from the mid-1960s to the early 1970s, did historiographic nationalism get onto the defensive. The challenge provided by the Social Democratic critics of the national tradition in German historiography was taken up by the conservative mainstream of the profession. Historians could feel themselves in line with conservative national politics. Richard von Weizsäcker, declared in the Bundestag in 1972: '...the year 1871 defines our understanding of the nation. From this point and only from there do we know today that we feel ourselves to be German. Hitherto this has not been replaced by anything else.'[70] In 1975 Hans-Peter Schwarz echoed Weizsäcker in describing it as moral necessity and good common sense to keep the national question open and on the agenda. The division of the country remained illegitimate, and the policy of the Federal Republic had to remain geared to achieving unity in the long term. *Ostpolitik* could not mean genuine cooperation with the GDR, it could only mean relieving the oppressive situation of the people of the GDR.[71]

On the extreme right wing of the *Zunft*, Helmut Diwald in 1978 published a 'History of the Germans' which was a blatant example of historiographic nationalism.[72] Diwald saw in the post-1945 occupation and division of the country the 'biggest ever danger' to Germany's existence, especially as, according to him, Allied re-education policies aimed at crippling German national identity. He warned: 'A people which ... covers its mirrors, gives up on its future.'[73] For him regaining sovereignity for a united Germany was the 'supreme' goal.[74] The boundaries of the future Germany, he argued, were defined by ethnicity. Hence he routinely mentioned Austria, South Tyrol, Sudetenland and the Eastern parts of Germany (in contrast to middle Germany, i.e., the GDR) when discussing the shape of the reunited nation to be. In his national history writing, 'the struggle for unity' became the central motif of one thousand years of German history. For Diwald the vocation of the historian remained linked to allowing a wider public to identify emotionally with *Volk* and fatherland.

Like Diwald, Hans-Joachim Arndt from the University of Heidelberg argued in 1979 that the Germans had been brainwashed by the Allied re-education policies after 1945. For Arndt, only the return to a 'historical consciousness of the *Volk*' and a healthy identification with the nation would halt the threatening moral and political decline of the German people.[75] Attacks on Western liberalism as alien to German *Geist* and calls for a policy which would put reunification of the country centre-stage can – together with the propagation of an overt nationalism – also be found in the writings of Hans-Dietrich Sander and Gerd-Klaus Kaltenbrunner.[76] References to geopolitics, to Romantic nationalism and to the strength of the German ethnic characteristics merge in a dangerous revisionist amalgam: 'The geographic position of Germany has ... maintained the original strength of our people ... through unrelenting demands upon its endurance.'[77] Henning Eichberg argued that only ethnically homogeneous nations could develop a stable collective identity.[78] Bernard Willms, of Bochum University, also took the critical historians to task for allowing the alien transplantation of 'puny liberal thinkers' *(liberale Schwachdenker)* and their theories to spread in the FRG.[79] Willms instead demanded a return to German idealism and its 'national imperative', i.e., the idea 'that a historical collective, a people, puts its very existence as a nation before everything else.'

Diwald, Sander, Eichberg, Arndt, Kaltenbrunner, Mohler, and Willms – the most vociferous representatives of traditional forms of nationalism, remained marginal to the historical profession in the 1970s and 1980s. Mainstream conservative historians like mainstream conservative politics in West Germany after 1945 had come to endorse a Westernised understanding of the nation-state. By 1966 one could find the argument that the old German concept of the nation lay buried in the ruins of Nazi Germany. However, there was still a chance to break through to an alleged Western normality of the nation-state.[80] The national tradition was thus decisively redirected in its form and content in the Federal Republic. To such a revamped national idea, there was a far more widespread commitment amongst historians in the 1970s and 1980s, as the subsequent paragraphs will aim to demonstrate.

In 1979 Ernst Schulin had already written perceptively of the worrying trend of 'numerous demands for resurrecting a homogenous German national history'.[81] Hans Mommsen found that such efforts still revealed the strong anti-pluralist potential within the *Zunft* and the political culture of the Federal Republic at large.[82] Wilfried von

Bredow and Hans F. Foltin feared that the renaissance of *Heimat* in West Germany might easily lead to the revival of nationalism in Germany.[83] Arno Klönne argued that 'national identity' had become the keyword of the intellectual discourse of the 1980s,[84] and Irmline Veit-Brause asked in 1984 whether the search for national identity would be the new topic which was to replace the Enlightenment ideals of the critical historians.[85]

In the 1970s the Staufer exhibition and the Wallenstein cult in the wake of Golo Mann's Wallenstein biography were signs that history was becoming more important in strengthening the national aware-ness of a wider public. In the summer of 1981 the exhibition on Prussia in Berlin produced a wave of publications on Prussia and its role in the making of Germany. More than half a million people vis-ited the central exhibition in West Berlin. There were about thirty further exhibitions and about one hundred events surrounding the main exhibition. A documentation of the media reaction to the exhi-bition filled three thick tomes. Conservative historians like Michael Stürmer, Hagen Schulze and Karl Dietrich Erdmann all evoked Prussia and Prussian history in order to cement the allegedly crum-bling national identity of West Germany.[86] Wehler explained this vogue in terms of a 'flight into a transfigured past'.[87] Prussomania, he argued, went hand-in-hand with a very one-sided positive re-assess-ment of Prussian values and achievements. Fritz Fischer felt obliged to call on his fellow Germans to renounce the fateful Prussian-Ger-man tradition and not fall prey once again to the charms of Prussia.[88]

Encouraged by Prussomania, conservative historians and publi-cists continued their national campaign with a revivalist rhetoric. Werner Weidenfeld argued that the 'deficit of German national iden-tity' spelt danger for the stability of the Bonn republic.[89] Guido Knopp, having come essentially to the same conclusion, recom-mended the idea of a united German nation that would fill the threatening abyss of a Germany without an identity,[90] and Roland Hahn argued that 'it will be of decisive importance in future whether we in the Federal Republic succeed in bringing about a positive iden-tification with German national history.'[91]

The major obstacle on the road to national identity, however, was Auschwitz. One strategy for overcoming this stumbling block was to end the public discussion and return to the silence of the 1950s. Her-mann Lübbe began to argue that the lack of discussion on National Socialism in the 1950s, far from being any great misfortune, was in fact the precondition for a successful and stable democracy in the Federal Republic. Only by excluding the consciousness of their own involvement with the Nazi regime was the majority of the West Ger-

man population able to turn to the new democracy with such amazing speed. Psychologically, Lübbe argued, the consolidation of the
Federal Republic in the 1950s rested on the forgetfulness of its citizens.[92] Thomas Nipperdey went one step further by arguing that the
critical historians' efforts to 'come to terms' with the Nazi past, far
from producing a deeper understanding of the historical phenomena,
had only contributed to a climate of public denunciation and accusation.[93] Such poisoned national consciousness, Nipperdey alleged, had
led the critical historians prematurely to declare the German question
answered. Nipperdey instead insisted on the continued unity of the
German nation and propagated a healthy national identity.[94]

From the early 1980s onwards the rediscovery of Prussia was
accompanied by the renaissance of geopolitical concepts. The strong
link between geopolitical thinking and Nazi concepts of *Lebensraum*
in the Second World War had discredited the idea after 1945. Now,
Karl Schlögel, Stürmer and Hillgruber in particular resurrected
geopolitics to portray the history of the German nation between 1871
and 1945 in an essentially tragic mode. However, it was not so much
the lack of domestic political unity, of democratic structures and the
persistence of authoritarian government which explained Germany's
instability and aggressive foreign policy. Rather it was the logic of
Germany's geographic position; located in the 'heart of Europe', it
was burdened with the 'curse of geography'.[95]

History was widely perceived as a mutual bond between FRG
and GDR, and many historians in the West perceived it as their duty
to keep the vision of a united Germany before the public's attentive
eye. In 1982 Joachim Fest wrote that the most important task in Germany at the time was to 'retain the consciousness of a common language, a common culture and the idea of the one nation'.[96] Awaiting
the collapse of Communism, some Cold War warriors like Konrad
Löw and Wolfgang Seiffert developed various scenarios for reunification. After all: 'Every normal healthy nation feels national'.[97] For
Tilman Mayer, to give up the principle of the unified nation was a
case of 'national self-surrender'.[98]

The fortieth anniversary of the end of the Second World War on
8 May 1985 produced a flurry of articles that were clearly affected by
the contemporary national debate. Schulze, for example, noticed a
'crisis of values' in West Germany. In his view, 'a society held
together simply by the ambition to constantly raising the GNP'
could not replace the nation. In the long run a society without a
nation would inevitably lead to 'loss of orientation' and 'doubts
about one's identity'.[99] Schulze's collected essays from 1982 to 1986
testify to the centrality of maintaining a collective national identity in

his thinking which he based on a common history and culture.[100]
Stürmer advised Germans to allow themselves 'mixed feelings' in
the face of defeat and liberation. For him national 'sorrow and bitterness' at the memory of the expulsion of twelve million Germans
from the East and the subsequent division of the country had to
remain as important as the gratefulness to the Allies for putting an
end to Nazi terror and humiliation.[101]

During the 1980s the whole question of national identity became
important for propagating a more power-conscious foreign policy for
a Federal Republic geared more clearly to pursuing national interests. Hans-Peter Schwarz scolded the Germans for their alleged
'obliviousness to questions of power' *(Machtvergessenheit).* In his view,
this was related, first, to the alleged German guilt complex about
their National Socialist past and, secondly to their Western orientation. The latter had facilitated a hedonistic materialism devoid of the
Prussian values of selfless duty and sacrifice.[102] Christian Hacke's
panegyric account of West German foreign policy was informed by
the same desire to link the question of German identity to the importance of accepting a wider international role. A tone of narcissistic
self-congratulation pervades the whole book. In the preface, the Federal Republic's foreign policy after 1949 is described as a 'breath-tak-
ing success story' and an 'unbelievable success story'.[103] Hacke was
disappointed that this success story had neither contributed to a 'new
self-confidence' amongst his countrymen nor to the creation of a stable 'German identity'.[104]

Some critics of the national tradition argued that the challenge of
the political right had to be taken up. The topic of national identity
was to be developed by the political left, but without falling prey to
nationalism.[105] Many of Wolfgang J. Mommsen's articles from 1978
to 1988 on the 'national question' confirm the importance he
attached to the topic. Attacking the way in which the national question was allegedly tabooed, he saw the creation of national identity
based on national history as a necessary task for historians.[106] Whilst
claiming that 'in principle the historiography of the FRG had cut
itself loose from a predominantly national perspective',[107] Mommsen
was adamant about anchoring any positive German identity in the
history of the FRG, its Western orientation, its European integration,
its federal structure and its achievements as a welfare state. Several
volumes in the early 1980s brought together right-wing and left-wing
historians to discuss questions of national and cultural identity and
national consciousness, *Sonderweg,* the difficult fatherland, the missing national normality, the divided identity and other familar topoi
of the national debate.[108] At the same time, the late 1970s and early

1980s saw a flurry of historical research on nation and nationalism in general and on the German nation and the national movement in its historical configurations in particular.[109] There was certainly no shortage of discussions on the nation.

Sonderweg theories were rapidly falling out of favour in the 1980s, partly because they were conceptually flawed, partly because they stood in the way of an attempted renationalisation of German identity. Even some of its erstwhile champions like Jürgen Kocka and Bernd Faulenbach moved away from or at least modified the *Sonderweg* concept.[110] Geiss, foreshadowing his defence of revisionist national positions in the *Historikerstreit*, explicitly called on historiography to pave the way for 'a new positive identification of the Germans with their collective national history'.[111] Rudolf von Thadden maintained throughout the 1980s that the topic of national identity was relevant, and called on fellow Germans not to get lost in 'European dreams or a vague cosmopolitanism'.[112]

Peter Brandt and Herbert Ammon, both close to the peace movement in the early 1980s, developed a left-wing nationalism intended to reclaim the concept of the nation for the political left. They claimed that, from the early nineteenth century onwards, a left-wing, radically democratic patriotism in Germany was opposed to an ethnic definition of the nation-state. This assumption allowed them to link scenarios for overcoming the Cold War division of Europe with reunification. The very real danger of 'exterminism' (E.P. Thompson) demanded the creation of a nuclear-free zone in Central Europe. Disengagement plans would necessarily bring up the question of a peace treaty with Germany, the neutralisation of Germany and the reunification of the country. Hence, peace policy was national policy. For Brandt and Ammon it was impossible to accept the division of Germany as the key stabilising element in the Cold War European order. For them the question of identity always remained the question of national identity, and this included the Federal Republic and the GDR. Only if the left recaptured the national question for itself and pushed the superpowers out of central Europe would a European community of peace be established. Such a post-Cold War peace would create the opportunities for a truly socialist Europe which would go a third way between the capitalism of the United States and the state Communism of the Soviet Union.[113]

However, Brandt and Ammon remained more the exception than the rule amongst left-liberal historians in the 1980s. A majority remained strongly opposed to the revival of the national discourse in historiography. For Wehler, any renewed preoccupation with the German problem only revealed the old tendencies of the Germans 'to get bound up with themselves' and 'escape into cloud-cuckooland'[114] In his scathing attacks on the nationalism that could be found on the margins of the peace movement, he even went so far as to defend Reaganite Cold War policies. For Wehler, the Western orientation had to take clear precedence over reunification, especially as the former had not taken firm root in the FRG's political culture, whilst the latter had become 'historically outdated and a mere paper tiger'.[115] Hans Mommsen was highly critical of the 'continued strong apologetic motivations' in German historical writings, and instead recommended comprehending 'the nation as only one group amongst diverse forms of human socialisation'.[116] He argued that national identity was neither necessary nor, in the disastrous German context, particularly desirable.[117] He went on to predict that in any case 'no social group in the FRG would even rhetorically support the material sacrifices necessary in the event of any incorporation of the GDR into the FRG'.[118] Kocka underlined Wehler's and Mommsen's scepticism. The nation, he argued, was neither a natural nor a necessary state form for Germans. In fact, he pointed out, they had lived without a nation for most of their history and had fared much better without one: 'national tradition had left little to build on in the present'.[119] Kocka was highly critical of the national tradition in historiography, which, as he argued in a review of two national histories by Schulze and Stürmer, all too easily lends itself to exculpating German responsibility for major desasters in the twentieth century.[120] According to Sebastian Haffner, the Bismarckian nation should best be viewed as a transition period after which Germany returned to the normality of division.[121] Two years later Rudolf Vierhaus echoed this verdict: 'In the course of German history, political unity has been the exception.'[122] Wilfried Loth was amongst those who throughout the 1980s had argued most vigorously for seeing the positive sides of German division as well as its negative consequences. He described the division of Germany as a 'solution to the "German problem", which had evolved historically'.[123] For Peter Alter 'Europe's experience of the German Reich after 1871 was too awful' for one to imagine any future scenarios of reunification.[124] Bracher, in an influential article, urged historians to abandon the discourse of national identity altogether as, in his view, most West Germans had long developed a postnational consciousness.[125] Along similar lines, Rainer Lepsius developed his concept of the FRG as a 'state nation' *(Staatsnation)* in contrast to the traditional 'nation-states' *(Nationalstaaten).*[126]

The rejection of efforts to renationalise German identity finally culminated in the *Historikerstreit* of 1986/87. It has itself by now been the topic of much research, and there is no need for further detailed analysis.[127] In the debate Stürmer argued most strongly that only such renationalisation would prevent Germany from drifting into civil war in the face of the alleged double threat constituted by the peace movement and Soviet Communism. Ernst Nolte's efforts to question the uniqueness of the holocaust and interpret Nazism as a justified reaction to Bolshevism fitted the bill, since his revisionism allowed for the spread of more positive national identity. Andreas Hillgruber's and Klaus Hildebrand's contributions similarly focussed on themes which stressed the positive sides of German history and accused critical historiography of spreading a pathological anti-nationalism. Habermas reacted by claiming that 'anyone wanting to recall the Germans to a conventional form of their national identity, destroys the only reliable base for our link with the West.'[128] Winkler suspected the true agenda of the conservative historians to be reunification of the country underpinned by a 'national apologetic wave' in historical writing: 'To demand the restitution of the German Reich today, history has to be rewritten. The regime that gambled away the unity of Germany, can no longer appear as what it truly was: the most inhumane regime in history ...'.[129] At the end of the debate it seemed as though a return to a narrow national identity in Germany had been prevented. Complex modern societies, Faulenbach argued, could not without difficulty develop consistent and homogeneous national identities. The real task of historiography was 'critical self-reflection'.[130] A pluralist society, Hans Mommsen concluded, would have to learn to live with competing social and political identities.[131] Eberhard Jäckel pleaded for 'a ruthless examination of one's own national past. The freedom which comes from such critical examination, can form the basis of civic pride.'[132] In the old struggle between the leading key terms of German historical consciousness after the 1960s, i.e. between 'emancipation' vs. 'identity',[133] it looked, as though the former had effectively halted the ideological advances of the latter. Yet perceptive analysts of the debate already noted the defensiveness of the Social-Democratic position of Habermas and others. Terms like constitutional patriotism and Western orientation had never been left-wing concepts. They had been taken over by parts of the left in a hapless attempt to stem the tide of political neo-conservatism after the so-called *Wende* in 1982 to which context the revival of the national idea firmly belonged. In referring to an alleged consensus on national matters that had existed before the neo-conservative revival (connected to the revamped patriotic rhetoric of Chancellor Kohl, to Bitburg, to the debates surrounding the fortieth anniversary of the end of the Second World War, to Lübbe's prominent call to end *Vergangenheits-*

bewältigung), critics of historiographic nationalism were adhering to homogenising strategies.[134]

It was, however, partly thanks to this continued rejection of national identity as focal point of German historiography that a genuine dialogue emerged in the 1980s between some left-liberal historians of the FRG and the Marxist historians of the GDR. Before the 1980s only a handful of Marxist historians like Wolfgang Abendroth and Reinhard Kühnl maintained contacts with their colleagues in the GDR. Kühnl had in fact denounced the revival of the national debate in the 1980s as an effort to delegitimate the GDR and its socialist society. Against the 'ghost worlds erected by constitutional lawyers', he had firmly pleaded for an independent national consciousness in the GDR and the FRG, agreeing, by and large, with his GDR colleagues. This went hand-in-hand with an embarrassingly kitschy admission of his own commitment to the idea of *Heimat,* reminiscent of Tucholsky's famous declaration of love for Germany.[135] In the 1980s a group of Social Democratic historians began breaking the ice as well. The conference organised by the Historical Commission of the SPD in March 1987 saw lively discussion between historians from both Germanies. The conference contributions were characterised by a strong willingness to end old ideological rivalries and come to a mutual acceptance of each other's achievements. A climate of cooperation and relatively open and free discussion seemed to prevail at last.[136] GDR historians had long been pleased by the increased recognition that representatives of historical social science were willing to grant to them, and had in turn signalled their willingness to enter into a dialogue.[137]

The partial renationalisation of GDR historiography throughout the 1980s no doubt helped such overtures and provided further proof for the thesis that GDR and FRG historiography had always remained closely related to each other in topics and debates.[138] In the post-Stalinist thaw of the late 1960s and early 1970s GDR historiography began to shift away from the ideological restrictions prescribed by the SED. The setting up of the 'Council for Historical Sciences' in 1968 marked the development of a more consultative process between the party and the historical profession. Even if, ultimately, the party still called the shots, historians now had at least a limited say. They used it to cover a broader spectrum of topics, and in some areas (e.g., agrarian history, economic history, everyday life history, social history of the working class, history theory) GDR research made significant contributions to international scholarship.

From the early 1980s onwards the concept of 'heritage' *(Erbe)* started to underpin the concept of 'tradition' *(Tradition)* which had divided German history neatly into positive and negative traditions. GDR historiography now declared its willingness to research, not only the positive lines of tradition, but the whole of German history.[139] Chronologically, the concentration on certain periods of German history was to be given up. Territorially, the formerly excluded areas like Prussia, Silesia and all those which had been incorporated into different East European states after 1945, were to be given new attention. And socially, the emphasis on the working class was to be superseded by research on other classes and their interest organisations.

Ingrid Mittenzwei's biography of Frederick of Prussia marked the beginning of a more intensive effort to come to terms with Prussian history.[140] Mittenzwei's biography, criticial of many of Frederick's policies, had not excluded its progressive elements. In much of the ensuing literature the old Hohenzollern myths surfaced again.[141] No wonder that Stürmer recommended the new GDR Prussianism to his West German colleagues: 'The GDR can adapt Prussia's history and national history for its needs, and we should take up this challenge productively'.[142] Many observers noted that the commemorations for the five-hundredth anniversary of Luther's birthday in 1983 brought a more positive re-assessment of the key figure of the German Reformation.[143] By the mid-1980s it was Bismarck's turn to be saved from Communist hell fire. Ernst Engelberg's fascination with the representative of German Junkerdom led to a more positive re-evaluation of his role in German national history. In fact, as Alter noted, Engelberg's views were at times indistinguishable from Gall's biography of the 'Iron Chancellor'.[144] The fortieth anniversary of the attempt on Hitler's life in 1984 also brought a more positive re-appraisal of the 'bourgeois' resistance to Hitler.[145] GDR textbooks on German history routinely referred to the war in 1813/14 as a national war of liberation. The national movement of the first half of the nineteenth century was one-sidedly portrayed as progressive. The war in 1870 against France was described as a 'national war of defence', and there was hardly any doubt that the Bismarckian solution to the German question in 1871 was both necessary and without alternatives.[146]

Part of the reason why the 1980s witnessed such partial renationalisation of GDR historiography, was the inadequate reception of Marxist theory by a number of scholars.[147] Ironically, at a time when Marxist theorists of history in the GDR like Wolfgang Küttler achieved international recognition,[148] many of their colleagues chose to ignore their writings. And yet, the much more important reason for the new national tone was its functional value for GDR political ambitions. Historical references to the national heritage legitimated concepts of the 'socialist German nation'.[149] As Georg Iggers wrote of the renationalisation of GDR historiography in the 1980s, it marked an effort 'to integrate traditions of the military, of state authority, and of national identity into the historical consciousness of a socialist society'.[150] Although it would probably mean overstating the extent and importance of the national perspective to argue that it had already set the mental predisposition towards unity,[151] it still is worthwhile to point out that GDR historiography never formulated a principled rejection of a unified German nation-state. German reunification would be on the agenda as soon as socialism had won the day in the FRG. In the teleological Marxist-Leninist concept of history that the SED officially believed in, this was only a matter of time. In the end, of course, it was not socialism 'which neither bull nor ass could stop in its tracks' (to paraphrase Erich Honecker), it was capitalism.

If historians in the GDR contributed to official efforts by the SED leadership to invent a socialist nation, conservative historians in the West lent a hand in underpinning the idea of a united German national identity. Erich Kosthorst, for example, predicted the futility of all efforts to replace national identity with constitutional patriotism. In a vague psychologising approach he argued that the critics of the national principle underestimated 'the very deep-reaching emotional ties involved in the process of nation building'.[152] Schwarz formulated what amounts to a Social Darwinist conception of foreign policy: 'A people whose will for self-assertion is weakened easily becomes the victim of stronger and unscrupulous predators.' What was therefore needed in Germany was an 'emergency patriotism' which would foster the readiness of the citizen to die 'the death of the hero' *(Heldentod)*.[153] Schwarz and Hillgruber belonged to the standard bearers of the national idea throughout the 1970s and 1980s, and it is not by chance that Schwarz referred to Hillgruber as 'a Prussian historian of the old school'.[154]

Michael Wolffsohn, a self-declared 'German/Jewish patriot', argued in 1988 that the Holocaust, seen as the national trauma of the Germans, had fostered a virulent 'anti-Germanism'. For Wolffsohn, German guilt should be put in the context of German efforts after 1945 to do everything possible to come to terms with that guilt. Therefore, according to Wolffsohn, the Germans should develop 'normal patriotism' which would look after German interests in Europe and the wider world.[155] Wolffsohn's argument is based on a simple role reversal. From being perpetrators, Germans are turned into present-day victims, and the Israelis and those 'anti-German' Germans are seen as perpetrators keeping Germany small and guilt-ridden and preventing a justified positive national identity from developing.

German history, sometimes including half of Eastern Europe,[156] sometimes 'only' the territory of the GDR, clearly continued to haunt the imagination of historians throughout the allegedly postnational decades of the 1970s and 1980s. On the occasion of the fortieth anniversary of the FRG, Konrad Repgen staunchly upheld demands for reunification.[157]

The educational-political climate began to reflect the renationalisation of German identity from the late 1970s onwards. In the autumn of 1978 the conference of ministers of culture in the Federal Republic endorsed a resolution whereby the German question should be more extensively discussed in schools. Teachers were to aim at making pupils conscious of the enduring aim and reality of a unified German nation-state.[158] In 1988 the ministers of culture of the West German Länder agreed to expand history as a subject and to increase its importance in schools. Conservative historians such as Schwarz and Diwald almost immediately applauded this decision. Schwarz argued that history served the purpose of allowing young Germans to develop a national identity.[159] And Diwald found that 'acquiring a basic knowledge of German history will be character-building and strengthen the pupils' self-esteem'.[160]

It is, of course, incredibly difficult to say anything definite about the historical consciousness of pupils in relation to their national identity. As far as school textbooks are concerned, it is revealing that in the 1980s there was a considerable amount of lament by largely conservative historians about the disappearance of Germany and the German question from German schoolbooks. Wolfgang Marienfeld worriedly asked: 'Will the history lesson be an effective counter to the erosion of the national idea?'[161] Yet, if we move away from the ideologically motivated whimpers and look at the empirical results of schoolbook and historical-consciousness studies, the pessimism that regularly befell neo-Prussians in the 1970s and 1980s is hardly born out.

On the one hand, it is certainly true to say that the glorification of national history has largely vanished from school textbooks. In fact, in the 1980s English history received much attention in German schoolbooks as a paradigm of what ought to have happened in Germany.[162] Thus more critical perspectives on German national history seemed to have found their way into German schoolbooks twenty years after their first airing. On the other hand it is hardly the case that the national dimension is absent from history lessons in schools. If anything, *Ostpolitik* stimulated an interest in the German question which is given more room in school textbooks. In the 1980s the question of German unity and the German nation was given extensive room in the history curricula at German schools.[163]

The research available on the historical consciousness of pupils has painted a very differentiated picture of the importance of national categories for pupils in the 1980s. In an early phase (nine and ten year olds) signs of national identity were often grounded in linguistic and ethnic difference which could show itself in open enmity to foreigners. Older pupils (thirteen and fourteen year olds), by contrast, tended to show a high potential for reflecting critically on the national idea. They often perceived national boundaries as limiting. In 1988 Hamburg pupils did not automatically equate history with national history and there was little correlation between studying German history and developing national pride. Yet the same pupils overwhelmingly clung to the idea of a united Germany. They strongly rejected the thesis that the FRG should give up the reunification demand, as unity had been the exception rather than the norm in Germany's history.[164] Whilst on the whole one would do well not to overemphasise the importance of 'school history' in shaping the historical consciousness of pupils, it does appear that they retained a sense of national identity while at the same time relativising its importance. It now forms only one focus of identity besides a whole range of other political, social and economic foci. As there was no correlation between the stability of the pupils' democratic convictions and their feelings of national loyalty, a good history lesson, one could argue, is one which does not legitimate but seeks to undermine any sense of collective identity by demonstrating how traditions are invented and communities imagined.[165]

Despite the staunch and principled national orientation of some historians, others, who traditionally belonged to the national camp, had by 1989 moved further away than ever from endorsing the Bismarckian solution to Germany's 'national problem'. Erdmann, for example, could write: 'Against the background of a thousand years of German history, the small German nation-state created by Bismarck has been a relatively short-lived construction, and by no means the normal state from which to judge all other times ... .'[166] Hacke, despite lamenting the lack of 'national yearnings' reluctantly gave expression to the belief that reunification was not a realistic option: 'it is not reunification but the right of self-determination which is decisive in the long term.'[167] Christian Meier argued that the national theme could be neglected for the time being as it was based on the illusion of a possible reunification.[168] Schulze described the unified German nation-state as a cul-de-sac.[169] Alexander Schwan commented that the German nation-state's undoing after 1945 was directly linked to its nineteenth and early twentieth century *Sonderweg* which led to the 'German catastrophe'. Only total defeat in 1945 allowed at least the West Germans to find the way to Western political culture, to genuine democratisation and freedom. In the light of this the CDU member Schwan rejected any plans for a renationalisation of German identity.[70] Even for Ernst Nolte, it seemed in the late 1980s that 'the question of German unity, of the country's reunification has been laid to rest for the time being.'[71]

Some historians developed alternative models of national identification for Germans. As national unity had been the exception, it had become difficult for Wolf Gruner to envisage any simple 'restoration of the German nation-state as it existed between 1870 and 1945'.[72] Instead Gruner continued to argue, right up to the years 1989/90, that the best chance of achieving a reunified Germany would lie in reviving the constitution of the German Federation (Deutsche Bund), i.e., in a confederation of the two Germanies.[73] In 1987 Franz-Josef Jakobi explicitly referred to the Holy Roman Empire as a period of relative national bliss and harmony, thereby turning on its head the disdain felt for this pre-national structure by all practitioners of historiographic nationalism. As a confederation of relatively autonomous states it once again seemed to be in keeping with the times.[74]

In May 1989 Karl Dietrich Bracher re-affirmed the key beliefs underpinning the critical stance vis-à-vis the national tradition: German history between 1871 and 1945 was confirmed as a *Sonderweg*; 1945 was portrayed as decisive break with hyper-nationalism; West Germany turned to the democratic traditions of the West; the concept of constitutional patriotism, the development of a postnational democracy and the increasing federalisation of Europe were described as underpinning the identification of West Germans with the Federal Republic; a collective national identity was rejected as it would endanger the Federal Republic's Western orientation; Jaspers' question, posed in the 1950s, of whether freedom came before unity was answered with an emphatic 'yes'.[75]

If one examines the two decades from the late 1960s to the fall of the wall, the picture which emerges in relation to historiography and the national question is far more complex than the one often painted after 1989. Methodologically, it seems impossible to speak of a paradigm shift in German historiography in the late 1960s, let alone of the emergence of a new social history orthodoxy after the 1960s. At best one can describe what happened as a pluralisation of methods, with neohistorist, everyday life, anthropologist and poststructuralist approaches all vying for influence and support. If the situation in 1989 was not characterised by methodological agreement, there were equally diverse opinions on the national tradition. From the late 1970s onwards it was becoming increasingly evident that it had been premature to speak of the death of the strong national tradition amongst German historians in the 1960s. Surviving well throughout the 1960s and 1970s, it gained in strength from the second half of the 1970s onwards and culminated in the *Historikerstreit*. The ideas of postnationalism, and constitutional patriotism were sometimes, as in the work of Sternberger, Bracher and Schwan, bound up with national sentiments. German historians rarely questioned the reunification demand enshrined in the Basic Law.

Certainly there was a more critical national historiography which argued that the Bismarckian nation-state had been an unfortunate episode and did not provide traditions to build the future on, but this never even came within sight of becoming the majority view – even if some of its proponents such as Winkler have belonged to the most industrious participants in public debates. This critical view of national history rejected the re-invention of a fictitious national collective and argued that the politics of national identity could not be justified within the framework of a rational academic discourse about history. As will be argued in the next chapters, the unexpected reunification of Germany in 1990 undermined this perspective.

NOTES

1. Jörn Rüsen prominently adapted Thomas Kuhn's idea of scientific progress via paradigm changes to historiography. On Rüsen see Alan Megill, 'Jörn Rüsen's Theory of Historiography between Modernism and Rhetoric of Inquiry', *History and Theory*, vol. 33, 1994, pp. 39-60.
2. Jörn Rüsen, *Für eine erneuerte Historik. Studien zur Theorie der Geschichtswissenschaft*, Münster, 1976, p. 46.
3. Jürgen Kocka, *Sozialgeschichte*, Göttingen, 1977, pp. 117-19.
4. Hans-Ulrich Wehler, 'Bismarcks Imperialismus und späte Rußlandpolitik unter dem Primat der Innenpolitik', in: Stürmer (ed.), *Das kaiserliche Deutschland*, p. 235. In the same vein Wehler, *Geschichte als Historische Sozialwissenschaft*, p. 26.
5. Kühnl, 'Anmerkungen', p. 10.
6. Jürgen Kocka, 'Veränderungen in der Geschichtswissenschaft', in: Wolfgang Prinz and Peter Weingart (eds), *Die sogenannten Geisteswissenschaften: Innenansichten*, Frankfurt-on-Main, 1990, pp. 134-7.
7. Jürgen Kocka, 'Paradigmawechsel? Die Perspektive der "Historischen Sozial-wissenschaft"', in: Bernd Mütter and Siegfried Quandt (eds), *Historie, Didaktik, Kommunikation. Wissenschaftsgeschichte und aktuelle Herausforderung*, Marburg, 1988, pp. 73-7.
8. Hans-Ulrich Wehler, *Aus der Geschichte lernen?*, Munich, 1988, p. 23.

9. Volker Berghahn, 'West German Historiography Between Continuity and Change: Some Cross-Cultural Comparisons', *Daedalus*, vol. 34, 1981, p. 256.

10. Manfred Hettling, Claudia Huerkamp, Paul Nolte and H.W. Schmuhl (eds), *Was ist Gesellschaftsgeschichte? Positionen, Themen, Analysen*, Munich, 1991, p. 9.

11. Karlheinz Weißmann, 'Der "Westen" in der deutschen Historiographie nach 1945', in: Rainer Zitelmann, Karlheinz Weißmann and Michael Grossheim (eds), *Westbindung. Chancen und Risiken für Deutschland*, Frankfurt-on-Main, 1993, pp. 353 f.

12. Stürmer, *Die Grenzen der Macht*, p. 147.

13. Gustav Seibt, 'Ein Drama ohne Helden. Historische Wissenschaft und gegenwärtige Erfahrung', *FAZ*, 5 June 1990.

14. Andreas Hillgruber, 'Politische Geschichte in moderner Sicht', *HZ*, vol. 216, 1973, pp. 529-52; Klaus Hildebrand, 'Geschichte oder "Gesellschaftsgeschichte"? Die Notwendigkeit einer politischen Geschichtsschreibung von den internationalen Beziehungen', *HZ*, vol. 223, 1976, pp. 328-57; Golo Mann, 'Die alte und die neue Historie', in: Clemens Graf Podewils (ed.), *Tendenzwende? Zur geistigen Situation der Bundesrepublik*, Stuttgart, 1975; Konrad Repgen, 'Methoden- oder Richtungskämpfe in der deutschen Geschichtswissenschaft seit 1945?', *GWU*, vol. 30, 1979, pp. 591-610; Hermann Lübbe, *Geschichtsbegriff und Geschichtsinteresse: Analytik und Pragmatik der Historie*, Basle, 1977; Thomas Nipperdey, 'Kann Geschichte objektiv sein?', *GWU*, vol. 30, 1979, pp. 329-42.

15. Joachim Fest's biography of Hitler (1973), Lothar Gall's biography of Bismarck (1980), Theodor Schieder's biography of Frederick the Great (1983) and Hans-Peter Schwarz's biography of Adenauer (1983-1991).

16. Michael Stürmer, 'Die Geburt eines Dilemmas. Nationalstaat und Massendemokratie im Mächtesystem von 1848', *Merkur*, vol. 36, 1982, pp. 1-12.

17. Nipperdey, 'Kann Geschichte', p. 341.

18. Hillgruber, 'Politische Geschichte', p. 549.

19. Thomas Nipperdey, 'Wehlers Kaiserreich: Eine kritische Auseinandersetzung', *GG*, vol. 1, 1975, pp. 539-60, where he famously characterised Wehler as 'Treitschke redivivus', was problably the most influential long-term critique of Wehler's book.

20. Hillgruber, 'Politische Geschichte', p. 542.

21. Hildebrand, 'Geschichte oder "Gesellschaftsgeschichte"', p. 349.

22. Thomas Nipperdey, *Deutsche Geschichte 1866-1914*, vol. 1: *Bürgergeist und Arbeitswelt*, Munich, 1989 and vol. 2: *Machtstaat vor der Demokratie*, Munich, 1992, especially p. 904.

23. Michael Stürmer, 'Nationalstaat und Klassengesellschaft im Zeitalter des Bürgers – Ein Versuch', *Merkur*, vol. 35, 1981, p. 477.

24. Lothar Gall, '"Deutsche Gesellschaftsgeschichte"', *HZ*, vol. 248, 1989 pp. 365-75.

25. Celia Applegate, *A Nation of Provincials. The German Idea of Heimat*, Berkeley, 1990; Alan Milward, *The European Rescue of the Nation State*, London, 1992.

26. Jürgen Reulecke, 'Von der Landesgeschichte zur Regionalgeschichte', *Geschichte im Westen*, vol. 6, 1992, pp. 202-8; see also the contributions in Lothar Gall and Dieter Langewiesche (eds), *Liberalismus und Region. Zur Geschichte des deutschen Liberalismus im 19. Jahrhundert*, Munich, 1995.

27. Horst Kuss, 'Geschichtsdidaktik und Geschichtsunterricht in der Bundesrepublik Deutschland (1945/49-1990), Teil 2', *GWU*, vol. 46, 1995, p. 8.

28. Hartmut Kaelble, 'Vergleichende Sozialgeschichte des 19. und 20. Jahrhunderts: Forschungen europäischer Historiker', *Jahrbuch für Wirtschaftsgeschichte*, 1993, pp. 173-200.

29. Carola Lipp, 'Writing History as Political Culture. Social History versus "Alltagsgeschichte". A German Debate', *Storia della Storiografia*, vol. 17, 1990, p. 70.

30. Lutz Niethammer, 'Anmerkungen zur Alltagsgeschichte', *Geschichtsdidaktik*, vol. 5, 1980, p. 239; idem, 'Das kritische Potential der Alltagsgeschichte', in: Ursula Becker and Klaus Bergmann (eds), *Geschichte – Nutzen oder Nachteil für das Leben?*, Düsseldorf, 1986, pp. 60-2; Hans Medick, '"Missionaries in the Row Boat?" Ethnological Ways of Knowing as a Challenge to Social History', *Comparative Studies in Society and History*, vol. 21, 1987, p. 93.

31. Peter Borscheid, 'Alltagsgeschichte – Modetorheit oder neues Tor zur Vergangenheit' (1986), reprinted in: Hardtwig, *Studium*, p. 406. For the influence of cultural anthropology on the history of everyday life see Hans Medick, 'Entlegene Geschichte? Sozialgeschichte im Blickfeld der Kulturanthropologie', in: Konrad Jarausch, Jörn Rüsen and Hans Schleier (eds), *Geschichtswissenschaft vor 2000. Perspektiven der Historiographiegeschichte, Geschichtstheorie, Sozial- und Kulturgeschichte*, Hagen, 1991, pp. 360-9.

32. Alf Lüdtke, 'Was ist und wer treibt Alltagsgeschichte?', in: idem (ed.), *Alltagsgeschichte. Zur Rekonstruktion historischer Erfahrungen und Lebensweisen*, Frankfurt-on-Main, 1989, pp. 26 f.

33. Hans-Ulrich Wehler, 'Geschichte von unten gesehen', *Die Zeit*, no. 19, 3 May 1985, p. 64; idem, 'Barfußhistoriker – woher sie kommen und was sie wollen', *Die Zeit*, no. 45, 2 November 1984. See also Jürgen Kocka, 'Sozialgeschichte zwischen Strukturgeschichte und Gesellschaftsgeschichte', in: Wolfgang Schieder, Volker Sellin (eds), *Sozialgeschichte in Deutschland*, vol. 1, Göttingen, 1986, p. 80.

34. Wehler, *Preußen*, p. 104.

35. Reinhard Rürup (ed.), *Historische Sozialwissenschaft*, Göttingen, 1977.

36. Compare the agendas of emancipation set out by Jörn Rüsen, 'Geschichte als Aufklärung?', *GG*, vol. 7, 1981, pp. 189-218 and by Alfred G. Frei, 'Die Zukunft beginnt in der Vergangenheit. Geschichtswerkstätten, Tendenzwende und demokratische Alternative', *Geschichtswerkstatt*, vol. 3, 1984.

37. For an introduction to the postmodern and poststructuralist challenges see Kütler, Rüsen, Schulin (eds), *Geschichtsdiskurs*, vol. 1, pp. 17-96; Derek Attridge, Geoff Bennington and Robert Young (eds), *Post-structuralism and the Question of History*, Cambridge, 1987; a very useful attempt to differentiate between different concepts of 'discourse analysis' and their usefulness for historical study can be found in Peter Schöttler, 'Wer hat Angst vor dem "linguistic turn"? Ein Diskussionsbeitrag', *Potsdamer Bulletin für Zeithistorische Studien*, no. 7, August 1996, pp. 5-21.

38. An exception is Wolfgang Ernst, 'Postmoderne Geschichtskultur', in: Klaus Fröhlich, H.-T. Grütter, Jörn Rüsen and Hans Schleier (eds), *Geschichtskultur, Jahrbuch für Geschichtsdidaktik*, vol. 3, 1991.

39. If I understand him correctly Michael Geyer, 'Geschichte als Wissenschaft für eine Zeit der Unübersichtlichkeit', in: Konrad Jarausch and Mathias Middell (eds), *Nach dem Erdbeben. (Re-) Konstruktion ostdeutscher Geschichte und Geschichtswissenschaft*, Leipzig, 1994, pp. 38-67 has pleaded for such a merger of poststructuralist and Enlightenment approaches.

40. See, for example, Jürgen Kocka, 'Theory Orientation and the new Quest for Narrative: some Trends and Debates in West Germany', *Storia della Storiografia*, vol. 10, 1986, pp. 170-81; Jörn Rüsen, 'Grundlagenreflexion und Paradigmawechsel in der westdeutschen Geschichtswissenschaft', *Geschichtsdidaktik*, vol. 11, 1986, pp. 388-405.

41. Jürgen Kocka, 'Das Haus der Geschichte hat viele Zimmer', *FR*, 20 June 1989.

42. Eberhard Schulz, *An Ulbricht führt kein Weg mehr vorbei. Provozierende Thesen zur deutschen Frage*, Hamburg, 1967.

43. Lutz Niethammer and Ulrich Borsdorf, 'Traditionen und Perspektiven der Nationalstaatlichkeit', in: *Außenpolitische Perspektiven des westdeutschen Staates*, vol. 2: *Das Vordringen neuer Kräfte*, Munich, 1972, pp. 13-107.

44. Kurt Sontheimer, 'Volk und Nation im Nachkriegsdeutschland', *Die Mitarbeit – Zeitschrift zur Gesellschafts- und Kulturpolitik*, vol. 18, 1969, pp. 98-113. By 1988 he still essentially thought of the German question as closed once and for all. See Kurt Sontheimer, in: *Reden über das eigene Land: Deutschland*, 2nd edn, Munich, 1989, pp. 37-66.

45. Hans-Günter Zmarzlik, *Wieviel Zukunft hat unsere Vergangenheit? Aufsätze und Überlegungen eines Historikers vom Jahrgang 1922*, Munich, 1970, p. 230.

46. For this new approach which de-facto accepted the end of the unified nation-state see Peter Christian Ludz, *Deutschlands doppelte Zukunft. Bundesrepublik und DDR in der Welt von morgen. Ein politischer Essay*, Munich, 1974; Rüdiger Thomas, *Modell DDR. Die kalkulierte Emanzipation*, Munich, 1972; Gert-Joachim Glaeßner (ed.), *Die DDR in der Ära Honecker*, Opladen, 1988.

47. Dolf Sternberger, 'Verfassungspatriotismus' (1979) and 'Verfassungspatriotismus' (1982), both reprinted in: *Verfassungspatriotismus*, Frankfurt-on-Main, 1990, pp. 13-31.

48. Bernd Faulenbach, 'Die These vom deutschen Sonderweg und die historische Legitimation politischer Ordnung in Deutschland', in: Karl-Ernst Jeismann (ed.), *Geschichte als Legitimation? Internationale Schulbuchrevision unter den Ansprüchen von Politik, Geschichtswissenschaft und Geschichtsbedürfnis*, Brunswick, 1984, p. 109.

49. Christoph Kleßmann, 'Verflechtung und Abgrenzung. Aspekte der geteilten und zusammengehörigen deutschen Nachkriegsgeschichte', *aus politik und zeitgeschichte*, 16 July 1993, p. 32.

50. Eugen Gerstenmaier, *Neuer Nationalismus? Von der Wandlung der Deutschen*, Stuttgart, 1965, pp. 82-5.

51. Cited in Matthias von Hellfeld, *Die Nation erwacht. Zur Tendenzwende der deutschen politischen Kultur*, Cologne, 1993, p. 75.

52. Erwin Hölzle, 'Griff nach der Weltmacht?', *Das Historisch-Politische Buch*, vol. 10, 1962, pp. 65-9.

53. Ritter, 'Kriegsschuldthese?', p. 668.

54. Armin Mohler, *Was die Deutschen fürchten. Angst vor der Politik, Angst vor der Geschichte, Angst vor der Macht*, Stuttgart, 1965, p. 146.

55. Hans Rothfels, 'Zum 150. Geburtstag Bismarcks', *VfZ*, vol. 13, 1965, pp. 329-43.

56. Karl Bosl, 'Die Verhandlungen über den Eintritt der süddeutschen Staaten in den Norddeutschen Bund und die Entstehung der Reichsverfassung', in: Theodor Schieder and Ernst Deuerlein (eds), *Reichsgründung 1870/71*, Stuttgart, 1970, p. 151.

57. Peter Graf Kielmannsegg, 'Was ist vom Reich geblieben?', *Die Zeit*, 15 January 1971.

58. Manfred Busowietz, 'Gedenkreden deutscher Historiker', *Das Argument*, no. 70, 1972, pp. 142-64.

59. Ernst Nolte, 'Zur Konzeption der Nationalgeschichte heute', *HZ*, vol. 202, 1966, p. 618.

60. Ibid., p. 621.

61. Werner Conze, *Die deutsche Nation. Ergebnis der Geschichte*, Göttingen, 1963. Transl. into English as *The Shaping of the German Nation. A Historical Analysis*, London, 1979.

62. Conze, *Shaping*, p. 109.

63. Ibid., p. 110.

64. Ibid., p. 130.

65. Werner Conze, 'Das Kaiserreich von 1871 als gegenwärtige Vergangenheit im Generationswandel der deutschen Geschichtsschreibung', in: Werner Pöls (ed.), *Staat und Gesellschaft im politischen Wandel. Beiträge zur Geschichte der modernen Welt*, Stuttgart, 1979, pp. 383-405.

66. Compare the eulogies on Schieder by Wolfgang J. Mommsen, 'Vom Beruf des Historikers in einer Zeit beschleunigten Wandels', *VfZ*, vol. 33, 1985, pp. 387-405; Hans-Ulrich Wehler, 'Einleitung', in: Schieder, *Das deutsche Kaiserreich*.

67. Angelika Ebbinghaus and Karl Heinz Roth, 'Vorläufer des "Generalplans Ost". Eine Dokumentation über Theodor Schieders Polendenkschrift vom 7. Oktober 1939', *1999*, vol. 7, 1992, pp. 62-94.

68. Theodor Schieder, *Nationalismus und Nationalstaat: Studien zum nationalen Problem im modernen Europa*, ed. by Otto Dann and Hans-Ulrich Wehler, 2nd edn, Göttingen, 1992, p. 136.

69. Ibid., pp. 218-70.

70. Richard von Weizsäcker in a speech before the *Bundestag*, 24 Feb. 1972, reprinted in: Peter Longerich (ed.), *'Was ist des Deutschen Vaterland?' Dokumente zur Frage der deutschen Einheit 1800-1990*, Munich, 1990, p. 245.

71. Hans-Peter Schwarz, 'Einheit der Nation?!', *Jahrbuch der Albertus Universität zu Königsberg/Preußen*, vol. 25, 1975, pp. 41-68.

72. Hellmut Diwald, *Geschichte der Deutschen*, Frankfurt-on-Main, 1978.

73. Hellmut Diwald, 'Deutschland – was ist es?', in: Wolfgang Venohr (ed.), *Die deutsche Einheit kommt bestimmt*, Bergisch-Gladbach, 1982, p. 26.

74. Ibid., p. 17.

75. Hans-Joachim Arndt, *Die Besiegten von 1945*, Berlin, 1979.

76. Hans Dietrich Sander, *Der nationale Imperativ. Ideengänge und Werkstücke zur Wiederherstellung Deutschlands*, Krefeld, 1980; Gerd-Klaus Kaltenbrunner (ed.), *Illusionen der Brüderlichkeit*, Munich, 1980.

77. Hans-Dietrich Sander, *Die Rückkehr des nationalen Elements in der Politik*, Göttingen, 1983, p. 14.

78. Henning Eichberg, *Nationale Identität. Entfremdung und nationale Frage in der Industriegesellschaft*, Munich, 1978.

79. Bernard Willms, *Idealismus und Nation. Zur Rekonstruktion des politischen Selbstbewußtseins der Deutschen*, Paderborn, 1986, p. 211.

80. Felix Messerschmid, 'Die Nation in der Politischen Bildung', *GWU*, vol. 17, 1966, p. 664.

81. Ernst Schulin, *Traditionskritik*, p. 142.

82. Hans Mommsen, 'Zum Problem des deutschen Nationalbewußtseins in der Gegenwart', *Der Monat*, vol. 31, 1979, pp. 75-83.

83. Wilfried von Bredow and Hans F. Foltin, *Zwiespältige Zufluchten. Zur Renaissance des Heimatgefühls*, Berlin, 1981.

84. Arno Klönne, *Zurück zur Nation? Kontroversen zu deutschen Fragen*, Cologne, 1984, p. 75.

85. Irmline Veit-Brause, 'Zur Kritik an der "Kritischen Geschichtswissenschaft": Tendenzwende oder Paradigmawechsel', *GWU*, vol. 35, 1984, p. 19.

86. On the debates amongst historians surrounding the Prussia exhibition see Karen Schönwälder, 'Preußen-Renaissance, "deutsche Frage" und geopolitische Ambitionen', *Blätter*, vol. 28, 1983, pp. 1,055-69; Barbara Vogel, 'Bemerkungen zur Aktualität der preußischen Geschichte', *AfS*, vol. 25, 1985, pp. 467-507.

87. Wehler, *Preußen*, p. 71.

88. Fritz Fischer, 'Eigene Leitbilder entwickeln', *Der Spiegel*, 26 Jan. 1981, pp. 8 f.

89. Werner Weidenfeld, 'Einführung', in: idem (ed.), *Die Identität der Deutschen*, Bonn, 1983, p. 9.

90. Guido Knopp, 'Brauchen wir die deutsche Einheit?', in: idem (ed.), *Die deutsche Einheit – Hoffnung, Alptraum, Illusion?*, Aschaffenburg, 1981, pp. 7-14.

91. Roland Hahn, 'Demokratie und Nation. Einleitende Bemerkungen zum Problem der deutschen Identität', in: Helmut Wagner, Alexander Schwan, Roland Hahn (eds), *Fragen und Antworten zur deutschen Identität*, Berlin, 1987, p. xvi.

92. Hermann Lübbe, 'Der Nationalsozialismus im politischen Bewußtsein der Gegenwart' (1983), in: idem, *Die Aufdringlichkeit der Geschichte. Herausforderungen der Moderne vom Historismus bis zum Nationalsozialismus*, Graz, 1989, pp. 334-50.

93. Thomas Nipperdey's remarks in the panel discussion, in: Martin Broszat (ed.), *Deutschlands Weg in die Diktatur*, Berlin, 1983, p. 370.

94. Thomas Nipperdey, *Nachdenken über die deutsche Geschichte: Essays*, Munich, 1986, pp. 206-17.

95. Andreas Hillgruber, *Die gescheiterte Großmacht. Eine Skizze des deutschen Reiches 1871 – 1945*, Düsseldorf, 1980; Michael Stürmer, 'Preußens Erbe an die deutsche Geschichte', FAZ, 14 October 1981; Karl Schlögel, *Die Mitte liegt ostwärts. Die Deutschen, der verlorene Osten und Mitteleuropa*, Munich, 1986.

96. Joachim Fest, 'Von der Unverlorenheit der deutschen Frage', *FAZ*, 28 Sept. 1982.

97. Wolfgang Seiffert, *Das ganze Deutschland. Perspektiven der Wiedervereinigung*, Munich, 1986, p. 57; Konrad Löw, 'Noch ist Deutschland nicht verloren', *Der Staatsbürger, Beilage der Bayerischen Staatszeitung*, Feb. 1985.

98. Tilman Mayer, *Prinzip Nation: Dimensionen der nationalen Frage, dargestellt am Beispiel Deutschlands*, Opladen, 1986.

99. Hagen Schulze, 'Schwierigkeiten mit einem Gedenktag', *Der Tagesspiegel*, 5 May 1985.

100. Hagen Schulze, *Wir sind, was wir geworden sind. Vom Nutzen der Geschichte für die deutsche Gegenwart*, Munich, 1986.

101. Michael Stürmer, 'Keine Angst vor gemischten Gefühlen', *Die Zeit*, 25 Jan. 1985, p. 4.

102. Hans-Peter Schwarz, *Die gezähmten Deutschen. Von der Machtbesessenheit zur Machtvergessenheit*, Stuttgart, 1985, p. 55.

103. Christian Hacke, *Weltmacht wider Willen. Die Außenpolitik der Bundesrepublik Deutschland*, Stuttgart, 1988, pp. 9-11.

104. Ibid., p. 453.

105. See, for example, Iring Fetscher, 'Die Suche nach der nationalen Identität', in: Jürgen Habermas (ed.), *Stichworte zur geistigen Situation der Zeit*, 2 vols, Frankfurt-on-Main, 1979, vol. 1, p. 130.

106. Mommsen, *Nation und Geschichte*.

107. Mommsen, 'Gegenwärtige Tendenzen', p. 165.

108. Weidenfeld (ed.), *Identität*; Otto Büsch and James Sheehan (eds), *Die Rolle der Nation in der deutschen Geschichte und Gegenwart*, Berlin, 1985; Josef Becker and Andreas Hillgruber (eds), *Die deutsche Frage im 19. und 20. Jahrhundert*, Munich, 1983; Eberhard Schulz, *Die deutsche Nation in Europa*, Bonn, 1982; Venohr (ed.), *Die deutsche Einheit; Die Frage nach der deutschen Identität*, Bonn, 1985; Klaus Weigelt (ed.), *Heimat und Nation – Zur Geschichte und Identität der Deutschen*, Mainz, 1984; Guido Knopp, Siegfried Quandt and Herbert Scheffler (eds), *Nation Deutschland? Erster Hambacher Disput*, Paderborn, 1984; Klaus Lange (ed.), *Aspekte der deutschen Frage*, Herford, 1986; Eberhard Andermann (ed.), *Die deutsche Frage*, Hannover, 1982.

109. See Heinz-Gerhard Haupt, 'Nationalismus als Emanzipationsideologie? Zur neueren Nationalismusforschung in der Bundesrepublik', *AfS*, vol. 24, 1984, pp. 576-88.

110. Bernd Faulenbach, '"Deutscher Sonderweg". Zur Geschichte und Problematik einer zentralen Kategorie des deutschen geschichtlichen Bewußtseins', *aus politik und zeitgeschichte*, no. 39, 1981, pp. 3-21; Jürgen Kocka, 'German History Before Hitler: The Debate about the German Sonderweg', *Journal of Contemporary History*, vol. 23, 1988, pp. 3-16.

111. Imanuel Geiss, 'Zwischen Auschwitz und Weimar. Nationale Identität als deutsche Frage', *Evangelische Kommentare*, vol. 12, 1984, p. 673. For his position in

the *Historikerstreit* see: Imanuel Geiss, *Die Habermas-Kontroverse. Ein deutscher Streit,* Berlin, 1988.

112. Rudolf von Thadden, 'Deutsches Geschichtsbewußtsein als historisches Problem', *Politik und Kultur,* vol. 9, 1982, p. 12.

113. Herbert Ammon and Peter Brandt, 'Patriotismus von links', in: Venohr (ed.), *Die deutsche Einheit,* pp. 118-59; Herbert Ammon and Peter Brandt, *Die Linke und die nationale Frage. Dokumente zur deutschen Einheit seit 1945,* Hamburg, 1981.

114. Wehler, *Preußen,* pp. 37-52.

115. Ibid, p. 51.

116. Mommsen, 'Zum Problem', p. 81.

117. Hans Mommsen, 'Auf der Suche nach der Nation. Zur Geschichte des deutschen Nationalbewußtseins', *Evangelische Kommentare,* vol. 10, 1979, pp. 565-7.

118. Hans Mommsen, 'Die Last der Vergangenheit', in: Habermas (ed.), *Stichworte,* vol. 1, p. 175.

119. Jürgen Kocka, 'Probleme der politischen Integration der Deutschen', in: Sheehan and Büsch (eds), *Rolle,* pp. 118-36; Jürgen Kocka, 'Nation und Gesellschaft. Historische Überlegungen zur "deutschen" Frage', *Politik und Kultur,* vol. 8, 1981, pp. 3-25.

120. Jürgen Kocka, 'Die Deutschen und ihre Nation', *Geschichtsdidaktik,* vol. 9, 1984, pp. 79-84.

121. Sebastian Haffner, 'Die Deutschen und ihre Nation', *Politik und Kultur,* vol. 10, 1983, pp. 60-7.

122. Rudolf Vierhaus, 'Historische Entwicklungslinien deutscher Identität', in: *Frage,* p. 21.

123. Wilfried Loth, *Ost-West Konflikt und deutsche Frage – Historische Ortsbestimmungen,* Munich, 1989, p. 24.

124. Peter Alter, *Nationalism,* London, 1989, p 131. Compare also with the understandably different assessment in idem, *Nationalism,* 2nd edn, London, 1994, pp. 95-7.

125. Karl Dietrich Bracher, 'Das Modewort Identität und die deutsche Frage', *FAZ,* 9 Aug. 1986.

126. Rainer Lepsius, 'Die Teilung Deutschlands und die deutsche Nation', in: Lothar Albertin and Werner Link (eds), *Politische Parteien auf dem Weg zur parlamentarischen Demokratie in Deutschland,* Düsseldorf, 1981, pp. 444 ff.

127. For the documentation of the *Historikerstreit* see *'Historikerstreit'. Die Dokumentation der Kontroverse um die Einzigartigkeit der nationalsozialistischen Judenvernichtung,* Munich, 1987 (an English edn was published under the title *Forever in the Shadow of Hitler?: Original Documents of the Historikerstreit, the Controversy Concerning the Singularity of the Holocaust,* New Jersey, 1993); an extensive bibliography of the writings on the *Historikerstreit* with more than 1,200 titles is provided by H. Donat and L. Wieland (eds), *Auschwitz erst möglich gemacht? Überlegungen zur jüngsten konservativen Geschichtsbewältigung,* Bremen, 1991, pp. 150-214.

128. Habermas, 'Eine Art Schadensabwicklung', in: *Historikerstreit,* p. 76.

129. Winkler, 'Auf ewig in Hitlers Schatten?', in *Historikerstreit,* pp. 262 f.

130. Bernd Faulenbach, 'Identität durch Geschichte?', in: *Streitfall deutsche Geschichte. Geschichts- und Gegenwartsbewußtsein in den achtziger Jahren,* Düsseldorf, 1988, pp. 237-50.

131. Hans Mommsen, 'Geschichte und politische Legitimation in der Bundesrepublik: Zum Dilemma gesteuerter historischer Konsensbildung', in: *Streitfall,* pp. 225-36.

132. Eberhard Jäckel, *Umgang mit Vergangenheit,* Stuttgart, 1989, p. 92.

133. Karl-Ernst Jeismann, '"Identität" statt "Emanzipation"? Zum Geschichtsbewußtsein in der Bundesrepublik', *aus politik und zeitgeschichte,* 20/21, 1986, pp. 3-16.

134. One of the most intelligent criticisms of the Habermas position in the debate is by Barbara Hahn and Peter Schöttler, 'Jürgen Habermas und "das ungetrübte Bewußtsein des Bruchs"', in: Heide Gerstenberger and Dorothea Schmidt (eds), *Normalität oder Normalisierung? Geschichtswerkstätten und Faschismusanalyse*, Münster, 1987, pp. 191-203.

135. Reinhard Kühnl, *Nation – Nationalismus – Nationale Frage. Was ist das und was soll das?*, Cologne, 1986, pp. 97-106, 110-1. Compare with Kurt Tucholsky, *Deutschland, Deutschland über alles*, Berlin, 1929, pp. 226-31.

136. All contributions to the debate between West and East German historians are conveniently collected in Susanne Miller, Malte Ristau (eds), *Erben deutscher Geschichte. DDR – BRD: Protokolle einer historischen Begegnung*, Reinbek, 1988.

137. Konrad Irmschler, 'Zum "Historisch-Sozialwissenschaftlichen Konzept einer bürgerlichen Gesellschaftsgeschichte in der Historiographie der BRD', *ZfG*, vol. 28, 1980, pp. 1,135-47.

138. Agnes Blänsdorf, 'Die deutsche Geschichte in der Sicht der DDR. Ein Vergleich mit der Entwicklung in der Bundesrepublik Deutschland und in Österreich seit 1945', *GWU*, vol. 39, 1988, pp. 263-90.

139. Wolfgang Küttler and Hans Schleier, 'Die Erbe-Konzeption und der Platz der preußischen Geschichte in der DDR-Geschichtswissenschaft', *German Studies Review*, vol. 6, 1983, pp. 535-57. The whole debate is documented in H. Meier and W. Schmidt (eds), *Erbe und Tradition in der DDR. Die Debatte der Historiker*, Berlin, 1988.

140. Ingrid Mittenzwei, *Friedrich II. von Preußen. Eine Biographie*, Berlin, 1979.

141. Barbara Vogel, 'Das alte Preußen in der Geschichtswissenschaft der DDR. Zum Wandel des Preußenbildes in der DDR', in: Fischer and Heydemann (eds), *Geschichtswissenschaft*, vol. 2, p. 434.

142. Michael Stürmer, 'Ein Preußen für die DDR – umstrittenes Erbe', in: Fischer and Heydemann (eds), *Geschichtswissenschaft*, vol. 2, p. 424.

143. Rainer Wohlfeil, 'Das wissenschaftliche Lutherbild in beiden deutschen Staaten', *Deutschland Archiv*, vol. 17, 1984, pp. 1140 ff.

144. Ernst Engelberg, *Bismarck*, 2 vols, Berlin 1985 and 1990.

145. Ulrich Neuhäusser-Wespy, 'Erbe und Tradition in der DDR. Zum gewandelten Geschichtsbild der SED', in: Fischer and Heydemann (eds), *Geschichtswissenschaft*, vol. 1, pp. 145 f.

146. Georg G. Iggers, 'New Directions in Historical Studies in the German Democratic Republic', *History and Theory*, vol. 28, 1989, p. 69.

147. For the failure of a Marxist theory of history to affect GDR research see Arnold Sywottek, '"Marxistische Historik": Probleme und Scheinprobleme', in: Fischer and Heydemann (eds), *Geschichtswissenschaft*, vol. 1, pp. 255-68.

148. For demanding discussions of 'history theory' *(Geschichtstheorie)* in the GDR see, for example, Ernst Engelberg and Wolfgang Küttler (eds), *Formationstheorie und Geschichte*, Berlin, 1978; Wolfgang Küttler (ed.), *Das geschichtswissenschaftliche Erbe von Karl Marx*, Berlin, 1983; Wolfgang Küttler (ed.), *Gesellschaftstheorie und geschichtswissenschaftliche Erklärung*, Berlin, 1985.

149. Walter Schmidt, 'Das Gewesene ist nie erledigt. Worauf muß sich eine Nationalgeschichte der DDR stützen?', *Sonntag*, 5 July 1981, p. 9.

150. Iggers, 'Historical Studies', p. 70.

151. This is argued by Jan Herman Brinks, *Die DDR-Geschichtswissenschaft auf dem Weg zur deutschen Einheit. Luther, Friedrich II. und Bismarck als Paradigmen politischen Wandels*, Frankfurt-on-Main, 1992.

152. Erich Kosthorst, 'Die Frage der deutschen Einheit im Spannungsfeld politischer Optionen und historischer Traditionen', in: Karl-Ernst Jeismann (ed.), *Einheit – Freiheit – Selbstbestimmung. Die Deutsche Frage im historisch-politischen Bewußtsein*, Bonn, 1987, pp. 19 – 42. For the quote see p. 33.

153. Hans-Peter Schwarz, 'Patriotismus', *Die politische Meinung*, no. 232, 1987, pp. 40-5.
154. Thus the respectful words of Hans-Peter Schwarz in his laudation on Hillgruber on the occasion of the latter's reception of the Konrad-Adenauer Preis für die Wissenschaft. Reprinted in *Deutschland-Magazin*, no. 7, 1988, p. 12. For Hillgruber's commitment to the national idea see, for example Andreas Hillgruber, 'Deutsches Nationalbewußtsein heute – in zeitgeschichtlicher Perspektive', *Geschichte, Politik und ihre Didaktik*, vol. 4, 1976, pp. 55-65; idem, 'Die Forderung nach der deutschen Einheit im Spannungsfeld der Weltpolitik nach 1949', in: Jeismann (ed.), *Einheit*, pp. 215-29. For Schwarz's early predictions of a possible chance for reunification see Hans-Peter Schwarz, 'Auf dem Weg zum post-kommunistischen Europa', *Europa-Archiv*, vol. 44, 1989, pp. 319-30.
155. Michael Wolffsohn, *Ewige Schuld? 40 Jahre deutsch-jüdisch-israelische Beziehungen*, Munich, 1988, p. 21.
156. Hartmut Boockmann, 'Die Geschichtswissenschaft und die deutschen Ost- bzw. polnischen Westgebiete seit 1945', in: Prinz and Weingart (eds), *Geisteswissenschaften*, pp. 56-74 argued not to reduce German history to '*Rhein-donauländische Heimatkunde*' but to include the history of the 'lost territories' in Eastern Europe.
157. Konrad Repgen, 'Deutschland als Teil Europas in seiner Geschichte: Verfassung, Recht und Staat', in: *Edition Deutschland Archiv. Von Weimar nach Bonn: Freiheit und Einheit als Aufgabe. Berliner Kongreß Mai 1989*, Berlin, 1989, pp. 25-37.
158. *Die 'Deutsche Frage' im Unterricht. Beschluß der Ständigen Konferenz der Kultusminister der Länder in der Bundesrepublik Deutschland vom 23.11. 1978*, Bonn, 1978.
159. Hans-Peter Schwarz, 'Immunisierung gegen die modischen Viren', *Die Welt*, 24 May 1988, p. 19.
160. Hellmut Diwald, 'Gelebtes Wissen: Geschichte gibt dem Charakter Profil', *Die Welt*, 15 June 1988.
161. Wolfgang Marienfeld, 'Die "Einheit der Nation" in der Schulgeschichtsschreibung beider deutscher Staaten seit 1945', in: Jeismann (ed.), *Einheit*, p. 46.
162. Volker Berghahn and Hanna Schissler (eds), *Perceptions of History. An Analysis of School Textbooks*, Oxford, 1987.
163. Karl-Ernst Jeismann, 'Einleitung', in: Wolfgang Jacobmeyer (ed.), *Deutschlandbild und deutsche Frage in den historischen, geographischen und sozialwissenschaftlichen Unterrichtswerken der Bundesrepublik Deutschland und der Deutschen Demokratischen Republik von 1949 bis in die 80er Jahre*, Brunswick, 1986, p. xxxix.
164. Bodo von Borries, Hans-Jürgen Pandel, Jörn Rüsen (eds), *Geschichtsbewußtsein empirisch*, Pfaffenweiler, 1991, pp. 41-3, 212-13.
165. Bodo von Borries, 'Legitimation aus Geschichte oder Legitimation trotz Geschichte? Zu einer Hauptfunktion von Geschichtsbewußtsein', *Geschichtsdidaktik*, vol. 8, 1983, pp. 9-21.
166. Karl Dietrich Erdmann, 'Drei Staaten – zwei Nationen – ein Volk? Überlegungen zu den deutschen Geschichte seit der Teilung', *GWU*, vol. 36, 1985, p. 673.
167. Hacke, *Weltmacht*, p. 470.
168. Christian Meier, *Vierzig Jahre nach Auschwitz. Deutsche Geschichtserinnerung heute*, Munich, 1987, p. 86.
169. Hagen Schulze, *Gibt es überhaupt eine deutsche Geschichte?*, Berlin, 1989.
170. Alexander Schwan, 'Verfassungspatriotismus und nationale Frage: Zum Verhältnis von deutschem Staats- und Nationalbewußtsein', in: Weidenfeld (ed.), *Politische Kultur und deutsche Frage*, pp. 143 f. Compare also for consistency Alexander Schwan, 'Frei vor Vereint', *Die politische Meinung*, vol. 28, 1983, pp. 31-9.
171. Ernst Nolte, 'Europa und die deutsche Frage in historischer Perspektive', in: Jens Hacker and Siegfried Mampel (eds), *Europäische Integration und deutsche Frage*, Berlin, 1989, p. 41.

172. Wolf Gruner, *Die deutsche Frage. Ein Problem der europäischen Geschichte seit 1800,* Munich, 1985, p. 205.

173. Wolf Gruner, 'Föderatives Denken und bündische Formen deutscher Staat-lichkeit: Überlegungen zur europäischen Dimension deutscher Geschichte und zur deutschen Dimension europäischer Geschichte', *Politik und Kultur,* vol. 16, 1989, pp. 11-28.

174. Franz-Josef Jakobi, 'Mittelalterliches Reich und Nationalstaatsgedanke. Zur Funktion der Mittelalterrezeption und des Mittelalterbildes im 19. und 20. Jahrhundert', in: Jeismann (ed.), *Einheit,* pp. 155-76.

175. Karl Dietrich Bracher, 'Kein Anlaß zu Teuto-Pessimismus', *Süddeutsche Zeitung,* 24 May 1989.

PART II

———

THE SEARCH FOR NORMALITY
AFTER 1990

Chapter 5

IMPERIAL GERMANY AND THE
SONDERWEG REVISITED

In November 1990, just one month after official reunification, Karl-Heinz Janßen, a historian working for the German weekly *Die Zeit*, attacked what he perceived as renewed efforts to whitewash Germans of their historical guilt in the twentieth century. Reminding historians of the profession's long nationalist legacy, he warned against repeating the mistakes of the past and engaging upon national apologias when critical self-examination was what was most needed.[1] That year, Schulin expressed his concern about the 'renaissance of attempting to endow Germans with national identity'.[2] In 1994, Konrad Jarausch perceived 'increasing signs that a new nationalism is spreading even amongst professional historians'.[3] And Sontheimer castigated 'the typical tendency in current historiography on National Socialism to relativise and sanitise' German twentieth-century history.[4] There have thus been voices warning against renewed efforts by largely conservative and male historians to use reunification to re-establish an apologetic national history. Yet the events of 1989/90, I would argue, have left critics of the national tradition rather uncertain both in terms of their methodology and their politics. Consequently some have been trying to adapt to the changed political circumstances by modifying their position on the national principle. The outcome has been different for different historians, and it is important to realise the great diversity of opinions amongst German historians. I do not wish to dramatise the situation which is still characterised fundamentally by a plurality of viewpoints and methods. However, the changes have been marked enough to merit their discussion in the context of an attempted rena-tionalisation of German historical consciousness.

Therefore it is necessary, first of all, to investigate the re-assess-ment of the history of the first German nation-state of 1870/71. Here the debates have centred on the question of whether the Bismarckian creation should and could serve as the starting point for national iden-tity in the reunified country after 1990. In line with a more positive re-interpretation of the 'achievements' of Imperial Germany, fewer and fewer historians are willing to subscribe to notions of the old *Sonder-weg* paradigm. In chapter six, one will have to examine re-interpreta-tions of National Socialism which lend themselves to legitimating and exculpating the nation from its darkest years. In particular one will have to review the debate on Nazism as a consciously modernising regime within the context of calls for a historisation of National Socialism. Furthermore, theories which have portrayed Nazism as a legitimate response to Bolshevism, various totalitarianist and excep-tionalist views of the Nazi period, a renewed marginalisation of the Communist resistance against National Socialism, as well as a resur-gent emphasis on portraying the Germans as victims of Hitler rather than perpetrators of crimes will have to be considered.

Efforts to renationalise German historical consciousness have not been restricted simply to the period from Bismarck to Bunker. They have involved new perspectives on post-Second World War German history. On the one hand, as will be discussed in chapter seven, the GDR and its historiography have been condemned lock, stock and barrel; on the other, as examined in chapter eight, the history of the Federal Republic has been portrayed as a provincial divertimento when compared with the 'normality' of the nation-state. If views of a *Sonderweg* prior to 1945 have been laid to rest, attempts to re-invent notions of a *Sonderweg* for the history of the Federal Republic have begun to surface. Attacks on *Vergangenheitsbewältigung* and *Ostpolitik* have been combined with indictments of Western integration, West-ern liberalism and European integration. The revival of *Mittellage* ideology goes hand-in-hand with a new espousal of the reunified country's alleged superpower status. Finally, chapter nine will analyse the rapid renewal of national commitment after 1989 which has found expression in national history museums, the revival of national symbols and the debate on the German capital. Reunification has brought calls for paradigm changes in German historiography and these strike at the very heart of critical structural social history.

The picture emerging from this analysis of the state of German historiography some six years after reunification is complex and

ambivalent. I do not believe in the existence of a manichaen struggle between the forces of light and darkness, i.e., the forces of the
national tradition and its critics. Nipperdey is worlds apart from
Zitelmann, Hildebrand is not Nolte, and Jäckel certainly does not
always see eye-to-eye with Hans Mommsen or Wehler. Yet a
renewed national commitment after 1989 is reflected in the political
and historical writings of a number of historians. Tracing such
attempts to renationalise German historical consciousness and plac-
ing it in the context of its long and unholy tradition is the aim of the
following chapters.

It is noticeable that a more positive view of the Bismarckian Reich
developed in German historiography after 1989. Its economic, technical and scientific achievements, its advanced welfare state, its modern, efficient bureaucracy, its constitutional and legal development
and potentials – these are all foregrounded in an effort to put aside
the more negative features of Imperial Germany. After years of a
more sober and sceptical assessment of Bismarck's genius, eulogies
about the 'iron chancellor' have begun to return to German historical writing. For Schwarz, Bismarck's foundation of Germany was
'urgently necessary if the Germans did not want to miss the path to
European modernity.'[5] It has been described alternately as 'artfully
undertaken'[6] and 'inevitable, without any alternative, expressing
the wish and the will of the nation'.[7] Ernst Nolte has perceived 'the
highest degree of historical necessity' in Bismarck's unification of
Germany.[8] By contrast, pointing to continuities in German history
from the Bismarckian foundation to National Socialism, has been
described as 'falsification of history'.[9] A masterly Bismarck eulogy of
recent times can be found in Klaus Hildebrand's work on German
foreign policy: 'Faced with a specific situation and without laying
extensive fires, it was Bismarck at last who let the fiery embers flare
up high to give to the Germans the long-missed warmth of the
nation-state without harming them directly through the belligerent
heat of the necessary [sic] battles.'[10] In the light of such elaborations,
one cannot but agree with Lothar Machtan who has perceived a
'return to the traditions of the Bismarckian Reich which belongs
once again to the arsenal of nationalist propaganda in Germany'.[11] If
the Bismarckian creation is to become the renewed focal point for
national consciousness, then historians have to deflect from its inherent structural weaknesses and instead emphasise the failure of Bismarck's successors. Wilhelm II in particular becomes the villain in
the national story – despite Nicolaus Sombart's rather strange
attempt to rehabilitate the last German Emperor. For Nipperdey,
Wilhelm II is simply the 'tragedy incarnate of German history'.[12]

Without Bismarck to guide Germany through its inherent difficulties of geopolitics, the nation went astray, antagonising every other major European power with the exception of Austria-Hungary until its *Mittellage* proved its undoing. Against the background of such scenarios the outbreak of the First World War is depicted as a tragedy rather than as a conscious effort on the part of Germany's ruling elite to gain hegemony in Europe.[13]

The concept of Germany lying in the middle of Europe, and being its heart, has experienced yet another renaissance in some of the historical literature after 1989. In Stürmer's German history, for example, almost all of Germany's catastrophes, from the Thirty Year's War via the First World War to the nationalist hubris of Hitler's 'Thousand Year Reich' are attributed to Germany's *Mittellage*.[14] For Gruner, the Germans are 'the European people of the centre', and Germany's history remains incomprehensible unless one considers the nation's geography.[15] Schulze has even returned to the idea that Germany's vulnerable geographic position made 'a rigorous policy at home' absolutely necessary. The notion is thus resurrected that the authoritarian 'German constitutionalism' was a reflection of foreign policy constraints.[16] Gregor Schöllgen has portrayed Germany's aggressive expansionism from Frederick the Great down to the First World War within the context of its alleged vulnerable position in the heart of Europe. Ideas of preventive war, he argued, could mature in such an insecure geographic position. German *Weltpolitik* in the age of imperialism was thus in line with the *Zeitgeist*. Its 'tragedy' was that it necessarily had to clash with the system of European security.[17] In similar fashion, Hildebrand's interpretation of German foreign policy between 1870 and 1945 rests on the assumption that Germany's geography was Germany's destiny: 'the danger of *Mittellage* ... encouraged ... the notorious restlessness of the Germans.' Germany's economic growth, its social change and political development, Hildebrand has argued, 'demanded expansion and hegemony on the continent'. In this view, it was not so much *Weltpolitik* which was the problem, but the fact that Germany embarked upon *Weltpolitik* before consolidating the nation-state.[18]

The *Mitte* ideology is clearly bound up with pre-Fischerite interpretations of the outbreak of the First World War.[19] Stürmer has insisted that there was no conscious effort by Germany's elites to achieve hegemony in Europe. He could detect no signs of a flight into war as a desperate attempt to escape the social tensions which had accumulated in the semi-constitutional state. His geo-political considerations do not allow such domestic considerations to come into play. Instead he returns to the notion of an accident for which no country bore clear responsibility: 'No one wanted the war to come about in the way it did'.[20] For Nolte 'there is every likelihood that the simplest of all explanations, the one given by Lloyd George, is correct – that the statesmen of all nations had "slithered" into this war.'[21] Weißmann has spoken of 'a dilemma from which there was no escape.'[22] 'World war', for Schulze, 'was sooner or later inevitable'.[23] Nipperdey and Schwarz have both referred to the Germans' sense of encirclement before 1914. In their view German aggressiveness sprang from an ultimately defensive mood which resulted from the country's geographic position in the middle of Europe.[24] Denying German war guilt for the First World War is linked to efforts to destroy a key link in Fischer's thesis of a basic continuity of German foreign policy from 1914 to 1939. It has thus become part and parcel of 'normalising' the national tradition of Germany.[25]

One can distinguish between two positions amongst the wider efforts to establish positive national traditions for the reunified country: on the one hand, there are those who want to link the reunited Germany to the Bismarckian creation and, on the other, those who want to go further back in history. Herbert Kremp has firmly supported the first option. According to him, Germany's status as a great power and its role as a mediator between east and west is best reflected in Bismarckian and old Prussian values and concepts.[26] With Prussian panache, Weißmann has denounced the *Kleinstaaterei* in Germany after 1648 as 'this wretched political condition.'[27] The new Germany would be well advised, in Weißmann's view, to recognise that 'surprisingly it has much in common with the Bismarckian Reich.'[28] Baring has expressed his firm conviction that 'as always Germany is the Reich created by Bismarck'.[29] For Hildebrand, Bismarck's nation-state remains 'the only conceivable form for Germany and the true scene of German history'.[30] And Harm Klueting has argued that after reunification one of the central tasks has to be to reinstate the Bismarckian creation as the 'historical point of reference' for the new Germany.[31]

In contrast, Stürmer's efforts to provide the reunified Germans with a presentable historical identity have pointed to the destructiveness of the national idea in the nineteenth century. He finds much to praise in the first German Reich, the Holy Roman Empire: the 'sixteenth century was the happiest century for the Germans'.[32] The multitude of major cities with their own impressive and proud history, the prevailing traditions of federalism, political freedoms and the rule of law, the predominant work ethic, and the idea of solidarity – these all endear the old Reich to Stürmer. It is here, he has argued, that the reunified Germans can find refuge from the more turbulent nineteenth and twentieth centuries: 'The heritage of the Old Reich has not been lost for the Germans ...'.[33] Günter Barudio, warning of linguistic and ethnic nationalism in contemporary Germany, has also insisted on the virtues of the universal traditions of the German empire between 1648 and 1806. Consequently, for Barudio, the true model for a future German nation-state should not be Bismarck's authoritarian and undemocratic creation but the Old Reich.[34] Such positions have found much support in the writings of the long-time head of the Institute for European History at Mainz University, Karl Otmar von Aretin, who has long been an extremely sympathetic interpreter of the history of the Old Reich in the seventeenth and eighteenth centuries.[35] Also, some historians, most notably Wolf Gruner, have adapted their earlier ideas of the German Federation as the model for Germany's reunification. After the process of nation-building was achieved without recourse to confederation plans, Gruner still recommends 'thinking back to confederate forms in German history and their contribution to the political and cultural development of Germany.'[36]

The search for positive national traditions has also affected some former critics of historiographic nation-building. For Geiss, the German revolutionaries of 1848 were unable to solve the German question in a positive and constructive fashion.[37] Hence, only Bismarck knew how to 'utilise decisively the favourable conditions of the moment'.[38] Winkler interpreted the events of 1989 as 'confirmation of the small German solution' of 1866/71.[39] For Wolfgang Mommsen 'even today the national identity of the Germans remains anchored in the German Empire.'[40] Whilst upholding his interpretation of the Empire as a 'nation-state deformed by authoritarianism', Mommsen now emphasised those structures which allegedly still positively affect the Federal Republic: the rule of law, the beginnings of a market-oriented capitalism, the development of an efficient educational system and of modernist avantgarde culture. These achievements of the Kaiserreich, according to Mommsen, have not been adequately recognised by historians. Hence 'the regained unity of the two German states gives us special cause for a retrospective on the history of the German Empire. ... It is conspicuous that the Germans stand in historical traditions the foundations of which were laid then.'[41]

If there has been a more positive reinterpretation of the first German nation-state after 1990, there still are those who continue to reject efforts to anchor the identity of the FRG in the history of Bismarckian Germany. For Eberhard Jäckel, the question has even been how to prevent a rerun, after 1990, of the events of the first half of the twentieth century. Jäckel pointed out the similarities between the sit-

uation in 1870/71 and that after 1989, and warned that the foundation of the German Empire in 1871 had led directly to two world
wars in Europe. Hence the overriding task after reunification has to
be 'to create conditions in which the following generations can make
as little mischief as possible'.[42] Kocka and Bernd-Jürgen Wendt have
explicitly denied the Bismarckian foundation any model status.[43] For
Kocka, any one-sided enhancement of the status of Imperial Germany spells danger.[44] Peter Glotz, who was born in Austria, has been
particularly conscious of 'the violence and arbitrariness of the state
building process initiated by Bismarck'.[45] Julius H. Schoeps has
underlined his doubts about seeing 1870/71 as a positive date in German history.[46] Even a more conservative historian like Erdmann
emphasised the great historical distance which separated the reunified Germany from the sentiments of the Bismarckian foundation of
the Reich.[47] Faced by attempts to ascribe the unification of Germany
to some kind of master plan of Bismarck, Kolb has stressed that there
was no such plan. Instead Bismarck had a variety of alternative
strategies, including the division of Germany into interest spheres
between Austria-Hungary and Prussia. Such a reminder that every
historical situation has alternatives can act as a useful corrective to
the renewed Bismarck hagiography.[48] Stig Förster's thesis that the
German general staff and in particular Moltke knew full well in the
summer of 1914 that the war might not be a limited local conflict but
would become a long drawn-out world war, should deter further
attempts to exculpate the German military and political elites from
their responsibility for the outbreak of the First World War.[49]

   Such continued critical perspectives on the first German nation-
state have to be put side-by-side with the search for positive traditions
in German history. The latter, however, has accelerated the further
demise of the *Sonderweg* paradigm after 1990. The revival of historiographic nationalism on the right goes hand-in-hand with an apod-
ictic condemnation of German 'peculiarities' as being irreconcible
with 'historical facts'. Stürmer declared the concept to be nothing but
'mirror counter-myths'.[50] The attacks on the German *Sonderweg* from
a national perspective have remained what they always were: a political tool on the path to a sanitised German national history. If the aim
is to paint Germany's national history in brighter colours, then historians have to deny the existence of problematic continuities in Germany's nineteenth and twentieth-century history.[51] Such politically
motivated condemnation of the *Sonderweg* has to be distinguished
from questions about its usefulness as master narrative of modern
German history. Whilst one should readily admit the fruitfulness of
the concept in encouraging a whole string of research monographs

into illiberal and antidemocratic traditions in Germany, the *Sonderweg* paradigm has also become a straitjacket for historical interpretation.[52] Reacting to their English critics in the early 1980s, Wehler, Puhle and Winkler vigorously defended the idea of a German special path.[53] One year before the fall of the wall Winkler wrote a classic restatement of the theory of the German *Sonderweg*, and emphasised the consequences of that special path for the future of the German nation-state. He explicitly rejected the aim of reunification, as formulated by the Basic Law. In his view it was both illusory and undesirable as a reunified Germany would mean an irresponsible concentration of power in the hands of one European state. Hence he urged Germans to 'leave behind Bismarck's shadow'.[54] Five years later, in the same journal, Winkler himself revived the iron chancellor's shadow. The German nation-state, far from being a *Sonderweg*, now marked a 'return to European normality'. The idea of the Federal Republic as a post national democracy deriving its identity from constitutional patriotism has now, in Winkler's eyes, become a dangerous illusion based on a number of ill-considered judgements.[55] The post-1945 development of the FRG was the real *Sonderweg*.[56] Geiss, who continues his drift to the right, has gone furthest in rejecting the *Sonderweg*. In his post-reunification history of the German question, he denounced it as narrow, dogmatic and moralising.[57] According to Geiss it provided a 'dogma of the new orthodoxy' which served the sole purpose of 'morally stigmatising' German history. It has been nothing but 'an instrument of subtle self-accusation'.[58] Wendt has also sceptically re-assessed the *Sonderweg* historians' 'handling of history which was marred by all too blatant normative and political-pedagogical ambitions.'[59] Kocka, who already modified the *Sonderweg* paradigm significantly in the late 1980s, seems resigned to the fact that, under the impact of reunification, it will further lose influence.[60]

Further modifications of the concept abound. Faulenbach, rather than emphasising a special path, has described the German development as a half-way house between the modernisation processes of the West and those of the East. In particular he has reiterated Plessner's view of Germany as a 'belated nation', thus stressing the various problems that the parallel modernisation processes of industrialisation, democratisation and nation-building created in Germany.[61] Hardtwig has framed an argument around the thesis that the German *Sonderweg* lies in the 'deeply fissured nature of German history' which was 'decisively conditioned by disjunctures in the modernisation processes of German society between Old and New Reich'. Tracing those disjunctures in the areas of society, politics and religion, he has come to the conclusion that the historical actors were unable adequately to assess the consequences of their actions, and thereby caused disaster. Hence, Hardtwig takes on the tragic emplotment of German history which usually belongs to the conservative national historiography.[62] For Winkler, the rise of Nazism in Germany can no longer be explained by referring only to a negative *Sonderweg*. Instead it was the mixture of authoritarian traditions and modern democratic structures which facilitated the victory of Hitler in Germany.[63]

However, not every sign of modification is a sign of renationalisation. It also needs to be pointed out that there still are a number of historians, including Winkler, Hardtwig and Faulenbach, who maintain that the German development was highly specific. In 1992, Fischer confirmed his view that there existed many lines of continuity between Wilhelmine Germany and Hitler's Germany. He maintained that the rhetoric of 'fate' and 'tragedy' employed by conservatives to explain Hitler never explained anything; rather it shrouded the phenomenon in a mysterious demonology. Nazism, he argued, was 'unthinkable without the social and mental conditions created in Imperial Germany and the Weimar Republic. Hitler neither came from hell nor from heaven, and he most certainly was no simple "accident".'[64] Now well into his eighties, Fischer is still a major opponent of any efforts to paint German national history in glowing colours.

In the third volume of Wehler's *Deutsche Gesellschaftsgeschichte* the discussion of German 'special conditions' *(Sonderbedingungen)* (rather than the German *Sonderweg*) is still the one organising theme which holds the volume together. Wehler has modified the terminology, yet such willingness to correct his own position stems primarily from the recognition that the picture of Imperial Germany he had painted in his hugely influential *Deutsches Kaiserreich* had to take on board some of the substantial criticisms that were made by Nipperdey, Black-bourn, Eley and many others. Thus Wehler now interprets 1848 not just as a failure. It is also recognised as a stepping stone for a whole range of liberal reforms in various German states. He admits the cultural strength of the *Bürgertum*, whilst maintaining that it was comparatively weak in the political arena. He is still convinced of the central role of Bismarck in the moulding of the German path into modernity, but the concept of 'bonapartist rule' is replaced by 'charismatic rule'. The 'great depression' turns into the 'great deflation', 'organised capitalism' becomes a strong corporatist tradition. Yet despite all this, Wehler insists on the existence of special conditions and has amassed an enormous amount of detailed data to underpin the notion of German peculiarities. Going through the list, one hardly gets the impression that the core concept of a *Sonderweg* is given up:

the monarchic tradition, the Prussian military state, the public esteem
of the military and the high public profile of the nobility, the emergence of authoritarian corporatism, the failure of political liberalism
to decisively shape the political system of the *Kaiserreich*, the unfinished 'civil society', the extreme nationalism as a response to rapid
modernisation, foreign policy as continuation of domestic policy with
other means, and, above all, the peculiar fact that industrialisation,
nation-state building and the social question were all on the agenda at
roughly the same time in Germany. In the context of the outstanding
strength of the bureaucratic tradition, Wehler even feels justified in
returning to the old word *Sonderweg.*[65] Notions of a *Sonderweg* are still
present elsewhere. For example, at the 1995 AGM of the German
History Society both Wolfgang and Hans Mommsen invoked the
notion of a German *Sonderweg* when addressing the topic 'Bureaucracy in German History'. As Wolfgang Mommsen pointed out, the
concept of bureaucratic government by experts *(Beamtenherrschaft)*
was highly popular amongst the middle classes in Wilhelmine Germany, whilst British party government hardly figured as a model.
Hans Mommsen, in a sweeping survey ranging from Weimar Germany to the Federal Republic, demonstrated the 'mentality of the
German way' which he located in the tensions between civil service
and citizens or, in other words, between state and individual liberty.[66]

So, whilst there are continued efforts to uphold and redefine the
peculiarities in German national history in the light of much justified
criticism, it seems also symptomatic for the state of German historiography that none of the participants at the 1994 spring conference
of the Evangelische Akademie Tutzing disagreed with the provoca-
tive statement: 'Good-bye to the German *Sonderweg*'.[67] The critical
perspectives provided by the *Sonderweg* paradigm stand in the way of
attempts to renationalise German historical consciousness. The place
of National Socialism in German history was reconsidered in the
light of German peculiarities. It is therefore hardly surprising that
renewed attacks on the *Sonderweg* idea have gone hand in hand with
attempts to refocus the historical memory of National Socialism.

Notes

1. Karl-Heinz Janßen, 'Von deutscher Schuld. Warum Deutschland den Schatten der Vergangenheit nicht entfliehen kann', *Die Zeit,* no. 47, 16 Nov. 1990, p. 48.
2. Schulin, 'Schlußbetrachtung', in: idem (ed.), *Geschichtswissenschaft,* p. 275.
3. Konrad Jarausch, 'Kritische Perspektiven zur deutschen Vergangenheit', in: Jarausch and Middell (eds), *Nach dem Erdbeben,* p. 28.
4. Kurt Sontheimer, 'Wider die Leisetreterei der Historiker', *Die Zeit,* 4 Nov. 1994, p. 15.
5. Hans-Peter Schwarz, *Die Zentralmacht Europas. Deutschlands Rückkehr auf die Weltbühne,* Berlin, 1994, p. 65.
6. Hagen Schulze, 'German Unification in the Context of European History', *German Studies Review,* winter 1992, p. 11.
7. Wolfgang Venohr, 'Argumente gegen zwei Staaten', *Rheinischer Merkur,* 15 Dec. 1989, p. 3.
8. Ernst Nolte, *Lehrstück oder Tragödie? Beiträge zur Interpretation der Geschichte des 20. Jahrhunderts,* Cologne, 1991, p. 103.
9. Ferdinand von Bismarck, 'Hier irren manche Geschichtsschreiber', *Die Welt,* 19 June 1993, p. G2.
10. Klaus Hildebrand, *Das vergangene Reich. Deutsche Aussenpolitik von Bismarck bis Hitler,* Stuttgart, 1995, p. 853.
11. Lothar Machtan, 'Einführung', in: idem (ed.), *Bismarck,* p. 9.
12. Nipperdey, *Machtstaat,* p. 421. This remains the dominant view despite the strange attempt by Nicolaus Sombart, *Wilhelm II. Sündenbock und Herr der Mitte,* Berlin, 1996 to rehabilitate the last German Emperor.
13. Nipperdey, *Machtstaat,* p. 882.
14. Stürmer, *Die Grenzen der Macht.*
15. Wolf D. Gruner, *Die deutsche Frage in Europa 1800-1990,* Munich, 1993, pp. 11, 60-4.
16. Schulze, 'German unification', p. 13.
17. Gregor Schöllgen, *Die Macht in der Mitte Europas. Stationen deutscher Außenpolitik von Friedrich dem Großen bis zur Gegenwart,* Munich, 1992, p. 66.
18. Hildebrand, *Das vergangene Reich,* p. 860, 869 f., 883. Mistrustful readers might well infer from such analysis to be aware of Germany in times to come, when the refound nation-state is consolidated.
19. Dirk Bavendamm, 'Deutscher Griff nach der Weltmacht?', *Das Parlament,* 11/18 Nov. 1994, p. 3.
20. Stürmer, *Die Grenzen der Macht,* p. 99. Similarly Gregor Schöllgen, *Das Zeitalter des Imperialismus,* 3rd rev. and ext. edn, Munich, 1994, p. 172; also idem, *Die Macht,* pp. 67-87.
21. Nolte, *Lehrstück oder Tragödie,* p. 106.
22. Weißmann, *Rückruf,* p. 80.
23. Schulze, 'German Unification', p. 13.
24. Nipperdey, *Machtstaat,* pp. 695, 698 f.; Schwarz, *Zentralmacht,* pp. 206 f.
25. Lothar Wieland, 'Der deutsche Griff nach der Weltmacht. Die Fischer-Kontroverse in historischer Perspektive', *Blätter,* vol. 37, 1992, pp. 742-52.
26. Herbert Kremp, 'Die Angst der Passagiere auf dem Luxusliner', *Die Welt,* no. 210, 8 Sept. 1990, p. 17.
27. Weißmann, *Rückruf,* p. 77.
28. Ibid., p. 49.
29. Arnulf Baring, *Deutschland, was nun?,* Berlin, 1991, p. 19.
30. Hildebrand, *Das vergangene Reich,* p. 868.
31. Harm Klueting, 'Hierarchische Strukturen, föderalistische Tendenzen', *Neue Zürcher Zeitung,* 11 March 1994, p. 46.

32. Stürmer, *Die Grenzen der Macht,* p. 24.

33. Ibid., p. 75.

34. Günter Barudio, 'Teutsche Freiheit statt Obrigkeit', *Rheinischer Merkur,* no. 39, 28 Sept. 1994, p. 4; see also idem, 'Die verspottete Nation', *Die Zeit,* no. 45, 4 Nov. 1994, p. 58.

35. Karl Otmar von Aretin, *Das alte Reich 1648-1806,* vol. 1: *Föderalistische oder hierarchische Ordnung (1648-1684),* Stuttgart, 1993.

36. Gruner, *Die deutsche Frage,* p. 79.

37. Imanuel Geiss, *Die deutsche Frage 1806-1990,* Mannheim, 1992, p. 40.

38. Ibid., p. 43.

39. Heinrich August Winkler, 'Nationalismus, Nationalstaat und nationale Frage in Deutschland seit 1945', in: Heinrich August Winkler and Hartmut Kaelble (eds), *Nationalismus – Nationalitäten – Supranationalität,* Stuttgart, 1993, pp. 30 f.

40. Mommsen, *Nationalstaat,* pp. 7-8.

41. Mommsen, *Das Ringen,* pp. 12, 17, 32.

42. Eberhard Jäckel, 'Furcht vor der eigenen Stärke? Das vereinigte Deutschland muß Versuchungen vorbeugen', *Die Zeit,* 2 Nov. 1990, p. 10. Also: idem, 'Nach der Einheit die Spaltung?', *Die Tageszeitung,* 7 Oct. 1992.

43. Kocka, *Vereinigungskrise,* p. 42; Bernd-Jürgen Wendt, 'Die Debatte über den "deutschen Sonderweg"', in: idem (ed.), *Vom schwierigen Zusammenwachsen der Deutschen. Nationale Identität und Nationalismus im 19. und 20. Jahrhundert,* Frankfurt-on-Main, 1992, p. 141.

44. Jürgen Kocka, 'Zwischen Sonderweg und Bürgergesellschaft', *Der Tagesspiegel,* 17 Sept. 1992.

45. Peter Glotz, *Die falsche Normalisierung. Essays,* Frankfurt-on-Main, 1994, p. 186.

46. Julius H. Schoeps, 'Die Deutschen und ihre Identität. Zwischen Kyffhäusermythos und Verfassungspatriotismus', in: Peter Krüger (ed.), *Deutschland, deutscher Staat, deutsche Nation. Historische Erkundungen eines Spannungsverhältnisses,* Marburg, 1993, p. 96.

47. Karl Dietrich Erdmann, 'Die Revolution Mitteleuropas – historische Perspektiven', *GWU,* vol. 41, 1990, p. 542.

48. Eberhard Kolb, 'Die kleindeutsche Reichsgründung. Bismarcks Konzeptionen und Strategien zur Lösung der nationalen Frage', in: Otto Dann (ed.), *Die deutsche Nation. Geschichte – Probleme – Perspektiven,* Greifswald, 1994, pp. 45-59.

49. Stig Förster, 'Mit Hurra und vollem Bewußtsein in die Katastrophe', *FR,* 9 Aug. 1994.

50. Stürmer, *Die Grenzen der Macht,* p. 112.

51. Lothar Wieland, 'Geschichtsrevisionismus und Kontinuitätsproblem in der deutschen Geschichte', in: Wieland and Donat (eds), *"Auschwitz erst möglich gemacht",* pp. 38-56.

52. Lutz Niethammer, 'Geht der deutsche Sonderweg weiter?', in: Antonia Grunenberg (ed.), *Welche Geschichte wählen wir?,* Hamburg, 1992, p. 31.

53. Wehler, *Preußen,* pp. 19-32. See also Hans-Jürgen Puhle, 'Deutscher Sonderweg – Kontroverse um eine vermeintliche Legende', *Journal für Geschichte,* no. 4, 1981, p. 45; Heinrich August Winkler, 'Der deutsche Sonderweg. Eine Nachlese', *Merkur,* vol. 35, 1981, pp. 793-803.

54. Heinrich August Winkler, 'Bismarcks Schatten. Ursachen und Folgen der deutschen Katastrophe', *Die neue Gesellschaft: Frankfurter Hefte,* vol. 35, 1988, pp. 111-21.

55. Heinrich August Winkler, 'Abschied von einem deutschen Sonderweg. Wider die postnationale Nostalgie', *Die neue Gesellschaft\ Frankfurter Hefte,* vol. 40, 1993, pp. 633-6.

56. Heinrich August Winkler, 'Rebuilding of a Nation: The Germans Before and After Reunification', *Daedalus,* vol. 123, 1994, p. 119.

57. Geiss, *Die deutsche Frage,* p. 13.
58. Imanuel Geiss, *Der Hysterikerstreit: ein unpolemischer Essay,* Bonn, 1992, pp. 156-61.
59. Bernd-Jürgen Wendt, 'Die Debatte', in: idem (ed.), *Vom schwierigen Umgang,* p. 138.
60. Kocka, *Die Auswirkungen,* pp. 18 f.
61. Bernd Faulenbach, '"Nation" und "Modernisierung" in der deutschen Geschichte', in: Zitelmann et al. (eds), *Westbindung,* pp. 103-26.
62. Hardtwig, *Nationalismus und Bürgerkultur,* pp. 165-90.
63. Winkler, 'Rebuilding of a Nation', p. 124.
64. Fischer, *Hitler,* p. 181.
65. Hans-Ulrich Wehler, *Deutsche Gesellschaftsgeschichte,* vol. 3: *Von der "Deutschen Doppelrevolution" bis zum Beginn des Ersten Weltkrieges 1849-1914,* Munich, 1995, p. 1,288. See also for a spirited defence of the *Sonderweg* notion idem, 'Raus aus der Sackgasse des "deutschen Sonderwegs"?', in: idem, *Die Gegenwart als Geschichte,* pp. 181-5.
66. Hans and Wolfgang J. Mommsen, 'Bureaucracy in German History', papers given to the AGM of the GHS, 25 Nov. 1995.
67. Carl Wilhelm Macke, 'Eiertänze und Denkverbote', *FR,* 15 March 1994, p. 7.

Chapter 6

———

GERMANY'S DARKEST YEARS
REVISITED

The renationalisation of German historiography has been closely linked to renewed attempts to exculpate the German nation from its darkest years. One can distinguish between four separate strategies: first, Ernst Nolte's theory of a European civil war which has endowed the Nazis and even genocide with historical 'legitimacy'; secondly, efforts to historise National Socialism which are combined with theories of Nazism as a consciously modernising force in twentieth-century German history; thirdly, various efforts to portray the German nation as Hitler's victims; and finally, a return to the view of the national-conservative opposition to Hitler as the 'true' Germany which upheld the 'good' national traditions throughout the twelve years of 'evil' dictatorship.

Ernst Nolte has declared his intention to write about National Socialism with his 'heart's blood' *(Herzblut)*.[1] Empathy and understanding replace sober judgment. Nolte's thinking has been directed by his notion that a European and later world civil war dominated the period from 1917 to 1989. It has allowed him to see National Socialism in the tradition of anti-Communism, and therefore National Socialism has become in a perverse way an ally of Western liberalism, not an adversary. In a sense, Nolte has inverted the Marxist notion of National Socialism as the ugly face of capitalism. Thus, for Nolte, National Socialism becomes the tough face of soft Western liberalism which proved unable to defend itself in the early 1930s against the advances of Bolshevism. The totalitarian antipluralism of

Hitler appears as the only alternative to the totalitarian antipluralism of Stalin. In line with this thinking, Nolte has had no difficulty rehabilitating National Socialist ideologues as defenders of cultural and national plurality against the levelling tendencies of Bolshevism.[2] In his eyes, one can even attribute greatness to Nazism because it was, after all, the most radical form of anti-Communism.

A number of scholars have taken up Nolte's extreme ideas. In a major monograph on the demise of the Weimar Republic, Christian Striefler has recently reiterated Nolte's thesis that National Socialism's 'rational centre' was its anti-Bolshevism. For Striefler, the real threat to the Weimar Republic came from the Communists. The Nazis by their *Machtergreifung* on 30 January 1993 thus only prevented a Communist take-over. By portraying democracy as being beyond rescue and by narrowing down the alternatives to Communism versus National Socialism, the Nazis, Striefler insisted, appeared to many the lesser evil: 'The main threat emanated from Bolshevism, and to many it seemed only a question of time, before Communist prophecies of destruction would carry the day in Germany.'[3] Striefler does not even discuss the fact that there was a strong democratic anti-Communism in the SPD and elsewhere, and that there were various alternative non-democratic solutions to the crisis of the Weimar Republic.

Stürmer's dictum that National Socialism was a 'revolution against all revolutions' also reminds one of Nolte's insistence that anti-Bolshevism was the central aspect of Nazism.[4] Weißmann has adopted Nolte's thesis of the world civil war in an attempt to exculpate Germans from their alleged guilt complex: 'It is part and parcel of the pathological condition of the post-war era that the Germans seriously believed that they had been at the hub of world events in the first half of the twentieth century. The collective consciousness of the nation hardly noticed that the international order and hence political developments in Europe were dominated by the "world civil war". Many illusions about the allegedly insoluble "German question" depended on such a distorted perspective.'[5] Rainer Zitelmann has explicitly defended Nolte whom he has described as the victim of left-wing intellectuals ruthlessly defending their cultural hegemony in the Federal Republic. Nolte, Zitelmann argued, has remained a serious historical scholar whose efforts to give a 'fair trial' even to Hitler have yielded many fruitful insights.[6] Nolte's critics are sometimes accused of neglecting the autonomy of historical research from politics, thereby erecting taboos which cement a static and unproductive view of the Nazi period. By contrast, Nolte's attempts to reinterpret Nazism are seen as a welcome change of perspective.[7] Fest has praised Nolte's 'passion for cool thinking' which produced convincing interpretations of Nazism. For Fest, these achievements cannot be eradicated by a deliberate anti-Nolte campaign of ahistorically minded moralists.[8] Horst Möller has commended Nolte's 'radical historisation' of National Socialism, calling his work 'both fascinating and irritatingly great'.[9] As these reactions indicate, it would certainly be a mistake to perceive Nolte as an extreme right-wing maverick without support amongst other conservative historians.

Yet, on the whole, Nolte's ideas continue to be met with overwhelming scepticism. Wehler has classified Nolte as an 'honest German nationalist',[10] whilst calling his theories 'bizarre' speculations without adequate empirical foundations.[11] For Wehler, it was not the duel between Bolshevism and National Socialism which dominated the twentieth century, but the struggle between liberal democracy and the totalitarian dictatorships.[12] According to Jäckel, the First World War and not the emergence of Bolshevism should be seen as the 'seminal catastrophe of the century'.[13] And Winkler, whose anti-Communist credentials are hard to undermine, has criticised both Nolte and Striefler for attributing rationality and historical legitimacy to Nazism.[14] Rolf Richter has argued that there should be no reason to correct the anti-Nolte position which had emerged as the consensus in the *Historikerstreit.*[15] Even a perennial centrist, like Christian Meier, has accused Nolte in harsh words of whitewashing the German past, relativising Nazi crimes and leaving the field of serious scholarship: 'It is sad to see how he destroys himself. I think: Enough is enough, Herr Nolte!'[16]

Indeed it is sad to see Nolte coming close to adopting the very race theories espoused by the Nazis, for example in his interpretation of the Law for the Restoration of the Professional Civil Services which, in his view, just simply proportionally readjusted the number of Jews and Germans in employment.[17] Despite overwhelming historical evidence to the contrary he denies that racism and anti-Semitism ever constituted the core of Nazism. Hence, in his writings, the Holocaust is moved from the centre to the margins: it becomes a byproduct of Nazism's fight against Communism. Nolte has given credibility to those revisionist critics like Fred Leuchter, Paul Rassinier and Robert Faurisson who have denied the existence of the extermination camps.[18] According to Nolte, the 'rational centre' of the Holocaust[19] was Hitler's fight against the 'eternal left', against 'Jewish Bolshevism'. Accordingly, the Bolsheviks' 'war of extinction' directed as it was against whole classes, was only mirrored by the Nazis' 'will for extinction' directed against the Jews. This will was equally rational: 'If the Jews have perceived themselves as "the light

of the people" ... then widespread enmity towards them is a necessary consequence ... If this self-definition is in reality mixed with
banal characteristics such as egotism and the will to power, then
such enmity is not without legitimacy, and the undifferentiated stig-
matisation of "anti-Semitism" has to be unmasked as a mere belli-
cose strategy, albeit an extremely successful one.'[20] Hence, it comes
as no surprise that Nolte has spoken up against a law which makes
the negation of the Holocaust a punishable offence in Germany.[21]

Dyed-in-the-wool revisionists have rejoiced that for the first time a
renowned historical scholar has taken their nonsense seriously.
Mohler has cited Nolte (as well as Broszat and Wolffsohn) at length to
prove that the former 'witchhunt' against revisionists is over.[22] However, the far right remains almost completely absent from the mainstream of professional historical writing about National Socialism in
Germany. Christian Streit has pointed out that anti-Bolshevism was at
best a 'catalytic marginal condition' for genocide which remained
firmly rooted in Nazism's *völkisch* anti-Semitism.[23] Wolfgang Benz has
reminded his fellow historians that Nolte's discussion of the number
of Jewish victims 'traditionally lies at the heart of the denial of the
Holocaust'.[24] Serious scholarly research on the Holocaust has
remained well established in the Federal Republic at institutions such
as the Berlin Zentrum für Antisemitismusforschung at the Technical
University Berlin, the Forschungsinstitut zur Geschichte des Nationalsozialismus in Hamburg, the Institut für Zeitgeschichte in Munich
or, most recently, the Fritz Bauer Institut in Frankfurt, which was
founded in January 1995. Internationally acclaimed scholars working
on the Holocaust include Germans such as Hans Mommsen and
Jäckel.[25] The president of the Federal Republic has recently sent a
positive signal that the Holocaust will remain at the centre of German
historical consciousness by declaring 27 January (the day that Soviet
soldiers liberated Auschwitz) as a national day of remembrance for
the victims of National Socialism. It was commemorated for the first
time in 1996. Even so, it remains worrying that Nolte seeks to
enhance the scholarly status of the far right in research about National
Socialism at a time when, after reunification, anti-Semitism is once
again gaining ground amongst Germans.[26]

Nolte has also contributed to a second re-interpretation of Nazi
Germany, which has stressed the modernising 'positive elements and
tendencies in National Socialism'.[27] In a best-selling biography of
Hitler published in 1987, Rainer Zitelmann portrayed the dictator as
a conscious moderniser and revolutionary. Zitelmann focussed on
Hitler's ideas about social and economic matters, concluding that
they were both coherent and modern. According to Zitelmann the

Führer anticipated an advanced technological and industrial society, increased social mobility, a planned economy and a comprehensive welfare state.[28] In contrast to older studies by Ralf Dahrendorf and David Schoenbaum, who had also drawn attention to what they described as unintentional modernising effects of the Nazi regime on German society,[29] Zitelmann emphasised that modernisation was a conscious strategy of the Nazi leadership. Following Nolte, who in 1984 had already declared Hitler a modern revolutionary,[30] Zitelmann has repeatedly demanded unreserved recognition of the historical achievements of National Socialism.[31]

Zitelmann has emerged as a key figure amongst new right historians after 1990. Born in 1957, he can already look back on an impressive carreer. Up until 1992 he was a lecturer at the Free University of Berlin, and became chief commissioning editor of the powerful Ullstein publishing house in 1992. Many of the key texts, attempting to contribute to a renationalisation of German historical consciousness, have been published there.[32] In their introductions, many new right authors thank Zitelmann for his 'encouragement'. Whilst continuing as commissioning editor, in 1993 he became head of the section 'Geistige Welt' within the conservative newspaper *Die Welt*. In May 1994 he had to resign after staff protested against what they perceived as Zitelmann's escalation of the paper's arch-conservatism. Despite a solidarity campaign by some of the leading conservative historians, such as Schwarz and Hildebrand, Zitelmann had to go.[33] Ever since, he has continued to lead an existence on the right-wing margins of German history-writing and German politics – a leading member of the nationalist grouping in the FDP headed by the former general state attorney Alexander von Stahl.

The latest scandal connected to the Ullstein publishing house involves the highly respected series on German history, *Propyläen Geschichte Deutschlands*. Hans Mommsen, an internationally renowned expert on Nazism and at the same time a leading critic of historiographic nationalism, had initially been commissioned to write the volume on the National Socialist period. However, when Mommsen did not come up with a final date for submission of his manuscript, the publisher abruptly decided to transfer the task to Karlheinz Weißmann, one of the young nationalist hawks which emerged in Germany after 1990.[34] Unsurprisingly, in this volume Weißmann finds praise for those on the right who, like Zitelmann, have emphasised the intentional modernising aspects of the Nazi regime whilst he attributes the blindness of other historians to their political-pedagogical inclination to taboo the debate on Nazism and modernisation. Nazism, in Weißmann's view, brought about its own 'economic miracle' and then set out to create a developed consumer society and a strong welfare state.[35] As Wolfgang Wippermann pointed out in a review of Weißmann's work, the whole book is motivated by one desire – to attribute 'positive' sides to the Nazi regime.[36] However, the critical reception of Weißmann's book by leading members of the profession ultimately led the Ullstein publishing house to withdraw Weißmann's volume in July 1996 and start a new search for a more respectable author. Ullstein not only got rid of Zitelmann but also severed its connection to the extreme right-wing publisher Herbert Fleißner. The new head of Ullstein, Wolfram Göbel, instead announced in July 1996 that he would seek to give a more liberal image to the publishing house.

Central to Zitelmann's modernisation concept is the assumption that modernisation is value-free and should consequently not be connected to concepts such as democratisation, parliamentarianism, humanitarianism, progress or pluralism.[37] Those historians who have subscribed to Zitelmann's perspective have portrayed the Nazis as technological innovators, social revolutionaries, great architects, economic innovators in the Keynesian tradition, and pioneers of the welfare state and mass consumerism. The Nazis, from this perspective, created the first modern catch-all party and contributed vitally to the dissolution of traditional social, confessional and regional milieus in Germany. Furthermore, the modernity of Nazi planning has been traced in particular in areas such as education, culture, science, town planning, psychiatry and the organisation of the army.[38] However much those advocating a historisation of National Socialism emphasise that they do not intend to justify the Nazi regime morally and politically,[39] it remains the case that any social history of Nazism which uses a value-free modernisation theory unduly emphasises that which is marginal about National Socialism. Michael Prinz seemed to have recognised this dilemma himself when he admitted that modernisation theory remains unconvincing as 'the general interpretative framework' for the period.[40] Prinz and others, however, have insisted on their mission to free historiography from the alleged stranglehold of 'popular educational motives'. Some, like Weißmann, have already argued that the debate on the historisation of National Socialism has marked a paradigm change in German historiography. In his view, a generation of young historians has rediscovered the radical revolutionary and modern aspects of the Third Reich while the 'ancien regime' of the old *Sonderweg* historians is doomed to perish on the garbage heap of history.[41]

Modernisation theory does not have to deny the Holocaust – unless one wants to agree with Nolte's argument that the essentially 'humane' methods employed in the genocide are a sign of the Nazis' modernity.[42] In fact, there have been extremely interesting interpretations of Nazism which have located its criminal energies within the context of an allegedly destructive modernity. One thinks of Peukert's idea of seeing Nazism as a pathological variant of modernisation or of Götz Aly's, Susanne Heim's or Karlheinz Roth's interpretation of Nazism within the framework of capitalist modernisation.[43] Yet the modernisation concept in the form employed by Rainer Zitelmann easily lends itself to the overall aim of the new right, namely a revival of positive national identity. For them, Auschwitz has long been the central stumbling block preventing the resurrection of a glorious national history. How easily the paradigm of 'value-free modernisation' pushes the horrendous inhumanity of National Socialism to the sidelines has been demonstrated in a series of biographical sketches of the Nazi elite, edited, amongst others, by Zitelmann. Here Joachim Lehmann, the biographer of Herbert Backe, for example, writes of the latter's detailed plans for the murder of millions of people in Eastern Europe as an 'idée fixe'.[44]

In relation to a recent biography of Werner Sombart, Kurt Sontheimer has raised the question of whether historians can write about National Socialism without taking a decisive political and moral stance against it. Friedrich Lenger's portrayal of Sombart – in many respects an admirable biography – avoids drawing a clear line between Sombart's initial support for the Nazis in 1933 and his past as an anti-Semite, racist and arrogant mandarin professor. Instead Lenger emphasises a multi-faceted perspective on Sombart's life. In his 'genetic-contextualising' approach to biography which aims to escape the 'biographical illusion' (Pierre Bourdieu) of the essential unity and homogeneity of any person's life, there are many Sombarts. For him the perspective on Sombart's life should not be determined by 'a totally contingent endpoint'.[45] The problem with such an approach, however, surely is that Sombart's sympathies for the Nazis were not merely contingent. Any biographer would not have to be unduly teleological to point out in a more systematic fashion the many facets of Sombart's life and ideas which made him end up as anti-republican sympathiser of the Nazi regime who, at the same time, reserved a *geistesaristokratisch* disdain for Nazism. For Sontheimer Lenger's approach amounts to 'the abdication of morality from historiography, the flight of the historian from his political responsibility'.[46] Lenger's response to Sontheimer's attack has also been revealing. First, he portrays himself as persecuted by those critical historians who have erected certain taboos in historical scholarship. Again one encounters the fiction of an alleged 'new orthodoxy' which I discussed in chapter four. It serves the purpose of portraying the new national overtones as a necessary corrective against a presumed left-wing hegemony over historical writing. The self-declared taboo breakers put on a show of 'persecuted innocence'. Secondly, Lenger refers to the neo-historist assumption that morality and politics should not have any place in the writing of history.[47] Thereby attempts to revive the national tradition are hiding behind demands for a value and politics-free scholarship. The problem with Lenger's book is not so much that it follows a conscious agenda of renationalisation (he does not belong to the Zitelmann and Nolte school of German historical writing). The problem lies rather in its methodology, which is rooted in the historist notion of *Verstehen* and aims to avoid normative judgements, thereby opening the prospect of yet another fateful merger between a revived neo-historism and the apologias of a national tradition.

Zitelmann, Nolte and their followers want to historise National Socialism in the hope that it will lose its importance for the presence.[48] Geiss, with the zeal of the converted, even demanded a rigorous historisation of the Holocaust.[49] Attempts to use the concept of 'historisation' for the purpose of making the national tradition more presentable routinely refer to Martin Broszat's initial 1985 suggestion that it was an appropriate time to historise the Nazi period. To this end, historical revisionists frequently cite the respected former head of the Institut für Zeitgeschichte in Munich in support of their 'historised' version of National Socialist history.[50] Broszat, without being able to substantiate his claim empirically, had already argued in 1985 that the German Labour Front (DAF) served as basis and prepared the ground for the social insurance laws of the Federal Republic in the 1950s. Yet Broszat's position could not have been more hostile to any renationalisation of German historical consciousness. His intention had been to overcome what he perceived as unhelpful moralism which, in its blanket condemnation of Nazism as evil, failed to understand much of the phenomenon itself. For Broszat this had become an essential task because he felt that the writing of history had to remain committed to the Enlightenment principles of critical understanding. The prophets of the 'self-confident nation', who bestow laurels upon him today, want to get rid of these critical perspectives. Broszat had always been among the sharpest critics of the national tradition in German historiography.[51] In his famous exchange with Saul Friedländer[52] he conceded that his concept of historisation would lend itself to nationalist misuse. Sadly Broszat died in 1989, and his name has been used since to justify the crudest apologias of German national history.

Broszat was increasingly interested in the view from below, in the everyday life history of National Socialism and the perspective of the ordinary man in the street.[53] The Bavaria project, initiated by Broszat at the Institut für Zeitgeschichte, largely adopted this perspective. Broszat would have agreed with Detlev Peukert that research on National Socialism had to shift its perspective from the institutions of power to 'the multiple ambiguities of "ordinary people" making their choices among the various greys of active consent, accommodation and nonconformity'.[54] Broszat's call for the historisation of Nazism only becomes understandable from this perspective. The national perspective, on the other hand, immediately invalidates the historisation approach since historisation becomes a byword for exculpation. Historisation, as Dan Diner has pointed out, may be a useful concept when a microhistorical and everyday life perspective on Nazism is adopted. The Holocaust, however, needs its own *Historik*.[55]

A number of historians have firmly rejected the argument that Nazism was a period of conscious modernisation. Roth has traced in detail the way in which the revisionists 'misappropriated and instrumentalised' modernisation theories in their effort to 'erect a system of "scientific" rehabilitation' of National Socialism.[56] Hans Mommsen has interpreted the National Socialist dictatorship as 'fake modernisation', arguing that 'a strong backward tendency lay hidden behind the facade of the new Reich'.[57] According to Mommsen, Zitelmann's willingness to interpret even the most brutal exploitation as value-free modernisation robs the historian of all capabilities seriously to analyse the structure of the Nazi regime.[58] Peter Reichel called the regime 'inimical to and incapable of modernisation'.[59] Norbert Frei has condemned the historisation approach of Zitelmann and company as misleading and apologetic. In his view the term modernisation does not do justice to the reality of the National Socialist regime: 'The Nazis did not lend an almost metaphysical credence to their claim to power by referring to what was timely, progressive and innovative, but by speaking up for "eternal values", the overcoming of all history and the "Thousand Year Reich". Hitler knew the word "modern" almost exclusively in a pejorative sense.'[60] Axel Schildt has perceived in the debates about the modernity of National Socialism the latest form of the *Historikerstreit*. He has insisted that the civilising, democratic and humanising elements of modernity stood in direct contrast to the amoral elements of alleged modernity under National Socialism.[61] Similarly, Michael Schneider has rejected efforts to reduce the term modernity to quantifiable technical rationality. He has written one of the most comprehensive indictments of the new right's attempts to use 'historisation' as a pretext for renationalisation.[62] The renewed efforts to dispose of National Socialism via modernisation theory should be seen as the ultimate precondition for the emergence of a new nationalism in Germany. Those, like Zitelmann, who loudly proclaim the modernity of National Socialism are first and foremost bent on a reappropriation of the National Socialist period for the whole of German national history.

Such 'normalisation' of German history through the back door of historisation has been profoundly disturbed by the Goldhagen debate which lasted from April to October 1996.[63] Goldhagen's study on the perpetrators of the Holocaust has been met by overwhelming condemnation by German historians from the right and from the left.[64] The criticism centred on his attempt to explain the Holocaust with the 'eliminationist mind-set' of 'the Germans'. A widespread and deeply ingrained anti-Semitism made all Germans potential 'willing executioners' of Hitler's paranoia. In fact, the Holocaust appears as a German 'national project'. Such a thesis which comes perilously close to the old argument about German collective guilt, was overwhelmingly rejected as too monocausal and conceptually weak. It rests on a number of circular arguments which are not backed up by sufficient evidence to justify the sweeping generalisations about German society at large. Whilst Goldhagen is no doubt justified in pointing towards the long tradition of anti-Semitism in German political culture, the question remains whether nineteenth-century German anti-Semitism was anymore violent or widespread as anti-Semitism in other Western European societies (and it was almost certainly less widespread and violent than in Eastern Europe).[65] Furthermore, the special circumstances of the Second World War, under which the perpetrators of the Holocaust acted, are not considered at all by Goldhagen. The more differentiated picture that Christopher Browning painted about the motives of those involved in the mass killings is papered over in Goldhagen's desire to demonstrate that the 'eliminationst anti-Semitism' of the Germans was the sole reason for the killing fields.[66]

Whilst the book most certainly rests on weak conceptual foundations, it is interesting to note that so few historians have commented on the fact that the ultimate intention of Goldhagen's study, namely to get to know the mentality of the killers and to ask why and under which circumstances 'ordinary' people become unscrupulous mass murderers, is a valid one. His case studies on the police battailons, the work camps and the death marches focus deliberately on the individual perpetrators, their barbarity and the choices they made. Such an angle on the Holocaust has been largely neglected by Holocaust research so far, and the only two studies which exist are by American scholars, not by Germans.[67] In this context, Hans-Ulrich Wehler has rightly pointed out that the rejection of Goldhagen's simplistic and monocausal explanation for the Holocaust should not lead to an automatic rejection of the very important questions raised in sections three to five of the book, i.e., in the case studies about the perpetrators. Which were the cultural and social preconditions which led to the brutalisation of German society under Nazism? Why do 'ordinary' human beings suddenly become mass murderers? Here, he sees a challenge for any future research about the Holocaust.[68] If historians begin to ask for the mentality of the perpetrators, then this raises another very important question. How should any such study portray its evidence, tell its story, depict the unspeakable. It is the question of which style of historical writing is best suited for the task in hand or rather whether there is an adequate style of historical writing at all. Interestingly, Goldhagen has been attacked for his alleged 'pornography of horror'. It was his technique of filmic description which invited comparisons between his book and Spielberg's film *Schindler's List*, or even the Hollywood series 'Holocaust'.[69]

Yet, quite apart from the debates about the scholarly merits of Goldhagen's volume, the question about its moral-political implications is the one which really interests us in the context of German historical consciousness post-1990. First of all, the moral-political implications of the book are clearly different for different national contexts. As Gulie Ne'eman Arad has pointed out, Goldhagen's book served a political-moral function in the United States: it promises to underpin the claims of American Jewry for a special status amongst the increasingly diverse ethnic groups who claim to be victims of one sort or another.[70] What does the debate and the reception of this study in Germany tell us about contemporary German identity and its relationship towards the Holocaust? Some commentators, in particular those on the left, have hailed Goldhagen's book, because they perceived it as a means by which to defeat those who want to 'normalise' German history by 'historising' National Socialism.[71] True enough, commentators on the right have condemned the book for its political implications: at a time when it had just seemed possible to overcome the talk about the German *Sonderweg* and to stop *Vergangenheitsbewältigung*, Goldhagen's book was greeted with dismay by those who wanted more 'normality' for the Germans.[72] Hanno Loewy has pointed out that 'the reactions [against Goldhagen] were so strong, as if the nation had been attacked.'[73] Indeed, there was a marked difference between the often arrogant dismissal of Goldhagen's book by professional German historians and the reaction of the German public. Whilst the Historians' Association which met in September 1996 refused to discuss Goldhagen,[74] 'ordinary Germans' showed more interest.

When Goldhagen attended public meetings in Hamburg, Berlin and Frankfurt in September 1996, the halls were packed and the audiences widely sympathetic. Both Volker Ullrich in *Die Zeit* and Frank Schirrmacher in the *FAZ* have talked about his visit as a 'triumph' *(Triumphzug)*.[75] Hence it seems that efforts in the 1970s and 1980s to develop a culture of remembrance vis-à-vis the victims of National Socialist rule in Germany and in particular the Jewish victims, have had some positive effect. The memory of the Holocaust seems to be part and parcel of many Germans' identity today, and the question of why it could happen and, more to the point, why it could happen in Germany, does not seem to have lost any of its relevance. Eighty-thousand copies of the German translation were sold after the first four weeks. In the *Spiegel* bestseller list of 16 December 1996 Goldhagen's book came second, beating Kohl's *Ich wollte Deutschlands Einheit* into third place. It seems as though the book has successfully torn down the intellectual barriers which had been erected to carefully protect German national identity, namely the distinction between the evil Nazis and the good Germans.[76] Whilst this is indeed a hopeful sign that anyone intent on pushing the twelve darkest years of German history to the sidelines, might be up against an impossible task, things unfortunately are not as straightforward as this.

At the end of the day, the outcome of the debate has been ambiguous. First of all, one cannot possibly imply that the strong interest of tens of thousands of Germans in Goldhagen's book is evidence for the willingness of all Germans to confront the Nazi past (just as Goldhagen cannot conclude that the tens of thousands of 'ordinary Germans' who massacred Jews in the Second World War were representative of a whole people.). More importantly still, if Goldhagen's book rests on weak conceptual foundations, might conservatives not hope for an opportunity to dismiss not only the scholarly but also the moral-political intention of the author? By rejecting the idea of the Holocaust as 'national project' of the Germans, conservatives will find it easy to evade the central question of the link which exists between an established anti-Semitism in German society long before 1933 and the Holocaust.[77] Whilst his German publisher, Wolf-Jobst Siedler, has publicly denied any political motivation in publishing a book which must be deeply antagonistic to a man co-authoring Baring's *Deutschland – was nun?*,[78] one cannot help wondering whether Siedler does not perceive Goldhagen's book as a subtle way of attacking those scholars who have already established, in a more differentiated and complex way, that large sections of the German population were involved in the criminal activities of the regime, and notably in the Holocaust.[79] In this respect, the Goldhagen book might in the long run prove a burden rather than an ally for those who want to ensure that the memory of the Holocaust and of the National Socialist regime more generally remains prominent in the reunified Germany.

A 'historised' National Socialism, be it in the form of interpreting it as legitimate anti-Bolshevism, or as a consciously modernising regime have been identified as two distinct efforts to change the impact of the 'German catastrophe' on German historical consciousness. A third effort has combined the old Hitler demonology with equally worn-out attempts to portray the Germans as victims of the Second World War. Stürmer has once again characterised Hitler as the 'incarnation of evil'[80], whilst for Hildebrand National Socialism developed from German history but ended up far beyond the original preconditions and aims of the national tradition.[81] Schöllgen has written of Hitler's foreign policy as 'a radical break with the foreign policy traditions of the Weimar Republic and of Prussia-Germany'.[82] Furthermore, Nolte has castigated German historians for serving the purpose of Allied re-education policy 'all too quickly and obsequiously' by one-sidedly writing German national history as the pre-history of National Socialism.[83]

Although a broad consensus exists amongst German historians on Nazi Germany's responsibility for the outbreak of the Second World War, occasional caveats keep creeping in. The appeasement policy of the West, it has been emphasised, has at least to share the burden of not preventing the Second World War when it was still possible to do so.[84] Some historians have laid ultimate responsibility for Hitler's rise to power firmly at the doorstep of the Allies. Ignoring much of the research of the 1970s and 1980s on the topic, they have argued that the end of the Weimar Republic was inextricably linked to the 'collective humiliation' of the Versailles Treaty.[85] The doyen of extreme right-wing conservatism in Germany, Armin Mohler declared unequivocally: 'The Third Reich was not the product of a "German character" or any other predisposition – it was clearly the child of the Treaty of Versailles.'[86]

Allegations of shared guilt are not only levelled against the Western democracies. Time and again conservative historians have dug out the tattered theory that Hitler fought a preventive war against the Soviet Union in 1941.[87] More recently Werner Maser, professor of history at the University of Halle, has argued that by 1939 Hitler was thinking of a peaceful settlement between Nazi Germany and the

Soviet Union, whilst Stalin had been intent on waging war on Germany, even if this meant breaking his word.[88] Joachim Hoffmann, historian at the Militärgeschichtliches Forschungsamt in Potsdam, has argued that Stalin had planned a 'war of conquest' against Germany. Hitler, in his analysis, only narrowly forestalled Stalin's intentions. Furthermore Hoffmann has not hesitated to positively contrast the German army's behaviour in the Soviet Union with that of the Red Army in Germany. The latter allegedly led a 'war of annihilation' against the whole German people. In Noltian fashion, Hoffmann also has doubted the number of Holocaust victims. The number of six million, he has asserted, is mere Soviet propaganda.[89] In Geiss's recent writings German agency in the outbreak of the Second World War has vanished behind technological prowess: 'The industrial-technical potential that had been assembled in Germany since 1800 exploded for the second time within twenty-five years.'[90] Against the background of such bizarre comments, Weißmann has written somewhat mysteriously on the subject of the outbreak of the Second World War: 'As with the First World War it was not the German leadership alone who made politics …'.[91] As Wolfgang Wippermann has pointed out, a new 'war guilt lie' has been in the making over recent years.[92]

Most of the nationalist myths about the Second World War have long been revealed as utter nonsense. On the occassion of the fiftieth anniversary of the outbreak of the Second World War, a number of historians made it perfectly clear that it was cool-headed planning on the part of the German government and its thirst for world domination which led to war.[93] For Schneider, any claims that Hitler's war against the Soviet Union was a preventive one derive from a 'German urge to relieve themselves of the Nazi burden'.[94] The criminal character of German warfare in the Second World War, and particularly on the Eastern Front, has been well documented.[95] The view of the Russians as 'sub-humans' and the picture painted of the Soviet Union in Nazi Germany contributed significantly to the barbarisation of warfare by German soldiers.[96] Furthermore, the entanglement of the German army in the machinery of the Holocaust increasingly is also being revealed in its full extent.[97]

However, the historiography of the Second World War has occasionally rediscovered the Germans as victims. General histories of the Second World War have always enjoyed a wide circulation amongst German readers. Here the war has often been portrayed from the position of the suffering German soldier. Atrocities of the Soviet army have been reported one-sidedly, and very little has been said of the trail of destruction and murder left by Germans in the Soviet Union and elsewhere.[98] Weißmann has portrayed the Ger-

mans in the Second World War mainly as the victims of Allied warfare. By referring to the 'war of extermination' against the Germans[99]
he has appropriated to the Allied bombing campaign against German cities a term usually employed in the context of German warfare in the East. In the context of such statements Olaf Groehler has
warned against tendencies amongst the Germans on the fortieth
anniversary of the destruction of Dresden 'to resort to self-pity and
self-righteousness and to see themselves exclusively as victims'.[100]

Despite an official twenty-two volume history devoted to the subject of the German prisoners of war, published between 1962 and
1974, Albrecht Lehmann has recently come to the conclusion that
these German victims of war have been largely ignored by German
historiography. According to Lehmann, historians have been all too
willing to commit self-censorship in order not to embarrass the Western allies; their extremely negative treatment of the German prisoners of war was allegedly pushed under the carpet.[101] The German
prisoners of war, however, are not the only group whose fate – if we
are to believe historians like Lehmann or Theisen – has been met
with public silence after 1945. The expulsion of Germans from Eastern Europe has remained for some an 'unmastered chapter in European contemporary history. The general ignorance about the crimes
committed against millions of German refugees and expellees reveals
the shortcomings of teachers, historians, politicians and journalists
who all failed to convey this. At the same time they also refused to
inform a wider public about the achievements and the fate of the historical regions of Eastern Germany, the Sudeten Germans and other
regions where expulsions had taken place.'[102] Is it characteristic of
the mood of the 1990s, one feels tempted to ask, that the refusal of a
reputable publishing house to go ahead with the publication of an
anti-Semitic and pseudo-historical account of Jewish Holocaust sur-
vivors' maltreatment of Germans on behalf of the Polish secret service in 1945, provoked storms of protest about censorship?[103]

On the occasion of the fiftieth anniversary of the end of the Second World War, Zitelmann and Nolte figured prominently on a list
of historians, publicists, journalists and politicians who published a
call 'Against Forgetting' in the *FAZ*.[104] Here they collectively
denounced the view that 8 May signified liberation from Nazi
tyranny. Instead they emphasised that Germans had been victims of
the Second World War and that 1945 marked the beginning of the
division of Germany and the 'expulsion terror' against Germans
from the 'German East'. Their evocation of 1945 in effect means
excluding the memory of the victims of Nazism and instead incor-
porating the memory of Germans as victims. However, it showed the

limited appeal of the new right on the conservative mainstream that this initiative turned out a complete failure.

Yet, in fact, any talk of liberation may equally serve the purpose of identifying Germans as victims of Nazism who had to be liberated from their 'evil oppressors'. Despite overwhelming evidence about the strength of the 'Hitler myth' (Ian Kershaw) up until and beyond 1945 and despite the lack of resistance to Nazism amongst wide sections of the German population, such an attitude has become all too visible in the urge of German politicians to participate in the victory celebrations of VE day in 1995. Both memories, the one of defeat and the one of liberation, thus derive their appeal from the longing of many Germans to deny their own share in Germany's historic guilt.[105] To speak of liberation only makes sense in that the total defeat in 1945 allowed Germans, at least in the West, to develop in the long term a civic political culture which resembled that of the Western democracies. In other words, 1945 can and should be stressed as a caesura which formed the necessary precondition for ending the fatal German *Sonderweg*.[106] The historiography on the Second World War, on expulsions and prisoners of war does not have significant blind spots nor should it have. It is important to write these histories, but in their proper context. This should include a recognition that nationalism was a prime cause of the widespread 'ethnic cleansing' carried out first by Germans and then against Germans during and after the Second World War.

Finally, re-interpretations of National Socialism have also included efforts to open up old debates on the history of the German resistance. The concentration on researching the German resistance has often been connected to conscious or unconscious efforts to sanitise German national history. The resistance has at times been portrayed almost as a German alibi for Auschwitz.[107] Certainly the historiography on the resistance still seems constantly threatened by the creation of historical myths, political instrumentalisation and apologetic tendencies.[108] A more pluralist understanding of the resistance movement against National Socialism, including for the first time a recognition of the Communist resistance, was only established in the Federal Republic during the 1970s and 1980s,[109] yet the most recent wave of literature has seen a return to the narrow concern with the national conservative opposition.[110] The social conservatives of the Kreisauer Kreis have been portrayed as models for the reunited Germany.[111] Once again one can find the neat distinction between good national conservative resistance and evil Communist treason which had been so characteristic of the work of Gerhard Ritter and Hans Rothfels.[112] Fest has written of the 'legacy of the resistance' lying in

its 'antitotalitarian consensus'. Naturally such an understanding has
to exclude the Communist resistance.[113]

The exclusion of the Communist resistance was also the focus of
a major controversy surrounding the Berlin permanent exhibition
'Resistance against National Socialism'. The defence minister Volker
Rühe, leading conservative politicians and a small number of historians joined to demand the removal of documents relating to the
'Nationalkomitee Freies Deutschland' (NKFD) and 'Bund deutscher
Offiziere' (BDO), in which leading Communists like Walter Ulbricht
and Wilhelm Pieck had worked against National Socialism. Right
from the very start the modest documentation of the Communist
resistance brought such massive protests from the political right that
Peter Steinbach seriously considered giving up the chairmanship of
the exhibition as personal animosities reached an unbearable level.[114]
When the exhibition finally opened in the summer of 1989 Georg
Meyer, a military historian from Freiburg, wrote a scathing article in
which he continued to classify the Communist resistance to National
Socialism as treason: 'The failure of NKFD and BDO lacked all dig-
nity.'[115] In 1994 the campaign reached new heights. For extreme
right-wingers, such as Zitelmann, Communists, of course, should
have no place at all in the memory of resistance against National
Socialism.[116] However, more mainstream conservatives also contributed. Konrad Repgen referred to the Communist resistance as
'desperados' and 'vassals of Stalin'.[117] For him they should never
have been in the exhibition because they are unsuitable role models
for today's Germans. The identity of young Germans, in other
words, should not even be touched by the memory of Communism.
Schwarz vehemently protested against 'the moral canonisation of
the Communist struggle'.[118] Horst Möller, in a different context, has
also argued that 'the contemporary democratic state should erect no
monument to those who simply wanted to replace the Nazi dictatorship by a Communist one.'[119]

However, Steinbach's refusal to give in to those party-political
demands and his courageous defence of the idea underlying the exhibition finally prevented the Communists from being completely
eliminated.[120] He was backed up by fellow historians who warned
against 'dividing the resistance into the "right" and "wrong" dead.'[121]
The attack on the Communist resistance was, for Karl-Heinz Janßen,
a sign that 'the restoration is on the march' again.[122] Hans Mommsen
and Christoph Kleßmann have both warned of harking back to the
old models of the 1950s. The Communists, they emphasised, had
been an integral part of the German resistance against National
Socialism.[123] For Faulenbach the renewed efforts to belittle the Com-

munist and indirectly all left-wing resistance to Hitler signals 'a problematic narrowing down of the picture of the resistance which is
clearly influenced by political interests.'[124] From an East German
perspective Werner Bramke has pointed out that it would be incomprehensible for many people in the former GDR if the Communist
resistance was to be erased from public memory.[125] A recent com-
pendium on the resistance published by the semi-official Bundeszentrale für politische Bildung as well as a number of other publications
have testified to the plurality of views on the German resistance.[126]

Most of the re-interpretations of National Socialism that have
been discussed above have been neither completely new nor particularly original. A wide range of professional historians in Germany
have expressed, in one form or another, their conviction that 'the
legacy of the Nazi past and its crimes will have to remain an important part of any German identity.'[127] Yet, after 1990, a small number
of new right historians, sometimes with the help of more mainstream
conservative allies, have attempted to pursue their agenda of renationalisation of historical consciousness via a whole variety of revisionist accounts of Germany's darkest years. Theories of and
arguments about a 'European civil war', the need for historising the
Nazi past, 'value-free modernisation', the 'preventive war' against
the Soviet Union, the Germans as victims of the Second World War
and the centrality of the 'national opposition' to Hitler all have their
place in these apologetic narratives. The same agenda of renationalising German historical consciousness has, it will be argued in the
next chapter, informed endeavours to reassess both the history and
the historiography of the GDR in the reunified Germany.

Notes

1. Ernst Nolte, *Streitpunkte: heutige und künftige Kontroversen um den Nationalsozialismus,* Frankfurt-on-Main, 1993, p. 423.
2. See his discussion of Nazi thinkers in Ernst Nolte, *Geschichtsdenken im 20. Jahrhundert. Von Max Weber bis Hans Jonas,* Berlin, 1991.
3. Christian Striefler, *Kampf um die Macht. Kommunisten und Nationalsozialisten am
   Ende der Weimarer Republik,* Berlin, 1993, p. 15.
4. Stürmer, *Die Grenzen der Macht,* p. 112.
5. Weißmann, *Rückruf,* p. 76.
6. Rainer Zitelmann, 'Am Stammtisch der Geschichte', *Die Welt,* 9 Jan. 1993, p. G1.
7. Volker Kronenberg, 'Fragen muß erlaubt sein', *Die politische Meinung,* vol. 40,
   May 1995, pp. 35-43.

8. Joachim Fest, 'Glückwunsch für Ernst Nolte', in: Thomas Nipperdey, Anselm Doering-Manteuffel and Hans-Ulrich Thamer (eds), *Weltbürgerkrieg der Ideologien. Antworten an Ernst Nolte*, Berlin, 1993, p. 16.
9. Horst Möller, 'Ernst Nolte und das liberale System', in: Nipperdey et al., *Weltbürgerkrieg*, pp. 58, 71.
10. Hans-Ulrich Wehler, 'Die Kontinuität der Unbelehrbarkeit. Ernst Noltes Nationalsozialismus – nur Reaktion auf den Bolschewismus?', in: Lohmann (ed.), *Extremismus der Mitte*, p. 143.
11. Wehler, *Die Gegenwart als Geschichte*, p. 193.
12. Ibid., p. 139.
13. Eberhard Jäckel, *Die zweifache Vergangenheit. Zum Vergleich politischer Systeme*, Bonn, 1992, pp. 6-8.
14. Heinrich August Winkler, 'Appell an die Angst', *Die Zeit*, 3 Dec. 1993, p. 24.
15. Rolf Richter in the discussion 'German History and German Nationalism. Seven Historians Give their Views', *Debatte*, vol. 1, 1993, p. 12.
16. Christian Meier, 'Totales Verwirrspiel', *Die Zeit*, 4 Nov. 1994, p. 16.
17. Nolte, *Streitpunkte*, p. 280.
18. Ernst Nolte, 'Ein historisches Recht Hitlers?', *Der Spiegel*, 3 Oct. 1994, p. 85. See also: idem, *Streitpunkte*, p. 308, 312.
19. Nolte, *Streitpunkte*, p. 373.
20. Ibid., p. 396.
21. Ernst Nolte, 'Ein Gesetz für das Außergesetzliche', *FAZ*, 23 August 1994, p. 7; compare also Gunter Hofmann, 'Eine Obsession', *Die Zeit*, 26 Aug. 1994, p. 8; Thomas Assheuer, 'Der infame Konjunktiv', *FR*, 27 Aug. 1994, p. 7. Julius H. Schoeps, 'Treitschke Redivivus? Ernst Nolte und die Juden', *Zeitschrift für Religions- und Geistesgeschichte*, vol. 40, 1988, pp. 170-6 already compared Nolte to Treitschke who, like Nolte disclaimed being an anti-Semite whilst fostering anti-Semitism via his publications.
22. Armin Mohler, *Der Nasenring: die Vergangenheitsbewältigung vor und nach dem Fall der Mauer*, Munich, 1991, p. 134.
23. Christian Streit, 'Ostkrieg, Antibolschewismus und "Endlösung"', *GG*, vol. 17, 1991, pp. 242-55.
24. Wolfgang Benz, 'Realitätsverweigerung als antisemitisches Prinzip: Die Leugnung des Völkermords', in: idem (ed.), *Antisemitismus in Deutschland. Zur Aktualität eines Vorurteils*, Munich, 1995, p. 137 f.
25. On tendencies in Holocaust research see also Raul Hilberg, 'Tendenzen in der Holocaust Forschung', in: Walter H. Pehle (ed.), *Der historische Ort des Nationalsozialismus*, Frankfurt-on-Main, 1990, pp. 71-80.
26. Thus the view of Wolfgang Benz, 'Rechte testen das Tabu', *Der Spiegel*, 30 January 1995, p. 39. See also the statistical results of Werner Bergmann and Rainer Erb, 'Wie antisemitisch sind die Deutschen? Meinungsumfragen 1945-1994', in: Benz (ed.), *Antisemitismus in Deutschland*, pp. 47-63, where they come to the conclusion that anti-Semitism has gained ground especially amongst the young in the reunited Germany. Manfred Brusten and Bernd Winkelmann, 'Wie denken deutsche Studenten in "West" und "Ost" nach der Wiedervereinigung über den Holocaust', *TAJB*, vol. 23, 1994, pp. 461-86 come to a different conclusion by looking only at students. See also: Werner Bergmann, 'Anti-Semitism and Xenophobia in the East German Länder', *German Politics*, vol. 3, 1994, pp. 265-76.
27. Nolte, 'Ein historisches Recht', p. 97. See also the representative survey published in *Der Spiegel*, 8 May 1995, p. 77, in which 41 percent of those questioned agreed that National Socialism had positive aspects. Only 55 percent argued that National Socialism had overwhelmingly negative aspects.
28. Rainer Zitelmann, *Hitler. Selbstverständnis eines Revolutionärs*, Hamburg, 1987.

29. Ralf Dahrendorf, *Gesellschaft und Demokratie in Deutschland*, Munich, 1965; David Schoenbaum, *Hitler's Social Revolution*, New York, 1966.
30. Ernst Nolte, 'Europäische Revolutionen des 20. Jahrhunderts', in: idem, *Lehrstück oder Tragödie*.
31. Rainer Zitelmann, 'Am Stammtisch der Geschichte', *Die Welt*, 9 Jan. 1993; idem, 'Das Erbe der Diktaturen', *Rheinischer Merkur*, 18 Oct. 1991, p. 3.
32. See, for example, Weißmann, *Rückruf*; Hacke, *Weltmacht*; and Hans-Hellmuth Knütter, *Die Faschismuskeule. Das letzte Aufgebot der Linken*, Frankfurt-on-Main 1994.
33. Karl Heinz Roth, 'Erfolglose Solidaritätskampagne für den rechtsextremistischen Historiker Rainer Zitelmann', *1999*, vol. 9, 1994, pp. 149-51.
34. Joachim Fried, who has written another volume in the *Propyläen Geschichte Deutschlands* has attacked the affair as 'scandal' and a 'stage-managed coup'. See 'Fried: "Skandal" war "inszenierter Coup"', *FR*, 4 Dec. 1995. Dieter Groh, one of the general editors of the series, has publicly distanced himself from Weißmann's book.
35. Karlheinz Weißmann, *Der Weg in den Abgrund – Deutschland unter Hitler 1933 bis 1945*, Berlin, 1995.
36. Wolfgang Wippermann, 'Ein Abgrund. Deutsche Geschichtsrevision im "Propyläen"-Verlag', *FR*, 9 Jan. 1996. For highly critical reviews of Weißmann see also Michael Jeismann, 'Kuckucksei', *FAZ*, 24 Nov. 1995; Walther Hofer, 'Der deutsche Arbeiter, der englische Lord', *FAZ*, 13 Feb. 1996; Jost Dülffer, 'Nicht ableugnen, aber verharmlosen', *SZ*, 20 Dec. 1995; Götz Aly, 'Die Banalisierung des Bösen', *Die Woche*, 8 Dec. 1995.
37. Rainer Zitelmann, 'Die totalitäre Seite der Moderne', in: Michael Prinz and Rainer Zitelmann (eds), *Nationalsozialismus und Modernisierung*, Darmstadt, 1991, pp. 1-20.
38. Central texts are Rainer Zitelmann, Eckhard Jesse and Enrico Syring (eds), *Die Schatten der Vergangenheit. Impulse zur Historisierung des Nationalsozialismus*, Frankfurt-on-Main, 1990; Prinz and Zitelmann (eds), *Nationalsozialismus und Modernisierung*; Michael Prinz, 'Der Nationalsozialismus – eine "Braune Revolution"?', in: Manfred Hettling (ed.), *Revolutionen in Deutschland 1789-1989*, Göttingen, 1991, pp. 70-89. It should be noted that only some of the contributors in the edited volumes by Prinz and Zitelmann seem to share the theoretical assumptions of the editors.
39. The denial is most explicit in Michael Prinz, 'Nachwort: Einige Bemerkungen zur neueren Debatte über Modernisierung und Nationalsozialismus', in: Prinz and Zitelmann (eds), *Nationalsozialismus und Modernisierung*, 2nd edn, Darmstadt, 1994, p. 355.
40. Ibid., p. 349.
41. Karlheinz Weißmann, 'Auf dem Sonderweg verirrt', *Rheinischer Merkur*, 28 Feb. 1992, p. 3.
42. Nolte, *Streitpunkte*, p. 399 f.
43. Detlev J.K. Peukert, 'The Genesis of the "Final Solution" from the Spirit of Science', in: David Crew (ed.), *Nazism and German Society 1933-1945*, London, 1994, pp. 274-99; Götz Aly and Susanne Heim, *Vordenker der Vernichtung. Auschwitz und die deutschen Pläne für eine neue europäische Ordnung*, Hamburg, 1991; Karl Heinz Roth (ed.), *'Autonomie', Erfassung zur Vernichtung. Von der Sozialhygiene zum 'Gesetz über Sterbehilfe'*, Berlin, 1984.
44. Joachim Lehmann, 'Herbert Backe – Technokrat und Agrarideologe', in: Ronald Smelser, Enrico Syring and Rainer Zitelmann (eds), *Die braune Elite II. 21 biographische Skizzen*, Darmstadt, 1993, p. 8.
45. Friedrich Lenger, *Werner Sombart 1863-1941. Eine Biographie*, Munich, 1995, p. 387.
46. Kurt Sontheimer, 'Wider die Leisetreterei der Historiker', *Die Zeit*, 4 Nov. 1994, p. 15 (Beilage).

47. Friedrich Lenger, 'Wider die falschen Eindeutigkeiten', *Die Zeit*, 25 Nov. 1994, p. 65.

48. Eckhard Jesse, 'Vergangenheitsbewältigung und politische Kultur', *Politische Bildung*, vol. 23, 1990; Rainer Zitelmann, 'Vom Umgang mit der NS-Vergangenheit', in: Rolf Italiaander (ed.), *Bewußtseins-Notstand. Thesen von 60 Zeitzeugen*, Düsseldorf, 1990, pp. 69-79; Mohler, *Der Nasenring*, p. 252. See also Hans-Ulrich Thamer, 'Nationalsozialismus und deutscher Nationalstaat', in: Krüger (ed.), *Deutschland*, pp. 125-38.

49. Geiss, *Der Hysterikerstreit*, p. 229 f.

50. Backes et al. (eds), *Die Schatten* is even dedicated to Broszat.

51. Broszat, *Nach Hitler*, pp. 98 ff. committed historiography to be 'resolutely self-critical' and aiming at 'radical national self-criticism'.

52. See the exchange between the two: Martin Broszat, Saul Friedländer, 'Um die "Historisierung des Nationalsozialismus". Ein Briefwechsel', *VfZ*, vol. 36, 1988, p. 340.

53. Christian Meier, 'Der Historiker Martin Broszat', in: Klaus-Dietmar Henke and Claudio Natoli (eds), *Mit dem Pathos der Nüchternheit: Martin Broszat, das Institut für Zeitgeschichte und die Erforschung des Nationalsozialismus*, Frankfurt-on-Main, 1991, p. 23 f.

54. Peukert, *Inside Nazi Germany*, p. 243.

55. Dan Diner, 'Perspektivenwahl und Geschichtserfahrung. Bedarf es einer besonderen Historik des Nationalsozialismus', in: Pehle (ed.), *Der historische Ort*, pp. 94-113.

56. Karl Heinz Roth, 'Revisionist Tendencies in Historical Research into German Fascism', *IRSH*, vol. 39, 1994, pp. 433, 444. See also idem, 'Verklärung des Abgrunds. Zur nachträglichen "Revolutionierung" der NS-Diktatur durch die Gruppe um Rainer Zitelmann', *1999*, vol. 7, 1992, pp. 7-11.

57. Hans Mommsen, 'Nationalsozialismus als vorgetäuschte Modernisierung', in: Pehle (ed.), *Der historische Ort*, p. 43.

58. Hans Mommsen, 'Noch einmal: Nationalsozialismus und Modernisierung', *GG*, vol. 21, 1995, pp. 398 f.

59. Peter Reichel, '"Vergangenheitstraum", "Fortgeschrittenheit" und Völkermord. Zur Diskusion um Modernität und Modernisierung im NS-Staat', *Historicum*, vol. 27, 1991, pp. 18-26, quote on p. 24.

60. Norbert Frei, 'Wie modern war der Nationalsozialismus?', *GG*, vol. 19, 1993, p. 385. See also his devastating critique of Zitelmann et al. (eds), *Die Schatten* under the title 'Die neue Unbefangenheit', *FR*, 5 Jan. 1991.

61. Axel Schildt, 'NS-Regime, Modernisierung und Moderne. Anmerkungen zur Hochkonjunktur einer andauernden Diskussion', *TAJB*, vol. 23, 1994, p. 22.

62. Michael Schneider, 'Nationalsozialismus und Modernisierung? Probleme einer Neubewertung des "Dritten Reiches"', *AfS*, vol. 32, 1992, pp. 541-5. See also his systematic refutation of new-right thinking on National Socialism in idem, *"Volkspädagogik" von rechts. Ernst Nolte, die Bemühungen um die "Historisierung" des Nationalsozialismus und die "selbstbewußte Nation"*, Bonn, 1995.

63. Daniel Jonah Goldhagen, *Hitler's Willing Executioners. Ordinary Germans and the Holocaust*, New York, 1996 provoked a controversy before it was even translated into German. The debate was started by Volker Ullrich, 'Hitlers willige Mordgesellen', *Die Zeit*, 12 April 1996, who predicted that this book would lead to a new *Historikerstreit*. The intellectual standing of this weekly in Germany almost ensured that this became a self-fulfilling prophecy. See Julius H. Schoeps (ed.), *Ein Volk von Mördern? Die Dokumentation zur Goldhagen-Kontroverse um die Rolle der Deutschen im Holocaust*, Hamburg, 1996.

64. It is remarkable in itself, how few historians of the right have commented on Goldhagen. One example is Michael Wolffsohn, 'Metaphysische Feinde', *Rheinischer*

Merkur, 26 April 1996. Most of the criticisms came from the left. See Norbert Frei, 'Ein Volk von "Endlösern"?', *SZ,* 13/14 April 1996; Hans Mommsen, 'Schuld der Gleichgültigen', *SZ,* 20/21 June 1996; idem, 'Die dünne Patina der Zivilisation', *Die Zeit,* 30 August 1996. The ultra-intentionalist Eberhard Jäckel, who found himself on the left in the *Historikerstreit,* condemned Goldhagen's book in no uncertain terms. See his review 'Einfach ein schlechtes Buch', *Die Zeit,* 17 May 1996.

65. Whilst Lothar Kettenacker denies that anti-Semitism in Germany had peculiarly strong roots in German political culture around the turn of the twentieth century in his review in *GHIL Bulletin,* vol. 28, no. 3, 1996, p.74, I would be more inclined to agree with Julius H. Schoeps, 'Vom Rufmord zum Massenmord', *Die Zeit,* 26 April 1996 that we need to know more about the precise nature and the extent of anti-Semitism in Imperial Germany.

66. Christopher Browning, *Ordinary Men: Reserve Batallion 101 and the Final Solution in Poland,* New York, 1992 stressed that the transformation of caring family men into barbarbians had multiple causes and thus were not solely linked to an 'eliminationist mind-set'. For the differences between Browning and Goldhagen see Christopher Browning, 'Dämonisierung erklärt nichts', *Die Zeit,* 19 April 1996.

67. However, two promising new German studies are Dieter Pohl, *Nationalsozialistische Judenverfolgung in Ostgalizien 1941-1944. Organisation und Durchführung eines staatlichen Massenverbrechens,* Munich, 1996; Thomas Sandkühler, *'Endlösung in Galizien'. Der Judenmord in Ostpolen und die Rettungsinitiativen von Berthold Beitz 1941-1944,* Bonn, 1996.

68. Hans-Ulrich Wehler, 'Wie ein Stachel im Fleisch', *Die Zeit,* 24 May 1996. This methodological challenge of Goldhagen's book is also picked up in Ingrid Gilcher-Holtey, 'Die Mentalität der Täter', *Die Zeit,* 7 June 1996.

69. A lucid discussion of these aesthetic problems can be found in Ulrich Raulff, 'Herz der Finsternis', *FAZ,* 16 August 1996.

70. Gulie Ne'eman Arad, 'Ein amerikanischer Alptraum', *FR,* 14 May 1996.

71. Thus already Volker R. Berghahn, 'The Road to Extermination', *The New York Times,* 14 April 1996. See also Hannes Heer, 'Die große Tautologie', *die tageszeitung,* 4 Sept. 1996, and the reaction of Wolfgang Wippermann cited in Volker Ullrich, 'Goldhagen und die Deutschen', *Die Zeit,* 13 Sept. 1996.

72. Frank Schirrmacher, 'Hitlers Code', *FAZ,* 15 April 1996; Jost Nolte, 'Sisyphos ist Deutscher', *Die Welt,* 16 April 1996.

73. Hanno Loewy, 'Wider die allzu schnelle Erledigung', *FR,* 15 June 1996.

74. For an acerbic portray of a 'conservative' and 'self-satisfied' profession see Gunter Hofmann, 'Die Welt ist, wie sie ist', *Die Zeit,* 27 Sept. 1996.

75. Ullrich, 'Goldhagen'; Frank Schirrmacher, 'Wunderheiler Goldhagen', *FAZ,* 13 Sept. 1996.

76. Wolfgang Sofsky, 'Normale Massenmörder', *Neue Züricher Zeitung,* 10/11 August 1996.

77. Ulrich Herbert, 'Aus der Mitte der Gesellschaft', *Die Zeit,* 14 June 1996.

78. 'Gespräch mit Wolf Jobst Siedler. Der Verleger soll sich hüten, ein Missionar zu sein', *FAZ,* 24 August 1996.

79. The book was, after all, rejected by a number of German publishing houses with more liberal reputations including Fischer and C.H. Beck, who concluded that the scholarly merits of the volume did not justify publication.

80. Stürmer, *Die Grenzen der Macht,* p. 114.

81. Hildebrand, *Das vergangene Reich,* p. 893.

82. Schöllgen, *Die Macht,* p. 94.

83. Nolte, *Lehrstück oder Tragödie,* p. 100.

84. Schöllgen, *Die Macht,* p. 91. See also Hans-Adolf Jacobsen, 'Der zweite Weltkrieg – eine historische Bilanz', *aus politik und zeitgeschichte,* 10 Feb. 1995, p. 4.

85. Weißmann, *Rückruf*, p. 83; Hagen Schulze, 'German Unification', p. 13; Guido Knopp and Ekkehard Kuhn, *Die deutsche Einheit. Traum und Wirklichkeit*, Erlangen, 1990.

86. Mohler, *Der Nasenring*, p. 82.

87. Ernst Topitsch, *Stalins Krieg. Die sowjetische Langzeitstrategie gegen den Westen als rationale Machtpolitik*, 3rd edn, 1990 (first published in 1985). See also: Klaus Hornung, 'Der Teufelspakt', *Rheinischer Merkur*, 18 Aug. 1989, p. 4; Klaus Hildebrand, 'Krieg im Frieden und Frieden im Krieg. Über das Problem der Legitimität in der Geschichte der Staatengesellschaft 1931-41', *HZ*, vol. 244, 1987, p. 23 f.

88. Werner Maser, *Der Wortbruch. Hitler, Stalin und der Zweite Weltkrieg*, Munich, 1994.

89. Jürgen Hoffmann, *Stalins Vernichtungskrieg 1941-1945*, Munich, 1995.

90. Geiss, *Die deutsche Frage*, p. 76.

91. Weißmann, *Rückruf*, p. 85.

92. Wolfgang Wippermann, 'Die Wiederkehr der Propaganda. Einige Anmerkungen zur grotesken Debatte um die "Kriegsschuldlüge"', *FR*, 31 Oct. 1995.

93. See, for example, Manfred Messerschmidt, 'Der Krieg, ein Kind des deutschen Machtwahns', *FR*, 1 Sept. 1989; Karl-Heinz Janßen, 'Griff nach der Weltherrschaft', *Die Zeit*, 18 Aug. to 8 Sept. 1989; Herman Graml, 'Der blutige Traum. Der nationalsozialistische Imperialismus als Ursache des zweiten Weltkrieges', *SZ*, 9/10 Sept. 1989.

94. Michael Schneider, 'Die Präventivkriegslüge', *Die Tageszeitung*, 17 Oct. 1989.

95. See especially amongst the most recent literature Reinhard Rürup and P. Jahn, *Erobern und Vernichten. Der Krieg gegen die Sowjetunion 1941-45*, Berlin, 1991; Mechthild Rössler and Sabine Schleiermacher (eds), *'Generalplan Ost'. Hauptlinine der nationalsozialistischen Planungs- und Vernichtungspolitik*, Berlin 1993; Hannes Heer and Klaus Naumann (eds), *Vernichtungskrieg. Verbrechen der Wehrmachtg 1941-44*, Hamburg, 1995.

96. Hans-Erich Volkmann (ed.), *Das Rußlandbild im Dritten Reich*, Cologne, 1994.

97. Hannes Heer, 'Killing Fields, Die Wehrmacht und der Holocaust', *Mittelweg*, vol. 36, no. 3, June/July 1994. Heer, historian at the Hamburg Institut für Sozialforschung, has also played a major role in organising the exhibition about the crimes of the German Wehrmacht which has been touring Germany since 1996 amidst massive protests by conservative and new-right historians and politicians alike.

98. A fine example is Günther H. Dahms, *Der zweite Weltkrieg in Text und Bild*, Munich, 1989.

99. Weißmann, *Rückruf*, p. 30.

100. Olaf Groehler, 'Dresden: Kleine Geschichte der Aufrechnung', *Blätter*, vol. 40, 1995, p. 141.

101. Albrecht Lehmann, 'Die Kriegsgefangenen', *aus politik und zeitgeschichte*, 10 Feb. 1995, pp. 13 f.

102. Alfred Theisen, 'Die Vertreibung der Deutschen – Ein unbewältigtes Kapitel europäischer Zeitgeschichte', *aus politik und zeitgeschichte*, 10 Feb. 1995, p. 20.

103. The book, John Sacks' *Auge um Auge. Opfer des Holocaust als Täter. Eine Parabel über die Gewalt* had already been heavily criticised when it first appeared in English. However, the Piper publishing house had agreed to bring out a paperback of the book. Only after initial protests (see Eike Geisel, 'Antisemitische Rohkost', *FR*, 26 Jan. 1995), the publisher announced that it would pulp the already printed books. However, after the protests against censorship, the book appeared under the above title in the small Hamburg-based Kabel publishing house late in 1995. The topic of Sack's book is, of course, an important one and an effort to deal with it adequately can be found in Helga Hirsch, 'Die Rache des Kommandanten', *Die Zeit*, 2 December 1994, pp. 20-3.

104. 'Gegen das Vergessen', *FAZ*, 7 April 1995. Compare also from the new right perspective the comments on 8 May in Rainer Zitelmann, *Wohin treibt unsere Republik?*, Berlin, 1995, p. 87.
105. Klaus Naumann, 'Die Sehnsucht des Mitläufers nach dem Schlußstrich', *Die Zeit*, 3 Feb. 1995, p. 46.
106. For such perspectives compare Hans Mommsen, 'Rückgriffe auf die deutsche Innerlichkeit', *FR*, 8 May 1995; Wilfried Loth, 'Epochenjahr 1945: Zäsuren und Optionen', *Blätter*, vol. 40, 1995, pp. 31-6; Rolf-Dieter Müller and Gerd R. Ueberschär (eds), *Kriegsende 1945. Die Zerstörung des Deutschen Reiches*, Frankfurt-on-Main, 1994, p. 7; Peter Bender, 'Ganz und gar am Ende. Über die Notwendigkeit der deutschen Niederlage 1945', *Merkur*, vol. 49, 1995, p. 450; Christian Krockow, *Von deutschen Mythen. Rückblick und Ausblick*, Stuttgart, 1995, pp. 141 ff.
107. Frank Stern, 'Wolfsschanze versus Auschwitz. Widerstand als deutsches Alibi', *ZfG*, vol. 42, 1994, pp. 645-50. On the apologetic tendencies of the early West German literature on the resistance see also Bernd Faulenbach, 'Auf dem Weg zu einer gemeinsamen Erinnerung? Das Bild vom deutschen Widerstand gegen den Nationalsozialismus nach den Erfahrungen von Teilung und Umbruch', *ZfG*, vol. 42, 1994, pp. 589-97.
108. Ulrich Heinemann, 'Arbeit am Mythos. Neuere Literatur zum bürgerlich-aristokratischen Widerstand gegen Hitler und zum 20. Juli 1944 (Teil 1)', *GG*, vol. 21, 1995, pp. 111-39.
109. Central texts include J. Schmädeke and P. Steinbach (eds), *Der Widerstand gegen den Nationalsozialismus. Die deutsche Gesellschaft und der Widerstand gegen Hitler*, 2nd edn, Munich, 1986; Hans Mommsen, 'Die Geschichte des deutschen Widerstands im Lichte der neueren Forschung', *aus politik und zeitgeschichte*, B50/1986, pp. 3-18.
110. Compare Wolfgang Venohr, *Patrioten gegen Hitler. Der Weg zum 20. Juli 1944*, Bergisch-Gladbach, 1994; Joachim Fest, *Staatsstreich. Der lange Weg zum 20. Juli*, Berlin, 1994; Marion Gräfin Dönhoff, *Um der Ehre willen*, Berlin, 1994; Ursula Adam (ed.), *Die 'Generalsrevolte'. Deutsche Emigranten und der 20. Juli 1944*, Berlin, 1994; Carl Hans von Hardenberg, *Ein deutsches Schicksal im Widerstand*, Berlin, 1994; Eberhard Zeller, *Oberst Claus Graf Stauffenberg*, Paderborn, 1994; Harald Steffahn, *Claus Schenk Graf von Stauffenberg*, Reinbek, 1994; Peter Hoffmann, *Claus Schenk Graf von Stauffenberg und seine Brüder*, Stuttgart, 1992; Bodo Scheurig, 'Der 20. Juli 1944 – damals und heute', *aus politik und zeitgeschichte*, 15 July 1994, pp. 15-21.
111. Klaus Hornung, 'Der Kreisauer Kreis und die deutsche Zukunft', *aus politik und zeitgeschichte*, 15 July 1994, pp. 22-30.
112. Ulrich Heinemann, 'Es gab nicht nur den 20. Juli', *Die Zeit*, no. 12, 18 March 1994, p. 20.
113. Joachim Fest, 'Die symbolische Tat', *FAZ*, 16 July 1994.
114. Marianne Heuwagen, 'Aufbegehren – akribisch dokumentiert', *SZ*, 19 July 1989.
115. Georg Meyer, 'Täuschung hinter Stacheldraht', *Rheinischer Merkur/Christ und Welt*, no. 30, 28 July 1989, pp. 3 f.
116. Zitelmann, *Republik*, p. 87.
117. Konrad Repgen, 'Keine Ehrung für Stalins Vasallen', *Rheinischer Merkur*, 24 June 1994, p. 3.
118. Hans-Peter Schwarz, 'Nach den Gedenktagen', *Die Welt*, 25 July 1994.
119. Cited in Carl Wilhelm Macke, 'Zeitgeschichte', *FR*, 29 August 1996, p. 8.
120. Peter Steinbach, 'Teufel Hitler – Beelzebub Stalin? Zur Kontroverse um die Darstellung des Nationalkomitees Freies Deutschland in der ständigen Ausstellung "Widerstand gegen den Nationalsozialismus" in der Gedenkstätte Deutscher Widerstand', *ZfG*, vol. 42, 1994, pp. 651-62.

121. Inge Marßolek, 'Der überwältigte Widerstand', *FR*, 16 July 1994.
122. Karl-Heinz Janßen, 'Ein Anschlag auf den Widerstand', *Die Zeit*, 8 July 1994, p. 25.
123. For their statements at a conference of the Protestant Academy Arnoldshain on '20 July: Resistance and German Identities' see the conference report in *FR*, 6 June 1994.
124. Faulenbach, 'Auf dem Weg zu einer gemeinsamen Erinnerung', pp. 594 f.
125. Werner Bramke, 'Das Bild vom deutschen Widerstand gegen den National-sozialismus nach den Erfahrungen von Teilung und Umbruch', *ZfG*, vol. 42, 1994, pp. 597-604.
126. Peter Steinbach and Johannes Tuchel (eds), *Widerstand gegen den Nationalsozialismus*, Bonn, 1994; Wolfgang Benz and Walter H. Pehle (eds), *Lexikon des deutschen Widerstandes*, Frankfurt-on-Main, 1994; Gerd R. Ueberschär, *Der 20. Juli 1944. Bewertung und Rezeption des deutschen Widerstandes gegen das NS-Regime*, Cologne, 1994.
127. Bernd Faulenbach, 'Probleme des Umgangs mit der Vergangenheit im vereinten Deutschland: Zur Gegenwartsbedeutung der jüngsten Debatte', in: Werner Weidenfeld (ed.), *Deutschland. Eine Nation – doppelte Geschichte. Materialien zum deutschen Selbstverständnis*, Cologne, 1993, p. 184.

Chapter 7

'THE SECOND GERMAN DICTATORSHIP'

The history of the GDR has become the most booming field of research within contemporary German historiography. Public interest in the topic has been high as it lends itself to being used as an effective weapon in the day-to-day political battles as well as in the broader identity debate, which since reunification has reemerged with renewed vigour. In this chapter I would like to assess the place of GDR history and historiography in efforts to renationalise the German identity. Therefore it will be necessary, first of all, to look at the revival after 1989 of totalitarianism as a framework for interpreting GDR history. Secondly, the often rather one-sided rewriting of GDR history will be discussed in the context of frequent calls for comparisons between 'the two German dictatorships'. Thirdly, the complete overhaul of the historical profession in the former GDR will be scrutinised and related to the attacks on alleged Communist fellow-travellers in West German historiography.

Conservative and new right historians have tirelessly reiterated their claim that Communist totalitarianism has to be the object of scholarly scrutiny to the same degree as the National Socialist period. For Schwarz the comparison of 'the two darkest totalitarianisms in European and German history'[1] has become one of the most pressing tasks for contemporary historiography. 'Playing down the most recent terror regime' in the GDR and 'measuring the German past with different yardsticks' as far as the 'red and brown dictatorships' are concerned, will no longer do, according to Weißmann.[2] Hockerts has criticised left-liberal historians for their alleged double standards which allowed them for years to castigate the Federal Republic's insufficient efforts to come to terms with the Nazi past whilst, post-1989, they were the first to show lenience towards representatives of the SED regime. For Hockerts this is clearly unacceptable and he has called on contemporary historians to demonstrate that both the Nazi and the SED dictatorships had many things in common.[3] According to Michael Wolffsohn, the 'red manure' equalled the brown.[4] Zitelmann has recommended returning to the anti-totalitarian consensus of the 1950s which allegedly had a clearer perception of the inner relationship between Nazism and Communism.[5] The comparison of dictatorships *(Diktaturenvergleich)* has become the catchword of the day, and the financially powerful *Volkswagenstiftung* was quick to announce plans to finance a major new project on the comparison of Nazi Germany and GDR.[6]

Calls for comparisons have led to a revival of the totalitarian paradigm. The 'quiet victory of a term'[7], however, throws up more problems than it promises to solve. In the forefront of those arguing for a renaissance of the concept has been Eckhard Jesse. For him, efforts to overcome the totalitarian paradigm in the 1970s and 1980s were unhelpful as they prevented the thorough analysis of government techniques in dictatorships.[8] Research on the GDR from this perspective has to be first and foremost research on the functioning of a dictatorship.[9] The Research Group on the SED State established at the Free University Berlin in 1992 has endorsed the totalitarian paradigm. Viewing the GDR as a 'totalitarian society', the Stasi and the SED as the 'central institutions' have been put in the centre of GDR research.[10] Castigating fellow historians for turning a blind eye to the evils of Communism, Geiss has demanded 'equidistance from both great totalitarianisms of our century'.[11] The GDR, in his view, is best described as 'left totalitarian rule'.[12]

Even amongst left-liberal historians there has been some support for the totalitarian paradigm. Kleßmann, in a far more differentiated look at the pros and cons of the totalitarian paradigm, has argued for its usage 'under well-defined conditions and as a means of seeking answers to very specific problems' in relation to the structures of political rule.[13] Kleßmann, trying to outline a comparative post-war national history, has insisted that the totalitarian paradigm alone will not be sufficient to explain the promises and failures in the history of the GDR. Indeed, in an article co-authored with Martin Sabrow, he insisted that 'the concept of dictatorship cannot be the general key to solve all problems of historical analysis' vis-à-vis GDR history.[14] Habermas has argued that 'the succession of two

dictatorships can serve as an instructive enforcement of what totalitarian systems have in common'.[15]

Other historians have been more forthright in their rejection of
revamped notions of totalitarianism. Whilst Kocka has pointed out
that comparing the Nazi and SED regimes might be helpful, if it
means more than simply equating the two, theories of totalitarianism,
in his opinion, remain too ideological and too vague to be of much
help.[16] Jäckel has warned of their inherent 'tendency to equate Nazism
with Communism'. He has pointed out that no aggressive wars and
no mass murder originated from the GDR. According to the Stuttgart
historian, the GDR also was never Stalinist in any real sense. The
Soviet purges of the 1930s found no real counterpart in the GDR.
And finally, Jäckel has reminded his readers that the GDR always
adhered to the humanitarian traditions of the German labour movement which were based on the vision of a better world. In stark contrast, National Socialism never pretended to be anything other than
the incarnation of the most base inhumanity.[17] For Hans Mommsen,
any similarities between the regimes are outweighed by the differences. Soviet imperialism was different from Hitler's aimless
self-destructive war of expansionism *(Amoklauf)*. The extent of the
regimes' consolidation and flexibility, party structures, character of
leadership, degrees of administrative and bureaucratic centralisation,
the extent to which the state apparatus was transformed and, above
all, the extent of the regimes' criminal energies were all different.[18]
Georg Fülberth has argued that the totalitarian paradigm can only be
usefully employed for the history of the Soviet Union between 1930
and 1956.[19] Peter Reichel has pointed out the irony behind reviving
one of the major weapons of the hot phase of the Cold War, totalitarianism, at exactly the time when Communism had lost the Cold War.
Its functionality in the concerted efforts of the political right to sanitise
German national history from its most problematic sides has, according to Reichel, invalidated the concept once and for all.[20] Ralph Jessen
has maintained that, quite apart from its political side effects, the totalitarian paradigm cannot adequately reflect the complexity of the
GDR's social history as it necessarily has to describe society as totally
dependent on the state. His plea that one should allow for an 'autonomy of the social dimension' in GDR history has produced a convincing framework for future research.[21]

The revival of the totalitarian paradigm, however, has at times
clearly served the purpose of removing the Nazi period from public
sight or of belittling its importance in modern German history.[22] Wolf-
Jobst Siedler, for example, has written of the Nazi dictatorship as 'an
authoritarian regime', contrasting it with the GDR which he has

described as 'a truly totalitarian regime'.[23] For Christa Hoffmann, 'the Nazi regime was not totalitarian in the same sense as the rule of the Communists'.[24] Horst Möller has argued that the SED dictatorship should in many ways be seen as 'more efficient' than the Nazi dictatorship. In his view, the mechanisms of power and repression were far more developed and the SED drove far more people into exile than the Nazis. Overwhelming parallels between the two regimes, he maintained, will make comparisons within the paradigm of totalitarianism both necessary and fruitful.[25] Schwarz has speculated with obvious glee that, in the medium term, the focus of attention will at long last shift from the Nazi period to the GDR, thus relieving Germans of their 'neurotic guilt complex': 'in the coming decades the Communist past will be the major topic of *Vergangenheitsbewältigung* for a younger generation … The [Nazi] trauma is not as powerful anymore.'[26] Knütter, Zitelmann, Baring but also Wolfgang Schuller have all argued that any coming-to-terms with the German past after 1989 would have to involve the explicit comparison between Stalinism and National Socialism in Germany.[27] Even the liberal-conservative Lothar Gall, chairman of the Historians' Association from 1993 to 1996, found that the 'structural similarities of the dictatorships' will give credence to those who in the *Historikerstreit* argued against the singularity of National Socialist crimes.[28] Here, one feels reminded of Manfred Kossock's bitter words on the process of *Geschichtsbewältigung* after 1989: 'If the German East has already paid the war bill for the whole of Germany, why should one not dispose of the unpalatable bits of the German past at its expense.'[29]

Indeed, any comparisons which relativise the importance of the German Nazi crimes, whilst attributing the unpalatable GDR past to foreign, i.e., Soviet responsibility,[30] may easily degenerate into national apologias. Historians will have to locate the place of the GDR in German history by pointing to the continuing existence of authoritarian structures and mentalities or the rootedness of GDR society in the class society of the Weimar Republic. However, the legitimate question about the roots of the GDR in German history can easily turn into a blanket condemnation of the traditions of the German labour movement, thereby discrediting some of the basic values of the old Federal Republic such as its welfare state and the social rights of citizens. It therefore seems more important than ever to insist on the labour movement's positive contribution in bringing about today's civil society. Its commitment to the democratisation of all areas of life, to the development of the welfare state as well as its fight for international solidarity and against nationalism, anti-Semitism and xenophobia need to be defended against efforts to tar everything with the broad brush of Stalinism.

The totalitarian paradigm with its emphasis on government appa-
ratuses and high politics has also contributed to the emergence of a
kind of tunnel vision in regard to GDR history. It has at times
reduced its topic to the problem of the Stasi, i.e., to coercion and
terror.[31] The complexities of everyday life under the Communist
regime thus get pushed to the sidelines. Nolte has already spoken of
the GDR as a mere 'Soviet protectorate',[32] whilst Schwarz has talked
of the Communists in the GDR as an 'association of slave-drivers'
who managed to foster a 'concentration camp mentality' within
the 'mega concentration camp' GDR.[33] Weißmann has described
the GDR as a 'completely peripheral historical phenomenon.'[34]
Whereas some authors have argued that the GDR only produced
something genuine in the form of the 1989 revolution,[35] others have
even dismissed the activity of the GDR dissidents as peripheral to
the collapse of the GDR.[36] Baring has denounced the country's elite
as second rate: 'The former GDR is largely a headless country. Anyone who showed initiative or was energetic and determined, had
either left in time or was thrown out later on.'[37] Hans Günther Hockerts has taken it upon himself to unmask the reality of the GDR's 'so-
called social achievements'.[38] And with increasing frequency one
stumbles across overall assessments such as the following: 'The
GDR was a dictatorship totally dependent on the Soviet Union;
it kept itself going over forty years through open and latent terror
against its population.'[39]

Even those who are opposed to the national agenda of the new
right have sometimes contributed to the vilification of the GDR.
Winkler has interpreted GDR society as a place where functional
elites had been replaced by inefficient and privileged *nomenklatura*.
For Winkler this 'irreparably failed socialism' will form part of the
massive '"hereditary burden" for the reunified country of four
decades GDR'.[40] Winkler has condemned the system from top to
bottom: 'Very few East German businesses were competitive. The
decay of the old buildings … had long ago turned into social catastrophe. The ravages of the environment went even further than
experts in the East and West had assumed. And the same was true
for the moral destruction which the SED caused with the help of the
Krake Stasi. The spying was so extensive that, in this field at least, the
GDR belonged to the international top class.'[41] Winkler'commitment to the eradication of Communist street names in Berlin, his
efforts to cleanse the Humboldt university of 'red professors' and his
phobia of the PDS all testify to the survival of anti-Communism
after the death of Communism. Wolfgang J. Mommsen has also
described as one of the central tasks of historiography in the reuni-

fied country to demonstrate 'how rotten and bankrupt the system of "really-existing socialism" had been right from the very beginning', and Hans-Ulrich Wehler recently referred to the GDR as a 'Russian satrapy'.[42] If, according to Kocka, historians had not recognised such deficits earlier, it was due to 'systematic deception' by their GDR colleagues who had for years fed them with manipulated statistics about the state of the GDR economy and society.[43]

West German historians have also begun to interpret the history of the GDR as a continuation of the German *Sonderweg*, implying that its ultimate failure was related to insurmountable modernisation deficits.[44] Such interpretations are often overdetermined by structural considerations and informed by a clear sense of superiority on the part of the Westerners vis-à-vis their Eastern cousins. Thus they have contributed to a feeling of uneasiness amongst East German historians who have criticised 'the dominance of West Germans in the debates on GDR history'.[45] It was in the context of such modernisation theories that some historians immediately after reunification were concerned about the continued Westernisation of Germany.[46] The GDR, in this view, with its modernisation deficits and its lack of thorough Westernisation threatened the democratic potential of the old Federal Republic. Thus it was argued that very little of the GDR could usefully be integrated into the reunited country. On the contrary: any impact the GDR might have on the FRG was likely to be negative. Therefore, a full-scale colonisation of the GDR by the old FRG was seen as beneficial. This included destroying any form of identification with the GDR. Its historiography was demolished, its historians dismissed, its historical museums redesigned to fit the old Federal Republic's self definitions. Exhibitions presented the population of the former GDR with a distorted image of their own biographies. Understandably, many reacted by stressing allegedly specific GDR mentalities, some of which only really surfaced after 1989.[47] Despite self-critical remarks on the 'limits of transferring the West German model to a society which had developed differently over forty years', historians like Kocka have come to the conclusion that the 'incorporation' of the East into the West has been a success story.[48] This ignores the fact that there had been alternatives to the 'colonisation' of the GDR in a whole variety of policy sectors which were dismissed for political reasons.[49]

GDR identity was and is closely bound up with anti-fascism. After 1989 the GDR's self-portrayal as anti-fascist has been severely criticised, because the SED functionalised the anti-fascist tradition to legitimate the regime. One is certainly justified in emphasising the extent to which the ruling elite in the GDR prevented internal criti-

cism and dissent by portraying it as 'the better Germany' in comparison to the FRG.[50] The anti-fascist paradigm encouraged a selective view of history, pushed unpalatable aspects to the sidelines,
created new *Feindbilder* and paralysed the intellectual opposition to
the SED regime. In this respect the anti-fascism of the GDR was the
functional equivalent to the anti-totalitarianism of the early Federal
Republic. It is equally beyond doubt that the officially prescribed
anti-fascism of the GDR prevented any thorough confrontation of
the Germans in the GDR with German guilt in the Nazi period.
Almost no-one would seriously dispute that GDR historiography
had an undue bias towards portraying the 'heroic struggle' of the
Communist resistance to National Socialism – despite efforts by,
amongst others, Werner Bramke, Dietrich Eichholtz, Kurt Pätzold,
Joachim Petzold, Werner Röhr, Wolfgang Ruge and Manfred
Weißbecker to produce a more differentiated view of National
Socialism. Most of these points are, in any case, readily accepted by
former GDR historians.[51]

To speak of a 'latent anti-fascist syndrome' of GDR historiography[52], however, is more incriminating than helpful. Like its Western
counterpart, the 'Auschwitz syndrome', it easily serves the purpose of
connecting efforts to remember the fascist dictatorship and its
consequences to forms of mental illness. Equally, Michael Wolffsohn's attempt to portray GDR anti-fascism as the propaganda coup
of a dictatorship which was little different from the Nazi one which
preceded it can barely hide its national apologetic function.[53] Anti-
fascism was never simply a legitimation for the SED regime. Hans-
Ulrich Thamer's dictum (consciously alluding to Ernst Bloch's quote
linking capitalism and fascism) that 'anyone who does not want to
talk about Stalinism has to keep quiet on anti-fascism'[54] is not only a
subtle way of equating National Socialism and Communism, it also
underestimates the different contexts in which the concept of anti-fascism has meaning. It neglects how important anti-fascist values and
sentiments were for many GDR citizens, especially in the immediate
post-war years.[55] One has to ask how people have been formed by
the anti-fascist traditions of the GDR, and what different everyday
experiences people had with the anti-fascist tradition. Only if one
recognises how embedded anti-fascist values had been in the everyday life experience of many Communists in the GDR who had experienced National Socialism, can one actually explain how the SED
was able to instrumentalise it so effectively. What seems necessary is
the distinction (which, for sure, cannot be all that neat) between a
'state and party anti-fascism' and an 'elementary anti-fascism present
amongst wide sections of the population'.[56] Public attempts to pre-

sent the Communist resistance in Buchenwald as mere group egotism and to put Communist concentration camp inmates, who managed much of the everyday life existence in the camp – and in this
capacity had to face extremely difficult moral decisions – on almost
the same level as the SS members who ran the camp, may neatly fit
the totalitarian equation, but there is little else to recommend it.[57]
Furthermore, to equate anti-fascism with anti-democratic sentiment,
Stalinist crime and the alleged guilt neurosis of the 1968 generation
in the West does not do justice to its history.[58] Neither is there much
sense in castigating critics of the national tradition for a 'ritualised
anti-fascism' which has allegedly belittled 'Communist crimes'.[59]
According to Klaus-Rainer Röhl, the term 'anti-fascism' should best
be replaced by 'anti-totalitarianism',[60] and in the eyes of some other
neo-nationalists, the ideology of anti-fascism has even served the
PDS to establish itself in post-reunification Germany.[61] Interpreting it
either as neurosis or as functional tool of Communists to win allies in
the non-Communist camp means scratching the surface of what has
made anti-fascism meaningful in the past and present. It has neither
been the last refuge of the political left nor can it be reduced to simply legitimating left-wing extremism. In one of the most abstruse
explanations of anti-fascism it has been described as rooted in the
extreme hedonism of the 1968 generation. This allegedly finds its
positive counterpart in 'hard, ascetic fascism which demands sacrifice
and enthusiasm'.[62] In the face of such hair-raising fantasies it needs to
be stressed that the belated acceptance of the anti-fascist struggle
against Nazism from the 1960s onwards served as an important
ingredient in the serious efforts made by West Germans self-critically
to face their most recent past in an unprecedented public debate.
Anti-fascism in the GDR, despite politically motivated efforts to discredit it, 'cannot be reduced to the dimension of prescribed political
norms.'[63] The delegitimation of anti-fascism in post-reunification
Germany threatens to contribute to a serious imbalance in the assessment of how the two Germanies faced up to their National Socialist
past. A rather rosy perspective on the West German experience con-
trasts with a rather one-sided condemnation of the anti-fascist tradition in the GDR. Any differentiated look at anti-fascism, its reality as
well as its myths, will act as an effective defence against those who
wish to call into question the moral integrity of Communists who did,
after all, pay for their political convictions with years of suffering in
Hitler's prisons and concentration camps. A revitalised anti-fascism
freed of its blatant function of legitimating the political system of the
GDR, may well have a positive part to play in the democratic political culture of the enlarged Federal Republic.

The results of an official parliamentary commission on GDR history as well as the research carried out by the Gauck Institute (which houses the Stasi papers) have further contributed to the one-sided perspectives on the GDR.[64] The commission, whose remit it was to look at the power structure of the GDR system of government, held 44 public meetings, and its members heard 327 historians, political scientists, philosophers and eyewitnesses. A total of 148 experts wrote lengthy reports and evaluations about the GDR. The work of the commission started in March 1992 and ended in June 1994. Within the six topics covered, the Stasi, the police, the ruling party as well as politically sensitive issues such as German-German politics and the role of the churches in the GDR were extensively debated. Other aspects such as the economic performance of the GDR or various aspects of the history of everyday life were barely mentioned. The Bochum historian Bernd Faulenbach, who served on the commission, had to admit: 'We have hardly been able to touch on the everyday life in the GDR without Stasi and without opposition which also existed.'[65] The present dominant trend of instrumentalising GDR history for party-political purposes became clearly visible in the election year of 1994 when the work of the commission ended in political disarray and a public mud-slinging match between government and opposition about which party, in the West, had supported the 'evil machinations' of the 'Stasi-regime'. A new commission which was set up in 1995 will hopefully shed some light on those aspects of GDR history which were excluded from the remit of the first commission.

The massive institutional support given to research into GDR history underlines how political interests make the GDR a prime focus of historical study. From 1950 a single institute, the Institut für Zeitgeschichte in Munich, had the special task of illuminating the history of National Socialism. After 1989 the number of institutes dealing with GDR history rapidly increased. The historians of the Gauck Institute are not the only ones filling the pages of the newspapers week after week with allegedly sensational revelations about the all-pervasive Stasi.[66] Its fourteen branches have been intensively engaged upon the task of political education. Other research institutes largely dedicated to the history of the GDR include the Zentrum für Zeithistorische Forschung in Potsdam, the Potsdam branch of the Munich-based Institut für Zeitgeschichte, and the Hannah-Arendt Institut für Zeitgeschichte, für Totalitarismusforschung in Dresden. In 1994 Kocka counted more than eight hundred ongoing research projects on the history of the GDR.[67] Universities, hoping to cash in on the new boom, have been quick to establish new centres for GDR history. Contemporary history departments in particular are finding a new and enticing field of study. After all, almost no era of contemporary history offers so much by way of freely accessible sources and information. A state which has collapsed cannot protect its sources, and thus historians are free to move even in the GDR's most recent past.[68]

Of course, it cannot possibly be argued that research on the GDR necessarily has an apologetic tendency and serves the agenda of renationalising historical consciousness. Much of the attention given to the GDR has been both fruitful and productive adding to our understanding of German history. Hans Mommsen, for example, has suggested analysing GDR social history within its regional contexts so as to understand better the 'way East Germans see themselves'.[69] Rather than serving the purpose of renationalising German identity on the back of the GDR, such an undertaking would improve understanding between East and West. The publications of the Zentrum für Zeithistorische Studien Potsdam, in particular, belong to the most differentiated analyses of the GDR.[70] It is also one of the very few places where historians from East and West have been cooperating in the difficult task of coming to terms with the complex legacy of the GDR. Jürgen Kocka, acting head of the institute until 1995, has argued time and again that GDR history should not be sensational history *(Enthüllungshistorie)*. Only a differentiated perspective on the GDR which does not view its history primarily from its demise, can, he insisted, come to grips with the hopes, desires and failures buried in the ruins of this German state.[71]

However, as part of the total condemnation of the GDR after reunification, some historians have been engaged in efforts to 'establish a kind of monopoly of interpretations' over GDR history: 'certain views on the GDR are decreed which are politically opportune in the current situation'.[72] It is not a matter of wanting to excuse the Stasi activities or the intolerable level of repression in the GDR. Of course, the economic and ecological policies of the GDR were disastrous. Yet, above and beyond those 'facts', there has been a tendency to make the GDR an evil spirit in German national history.[73] Characterising the GDR as a 'totalitarian dictatorship' and condemning it to the rubbish heap of historical 'trial and error' experiments will also hardly facilitate the integration of those East Germans who partly identified with the regime. Walter Schmidt, the former head of the Institute for History in the old GDR Academy of Sciences, wrote in May 1990: 'The identity of all those who have worked here [in the GDR] cannot be maintained if everything that has been done and achieved in more than four decades is simply invalidated and declared useless. My identity is incomprehensible without the GDR, its hopes and disappointments, its achievements and errors, its expectations and its ultimate failure.'[74] Seen in this context, Western criticisms of GDR nostalgia ignore what led to this curious phenomenon in the first place: the annulment of personal biographies of people who grew up and lived in the GDR.

Nowhere has this annulment become more visible than in the destruction of the historical profession in the GDR in which Western historians of different political persuasions participated. It is worthwhile reminding oneself of the judgement passed by West German historians on their GDR counterparts before 1989. In the late 1980s, Alexander Fischer and Günther Heydemann offered a fairly positive evaluation of GDR historiography. It had successfully managed the 'transition from a selective representation of German history to an integrated one'. Its legitimating function 'cannot be the sole criterium for its assessment'. In various fields, the GDR had achieved 'international recognition'. In view of the 'considerable historiographical achievements' of GDR historians, their counterparts in the FRG were taken to task for 'their failure to engage in a critcal dialogue with Marxist-Leninist historiography in the GDR'.[75]

After 1989 the parameters governing the assessment of GDR historiography quickly changed. The Independent Historians' Association of the GDR, established in 1990, has played a major role in discrediting GDR historiography, often by blanket denunciations and personal attacks. Armin Mitter and Stefan Wolle, who often act as spokespersons for the Association, have been in the forefront of those castigating GDR historians for their political opportunism and moral failings. One certainly has to accept that some had been unable to uphold minimum standards of moral decency in extremely difficult personal circumstances. One can also understand that dissident GDR historians, especially those who had suffered persecution under the GDR, were justifiably angry about their more established colleagues. A genuine debate on the past of GDR historiography would indeed have been helpful.[76] However, the total condemnation of GDR historiography has made a thorough and complex debate about a difficult and painful matter almost impossible. All too soon the hesitant beginnings of an honest questioning of their own roles in the GDR were pushed to the sidelines by historians' fears that they were about to lose their jobs. Their personal biography became a serious risk factor. Shrill demands for public tribunals dealing with historians who allegedly legitimated the SED regime increased the defensiveness of GDR historians. Furthermore, as Jürgen Danyel has pointed out, the public debate on the role of historians in the GDR is not necessarily as sign of the intensity of the private self-questioning of historians.[77]

If, for example, the very first call to form an Independent Historians' Association described GDR historiography as 'an unpalatable mash made from lies and half-truths' in which 'scholastic nonsense' and 'stale commonplaces' dominated, this hardly does it justice. Neither do blanket accusations of 'provincialism' and 'incompetence'.[78] Furthermore it was hardly helpful to call the whole of GDR historiography 'something which had intellectually gone to the dogs, ... which was rotten.'[79] The routine description of GDR historiography as 'scholarship legitimating the political regime' (*Legitimationswissenschaft*) ignores the link between history and politics in every country and also implies that GDR historiography was nothing but legitimation and had no other merits. Or, if it was considered that it had made positive contributions, they were described in terms of having developed within certain isolated oases amidst a vast desert.[80] GDR historians have found themselves alternately described as 'mediocre SED henchmen' or 'plebeians of the mind' who 'degraded historiography'[81] Predictably, East German criticisms have been quickly taken up by West German historians who indulged themselves in demonstrating time and again the complete dependence of GDR historians on the SED. Harm Klueting, citing official GDR dictionary articles (hardly the place to look for deviance), found that toeing the party line was always more important to GDR historians than genuinely searching for historical 'truth'.[82] Christian Meier called for the greatest possible number of GDR historians to be dismissed arguing *in dubio contra reo*,[83] and Wolfgang Schuller, professor of ancient history at the University of Konstanz, argued that it was an act of hygiene to cleanse the GDR universities of the representatives of Communist dogma.[84]

Between June and September 1990 there was also a marked cooling in the tone of the West German Historians' Association towards GDR colleagues. In June one of its resolutions still read modestly: 'The attempts thoroughly to renew GDR historiography, which at present is seeking to make sure of its character as a science bound by the principles of objective historical research, have to be supported with all available means by the relevant institutions in both the GDR and the FRG.' By September the tone had become harsher: 'Before 9 November 1989 GDR historiography was a governmental science, whose task it was above all to legitimate the SED regime.'[85] Now West German professors began demanding the reorganisation of East German universities, widespread dismissals and checks on the scientific qualifications of their East German colleagues. Four years later the Association, at its Leipzig meeting, justified the destruction of GDR historiography as 'unavoidable'.[86] For Lothar Gall the real

problem with East German historians was that they 'did not adapt
quickly enough to certain customs of the Western form of academic
community and its norms and conventions'.[87]

The blanket condemnation of GDR historiography was also
echoed by historians who had previously praised its achievements.
For Wehler 'maybe two dozen historians [in the former GDR] ... do
justice to the assessment principles that are regarded as normal in the
West ... One can forget tons of East German literature. I belonged to
a generation which believed in keeping track of GDR publications,
and I have consistently read the dozen or so most important journals
and publications on modern history. Almost everything ... that has
been written on the German labour movement can be binned.'[88] In
1990 Kocka, who, as chairman of the humanities working party of
the Academic Council (*Wissenschaftsrat*), occupied an influential position in the evaluation of GDR research institutes in 1990/1991, had
already come to the conclusion: 'Wide areas of GDR historiography
are underdeveloped.'[89] A 'legitimation science' without merits and
potential, it would, he predicted, become 'a heavy burden for the
united German historical profession'. As a solution to the dilemma,
he recommended decimating and transforming GDR historiography.[90] In September 1990 Wolfgang J. Mommsen was still finding
praise for his East German colleagues, arguing (correctly, in my
view) that within the last ten years in particular 'very interesting
results' had emerged from historical research in the GDR on areas
such as the Reformation, the peasant wars and non-European history, especially the history of Africa and the Developing World more
generally. He stressed the need to differentiate carefully between the
situations of different East German historians and argued that the latter should, if at all possible, retain their positions within the academic
community.[91] Four years later the same Mommsen characterised
Marxist historiography in the GDR as an 'ossified scholastic system
of empty phraseology'. Ernst Engelberg, one of the doyens of East
German historiography, is described as a 'petty-bourgeois' historian
who 'sold himself uncritically to the SED regime'.[92] GDR historians
became manipulators in the pay of the SED: 'historiography widely
became intellectually stunted and developed into a system which
simply acclaimed the ruling tendencies'.[93] Fischer, in direct contrast
to much of his pre-1989 writings, has described GDR historiography
as 'one of the last socialist strongholds' and its representatives as
'anything but an academic elite'. Therefore, according to Fischer, no
GDR institutions had been worth preserving, and the 'propagandists of the socialist system' have well deserved their fate.[94] As GDR
historiography was allegedly in the 'straitjacket' of ideology, history

teaching on all levels from the classroom to the universities would, according to Joachim Rohlfes, need a complete overhaul to bring them in line with Western standards and traditions.[95] Attacks on East German historiography after reunification has been aimed at delegitimising Marxist historiography generally as well as at the more profane aim of securing the career prospects of a whole generation of West German historians.[96]

There have, however, also been more balanced assessments of GDR historiography after 1989. In identifying areas of research which had, for ideological reasons, been ignored by GDR social scientists, Hermann Weber acknowledged a 'slow and painful learning process' among those East German historians 'wanting to cast off their past'.[97] Dietrich Staritz gave a balanced account of the strength and weaknesses of GDR contemporary historians, insisting that in 1989/1990 many had genuinely debated their past roles in stabilising the political system in the GDR.[98] Wolfgang Benz has written of the 'annoying posturing' of the victorious Western historians vis-à-vis their Eastern colleagues.[99] The indignation of Western historians about the ideological restrictions under which East German historians laboured has been especially facile if one considers the situation of the West German historical profession until the 1960s. In this respect Hermann Glaser has correctly characterised the attitude of many Westerners towards their East German colleagues as one of hypocrisy.[100] Kleßmann explicitly justified the increasing tendency of Western historians to read and engage with GDR research, for – apart from the dreary Marxist-Leninist gloss – it had become a serious challenge to West German historiography.[101] Jörn Rüsen argued not to silence GDR historiography, because any such exclusion would eradicate a historical consciousness which had become part of an East German identity.[102] Martin Sabrow has pointed out that the virtual extinction of Marxist-Leninist historiography in the former GDR has 'encouraged a narrow perspective according to which GDR historiography was symbiotically tied to the SED state and research was of little value apart from legitimating the rule of the SED.'[103]

However, considering the united front of those condemning GDR historiography, it cannot really be surprising that many East German historians found themselves frozen out. The debate is often conducted in such a way as if there had only been two choices: legitimating the regime or opposing it. In between those two extremes, however, was a whole range of positions. The struggle for survival has largely dissolved solidaristic behaviour amongst former academics in the GDR and contributed to a feeling of 'Every man/woman for himself/herself'.[104] According to Olaf Groehler's estimates, about

70 percent of the leading GDR elite, including academics, have left their positions after 1989. Weißbecker estimated that in the humanities subjects, around 95 percent of those who had been employed in institutions of higher education were dismissed after 1990.[105] And Helga Schultz calculated that only 25 percent of historians working in former Academy institutes and about 10 percent of university professors survived the Western onslaught, many on fixed-term contracts with a rather unsure future.[106] In 1992 Kurt Pätzold spoke about the 'end of historical study in the GDR'.[107] At times Western historians tried to set up a smokescreen of disinformation behind which the full extent of the demolition job was hidden. Thus Kocka has written that the aspects of continuity in GDR historiography far outweigh any elements of change.[108] Gerhard A. Ritter, in a reply to Kurt Pätzold's protestation about the destruction of GDR historiography, denied all such charges. Instead he referred to the 'deficiencies of historical study in the former GDR and the inadequate role played by established historians during the revolution of 1989.' Justifying his own work in the evaluation commission of the Humboldt university, Ritter found: 'The *Wende* did not bring about the end of historical study in the states of the former GDR. Rather it has meant … the opportunity to make a real new start.'[109] A new beginning certainly, but, one feels tempted to add, without GDR historians. Wolfgang Frühwald, in an otherwise extremely apologetic article on the process of evaluation, has admitted that 'of the core areas of the social sciences nothing much has survived.'[110] Niethammer also seems to have been closer to the actual problem than Kocka or Ritter when he described the lack of East German historians still in employment as one of the major problems of coming to terms with the East German past.[111] In the field of historical pedagogy *(historische Didaktik)*, all GDR representatives, about one hundred in number, had been thrown out of the universities four years after reunification.[112] According to Kossock, GDR historians never had the opportunity to come to some form of re-assessment of their own past and their profession's failures and shortcomings: 'The potential for a reform of GDR historiography by its own efforts has been completely eradicated by the conscious destruction of its intellectual life as a possible source of an unwanted identity (counter-culture).'[113]

How did GDR historians react to the unenviable position they found themselves in after 1989? Before 1989 there had been very few truly oppositional historians amongst the profession in the GDR. Those who had dared to be oppositional were silenced – often with dire consequences for their carreer.[114] Yet behind closed doors, there were increasing criticisms of the inflexibility and stubbornness of the

SED leadership – especially after 1985. When the regime finally collapsed, not a few amongst those who had supported the system, felt
a sense of relief.[115] During the *Wende* a minority of GDR historians
discussed their own role in the state with remarkable frankness and
showed a considerable degree of self-criticism in assessing their own
position as apologists for the politically powerful. In the summer of
1989 Fritz Klein reflected on his sixty-fifth birthday: 'The idea that
serving one's own side means covering up its less palatable aspects
is as wrong as the notion that one deals with the other side more
effectively by ignoring its virtues.'[116] True, for the most part, they did
not play an active role in bringing about the East German revolution, and few identified with the movement of dissent even after it
had reached unparalleled proportions. Hartmut Zwahr, of Leipzig
university, and maybe a handful of others were early and notable
exceptions. Many went on the defensive as they felt overwhelmed
by the victorious West Germans.[117] Yet from 1990 onwards an
increasing number have tried, in the words of Hans Schleier, to
'account to themselves and the scientific community for the degree
to which the misuse of history as legitimating the politics of the SED
regime has deformed their own work'.[118] At times, however, as
Weißbecker recalls, their own willingness to enter into a dialogue
about GDR historiography met with embarrassed silence. Western
colleagues, whom he had known for years, suddenly turned cold.[119]
Interestingly, what critics like Zwahr and Helga Schultz hoped for in
1989 and 1990 was a strengthening of GDR social history and an
end to the streamlining of history by what Zwahr has called the
'administrative system'.[120] The earliest self-critical contributions of
established GDR historians argued for renewal, reform and a thorough rethinking of the methodological straitjackets that had stifled
innovation in GDR historiography for too long: 'A renewed socialism is in need of a new understanding of history'.[121] Few could predict what lay ahead for GDR historiography.

Towards the end of 1989 leading GDR historians could still
sound self-confident: 'The results of the historical sciences in the
GDR have satisfied and encouraged a growing interest of GDR citizens in various fields of history. Their research achievements in
many areas have been internationally recognized.'[122] By October
1990 the GDR historians' association sounded worried: 'We support
the necessary process of radical renewal. Yet we are also worried to
see to what degree this process is connected to a dismissal of scientific achievements and successful institutions. Professional decisions
have been influenced by political pre-condemnations.'[123] In 1991
Helga Schultz could already compare GDR historiography to 'a

dead dog ... It is about to vanish totally, with all its research institutes, university chairs, journals and professional associations.'[124]
Faced by the virulence of Western anti-Communism after the fall of
Communism,[125] few have been courageous enough as Küttler to
maintain after 1989 that Marxist historiography will have a future in
the re-unified Germany. Emphasising the very real crisis and shortcomings of Marxist historiography both before and after the fall of
the wall, Küttler nevertheless self-confidently has pointed to a number of achievements in areas such as formation, revolution and class
theory. Arguing that the Marxist historiography in the GDR in fact
developed parallel to the historical social science in the FRG, he has
taken the view that in the future debates on a modern versus a postmodern historiography, the two former adversaries should take the
side of the former against the latter.[126] As Helga Schultz has emphasised, there had not only been innovative research groups but also
the retention of good historiographical traditions in the GDR. If it
had not been for the West, many GDR historians from the Academy
would have been taken on by the university sector. If it had not
been for the non-Marxist evaluation criteria of Western historians,
the results of Marxist historiography would have looked even more
impressive. And if it had not been for the confusion between personal misuse of power and political convictions amongst Western
evaluators, maybe the destruction of GDR historiography would
not have turned out to be quite as wholesale.[127]

The fact that there was indeed an increasingly fruitful dialogue
between East and West German historians in the 1980s has been a
welcome opportunity for new-right and conservative historians
since 1990 to attack the professional judgment and moral integrity of
everyone in the West who had not collected their credentials as a
battle-hardened Cold Warrior. Their accusations have routinely
started with the charge that anti-anti-Communism allegedly blinded
Western historians and led them to eulogise the achievements of the
GDR. Anti-anti-Communism had become, according to Geiss, the
'great sham' *(Lebenslüge)* of left-liberal historians in the West.[128]
Wolffsohn has asked all those who had accepted the division of the
country before 1989 for moral retribution of their 'guilt'.[129] Konrad
Löw triumphantly claimed that left-liberal social scientists were
caught wrong-footed by the events of 1989/1990. According to Löw,
they should at last repent and admit the mistakes of their past –
their anti-anti-Communism, anti-totalitarianism, modish Marxism
and undue reference to 1968. Over the years, so Löw's conclusion,
many had willingly adapted their research to the expectations of the
SED regime.[130] Equally Jens Hacker, in an excruciatingly self-right-

eous manner, has tarred with the brush of political opportunism, collaboration and immorality all those politicians, historians and political scientists who dared to have contacts with or spoke up in any way for dialogue with GDR representatives.[131] Schuller rhetorically asked all those historians 'who had used the word nation only in a pejorative sense ...: how could one possibly have been so blind?'[132] Nolte's 'final word' on the *Historikerstreit* rested heavily on the argument that his opponents had lost all credibility as they had for decades uncritically eulogised the Communist dictatorships.[133] For Zitelmann the real coming-to-terms with the past has to be a West German one since 1989, as it was only due to those in the West who sympathised with the SED regime that 'historical legends' had been created.[134] Furthermore, Fest has explained the alleged silence of the left-wing intellectuals in Germany on the revolutionary change in the GDR in terms of their role as fellow-travellers of the Communist dictatorship.[135]

Cases like that of Dietrich Staritz have strengthened the self-confidence of the conservatives. In the autumn of 1994 it became public that the distinguished scholar on the GDR had been an informant of the Stasi and, at the same time, of the West German *Verfassungsschutz* from the early 1960s to 1972. Conservatives quickly interpreted the incident as confirmation of their Cold War prejudices against left-liberal social scientists as puppets of the 'evil empire' behind the iron curtain. GDR research in the West, had, according to the blanket condemnations which set in after the fall of the GDR, without undue pressure, on several occasions belittled the 'criminal energies' of the 'second German dictatorship'.[136] Rainer Eckert has found the liberal mouthpiece of West German research on the GDR, the *Deutschlandarchiv*, guilty of persistently ignoring oppositional tendencies within GDR historiography, despite the fact that it reported extensively on the development of the profession in the 1970s and 1980s.[137] In another case, in August 1993, an attack on GDR historiography was explicitly combined with an attack on key representatives of Western historical social science. Wolle and Mitter accused them of forming networks with their erstwhile friends amongst GDR historians. Allegedly, some morally discredited Communist historians had found refuge at the Zentrum für Zeithistorische Studien Potsdam, headed by Kocka and Kleßmann. False allegations and patched-up misrepresentations formed the basis for Mitter's and Wolle's attacks on the Institute's academic credentials and its alleged lack of productivity. Nevertheless they received wide publicity by being published in Germany's biggest conservative quality newspaper.[138] The Institute has been the focus of conservative attacks which

time and again depict its rationale as Social Democratic and its aim
as trying to win back the threatened hegemony of a left-liberal historiography in the reunited Germany.[139]

Jürgen Kocka and Wolfgang Mommsen have both vigorously
rejected the accusations levelled against the Potsdam institute, arguing that cooperation, not colonisation, must remain the aim and that
former GDR historians were not necessarily either incompetent or
morally corrupt, nor were those who had shaken hands with them
before 1989.[140] According to Kleßmann the conservatives in the profession are intent on creating a climate in which 'those who had not
let themselves be governed by the preamble of the Basic Law, which
apparently, like the ten commandments, came direct from heaven,
is given a hammering and denied the legitimacy of his research
methodology'.[141] Weber, commenting on the Staritz case, defended
the bulk of GDR research carried out in the West before 1989: 'In
difficult circumstances, this subject has made a great contribution to
scholarship, and, all due self-criticism apart, its representatives have
no reason to appear in penitential robes now.'[142]

On balance, many Western historians from diverse political
camps have contributed to the demolition of GDR historiography
after 1990. However, many have also spoken up against any return
to an uncritical national history on the back of the GDR's corpse.
Thus Faulenbach, for example, has argued that the task of coming to
terms with GDR history should under no circumstances 'relegate the
critical examination of National Socialist history'.[143] And Kocka has
pleaded for a history of the GDR which would be carried out 'with
perceptiveness, precision and justice'.[144] In the climate of self-right-
eous, anti-Communist hysteria produced by attempts on the political
right to renationalise German historical consciousness, this will no
doubt be both a difficult task and an important one.

168   *The Search for Normality*

NOTES

1. Hans-Peter Schwarz, 'Mit gestopften Trompeten. Die Wiedervereinigung Deutschlands aus der Sicht westdeutscher Historiker', *GWU*, vol. 44, 1993, p. 693.
2. Karlheinz Weißmann, 'Trauerarbeit und Schönfärberei', *Die Welt*, 12 Feb. 1994, p. G1.
3. Hans Günter Hockerts, 'Schwamm drüber?', *Die politische Meinung*, vol. 40, August 1995, pp. 35-40.
4. Michael Wolffsohn, 'Doppelte Vergangenheitsbewältigung', in: Klaus Sühl (ed.), *Vergangenheitsbewältigung 1945 und 1989, ein unmöglicher Vergleich? Eine Diskussion*, Berlin, 1994, p. 39.
5. Zitelmann, *Republik*, pp. 13-15.
6. Edgar Wolfrum, 'Diktaturen im Europa des 20. Jahrhunderts. Ein neuer zeitgeschichtlicher Förderschwerpunkt der Stiftung Volkswagenwerk', *VfZ*, vol. 40, 1992, pp. 155-8.
7. Jürgen Braun, 'Stiller Sieg eines Begriffs', *Das Parlament*, 11/18 Nov. 1994, p. 1.
8. Eckhard Jesse, 'Der Totalitarismus-Ansatz nach dem Zusammenbruch des realexistierenden Sozialismus', *Die neue Gesellschaft/Frankfurter Hefte*, vol. 38, 1991, pp. 983-92.
9. Eckhard Jesse, 'War die DDR totalitär?', *aus politik und zeitgeschichte*, 7 Oct. 1994, p. 22. See also idem (ed.), *Totalitarismus im 20. Jahrhundert. Eine Bilanz der internationalen Forschung*, Schriftenreihe der Bundeszentrale für politische Bildung, vol. 336, Bonn, 1996.
10. Klaus Schroeder (ed.), *Geschichte und Transformation des SED-Staates*, Berlin, 1994 presents the first results of the Berlin research group. For a ringing endorsement of the totalitarian paradigm see especially pp. 11-3, 320.
11. Imanuel Geiss, 'Europäische Perspektiven nach der deutschen Einigung', *aus politik und zeitgeschichte*, 21 Dec. 1990, p. 42.
12. Geiss, *Die deutsche Frage*, p. 94.
13. Christoph Kleßmann, 'Zwei Diktaturen in Deutschland – Was kann die künftige DDR-Forschung aus der Geschichtsschreibung zum Nationalsozialismus lernen?', *Deutschland-Archiv*, vol. 25, 1992, pp. 601-6. Equally Sigrid Meuschel, 'Überlegungen zu einer Herrschafts- und Gesellschaftsgeschichte der DDR', *GG*, vol. 19, 1993, pp. 5-14 has been arguing in favour of a flexible and differentiated use of the totalitarian paradigm.
14. Christoph Kleßmann and Martin Sabrow, 'Zeitgeschichte in Deutschland nach 1989', *aus politik und zeitgeschichte*, 20 Sept. 1996, p. 11. The heuristic weaknesses of the totalitarianism paradigm are also analysed in Christoph Kleßmann, 'Verflechtung und Abgrenzung – Umrisse einer gemeinsamen deutschen Nachkriegsgeschichte', in: Schönhoven and Staritz (eds), *Sozialismus*, pp. 486-99.
15. Habermas, 'Die Last', p. 54.
16. Kocka, *Die Auswirkungen*, p. 16; idem, *Vereinigungskrise*, p. 101.
17. Jäckel, *Die zweifache Vergangenheit*. Also: idem, 'Die doppelte Vergangenheit', *Der Spiegel*, no. 52, 1991, pp. 39-43.
18. Hans Mommsen, 'Nationalismus und Stalinismus. Diktaturen im Vergleich', in: Sühl (ed.), *Vergangenheitsbewältigung*, pp. 109-26.
19. Georg Fülberth, 'An der Grenze', *Konkret*, 1 Aug. 1994, pp. 14-16.
20. Peter Reichel, 'Bitte keine neue Totalitarismus-Debatte!', *Die Tageszeitung*, 4 March 1992.
21. Ralph Jessen, 'Die Gesellschaft im Staatssozialismus. Probleme einer Sozialgeschichte der DDR', *GG*, vol. 21, 1995, pp. 96-110.
22. Herbert Obenaus, 'Stasi kommt – Nazi geht?', *Die Zeit*, 31 July 1992, p. 40.
23. Baring, *Deutschland*, pp. 55 f.

24. Christa Hoffmann, *Stunden Null? Vergangenheitsbewältigung in Deutschland 1945 und 1989*, Bonn, 1992, p. 304.
25. Horst Möller, 'Die Geschichte des Nationalsozialismus und der DDR: ein (un)möglicher Vergleich?', in: Sühl (ed.), *Vergangenheitsbewältigung*, pp. 127-38.
26. Hans-Peter Schwarz, 'Ende der Gedenktage?', *Die Welt*, 29 June 1991.
27. Hans-Helmuth Knütter, 'Vergangenheitsbewältigung nach der Wende im Herbst 1989', *Deutsche Ostkunde*, vol. 36, 1990, pp. 122-36; Rainer Zitelmann, 'Historiographische Vergangenheitsbewältigung und Modernisierungstheorie. Nationalsozialismus, Faschismus, Stalinismus', in: Bernd Faulenbach, Martin Stadelmaier (eds), *Diktatur und Emanzipation. Zur russischen und deutschen Entwicklung 1917-1991*, Essen, 1993, pp. 111-35; Arnulf Baring, 'Nur die Erinnerung erlöst', *FAZ*, 5 April 1995; Wolfgang Schuller, 'Vergangenheitsbewältigung in Deutschland', *FAZ*, 12 March 1996.
28. Lothar Gall, 'Die Geschichte ist nicht das Waffenlager der Politik', *Die Welt*, 26 Sept. 1994.
29. Manfred Kossock, 'Im Gehäuse selbstverschuldeter Unmündigkeit oder Umgang mit Geschichte', *BZG*, vol. 35, 1993, p. 36.
30. See, for an example, Arnulf Baring, 'Am Ende liegen sich alle in den Armen', *Berliner Zeitung*, 4/5 April 1992.
31. An example is Armin Mitter and Stefan Wolle, *Untergang auf Raten. Unbekannte Kapitel der DDR Geschichte*, Munich, 1993. Compare also the treatment of GDR history in the special issue of the journal *Das Parlament*, 17 June 1994.
32. Ernst Nolte, 'Die fortwirkende Verblendung', *FAZ*, 22 Feb. 1992.
33. Hans-Peter Schwarz, 'Wenn der Namenspatron ein Massenmörder war', *Die Welt*, 17 Jan. 1992; idem, 'Das Ende der Identitätsneurose', *Rheinischer Merkur*, 7 Sept. 1990, p. 3.
34. Weißmann, *Rückruf*, p. 49.
35. Patrick Bahners, 'Wie fesselt man den deutschen Gulliver', *FAZ*, 13 March 1990.
36. Karl Rudolf Korte, *Die Chance genutzt? Die Politik zur Einheit Deutschlands*, Frankfurt-on-Main, 1994, p. 12.
37. Baring, *Deutschland*, p. 55.
38. Hans Günter Hockerts, 'Soziale Errungenschaften? Zum sozialpolitischen Legitimitätsanspruch der zweiten deutschen Diktatur', in: Jürgen Kocka, Hans-Jürgen Puhle and Klaus Tenfelde (eds), *Von der Arbeiterbewegung zum modernen Sozialstaat*, Munich, 1994, pp. 790-804.
39. Klaus Schroeder and Jochen Staadt, 'Der diskrete Charme des Status-quo: DDR Forschung in der Ära der Entspannungspolitik', in: Schroeder (ed.), *Geschichte*, p. 309.
40. Heinrich August Winkler, '1989/90', in: idem and Carola Stern (eds), *Wendepunkte deutscher Geschichte 1848-1990*, rev. edn, Frankfurt-on-Main, 1994, pp. 206, 221 f.
41. Winkler, 'Rebuilding of a Nation', p. 115 f.
42. Wolfgang J. Mommsen, 'Fata Morgana aus Plattenbauten', *Die Welt*, 27 March 1993; Hans-Ulrich Wehler, 'Ein deutsches Säkulum?', *Die Zeit*, 8 Nov. 1996, p. 16.
43. Kocka, 'Überraschung und Erklärung', pp. 12 f.; Kurt Sontheimer, 'Real war nur der schöne Schein', *Rheinischer Merkur*, 23 Feb. 1990.
44. Jürgen Kocka, 'Ein deutscher Sonderweg. Überlegungen zur Sozialgeschichte der DDR', *aus politik und zeitgeschichte*, 7 Oct. 1994, pp. 34-45; Arnold Sywottek, 'Nationaler Attentismus und anachronistischer Sozialismus. Die DDR in der deutschen Geschichte', in: Schönhoven and Staritz (eds), *Sozialismus*, pp. 467-85. Historians here often follow Jürgen Habermas' interpretation of the revolutions in Eastern Europe as 'catching up revolutions'. Whereas in the West modernisation proceeded quickly after 1945, the East European countries had been

retarded by Communism's stranglehold. The velvet revolutions of 1989 sought to correct this imbalance. See Jürgen Habermas, *Die nachholende Revolution. Kleine Politische Schriften VII*, Frankfurt-on-Main, 1990.

45. Werner Bramke, 'Widerstand und Dissens. Gedanken über die Vergleichbarkeit von Widersetzlichkeit im Faschismus und im "realen Sozialismus"', in: Jarausch and Middell (eds), *Nach dem Erdbeben*, p. 223.

46. Jürgen Kocka, 'Nur keinen neuen Sonderweg', *Die Zeit*, 19 Oct. 1990, p. 11; Thomas Schmid, 'Die Eroberung der Bundesrepublik durch die ehemalige DDR', *Die Tageszeitung*, 14 Dec. 1990.

47. Rosmarie Beier, 'Deutsch-deutsche Befindlichkeiten', *GWU*, vol. 46, 1995, pp. 206-22. See also Thomas Gensicke, 'Vom Staatsbewußtsein zur Oppositions-Ideologie. DDR-Identität im vereinten Deutschland', in: Axel Knoblich, Antonio Peter and Erik Natter (eds), *Auf dem Weg zu einer gesamtdeutschen Identität?*, Cologne, 1993, pp. 49-65.

48. Jürgen Kocka, 'Crisis of Unification: How Germany Changes', *Daedalus*, vol. 123, 1994, pp. 173-92.

49. Wolfgang Dümcke and Fritz Vilmar (eds), *Kolonialisierung der DDR. Kritische Analysen und Alternativen des Einigungsprozesses*, Münster, 1995.

50. Ulrich Herbert and Olaf Groehler, *Zweierlei Bewältigung. Vier Beiträge über den Umgang mit NS-Vergangenheit in den beiden deutschen Staaten*, Hamburg, 1992, pp. 18-26; 29-40; Jürgen Danyel (ed.), *Die geteilte Vergangenheit. Zum Umgang mit Nationalsozialismus und Widerstand in beiden deutschen Staaten*, Berlin, 1995.

51. Kurt Pätzold, 'Research on Fascism and Antifascism in the German Democratic Republic: a Critical Retrospective', *Radical History Review*, vol. 54, 1992, pp. 87-109; Manfred Weißbecker, 'Wahrheit und Irrtum in den Faschismusforschungen der DDR. Historiographische und andere Reminiszenzen', *Deutsche Studien*, no. 116, 1992, pp. 397-415.

52. Schulze, '"Das traurigste Los"', p. 688. For a rather undifferentiated view of 'the ideology of antifascism' in both West and East Germany see Dan Diner, 'On the Ideology of Antifascism', *New German Critique*, no. 67, winter 1996, pp. 123-32.

53. Michael Wolffsohn, *Die Deutschland-Akte. Juden und Deutsche in Ost und West*, Munich, 1995.

54. Hans-Ulrich Thamer, 'Thesenpapier zu Antifaschismus und die Auseinandersetzung mit der Geschichte des Nationalsozialismus in den zwei deutschen Staaten', in: J. Calließ (ed.), *Getrennte Vergangenheit – gemeinsame Geschichte. Zur historischen Orientierung im Einigungsprozeß*, Rehburg-Loccum, 1992, p. 108.

55. For a telling personal account of the importance of anti-fascist motivations see Fritz Klein, 'Ein schlimmes gemeinsames Erbe kritisch und selbstkritisch auf beiden Seiten aufarbeiten', in: Danyel (ed.), *Die geteilte Vergangenheit*, pp. 139-41.

56. Manfred Weißbecker, 'Zwischen Beharrung und neuen Grenzen. Problematisches im heutigen deutschen Zeitgeschichtsdenken', in: Ekkehard Wagner and Hannes Kaschkat (eds), *Daß Deutschland eins werde*, Lauf an der Pegnitz, 1994, p. 145.

57. 'So halfen Kommunisten den Nazis beim Morden', *Bild Zeitung*, 20 Feb. 1994; The public debate was instigated by Lutz Niethammer (ed.), *Der "gesäuberte" Antifaschismus. Die SED und die roten Kapos von Buchenwald. Dokumente*, Berlin, 1994. Whilst Niethammer tried to find a differentiated approach to the complex problem of Buchenwald, the new right gleefully picked up some of his findings to equate Communism and Nazism. Thus, Niethammer's book was reviewed positively in the extreme right-wing *National-Zeitung* and *Junge Freiheit*. For the public debate surrounding Niethammer's publication see the sound judgment of Jürgen Danyel, 'Wandlitz auf dem Ettersberg? Zur Debatte um die roten Kapos von Buchenwald', *ZfG*, vol. 43, 1995, pp. 159-66.

58. All too one-sided, in my view, are Antonia Grunenberg, *Antifaschismus – ein deutscher Mythos*, Reinbek, 1993; Herbert Ammon, 'Antifaschismus im Wandel? Historisch-kritische Anmerkungen zur Aktualität eines Begriffs', in: Jesse, Backes and Zitelmann (eds), *Was heißt Historisierung*, pp. 568-94.
59. Geiss, '"Wende" und Ende', pp. 122-4.
60. Klaus Rainer Röhl, *Linke Lebenslügen. Eine überfällige Abrechnung*, Frankfurt-on-Main, 1994, pp. 12-26.
61. Christian Striefler and Wolfgang Templin (eds), *Von der Wiederkehr des Sozialismus. Die andere Seite der Wiedervereinigung*, Berlin, 1996.
62. Hans-Helmuth Knütter, 'Sozialpsychologie des Antifaschismus', in: Filbinger and Karst (eds), *Identität*, p. 69.
63. Jürgen Danyel, Olaf Groehler, Mario Kessler, 'Antifaschismus und Verdrängung. Zum Umgang mit der NS-Vergangenheit in der DDR', in: Jürgen Kocka and Martin Sabrow (eds), *Die DDR als Geschichte. Fragen – Hypothesen – Perspektiven*, Berlin, 1994, pp. 148-52.
64. Deutscher Bundestag (ed.), *Aufarbeitung von Geschichte und Folgen der SED-Diktatur in Deutschland. Materialien der Enquete-Kommission des Deutschen Bundestages*, 18 vols, Frankfurt-on-Main, 1995.
65. '"Viele Folgen noch gar nicht erkannt." Der Historiker Faulenbach über die Kommission zur Aufarbeitung der SED-Diktatur', *FR*, 2 May 1994.
66. For the institute's research foci see Siegfried Suckut, 'Zugang zu Stasi-Akten für Wissenschaftler erleichtert', *Das Parlament*, 17 June 1994, p. 8.
67. 'Ein deutscher Sonderweg im Osten', *Der Tagesspiegel*, 17 June 1994.
68. Hans Günter Hockerts, 'Zeitgeschichte in Deutschland. Begriff, Methoden, Themenfelder', *aus politik und zeitgeschichte*, 16 July 1993, pp. 6, 18.
69. Hans Mommsen's contribution to the panel discussion 'Sackgasse aus dem Sonderweg', in: Kocka and Sabrow (eds), *Die DDR als Geschichte*, p. 234.
70. Jürgen Kocka (ed.), *Historische DDR Forschung. Aufsätze und Studien*, Berlin, 1993. For an explication of the institute's concept and aims see Christoph Kleßmann, 'Die Chance der Erneuerung jetzt auch nutzen', *Das Parlament*, 10 March 1995, p. 11. Other good examples of how to deal with GDR history without moving into the area of national apologetics are provided by Hartmut Kaelble, Jürgen Kocka, Hartmut Zwahr (eds), *Sozialgeschichte der DDR*, Stuttgart, 1994; Richard Bessel and Ralph Jessen (eds), *Die Grenzen der Diktatur: Staat und Gesellschaft in der DDR*, Göttingen, 1996.
71. Jürgen Kocka, 'Chance und Herausforderung. Aufgaben der Zeitgeschichte beim Umgang mit der DDR Vergangenheit', in: Bernd Faulenbach, Markus Meckel and Hermann Weber (eds), *Die Partei hatte immer recht. Aufarbeitung von Geschichte und Folgen der SED-Diktatur*, Essen, 1994, pp. 239-49.
72. Christoph Kleßmann's contribution to the panel discussion 'Sackgasse aus dem Sonderweg', in: Kocka and Sabrow (eds), *Die DDR als Geschichte*, pp. 224 f.
73. Bernd Faulenbach, 'Die doppelte Vergangenheitsbewältigung', in: Danyel (ed.), *Die geteilte Vergangenheit*, p. 185 speaks of a '*Verbösung*' of the GDR.
74. Walter Schmidt, 'DDR-Geschichtswissenschaft im Umbruch. Leistungen – Grenzen – Probleme', in: Rainer Eckert, Wolfgang Küttler, and Gustav Seeber (eds), *Krise-Umbruch-Neubeginn.Eine kritische und selbstkritische Dokumentation der DDR-Geschichtswissenschaft 1989/90*, Stuttgart, 1992, p. 175.
75. Fischer and Heydemann (eds), *Geschichtswissenschaft*, vol. 1, pp. 3-30.
76. Rainer Eckert, 'Vergangenheitsbewältigung oder überwältigt uns die Vergangenheit? oder Auf einem Sumpf ist schlecht bauen', *IWK*, vol. 28, 1992, pp. 228-32. The early history of the Independent Historians' Association and its various activities have been documented in Rainer Eckert, Ilko-Sascha Kowalczuk and Isolde Stark (eds), *Hure oder Muse? Klio in der DDR. Dokumente und Materialien des Unabhängigen Historiker-Verbandes*, Berlin, 1994.

77. Jürgen Danyel, 'Die Historiker und die Moral. Anmerkungen zu einer Debatte um die Autorenrechte an der DDR Geschichte', *GG*, vol. 21, 1995, pp. 291, 295.

78. 'Aufruf zur Bildung einer Arbeitsgruppe Unabhängiger Historiker in der DDR', in: Eckert, Küttler and Seeber (eds), *Krise*, pp. 231-5.

79. Andreas Graf, 'Wende und Wände. Zur Selbstfindung der (DDR-) Geschichtswissenschaft', in: Konrad Jarausch (ed.), *Zwischen Parteilichkeit und Provinzialität. Bilanz der Geschichtswissenschaft der DDR*, Berlin, 1991, p. 37.

80. Winfried Schulze, '"Das traurigste Los"', pp. 683-9; Ilko Sascha-Kowalczuk, '"Wo gehobelt wird, da fallen Späne." Zur Entwicklung der DDR Geschichtswissenschaft bis in die späten 50er Jahre', *ZfG*, vol. 42, 1994, pp. 302-18; Rainer Eckert, 'Ein gescheiterter Neuanfang?', *GG*, vol. 20, 1994, pp. 609-15; idem, 'Geschichtswissenschaft in der ehemaligen DDR: eine ostdeutsche Sicht', *Deutschland-Archiv*, vol. 25, 1992, pp. 175-80.

81. Karlheinz Blaschke, 'Akademiker als Pförtner', *FAZ*, 27 June 1990; Herbert Gottwald, 'Es gab nicht nur Anpassung und Stagnation. Plebejer des Geistes degradierten die Geschichtswissenschaft in der ehemaligen DDR', *FAZ*, 10 Dec. 1990.

82. Harm Klueting, 'Parteilichkeit war wichtiger als Objektivität. Die marxistisch-leninistische Geschichtsschreibung der DDR', *FAZ*, 8 May 1990, p. 13.

83. Christian Meier, 'Im Zweifel lieber abwickeln', *FAZ*, 21 Sept. 1990. For a strict argument in favour of ending all prospects for GDR historians see also Gustav Seibt, 'Kader. Überlebt die SED-Historie?', *FAZ*, 5 Sept. 1990, p. 33.

84. Wolfgang Schuller, 'Zwei Nationen – zwei Wissenschaften? Eindrücke vom Wiederaufbau der Wissenschaftsorganisationen in den neuen Bundesländern', *Deutschland-Archiv*, vol. 27, 1994, pp. 470-7. In any case, as Udo Wengst has argued, the take-over of GDR history by Westerners was justified on the basis of the latter's superior scholarliness. Cited in 'Geschichte als Wundpflaster', *FAZ*, 8 July 1995.

85. Both resolutions are reprinted in Eckert, Küttler, and Seeber (eds), *Krise*, pp. 211 f., 228-30.

86. 'Resolution zur Förderung der geisteswissenschaftlichen Forschungsschwerpunkte in den neuen Bundesländern', *GG*, vol. 21, 1995, p. 157.

87. Lothar Gall, 'Interview', *ZfG*, vol. 42, 1994, p. 1,062.

88. Hans-Ulrich Wehler, 'Hart widersprechen und mit dem Unfug stets konfrontieren', *FR*, 24 Sept. 1992. Also idem, *Gegenwart*, pp. 118, 212.

89. Jürgen Kocka, 'Es droht die Zementierung der alten Verhältnisse', *Die Welt*, 19 Dec. 1990.

90. Kocka, *Vereinigungskrise*, pp. 47-8, 54, 75-80.

91. Wolfgang J. Mommsen, 'Die Deutschen haben einiges dazugelernt', *Die Welt*, 25 Sept. 1990.

92. Wolfgang J. Mommsen, 'Die Geschichtswissenschaft nach der "demokratischen Revolution" in Ostmitteleuropa', *Neue Rundschau*, vol. 105, 1994, p. 78.

93. Wolfgang J. Mommsen, 'Die DDR in der deutschen Geschichte', *aus politik und zeitgeschichte*, 16 July 1993, p. 27.

94. Cited in Volker Erhard, 'Historische Wissenschaften und neue Bundesländer', *Deutschland-Archiv*, vol. 25, 1992, p. 1,073.

95. Joachim Rohlfes, 'Geschichtsdidaktik in der Zwangsjacke. Kritische Gedanken zum Geschichtsunterricht im SED-Staat', *GWU*, vol. 41, 1990, pp. 705-19.

96. Karl Heinz Roth, 'Anschlußhistoriker – Historikeranschluß', *1999*, vol. 6, 1991, pp. 8-12.

97. Hermann Weber, 'Die DDR-Geschichtswissenschaft im Umbruch? Aufgaben der Historiker bei der Bewältigung der stalinistischen Vergangenheit', *Deutschland-Archiv*, vol. 23, 1990, pp. 1,058-70; idem, 'Weiße Flecken in der DDR Geschichtsschreibung', *aus politik und zeitgeschichte*, 9 March 1990, p. 15.

98. Dietrich Staritz, 'Auf der Suche nach der verlorenen Zeit. Die DDR-Histori-ographie in der "DDR" nach der "Wende"', *BZG*, vol. 32, 1990, pp. 759 ff.

99. Wolfgang Benz, 'Das Ärgernis der Siegerpose', in: *Neues Deutschland. Innenansichten einer wiedervereinigten Nation*, ed. by J. Kogel, W. Schütte and H. Zimmermann, Frankfurt-on-Main, 1993, pp. 30-2.

100. Hermann Glaser, 'Wohl und Wehe den Besiegten', *Die Zeit*, 10 March 1995, p. 60.

101. Christoph Kleßmann, 'Die DDR Geschichtswissenschaft aus der Sicht der Bundesrepublik', in: Jarausch (ed.), *Zwischen Parteilichkeit und Professionalität*, pp. 43-55.

102. Jörn Rüsen, 'Partizipation in der Geschichtskultur', *Berliner Debatte Initial*, no. 2, 1994, p. 204.

103. Martin Sabrow, 'DDR-Bild im Perspektivenwandel', in: Kocka and Sabrow (eds), *Die DDR als Geschichte*, p. 248. Sabrow's article about the attempt of a handful of GDR historians – amongst them Fritz Klein and Günter Paulus – to organise contacts with their West-German colleagues in 1964 is an excellent example of how complex (and volatile) the positioning within the established GDR historiography was in the period of the Cold War. See Martin Sabrow, 'In geheimer Mission', *Die Zeit*, no. 16, 12 April 1996, p. 34.

104. Jochen Gläser, 'Die Akademie der Wissenschaften nach der Wende: erst reformiert, dann ignoriert und schließlich aufgelöst', *aus politik und zeitgeschichte*, 11 Dec. 1992, p. 46; for the bitterness of the process of *Abwicklung* at East German universities like Jena and Halle, see Ulrich Schneckener, 'Vertane Chancen und die "Dialektik der Abwicklung"', *FR*, 17 Nov. 1994.

105. Weißbecker, 'Zwischen Beharrung', p. 148.

106. Helga Schultz, 'Das Fiasko der historischen Gerechtigkeit – Ostdeutsche Geisteswissenschaften im Umbruch', *GG*, vol. 21, 1995, pp. 430-2. See also on the failure of the reintegration programme WIP Dieter E. Zimmer, 'Amtlich betrogen', *Die Zeit*, 2 Aug. 1996, p. 35, and idem, 'WIP und weg', *Die Zeit*, 13 Dec. 1996, p. 33.

107. Kurt Pätzold, 'What New Start? The End of Historical Study in the GDR', *German History*, vol. 10, 1992, pp. 392-404.

108. Kocka, *Die Auswirkungen*, pp. 6-15.

109. Gerhard A. Ritter, 'The Reconstruction of History at the Humboldt University: A Reply', *German History*, vol. 11, 1993, pp. 339, 345.

110. Wolfgang Frühwald, 'Erneuerung oder Kolonisierung?', Deutschland-Archiv, vol. 27, 1994, p. 877.

111. For Groehler's and Niethammer's views see 'Ohne Wahrheit keine Versöhnung', *Die Tageszeitung*, 1 June 1992.

112. Wendelin Szalai, 'Die DDR Geschichtsmethodik im Spannungsfeld zwischen äußerer und innerer Disziplinierung', *aus politik und zeitgeschichte*, 14 Oct. 1994, p. 31; for the situation of GDR history of science see Reinhard Siegmund Schultze, 'Die "Abwicklung" der Naturwissenschaftshistoriographie der ehemaligen DDR. Vorläufige Bilanz eines Ostdeutschen, *GG*, vol. 22, 1996, pp. 417-27.

113. Kossock, 'Im Gehäuse', p. 30.

114. Rainer Eckert, 'Die Berliner Humboldt-Universität und das Ministerium für Staatssicherheit', *Deutschland-Archiv*, vol. 26, 1992, pp. 770-86.

115. Danyel, 'Die Historiker und die Moral', p. 295.

116. Cited in Stefanie Schüler-Springorum and Christl Wickert, 'Unversöhnte Geschichte(n). Historiker in Ost und West', in: Karsten Rudolph and Christl Wickert (eds), *Geschichte als Möglichkeit: über die Chancen von Demokratie. Festschrift für Helga Grebing*, Essen, 1995, p. 25.

117. Kurt Pätzold, 'Sich totstellen oder wehren? Das ist die entscheidende Frage. Gedanken eines Historikers zur "Abwicklung" in den neuen Bundesländern', *ND*, 29/30 Dec.1990.

118. Hans Schleier, 'Vergangenheitsbewältigung und Traditionserneuerung? Geschichts-wissenschaft nach 1945', in: Walter H. Pehle and Peter Sillem (eds), *Wissenschaft im geteilten Deutschland. Restauration und Neubeginn nach 1945*, Frankfurt-on-Main, 1992, p. 219.

119. Weißbecker, 'Zwischen Beharrung', p. 149.

120. Hartmut Zwahr, 'Zu einer beginnenden Diskussion', in: Eckert et.al. (eds), *Krise*, p. 31. Helga Schultz, 'Was bleibt von der Geschichtswissenschaft der DDR?', in: Eckert et.al. (eds), *Krise*, p. 459 argued that it was one of the advantages of the GDR social history '*nicht national begrenzt zu sein*'.

121. Jürgen John, Wolfgang Küttler and Walter Schmidt, 'Für eine Erneuerung des Geschichtsverständnisses in der DDR', in: Eckert et.al. (eds), *Krise*, p. 159. For a self-critical re-evalution of GDR historiography by GDR historians see also Wolfgang Küttler, 'Geschichtstheorie und -methodologie in der DDR', *ZfG*, vol. 42, 1994, pp. 8-20; Joachim Petzold, 'Die Auseinandersetzung zwischen den Lampes und den Hampes', *ZfG*, vol. 42, 1994, pp. 101-17; Gerald Diesener, 'Überlegungen zu einer Geschichte der DDR-Geschichtswis-senschaft', in: Jarausch and Middell (eds), *Nach dem Erdbeben*, pp. 68-87. The lat-ter has explicitly rejected the 'picture of a sheep-like recipient of orders' for describing GDR historians.

122. John, Küttler and Schmidt, 'Für eine Erneuerung', in: Eckert et.al. (eds), *Krise*, p. 153.

123. 'Erklärung des Präsidiums der Historiker Gesellschaft e.V.', in: Eckert, Küttler, and Seeber (eds), *Krise*, p. 256 f.

124. Helga Schultz, 'Was bleibt von der Geschichtswissenschaft der DDR?', in: Eck-ert et.al. (eds), *Krise*, p. 452.

125. See Stefan Berger, 'Anti-communism after the Fall of Communism? The Anti-Left Syndrome of the SPD and its Impact on Contemporary German Politics', *Debatte*, vol. 3, 1995, pp. 66-97.

126. Wolfgang Küttler, 'Hat "marxistische" Geschichtsschreibung noch eine Zukunft?', in: Jarausch (ed.), *Zwischen Parteilichkeit und Professionalität*, pp. 165-84; Küttler, 'Marxistische Geschichtswissenschaft – was bleibt? Das Beispiel DDR', in: Jarausch, Rüsen and Schleier (eds), *Geschichtswissenschaft vor 2000*, pp. 82-99. See also the pessimistic assessment of the future of a Marxist historiography in the reunited Germany of Eckhard Fuchs, 'Geschichtswissenschaft und Krise des Marxismus. Zum marxistischen Diskurs in der englischen Geschichtsschreibung seit 1945 und zu den Perspektiven marxistischen Geschichtsdenkens in Deutsch-land', in: Jarausch and Middell (eds), *Nach dem Erdbeben*, pp. 132-56.

127. Schultz, 'Das Fiasko', pp. 433-9.

128. Geiss, '"Wende" und Ende', p. 124; idem, 'Anti-Antikommunismus auf dem trockenen', *FAZ*, 2 Dec. 1995.

129. Wolffsohn, 'Doppelte Vergangenheitsbewältigung', in: Sühl (ed.), *Vergangenheits-bewältigung*, p. 37.

130. Konrad Löw, 'Die bundesdeutsche politikwissenschaftliche DDR Forschung und die Revolution in der DDR', *Zeitschrift für Politik*, vol. 38, 1991, pp. 237 – 254. Also idem, ... *bis zum Verrat der Freiheit. Die Gesellschaft der Bundesrepublik und die 'DDR'*, 2nd edn, Munich, 1994, chapters 5 and 7, pp. 135-53, 174-96; and in a similar vein of blanket condemnation of critical social scientists for their allegedly analytically facile and morally questionable behaviour see Eckhard Jesse, 'Wie man eine Schimäre zum Leben erweckt', *FAZ*, 24 Aug. 1990; Klaus Schröder and Jochen Staadt, 'Der diskrete Charme des Status quo: DDR-Forschung in der Ära der Entspannungspolitik', in: Schröder (ed.), *Geschichte*, pp. 309-46.

131. Jens Hacker, *Deutsche Irrtümer: Schönfärber und Helfershelfer der SED-Diktatur im Westen*, Frankfurt-on-Main, 1992.

132. Wolfgang Schuller, 'Wie sich das Ende der DDR abzeichnete', *FAZ*, 12 Oct. 1992.

133. Ernst Nolte, 'Abschließende Reflexionen über den sogenannten Historikerstreit', in: idem, *Lehrstück oder Tragödie?*, pp. 225-50.

134. Zitelmann, *Republik*, pp. 163-6.

135. Joachim C. Fest, 'Schweigende Wortführer', *FAZ*, 30 Dec. 1989.

136. Schroeder and Staadt, 'Der diskrete Charme', in: Schoeder (ed.), *Geschichte*, pp. 309-46.

137. Rainer Eckert, 'Die Geschichtswissenschaft der DDR im Deutschlandarchiv', *Deutschland-Archiv*, vol. 28, 1995, pp. 948-63.

138. Armin Mitter and Stefan Wolle, 'Der Bielefelder Weg. Die Vergangenheitsbewältigung der Historiker und die Vereinigung der Funktionäre', *FAZ*, 10 Aug. 1993; idem, 'Inquisitoren auf der Faultierfarm. Gestern Bielefeld und Ostberlin, heute Potsdam', *FAZ*, 9 Sept. 1993.

139. A perfect example is Klaus Schroeder, 'Fröhliche Parteiwissenschaft', *FAZ*, 22 July 1995. For accusations of networking between incriminated GDR researchers and Western colleagues leading to the danger of continued historical misrepresentation see also Schroeder (ed.), *Geschichte*, pp. 16, 19.

140. Jürgen Kocka, 'Auch Wissenschaftler können lernen' and Wolfgang Mommsen, 'Von Bevormundung zu intellektueller Kolonisierung', both in *FAZ*, 25 Aug. 1993.

141. Christoph Kleßmann's contribution to the panel discussion 'Sackgasse aus dem Sonderweg', in: Kocka and Sabrow (eds), *Die DDR als Geschichte*, pp. 224 f.

142. Hermann Weber, 'Das Büßergewand bleibt im Schrank', *FAZ*, 10 Sept. 1994, p. 30. Largely defending West German research on the GDR and its results also: Gert-Joachim Glaeßner (ed.), *Kommunismus – Totalitarismus – Demokratie*, Frankfurt-on-Main, 1994 and Gisela Helwig (ed.), *Rückblicke auf die DDR*, Cologne, 1995.

143. Bernd Faulenbach, 'Zur Bedeutung der Umwälzungen in Mittel- und Osteuropa für das Geschichtsverständnis der deutschen Arbeiterbewegung', *BZG*, vol. 34, 1992, p. 42.

144. Jürgen Kocka, 'Von der Verantwortung der Zeithistoriker', *FR*, 3 May 1994.

Chapter 8

THE OLD FEDERAL REPUBLIC AS
THE NEW *SONDERWEG*

We have already seen above that *Sonderweg* notions pre-1945 have been further eroded after 1989/1990. Those who are intent on renationalising German historical consciousness instead began to interpret the history of the Federal Republic between 1949 and 1990 as the new *Sonderweg*. A new framework for the history of the old FRG was provided by Karl-Heinz Bohrer who saw its society and politics characterised by its alleged provincialism.[1] From being a success story, the history of the Federal Republic has become a mere divertimento in German national history. For Weißmann, the Federal Republic lacked 'all those historical characteristics as leave their mark' on the nation.[2] Fest has characterised the Federal Republic's *Sonderweg* as 'its curiously dreamless existence, untragic, even a bit happy in the depth of consumerism and leisure time worlds'.[3] And Christian Meier has criticised the FRG's bloodless existence: 'No doubt the FRG was worthy, successful and sometimes even endearing, and yet at the same time it was narrow, all too abstract in its public thought and last but not least also extremely tense ... Is it fair to say that it had no authenticity and originality?'[4] For Meier it has become one of the central tasks of the present to overcome, not only the 'GDR nostalgia', but also the 'FRG nostalgia'. The FRG had allegedly alienated its citizens from the 'hard realities' of life which will have to be learnt again after 1989.[5]

The re-writing of the history of the Federal Republic has been particularly visible in four areas. First, it has been questioned whether

---

Germans had actually balked at the task of coming to terms with the Nazi past *(Vergangenheitsbewältigung)* in the immediate post-war era. Instead, it has been suggested that, from the 1960s onwards, the constant public breast-beating about the Nazi past was so excessive as to produce a neurotic guilt complex which Germans are now having to overcome after reunification. Secondly, attacks on the consequences of Allied and German re-education policies after 1945 have occasionally turned into a more general questioning of the Federal Republic's Western orientation. Criticisms of Western liberalism and European integration have merged with the revival of geopolitical ideas of Germany's position in the middle of Europe *(Mittellage)* to provide an explosive mixture of anti-Western sentiment. Thirdly, historians have propagated a more forceful foreign and military policy which would, in their view, adequately reflect the new Federal Republic's alleged superpower status in the world. And finally, *Ostpolitik* and its alleged moral and political failings have come under renewed attack in order to discredit the erstwhile champions of dialogue with Communist Eastern Europe.

The Germans' success in coming to terms with their Nazi past has, for the past six years, been a central debate in the reunified country. The traditional wisdom that the Nazi past was largely ignored in the 1950s has been severely questioned.[6] As early as 1981 Peter Steinbach pointed out that the 1950s had seen a considerable amount of *Vergangenheitsbewältigung.* It had become part of the basic political consensus amongst the major parties in the FRG.[7] Especially those historians in special research institutes outside the universities, Udo Wengst has recently argued, had been central to early efforts to come to terms with the Nazi past.[8] In a comparative treatment of *Vergangenheitsbewältigung* after 1945 and after 1990 Christa Hoffmann has praised the continuous and intensive judicial efforts at *Vergangenheitsbewältigung* after 1945. The current debates about the GDR past will, in her estimation, lead to a far more positive assessment of the achievements after the end of the Second World War.[9] For Jürgen Steinle, historians never really adhered to the thesis that National Socialism should be seen as an accident *(Betriebsunfall)* in German history. This notion, he argued, had been 'invented' by Fischer and his followers in the 1960s.[10] After 1989 diverse representatives of the new right have refashioned Steinbach's thesis with clear political intent. The argument about the *unbewältigte Vergangenheit* had to be undermined, as it de facto functioned as a barrier on the path towards the newly found 'normality' of the nation-state. Hence Weißmann and Wolffsohn, for example, have insisted that the Nazi past had been 'the decisive reference point for intellectual life' in the

Federal Republic from the very beginning.[11] For Zitelmann the thesis that the 1950s had been characterised by a widespread silence on Nazism belongs to one of the canonised legends of the 1968 generation.[12] Concentrating on the government, parliament, the justice system and the media, Manfred Kittel has devoted a substantial monograph to the thesis that a serious, successful and coherent effort to come to terms with the Nazi past was undertaken in the 1950s.[13] Kittel's argument, however, at least partly rests on a conceptual trick. By distinguishing normal crimes from Nazi crimes, he has excluded from the discussion certain topics, such as the crimes committed by the *Wehrmacht*. In other areas, for example when he writes about the prompt and efficient way in which the West German justice system dealt with Nazi crimes, he has simply chosen to ignore the overwhelming evidence to the contrary.[14] Kittel's focus on the public discussion of the Nazi past of individuals and on de-Nazification more generally shows up problems of continuity, but it does not say much about efforts to come to terms with that past. Furthermore, there remains a fundamental difference between a 'published opinion' and a 'public opinion'.[15] The fact that involvement in Nazi crimes was not a hindrance to a successful career in post-war West Germany is as absent from his arguments as the fact that only certain topics were addressed by Germans vis-à-vis the recent Nazi past. German suffering in the Second World War, together with the totalitarian character of the Nazi regime – those were indeed topics frequently found in public debates in the 1950s. Yet it was a taboo until the 1960s to draw any link between the German *Sonderweg* before 1945 and the Holocaust. The very insistence on the centrality of genocide for an understanding of National Socialism was largely absent from the early period of historiographical research on National Socialism in the Federal Republic.[16]

By ignoring these aspects of *Vergangenheitsbewältigung*, Kittel has concluded that the prevailing feeling in post-war Germany was one of guilt, re-enforced by the re-education policies of the Allies which allegedly were motivated by their 'puritanical enthusiasm for purges'.[17] Schöllgen has inferred that the destruction of Germany's power-consciousness by the Allies still prevents a 'healthy' return to superpower politics in the reunified Germany.[18] Even the foundation of the arch-conservative *Ranke-Gesellschaft* has been justified as the desperate attempt of 'upright patriots' to defend themselves against an imposed Allied historiography which fostered 'anti-Germanism'.[19] Dirk Rumberg, for one, has already asked impatiently: 'Will the reference to Auschwitz be forever used to blackmail us, make us compliant and keep us modest?'[20] According to Jochen Thies, editor-in-chief of the journal *Europa-Archiv*, Germans would do well to escape from the prison of constantly memorising the twelve years of the National Socialist dictatorship.[21] For Baring all efforts to come to terms with the past have been, in any case, a mere 'luxury because they do not belong [to a people's] elementary necessities of life'.[22] Such views have come close to adopting the old extreme right-wing attacks on the Allied re-education programmes as a brainwashing of the German nation.[23]

The real mistake, it is now argued with increasing frequency, was not the lack of *Vergangenheitsbewältigung* in the 1950s. On the contrary, the mistake was to have overdone it from the 1960s onwards. For Eckhard Jesse an 'excessive *Vergangenheitsbewältigung*' which he has described as exhibitionist and enforced, had successfully established an 'atavistic notion of atonement' in Germany as a 'substitute for the missing unifying identity'.[24] Authors like Kittel, Jesse and Zitelmann have expressed their disdain for the moralism and the 'false notions of a public pedagogy' which, in their view, characterised much of the historiography on Nazism. Pointing to Italy and Japan, they have argued that Germany's 'morbid' concentration on the Nazi past has been exceptionally thorough. Amongst historians in particular they have identified a 'mentality of remorseful rumination' *(Zerknirschungs-mentalität)*[25] which has led to anti-Germanism.[26] Enrico Syring has warned against a 'partisan historiography' which would ban anything positive about the Germans.[27] In this view many left-liberal historians allegedly fled their own past by accusing previous generations and denying their own national identity.[28] In almost masochist fashion, they allegedly instrumentalised the Nazi past to stigmatise and ulti-mately silence their political enemies.[29] *Vergangenheitsbewältigung* has thus become connected to what is referred to as 'the under-estima-tion of the national question in the FRG'.[30] Historiography became engaged in efforts to prove conclusively to the Germans that history itself had disapproved of their nation-building efforts. The 'anti-nationalist' 1968 generation supposedly invented the idea of postna-tionalism as a bloodless alternative.[31] Abandoning the postnational *Sonderweg* means, according to Löw, giving future generations of Ger-mans a consciously national education and thereby overcoming the present German self-hatred.[32] Baring has called upon his fellow his-torians to recognise at long last the simple truth that 'our people was for centuries regarded as one of the most competent, if not the most competent in the world at large.'[33] Hence 'the negative fixation on the National Socialist period has to be abandoned'.[34]

Given their perception of *Vergangenheitsbewältigung* as anti-nation-alism, it would be logical for neo-nationalists to call for an early end to the debate on the GDR past. Indeed, some, like Armin Mohler, have urged fellow historians not to repeat the mistakes of the past.[35] Wolffsohn has warned against letting zealotry destroy the opportunity for integrating vast numbers of East Germans into the FRG.[36] In contrast, others have openly come out in favour of rigorously confronting the GDR legacy. Talking of the need for a 'comparison of dictatorships' and insisting on the moral argument that the same yardsticks should be applied to the two systems, some historians conveniently forget that the two regimes have in fact been very different.[37] What tends to get pushed under the carpet in comparisons of various efforts to come to terms with different pasts, is the fact that the National Socialist past was not simply about dictatorship but about the Holocaust.

A widespread public discourse on Nazism involving all its criminal aspects only occurred from the 1960s onwards.[38] Norbert Frei's detailed study on *Vergangenheitspolitik* in the post-1945 era leaves no doubt about the moral failure and the political mistakes which were made in the early Federal Republic due to the fact that the National Socialist past was met by silence.[39] Simplistic pedagogical models which would equate critical reappraisal with demonstrating the terroristic, criminal elements of dictatorial regimes might indeed not be very helpful. Instead, as Lutz Niethammer has pointed out, any successful *Vergangenheitsbewältigung* would necessarily have to give space to the subjective experiences of individuals under the dictatorship.[40] On the whole *Vergangenheitsbewältigung* has benefitted Germany's democratic political culture. The caesura of 1989 will only remain a happy one provided Germans do not forget the importance of the caesura of 1945. A thorough confrontation with German barbarity will have to continue to play a major role in the reunified country.[41]

New right historians have not only attacked *Vergangenheitsbewältigung* as anti-Germanism. They have also linked efforts to come to terms with the Nazi past to the ideas of Westernisation and Western integration. Those ideas, the new right has argued, have been amongst the 'alien' identities instilled into the Germans via *Vergangenheitsbewältigung*. Describing such ideas as political utopias with almost totalitarian pretensions, Zitelmann and his followers have accused critical historians of 'metaphysically transfiguring' these concepts in the past through over-identifying with the West in an irrational fashion. As 'quasi-religions' such utopias could allegedly neither be questioned nor discussed openly in the Federal Republic.[42] Yet in their view that is exactly what is needed. Once again they have harked back to geopolitical arguments about Germany's *Mittellage* in order to reinterpret its past and demand a reorientation of its future European policies.[43] Such perspectives have worked real miracles for the disposal of an unwanted German past. Germany can thus be portrayed as having been first and foremost 'a permanent battlefield in Europe on which its neighbours ... fought out their rivalries'.[44] Conservative historians, like Schöllgen, have also warmed to the tune. For him, the 'tragedies' of German history are all – in one way or another – related to its geographic position in the middle of Europe.[45] In 1989, Stürmer argued, 'Germany has once again become the centre ... For Germany it will be the decisive question of the future, if it is able to develop enough statesmanship to evade the temptations and the damnations of the old *Mittellage*, Western Europe still has to learn ... that its own fate fulfils itself in the Centre and in the East.'[46] Geiss' recent analysis of the German question has been steeped in *Mitte* metaphors: 'In their foreign policy the Germans cannot evade their eternal dilemma in the centre of Europe ... Mercilessly the reunited Germans have been caught up by their basic dilemma, i.e., their position in the middle of cultural and economic gradients between West and East and North and South.'[47] Baring has described the reunified Germany as 'squatting once again in the old central European difficulties'.[48] In connection with Germany's supposed *Mittellage* some authors have revived the concept of Germany acting as a bridge between East and West.[49] For Hacke, 'Western integration will not suffice as a guideline for the future foreign policy of the reunified Germany'.[50] As historiography had allegedly forgotten such fundamental geographic facts, the so-called 1989 generation will have 'to rise to the challenge and return to Germany its true identity as nation of the centre'.[51] And Schwarz has already dreamt of renewed German hegemony over the countries of *Mitteleuropa*. Germany, he argued, will help their economic development and their integration into the EU and NATO, but, of course, 'everything has its price' – and the price for the smaller nations of central Europe is to support Germany on the stage of international politics.[52] It should, however, also be pointed out that the revival of geopolitical thought in post-reunification Germany has met with considerable opposition. In particular Wehler has remained sceptical of the 'germanocentric arrogance' of those 'adhering to the utopia of *Mittellage*'.[53] The concept of central Europe *(Mitteleuropa)* had such a fatal tradition in German foreign politics as a pretext for justifying German hegemony that it is beyond resurrection.[54]

A more sceptical evaluation of the European Union amongst new-right historians has been in line with the attacks on the Westernisation of the Federal Republic. Such anti-European sentiments should be carefully separated from the justifiable scepticism about the road to further European integration which has been voiced by, amongst others, Dahrendorf and Kielmannsegg. The latter have argued that any immediate hope of a Europe that would transcend national allegiances has to remain wishful thinking, for the time being at least. As they have pointed out, the nation-state will remain the only effective guarantor of basic civil liberties and rights for some time to come. Constitutional patriotism thus only makes sense within nation-states. Therefore, according to Dahrendorf, the renaissance of the nation-state as a constitutional entity guaranteeing civil liberties is not necessarily to be deplored, at least not until the European Union has developed reliable institutions to guarantee the same civil liberties and basic rights across Europe.[55] While no-one could denounce Dahrendorf or Kielmannsegg as anti-European national-ists, their rather one-sided positive re-endorsement of the nation-state has been gleefully picked up by those who would fit this description more neatly. For them, the current shortcomings of the EU are evidence of the unchanging superiority of the nation-state over supra-national organisations. The nation-state thus becomes the natural anchorage point for people's emotions which cannot be replaced by an allegedly artificial European identity.[56] For Tilman Mayer, nations 'simply exist ... They do not have to be constructed or invented'.[57] In this view Europe can at best develop as 'welcome supplement' to the everlasting nation-states.[58] Against the back-ground of such theories, Weißmann has declared apodictically: 'There will be no "European nation" ... .'[59] For some, the European Union has become a kind of master plot to exploit Germany eco-nomically and politically,[60] whilst others have asserted that a 'multi-national European mega-society will rob Germany of the last contours of national identity'.[61]

However, it has to be emphasised that anti-Western and anti-Euro-pean sentiments remain on the margins of historical discourse in Ger-many. Even amongst a majority of conservative historians, there is still a clear commitment to the European Union and the West more generally. Stürmer and Weidenfeld have explicitly warned against questioning Western integration.[62] He has certainly been critical of the Maastricht Treaty and of any tendency to level the differences between European nations. Boundaries, rivalries and differences, in his view, will have to remain as they constitute that which is specific about Europe. Yet ultimately this is a debate about what sort of Europe its citizens want to create. It is an important debate within a wider pro-European consensus. For Gruner, Germany has to become 'the motor of European unity'.[63] Others have hailed the end of the Cold War as a genuine opportunity to build a Europe that would

extend to the states of Eastern Europe.[64] German and European unification have often been perceived as the twin tasks for politics in the
future.[65] There have been some squabbles about the question
whether rapid integration of the EU countries should take precedence over the integration of Eastern European countries. At times
one can find the notion that Germany's *Mittellage* predestines the
country to mediate between East and West and there has been much
talk about the special responsibility of Germany for the smooth integration of Eastern Europe into the EU.[66] But on the whole a broad
consensus has emerged which combines commitment to the West
with help for the East. Developing and stabilising Eastern Europe is
portrayed as the EU's 'historical task'. A deepening of cooperation in
the West should be combined with extending the EU's remit eastwards.[67] Amongst left-liberal historians, calls for an acceleration of the
democratisation and further integration of the EU have also been
loud and clear.[68] The European dimension of reunification thus
indeed marks one of the most important differences to the Bismarckian foundation of the Reich in the nineteenth century. In a very optimistic assessment of the current situation, Hartmut Kaelble has come
to the conclusion that the renaissance of the nation-states has been
paralleled by a 'new enthusiasm' for the EU. For Kaelble, German
reunification will ease the task of European integration as it has done
away with the artificial replacement of national identity by European
identity. Instead, he argued, as with other 'normal' nation-states, Germany will in future develop a national identity which will comple-
ment its European identity.[69] For Schulze, it will be up to the 'spiritual
brotherhood' of European intellectuals to write history in such a way
as to underline the common roots of European civilisation.[70]

Despite the genuine commitment of many German historians to
the unification of the European continent, there has also been at times
something egocentric and even megalomaniacal in their assessment
of Germany's role in that process. For Gruner, Germany can either
become Europe's 'blessing' or its 'evil spirit', depending on whether it
fulfils its European mission or not.[71] A German-centred Europe has
also been behind Schöllgen's pleas that 'Europe's heart needs
strength',[72] or that Germany is to determine 'the fate of Europe'.[73]
Stürmer has even harked back to the pompous words of MacKinder's
1904 dictum that 'it will be decided in Europe's centre who inherits
the earth'.[74] Even critical observers of the neo-Prussian tendencies
have talked of Germany as 'the key country'[75] and 'the soft belly of
Europe. If colics develop here, then the whole continent is in agony.'[76]

New right attacks on Western integration have occasionally been
combined with a sceptical reevaluation of 'Western values' such as

liberalism, rationalism and universalism. 'Increased liberalism' in West Germany has become a 'gateway for the activities of left-wing extremism'[77] and this, in turn, has threatened the stability of liberal society and the very existence of the nation. In apocalyptic terms Nolte has written: 'one simply cannot overlook the fact that liberalism, if it develops into libertarianism [*Libertismus*], kills the nations and may well, after a gigantic migration of peoples, kill humankind.'[78] The rationalism of liberal societies is perceived as their major weakness. A perceived crisis of the liberal system is attributed to liberalism's lack of a 'decisive readiness to act' and its inability to develop 'an ethos of courage and sacrifice'.[79] In times of crisis, according to Nolte, liberal societies may do well to return to a more rigorous presidential dictatorship.[80] Conservatives, like Fest, have suggested less radical cures for the ills of liberalism, for example, the reestablishment of transcendental values such as religion, authority and the nation-state.[81] The strengthening of national feeling in particular has been rediscovered as an antidote to individual egotism and one-sided cosmopolitanism which allegedly prevailed in the Federal Republic. Hard-boiled nationalists like Weißmann have already declared their preference for a strong German state rather than for Western civil society: 'Can a society of shopkeepers [sic] ... continue to exist? Will it be able to overcome crises, and can it demand sacrifices (maybe even the sacrifice of life) from its citizens to guarantee the continued existence of the whole?'[82]

Any return to anti-Western forms of conservatism in Germany, long thought of as dead, would badly divide the conservative camp. Differences over Westernisation have become most visible in the debates surrounding Adenauer's policies. Many conservatives have continued to be admirers of Adenauer. Together with Bismarck he has been put firmly into the national gallery of good Germans.[83] Baring, Fest, Morsey, Schwarz, Erdmann, and also Sontheimer, have all, in one way or the other, endorsed Adenauer as an ingenious pathfinder on the road to German unity.[84] In this view, German reunification need not be worrying as the FRG's commitment to Westernisation would continue.[85] The new right, however, has rediscovered the anti-Western nationalist politics in the early history of the Federal Republic. Zitelmann, for example, has published short biographical portraits of Jakob Kaiser, Kurt Schumacher, Gustav Heinemann, Thomas Dehler and Paul Sethe in order to demonstrate the existence of a consciously national policy as an alternative to Adenauer's course of Western integration. The latter is interpreted as a conscious abandonment of the national principle. Adenauer, in this view, is held responsible for the deepening gulf between the two

Germanies. By contrast, his opponents deserve, according to Zitelmann, an 'honoured position in German post-war history' as they managed to keep alive the thought of German unity.[86] Zitelmann chooses representatives of all traditional political parties. The message is clear: all political parties will now have to come together and contribute to the necessary renationalisation of German identity.

Worried by such signs that the reunified Germans might in the end prove to be 'shallow-rooted Westerners' *(westernisierte Flachwurzler)*,[87] many historians have maintained that any erosion of Westernisation would simultaneously endanger the foundations of liberal parliamentary democracy in the FRG. Gesine Schwan has spoken of 'vestiges of antiliberal mentalities' resurfacing after 1989.[88] Hermann Glaser has diagnosed an 'erosion of the republic which is already far advanced'.[89] Wehler has accused the new right of 'reverting to the anti-Western resentment contained in the cultural pessimism so prevalent in Imperial Germany'.[90] Diner has warned of a slowly progressing de-Westernisation of German political culture,[91] and Hubert Kiesewetter has criticised Nolte as enemy of the 'open society'.[92] Critics of the renationalisation process are agreed that only the Europeanisation of the German question can defuse Germany's potential for political and economic hegemony over Europe. For Loth, what is on the agenda after 1989 is not renationalisation of the German identity but denationalisation within a European framework.[93] Kocka has warned: 'Each new *Sonderweg* leading to a renewed German divergence from the West has to be prevented.'[94] Furthermore, Winkler has argued that the Westernisation of the Federal Republic's political culture should be regarded as *'the* great intellectual achievement of the post-war period'.[95]

Far more prominent than anti-European or anti-Western sentiments have been calls for a more important world political role for the reunified Germany in the light of its alleged superpower status.[96] Recommendations for its future foreign policy have been informed by various fantasies of Germany becoming the 'leading power in a united Europe'.[97] Thus the 'luxurious provincialism' of the Federal Republic's foreign policy will have to be overcome.[98] It will be impossible for the future Germany to remain a 'political dwarf'.[99] There will be no more withdrawals to any kind of 'dream island'.[100] The Germans' 'world-political niche existence' has come to an end.[101] Hildebrand, for one, has expressed his hopes that a new era of glory might be just round the corner for Germany after fifty years of enforced division and powerlessness.[102] Occasionally there have been worries that the signal to depart on the road to a more powerful Germany has not yet been given.[103] If the country is about to miss a golden opportunity, then this supposedly is due to the burden imposed upon the republic by the left-wing 1968 generation. According to Hacke, Germany has for too long indulged in self-pity, anti-nationalism, indecisiveness, cowardice and endless controversy: 'Our country has to give itself a kick up the backside ... What we need is not moralistic nagging, but vigorous decisions.'[104] Central to such a change of *Zeitgeist* will be the revival of 'love and pride in one's country and its traditions'.[105] A clear definition of Germany's national interests, for Hacke, will have to include the remilitarisation of Germany's foreign policy.[106] Stürmer has written somewhat ominously that in future German foreign policy will have to face 'decisions of strategic importance and moral tragedy'.[107]

The mental remilitarisation of Germany has also found expression in the increased pressure on historians employed by the official Research Institute for Military History (Militärgeschichtliches Forschungsamt, MGFA) and the army universities (Bundeswehrhochschulen) to redirect their research to matters of direct strategic relevance and stop what is perceived by the military commanders as an overcritical view of the traditions of the German army. How ill-construed such accusations have been, becomes clear if one considers Omer Bartov's recent criticism of German military history. According to Bartov, a leading military historian of Germany, the German profession has for too long ignored social and cultural history, clinging to an outdated conservative methodology, and ignoring those areas like the Holocaust which would show up the negative traditions of the German military.[108] Indeed the idea that military historians have the task of establishing positive traditions for the military personnel can be traced throughout the history of the MGFA since its foundation in 1952.[109] Now, with the end of the Cold War and with German soldiers facing combat situations for the first time since 1945, there is a renewed demand for military history as a preparatory school for war and as a means of polishing up the diminished status of the military in German society.[110] The decision, taken in 1994, to move the MGFA from Freiburg to Potsdam and leave the military archives behind, has been interpreted as a conscious decision to weaken the productivity of critical historians at the MFG. The army's Institute for Social Science (Sozialwissenschaftliches Institut) has been increasingly turned into a mere PR institution. There have been efforts to tamper with the curricula of the army universities, and there have been incidents when the publications written by critical military historians have been censored. These are clear signs of efforts to dispose of critical perspectives with reference to 'the propagated "normality" of the refound nation-state'.[111]

The new emphasis on national interests has been combined with calls for a more independent foreign policy and for the rediscovery of a healthy 'national egotism'.[112] Germany, in this perception, has, for too long, been the plaything of other powers' interests. Hence, what is needed is a firmer demarcation of German from other Western European interests. Germany in this view, will increasingly have to rely on 'our own long-term interests as a superpower in the middle of Europe'.[113] According to Sven Papcke, Germany has in the past been too willing to accommodate Western European wishes, and this has led to a situation where other nations take for granted 'a kind of hereditary tendency of the Germans to please others. In future we will not be able to finance this … .'[114] According to Rolf Peter Sieferle 'the German zone of prosperity is quickly becoming the object of prey for all those who are determined enough to satisfy themselves without hesitation.'[115] Schöllgen has called on his fellow Germans to develop what he calls a 'responsible German power politics' to end the alleged *Sonderweg* of foreign policy abstentionism. As part of a renewed commitment to power politics it would, according to Schöllgen, be necessary to prepare Germany mentally for war.[116] For Baring, such remilitarisation will have to include Germany's right to obtain atomic weapons at long last.[117] But, alas, the country, according to Schwarz, still resembles a 'traumatised giant' who does not yet recognise his own greatness and therefore needs to be reawakened to 'full manhood' – presumably by manly historians.[118] Ultimately, according to Schwarz, the new foreign policy direction of Germany would have to follow the rationale: 'Germany has to lead without the others feeling dominated.'[119] Germany has to become for Europe what the United States has been for the Americas in the twentieth century.

In the late 1980s Baring criticised as suffering from delusions of grandeur those who envisaged a more independent role for Germany between East and West. A couple of years later his commitment to *Mittellage* ideology has led him to speculate on a change of borders: 'Suddenly very old questions reappear, questions about the position of Germany in the middle of Europe, about the relationship between east and west.'[120] A new 'Eastern settlement movement' *(Ostsiedlung)* might well be needed to save Eastern Europe from the ravages of Communism.[121] The new Germany and Poland are, after all, bound together by 'common territories',[122] and if Germans were to think more about Poland, then 'inevitably the lost, run-down eastern territories of Germany would be constantly on our minds.'[123] But a solution may be to hand '[for] if the Poles could do as they like, they would probably decide by a huge majority to join the Federal Republic.'[124]

Reunification has also tempted other historians to come forward with rather unclear utterances regarding German frontiers in the future Europe. Erdmann, for example, rediscovered not two but three German states in Central Europe. As a member of the EU, Austria, he argued, might once again find closer ties to Germany. Furthermore, he even included Kaliningrad amongst a list of cities 'from which the Federal Republic will never be able to separate itself'.[125] Michael Salewski, the current chairman of the Ranke society, has similarly stressed the 'immortality' of the German east. For Salewski, the 'German East' has survived within Germany as 'spiritual history'. Its values and norms will allow the future Germany to act as 'a bridge' between Eastern and Western Europe. From there his perspective gets very long term when he writes ominously of 'historical raw material, from which maybe in centuries to come new historical-political units will emerge.'[126] Peter Moraw has revived all the medieval myths about German national history by describing nation-building as a 'process of growing together ... which started in the tenth/eleventh centuries'. Reminding his readers that today's Germany has been reconstituted on less than half of its fifteenth century territory, he has concluded that 'a reunited Germany which simply encompassed the four zones of occupation, would only really seal the greatest catastrophe in German history.'[127] On the extreme right of the historiographical spectrum Hellmut Diwald has expressed dissatisfaction about the 'partial reunification' of Germany. Its eastern parts, he insisted, remained under Polish and Russian occupation.[128]

In the light of changed perspectives on Germany's foreign policy, Wehler has warned fellow historians not 'to romp about unreservedly in power politics'.[129] In view of the fact that the sheer size and potential of the reunified Germany might lead to dangerous foreign policy experiments, there have been calls to avoid 'excessive aspirations', 'craving for status' and national 'bigotry'.[130] Nation-states, in this view, have long ceased to be autonomous entities, and any return to nineteenth-century concepts of national interests would end in the possibility of Germany 'running amok' once again.[131] Whilst there is certainly a pressing need to discuss Germany's new foreign policy under the entirely changed conditions of the post-Cold War world, the modesty of the old FRG's foreign policy is often perceived as the best recipe for the future. Hence 'Germany cannot and should not aim to become Europe's leading power.'[132]

Finally, the re-interpretation of the FRG's past has led to renewed attacks on *Ostpolitik* which had become fairly uncontroversial in the Federal Republic by the late 1980s.[133] Some, like Jens Hacker, have insisted with hindsight on the basic difference between the *Ostpolitik* of the conservative governments after 1982 and the social-liberal version in the 1970s. Whilst the latter one-sidedly stabilised the GDR and pushed the German question to the sidelines, the former has been interpreted as the precondition for the reunification of the country in 1990.[134] According to Wolffsohn, *Ostpolitik* tended to ignore the dictatorial sides of the GDR. In the name of peace and co-existence an inhumane dictatorship was accepted by the West.[135] Furthermore, the ideal of the undivided nation-state was given up by the advocates of *Ostpolitik*. For Weißmann, the disappearance of the German question from the government agenda and public discourse belonged to the 'direct consequences' of *Ostpolitik*.[136] Schwarz has described the Federal Republic as a 'penetrated system'. *Ostpolitik* had allowed the GDR undue influence on the political system of the Federal Republic – in particular on the SPD and the Protestant churches.[137] *Ostpolitik*, it is argued, did not contribute to the fall of communism. If anything, it prolonged it by giving legitimacy to the dictatorships and weakening its internal opposition.[138] Left-liberal historians and social scientists are put on trial for allegedly immoral conduct, i.e., rubbing shoulders with Communists.[139] The real coming-to-terms with the past, in this view, has to be done by those West Germans who, through *Ostpolitik*, prolonged the life of the 'second German dictatorship'. Such arguments tend to ignore that the legitimacy of the Eastern European regimes was eroded by the CSCE process and that the peaceful revolutions of 1989 would have been unthinkable without *Ostpolitik*. After all, the destabilisation of the Communist regimes started with reforms undertaken by the regimes themselves, most notably in Hungary and the Soviet Union.[140] Any 'post-eventum historical certainty'[141] hence cannot discredit the ultimate success of *Ostpolitik*. The 'softening up' of the GDR which was forced into a 'slow and controlled opening towards the FRG' will remain its lasting achievement.[142]

So far, it has been established that a post-reunification reinterpretation of the history of the old FRG postulated, first, a neurosis about coming-to-terms with the Nazi past, secondly, one-sided Westernisation, thirdly, the absence of any foreign policy concerned with power and German interests and, fourthly, the abandonment of the national question in the wake of *Ostpolitik*. All those elements have allegedly produced the *Sonderweg* of a postnational identity. In the light of reunification, new-right and conservative historians found it relatively easy to argue that such postnationalism was one of the most abstruse concepts and best-nurtured illusions of the Federal Republic.[143] For Zitelmann they were expressions of the 'national masochism' prevailing amongst the Federal Republic's intellectuals.[144] For Meier the events of 1989/1990 proved conclusively that Germans 'are not at all postnational, but of latent nationality'.[145]

In the wake of the national revival in Germany many historians who had previously adhered to ideas of postnationalism readjusted their positions. Schulze, who in 1989 had described the German nation-state as a cul-de-sac, could write four years after reunification about the durability and longevity of the phenomenon of the nation.[146] Wolfgang Mommsen has called all notions of postnational identity 'rubbish'.[147] Kocka has conceded that the nation-state had been more firmly rooted in Germany than he had previously thought.[148] It would, according to him, remain 'the normal form of political organisation of European societies'.[149] For Winkler, theories of postnationalism have been largely invalidated concepts which effectively marked the end of the Federal Republic's *Sonderweg*.[150]

The prolonged unification crisis has led some historians to reemphasise that there may after all have been some merit in the concept of postnationalism.[151] The division of the country over forty years has meant the development of very different mentalities and attitudes which cannot easily be assimilated.[152] Kocka has returned to his pre-1989 position when claiming: 'It remains wrong even today to perceive the nation-state as the natural organisational form of modern societies. It remains legitimate to adhere to the aim of a postnational order.'[153] For Loth, the citizens of the FRG were able to master the reunification process without any major negative upheavals precisely because their state of mind was a postnational one, at least in the West.[154] Similarly Bracher has expressed his hope that the unified country would quickly find its way into a postnational federal state within the framework of the EU.[155]

Zitelmann's fear of a renewed 'leftward drift' *(Linksverschiebung)* of the political climate in the Federal Republic is a sure sign that the new right feels marginalised. Its attempted reinterpretation of the FRG history has met with considerable opposition.[156] Many left-liberal and liberal-conservative historians have defended the achievements of the old Federal Republic against its new enemies on the political right. To some degree this has been a kind of role reversal. Whereas conservatives used to defend the Federal Republic against its left-liberal critics, in the reunified country the traditions of the Federal Republic are hailed as a success story by left-liberal historians whilst the new right wants to set out for new shores, which may well be very old ones. A 'posthumous pro-Adenauer left'[157] is defending Western integration against the renationalisation of German identity. As Bernd Weisbrod has pointed out, such explicit endorsement of the FRG might well push into the background the more unpalatable sides of its history such as the social inequality produced by the 'economic miracle', the difficulties in integrating the refugees, the periodical resurfacing of neo-Nazism and the lack of *Vergangenheitsbewältigung*.[158] Therefore, Western historians would do well to remember at times that the old FRG was not the ideal state which justified posing as the victors of history in 1989/1990. Any consideration of the two German histories between 1945 and 1989 can hardly be based on the denunciation of a 'Soviet protectorate' which is juxtaposed to eulogies on the West German paradise.[159] If, however, the new right interpretation of the Federal Republic's history as a *Sonderweg* gains wider currency, and if the development of a postnational consciousness amongst West Germans is more widely perceived as nothing but a curious abberation from the norm of national identity, then historians will increasingly justify the return to the nation as the prime object of their study. Therefore it is necessary in the next chapter to ask whether since 1989 there have been any changes in historians' attitudes towards the concept of the nation.

Notes

1. Karl-Heinz Bohrer, 'Provinzialismus', *Merkur*, vol. 44, 1990, pp. 1,096-102, vol. 45, 1991, pp. 255-66, 348-56, 537-46, 719-27, vol. 46, 1992, pp. 88-90.
2. Weißmann, *Rückruf*, p. 43.
3. Joachim Fest, 'Nicht wie alle Welt', *FAZ*, 13 June 1992.
4. Meier, *Deutsche Einheit*, p. 51.
5. Christian Meier, 'Am Ende der alten Bundesrepublik', *Merkur*, vol. 48, 1994, pp. 561-72.
6. For the traditional view see especially Alexander and Margarete Mitscherlich, *Die Unfähigkeit zu trauern. Grundlagen kollektiven Verhaltens*, Munich, 1967; Ralph Giordano, *Die zweite Schuld oder von der Last, Deutscher zu sein*, Hamburg, 1987.
7. Peter Steinbach, *Nationalsozialistische Gewaltverbrechen. Die Diskussion in der deutschen Öffentlichkeit nach 1945*, Berlin, 1981, p. 8.
8. Udo Wengst, 'Geschichtswissenschaft und "Vergangenheitsbewältigung" in Deutschland nach 1945 und nach 1989/90', *GWU*, vol. 46, 1995, pp. 189-205.
9. Hoffmann, *Stunden Null?*, pp. 42 f., 51.
10. Jürgen Steinle, 'Hitler als "Betriebsunfall in der Geschichte". Eine historische Metapher und ihre Hintergründe', *GWU*, vol. 45, 1994, pp. 288-302. Compare chapters one and two of how unrealistic such assumptions remain.
11. Weißmann, *Rückruf*, p. 41; Michael Wolffsohn, *Keine Angst vor Deutschland*, rev. edn, Frankfurt-on-Main, 1992, pp. 91 f.
12. Zitelmann, *Republik*, p. 16.
13. Manfred Kittel, *Die Legende von der "Zweiten Schuld". Vergangenheitsbewältigung in der Ära Adenauer*, Frankfurt-on-Main, 1993.

14. Ingo Müller, *Furchtbare Juristen. Die unbewältigte Vergangenheit unserer Justiz*, Munich, 1987; Barbara Just-Dahlmann and Helmut Just, *Die Gehilfen. NS-Verbrechen und die Justiz nach 1945*, Frankfurt-on-Main, 1988; Jörg Friedrich, *Die kalte Amnestie. NS-Täter in der Bundesrepublik Deutschland*, Frankfurt-on-Main, 1984.

15. Arno Mohr, 'Das Auschwitz Syndrom – Geschichte der Juden in Deutschland nach 1945', *NPL*, vol. 40, 1995, p. 71.

16. Helmut Peitsch, 'Dicovering a Taboo: The Nazi Past in Literary-Political Discourse 1958-67', in: David Jackson (ed.), *Taboos in German Literature*, Oxford, 1996.

17. Kittel, *Legende*, p. 36.

18. Schöllgen, *Die Macht*, p. 173.

19. F.E.O. Jerzykiewicz-Jagemann, 'Geschichtsbilder. Anmerkungen zur Ranke-Gesellschaft', *Historische Mitteilungen*, vol. 5, 1992, pp. 130-49.

20. Baring, *Deutschland*, p. 146. Very similar Klaus Michael Groll, *Wie lange haften wir noch für Hitler? Zum Selbstverständnis der Deutschen heute*, Düsseldorf, 1990.

21. Jochen Thies, *Deutschland von Innen. Beobachtungen aus wechselnder Perspektive*, Stuttgart, 1990.

22. Arnulf Baring, 'Am Ende liegen sich alle in den Armen', *Berliner Zeitung*, 4/5 Apr. 1992.

23. In particular Caspar von Schrenck-Notzing, *Charakterwäsche*, Stuttgart, 1965; Armin Mohler, *Vergangenheitsbewältigung. Von der Läuterung zur Manipulation*, Stuttgart, 1968; idem, *Der Nasenring*, pp. 124, 203.

24. Jesse, '"Vergangenheitsbewältigung"', pp. 53, 54, 57.

25. Kittel, *Legende*, p. 11.

26. Zitelmann, *Republik*, pp. 89 ff, 131; idem, 'Wiedervereinigung und deutscher Selbsthaß: Probleme mit dem eigenen Volk', in: Weidenfeld (ed.), *Deutschland*; Jesse, '"Vergangenheitsbewältigung"', p. 61. Also: Hans-Helmuth Knütter, *Deutschfeindlichkeit gestern, heute und morgen …?*, Asendorf, 1991; Wolfgang Schuller, 'Alle Deutschen stehen vor einem Neuanfang', *FAZ*, 16 Dec. 1989.

27. Enrico Syring, 'Spurensuche nach altem Ungeist contra Rückkehr zur Normalität', *Das Parlament*, 11/18 Nov. 1994, p. 16.

28. Friedrich Tenbruck, 'Zeitgeschichte als Vergangenheitsbewältigung?', in: Nipperdey, Doering-Manteuffel, and Thamer (eds), *Weltbürgerkrieg*, p. 487.

29. Hoffmann, *Stunden Null?*, pp. 39, 42, 44.

30. Jesse, 'Vergangenheitsbewältigung', p. 61.

31. Weißmann, *Rückruf*, chapter one.

32. Konrad Löw, 'Die Deutschen und der totalitäre Kommunismus', in: Filbinger and Karst (eds), *Identität*, pp. 41, 50 f.

33. Baring, *Deutschland*, p. 149.

34. Zitelmann, *Republik*, p. 191; Karlheinz Weißmann, 'Trauerarbeiter und Schönfärber, *Die Welt*, 12 Feb . 1994, p. G1.

35. Mohler, *Der Nasenring*, pp. 320, 342-44; Weißmann, *Rückruf*, pp. 145-51. See also Mohler's argument that by its very peacefulness the events of 1989 did not allow for a gesture of forgiveness in later years. In this logic only a bloodbath would have prevented the nation from getting paralysed in the Stasi debate. See Armin Mohler, 'Dornröschen liegt in der Traufe', *Die Welt*, 17 Oct. 1992.

36. Michael Wolffsohn, 'Umkehr statt Rache zur Verhinderung der Wiederkehr oder Brauchen wir eine neue Vergangenheitsbewältigung?', in: *Ein Volk am Pranger? Die Deutschen auf der Suche nach einer neuen politischen Kultur*, Berlin, 1993.

37. Eckhard Jesse, 'Zwei Diktaturen auf dem Prüfstand', *Rheinischer Merkur*, 14 Aug. 1992; Wengst, 'Geschichtswissenschaft', p. 205.

38. Bert Pampel, 'Was bedeutet "Aufarbeitung der Vergangenheit"?', *aus politik und zeitgeschichte*, 6 Jan. 1995, pp. 27-38 even speaks of extensive deficits throughout the 1970s and 1980s.

39. Norbert Frei, *Vergangenheitspolitik. Die Anfänge der Bundesrepublik und die NS-Vergangenheit*, Munich, 1996, see also Ulrich Herbert, 'Als die Nazis wieder gesellschaftsfähig wurden'. *Die Zeit*, no. 3, 10 Jan. 1997, p. 34.
40. Lutz Niethammer, 'Erinnerungsgebot und Erfahrungsgeschichte. Institutionalisierungen im kollektiven Gedächtnis', in: Hanno Loewy (ed.), *Holocaust. Die Grenzen des Verstehens. Eine Debatte über die Besetzung der Geschichte*, Reinbek, 1992.
41. Jürgen Habermas, 'Zur Normalität der künftigen Berliner Republik', *FR*, 8 May 1995; Jürgen Kocka, 'Der neue Nationalstaat: Suche nach Identität', *Wirtschaftswoche*, 15 Feb . 1991, pp. 28 f.; Rudolf von Thadden, 'Ein 80-Millionen-Staat ohne klare Konturen?', *Tagesspiegel*, 3 Oct. 1993.
42. This is the central argument in Rainer Zitelmann, Karlheinz Weißmann and Michael Grossheim (eds), *Westbindung. Chancen und Risiken für Deutschland*, Frankfurt-on-Main, 1993.
43. Zitelmann, Weißmann, and Grossheim (eds), *Westbindung*, pp. 12 f.
44. Heinz Brill, 'Deutschland im geostrategischen Kraftfeld der Super- und Großmächte (1945-1990)', in: Zitelmann, Weißmann and Grossheim (eds), *Westbindung*, p. 272.
45. Schöllgen, *Die Macht in der Mitte*.
46. Michael Stürmer, 'Was ist das Europäische an Europa?', *Die politische Meinung*, vol. 40, Feb. 1995, p. 15.
47. Geiss, *Die deutsche Frage*, pp. 112 f.
48. Baring, *Deutschland*, p. 25.
49. Tilman Mayer, 'Fragmente zur Bestimmung der deutschen Nationalstaatlichkeit', in: Zitelmann, Weißmann and Grossheim (eds), *Westbindung*, p. 514.
50. Christian Hacke, 'Die Entscheidung für die politische Westbindung nach 1945', in: ibid., p. 148.
51. Ansgar Graw, '(Historiker-)Streit unter Adenauers Enkeln', in: ibid., p. 381. Also: Karl Schlögel, 'Deutschland: Land der Mitte, Land ohne Mitte', in: ibid., pp. 441-57. Similarly Weißmann, *Rückruf*, pp. 65 and 128-33.
52. Schwarz, *Zentralmacht*, pp. 240-57, esp. pp. 256 f.
53. Wehler, 'Hart widersprechen'. See also Rudolf Walther, 'Man braucht mehr Platz', *Die Zeit*, 21 July 1995.
54. Martin Bennhold, 'Mitteleuropa – eine deutsche Politiktradition. Zu Friedrich Naumanns Konzeption und ihren Folgen', *Blätter*, vol. 37, 1992, pp. 977-89; Wehler, *Gegenwart*, p. 136; Wilfried Loth, 'Die Deutschen und das Projekt der europäischen Einigung', in: Wolfgang J. Mommsen (ed.), *Der lange Weg nach Europa. Historische Betrachtungen aus gegenwärtiger Sicht*, Berlin, 1992, pp. 39-69.
55. Ralf Dahrendorf, 'Die Sache mit der Nation', *Merkur*, vol. 44, 1990, p. 831; more recently idem, 'Die Zukunft des Nationalstaats', *Merkur*, vol. 48, 1994, pp. 751-61; idem, 'Warum Europa? Nachdenkliche Anmerkungen eines skeptischen Europäers', *Merkur*, vol. 50, 1996, pp. 559-77 which includes the express notion that ever-closer union is a worthwhile political aim; Peter Kielmannsegg, 'Ein Maß für die Größe des Staates: Europa fehlt die Zustimmung der Bürger', *FAZ*, 2 Dec. 1992. Also: Hagen Schulze, 'Mit dem Segen der Nachbarn', *Die Zeit*, 30 Nov. 1990, p. 2.
56. Ludwig Watzal, 'Der Irrweg von Maastricht', in: Zitelmann, Weißmann and Grossheim (eds), *Westbindung*, pp. 477-500.
57. Tilman Mayer, 'Die nationalstaatliche Herausforderung in Europa', *aus politik und zeitgeschichte*, 2 April 1993, pp. 11-20.
58. Karl-Rudolf Korte, 'Allerorten Nachholbedarf? Nation und Nationalstaat im Konzept der europäischen Integration', *Deutschland-Archiv*, vol. 25, 1992, pp. 1,190-4.
59. Weißmann, *Rückruf*, p. 134.

60. Tilman Mayer, 'Die nationalstaatliche Herausforderung in Europa', *aus politik und zeitgeschichte*, 2 Apr. 1993, pp. 11-20.
61. Gunther Mai, 'Vom Obrigkeitsstaat zur Demokratiefähigkeit? Westdeutsche Einstellungen seit Kriegsende', in: Knoblich, Peter and Natter (eds), *Auf dem Weg*, p. 81. For a marked enmity towards further European integration see also Schwarz, *Zentralmacht*, pp. 27-100; Knütter, *Deutschfeindlichkeit.*
62. Stürmer, *Die Grenzen der Macht*, pp. 222 f; Werner Weidenfeld, *Kulturbruch mit Amerika? Das Ende transatlantischer Selbstverständlichkeiter*, Gütersloh, 1996.
63. Gruner, *Die deutsche Frage*, p. 352.
64. Eckart Conze, 'Deutsche Frage und europäische Integration 1945-1990', *Historisches Jahrbuch der Görres-Gesellschaft*, vol. 114, 1994, pp. 412-26.
65. Korte, *Die Chance*, pp. 217-21; Hermann Schäfer, 'Europas Einheit: Herkunft, Ziel, Form', in: Josef Isensee (ed.), *Europa als politische Idee und als rechtliche Form*, 2nd edn, Berlin, 1994, pp. 26, 33.
66. Already Karl Dietrich Erdmann, 'Die Revolution Mitteleuropas – historische Perspektiven', *GWU*, vol. 41, 1990, pp. 529 f.
67. Kocka, *Vereinigungskrise*, p. 178; Imanuel Geiss, 'Europäische Perspektiven nach der deutschen Einigung', *aus politik und zeitgeschichte*, B52-53, 1990, pp. 45 f.; Ernst-Otto Czempiel, 'Zeitläufte (II)', *Merkur*, vol. 49, 1995, p. 245.
68. Wehler, *Gegenwart*, pp. 135, 258; Wilfried Loth, 'Das Ende der Nachkriegsordnung', *aus politik und zeitgeschichte*, 26 April 1991, pp. 3-10; Winkler, 'Rebuilding of a Nation', p. 121.
69. Hartmut Kaelble, 'Supranationalität in Europa seit dem zweiten Weltkrieg. Einleitende Bemerkungen', in: idem and Winkler (eds), *Nationalismus*, pp. 189-206. For a similar argument compare Christian Meier, *Deutsche Einheit als Herausforderung. Welche Fundamente für welche Republik?*, Munich, 1990, pp. 87-108; Kurt Sontheimer, 'Nationale Identität in Europas Haus', *Die Welt*, 15 Sept. 1991; idem, 'Nationalstaat und vereintes Europa', *Die Welt*, 13 Jan. 1992; Wolfgang J. Mommsen (ed.), *Der lange Weg nach Europa*, pp. vii, ix.
70. Hagen Schulze, 'In manchem überholt, aber nicht überwunden. Über Geschichte und die Zukunft des Nationalstaats', *FAZ*, 27 Apr. 1991 (Beilage).
71. Gruner, *Die deutsche Frage*, pp. 354 f.
72. Gregor Schöllgen, 'Ängstlicher Riese im Vakuum', *Die Welt*, 20 Feb. 1993, p. G1.
73. Schöllgen, *Angst vor der Macht*, p. 156.
74. Stürmer, *Die Grenzen der Macht*, pp. 131 f, 135.
75. Loth, 'Die Deutschen', in: Mommsen (ed.), *Der lange Weg nach Europa*, p. 63; Peter Glotz, *Irrweg*, p. 147.
76. Glotz, *Normalisierung*, p. 29.
77. Jesse, '"Vergangenheitsbewältigung"', p. 57.
78. Ernst Nolte, 'Links und rechts – Über Geschichte und Aktualität einer politischen Alternative', in: Schwilk and Schacht (eds), *Nation*, p. 160.
79. Ernst Nolte, 'Die Fragilität des Triumphs', *FAZ*, 3 July 1993.
80. Thomas Assheuer, 'Der Staatsnotstand oder: Die Liebe zur Diktatur auf Zeit', *FR*, 21 May 1994.
81. Joachim Fest, 'Offene Gesellschaft mit offener Flanke', *FAZ*, 21 Oct. 1992; idem, *Die schwierige Freiheit. Über die offene Flanke der offenen Gesellschaft*, Berlin, 1994.
82. Weißmann, *Rückruf*, pp. 179 f.; Baring, *Deutschland*, pp. 211 ff. has denounced the German 'shopkeeper's soul' with similar vigour.
83. Kremp, *Die Angst der Passagiere.*
84. Arnulf Baring, 'Magnetfeld Europa', *FAZ*, 29 Sept. 1990; Joachim Fest, 'Land des Westens', *FAZ*, 29 Sept. 1990; Rudolf Morsey, *Die Deutschlandpolitik Adenauers*, Opladen, 1991, p. 49; Hans-Peter Schwarz, 'Die Bedeutung Adenauers für die deutsche und europäische Geschichte', in: Josef Becker (ed.), *Wiedervereinigung in*

Mitteleuropa. Außen- und Innenansichten zur staatlichen Einheit Deutschlands, Munich, 1992, p. 183; Kurt Sontheimer, *Die Ära Adenauer,* Munich, 1991, p 7; Karl Dietrich Erdmann, 'Vierzig Jahre Bundesrepublik – geteilte Nation im geteilten Europa', *GWU,* vol. 41, 1990, p. 267. Compare also as a corrective against the 'conservative myths' surrounding Adenauer Josef Foschepoth, 'Hat Kohl das verwirklicht, was Adenauer wollte?', *FR,* 13 Feb. 1993.

85. See, for example, Kurt Sontheimer, 'Kein Abschied von der Bundesrepublik', *Die Welt,* 1 Oct. 1990; idem, 'Die Einheit ist kein Kuckucksei', *Rheinischer Merkur,* 30 Nov. 1990.

86. Rainer Zitelmann, *Adenauers Gegner – Streiter für die Einheit,* Erlangen, 1991, p. 22; Weißmann, *Rückruf,* pp. 120-2.

87. Anselm Doering-Manteuffels' contribution to the panel discussion ' Sackgasse aus dem Sonderweg', in: Kocka and Sabrow (eds), *Die DDR als Geschichte,* pp. 211-2, 232.

88. Gesine Schwan's contribution to the panel discussion 'Sackgasse aus dem Sonderweg', in: Kocka and Sabrow (eds), *Die DDR als Geschichte,* pp. 207 f.

89. Hermann Glaser, 'Von einigen meiner deutschen Augenblicke', *aus politik und zeitgeschichte,* 10 June 1994, p. 9.

90. Hans-Ulrich Wehler, 'Gurus und Irrlichter', *FAZ,* 6 May 1994. For a clear endorsement of Westernisation on every level of German politics see also idem, *Gegenwart,* pp. 138-43.

91. Dan Diner, 'Deutschland im Epochenwechsel', *Blätter,* vol. 38, 1993, p. 1,113.

92. Hubert Kiesewetter, 'Die offene Gesellschaft ohne ihre Feinde', *Historische Mitteilungen,* vol. 6, 1993, pp. 225-34.

93. Wilfried Loth, 'Deutsche Einheit, Europäisches Haus. Von der europäischen Dimension der deutschen Einigung', in: Arthur Heinrich and Klaus Neumann (eds), *Alles Banane – Ausblicke auf das endgültige Deutschland,* Cologne, 1990, pp. 29-38.

94. Kocka, *Vereinigungskrise,* pp. 176 f.

95. Winkler, '1989/90', in: idem and Carola Stern (eds), *Wendepunkte,* p. 226.

96. Schöllgen, *Die Macht,* p. 7; idem, *Angst,* p. 123; Hacke, *Weltmacht,* p. 583. See also Arnulf Baring (ed.), *Germany's New Position in Europe. Problems and Perspectives,* Oxford, 1994.

97. Ernst Nolte, 'Ein historisches Recht Hitlers?', *Der Spiegel,* 3 Oct. 1994, p. 103.

98. Meier, *Deutsche Einheit,* p. 34.

99. Baring, *Deutschland,* p. 23.

100. Hacke, *Weltmacht,* p. 12.

101. Christian Meier, 'Halbwegs anständig über die Runden kommen, ohne das zuviele zurückbleiben', in: Siegfried Unseld (ed.), *Politik ohne Projekt? Nachdenken über Deutschland,* Frankfurt-on-Main, 1993, p. 164.

102. Hildebrand, *Das vergangene Reich,* p. 897.

103. Hacke, *Weltmacht,* p. 529.

104. Ibid., p. 539.

105. Ibid., pp. 539, 558.

106. Ibid., p. 558.

107. Stürmer, *Die Grenzen der Macht,* pp. 247 f.

108. Omer Bartov, 'Wem gehört die Geschichte? Wehrmacht und Geschichtswissenschaft', in: Heer and Naumann (eds), *Vernichtungskrieg,* pp. 601-19.

109. This has been carefully documented by Rainer Wohlfeil, 'Militärgeschichte. Zu Geschichte und Problemen einer Disziplin der Geschichtswissenschaft (1952-67)', *Militärgeschichtliche Mitteilungen,* vol. 52, 1993, pp. 323-44; Klaus A. Maier, 'Überlegungen zur Zielsetzung und Methode der Militärgeschichtsschreibung im Militärgeschichtlichen Forschungsamt und die Förderung nach dem Nutzen für

die Bundeswehr seit der Mitte der siebziger Jahre', *Militärgeschichtliche Mitteilungen*, vol. 52, 1993, pp. 359-70.

110. Wolfram Wette, 'Rückkehr zu "Normalität" und Weltmachtdenken. Die Renaissance des Militärischen im neuen Deutschland', *Blätter*, 1994, pp. 981-90.
111. Wilhelm Deist, 'Die Militärgeschichte gerät erneut in den Griff der Armee', *FR*, 24 May 1994. See also Detlef Bald, Martin Kutz, Manfred Messerschmidt and Wolfram Wette, 'Zurück, Marsch, Marsch!', *Die Zeit*, 6 May 1994, p. 52. For political censorship see 'Politik an die Front', *Der Spiegel*, 7 Nov. 1994, p. 76.
112. Schwarz, *Zentralmacht*, pp. 20, 84.
113. Hans-Christof Kraus, 'Die deutschen Konservativen, England und der Westen', in: Zitelmann, Weißmann and Grossheim (eds), *Westbindung*, p. 89; Weißmann, *Rückruf*, pp. 12, 172 f.
114. Sven Papcke, 'Deutschland auf der Suche nach politischem Profil', *Das Parlament*, 27 Sept. 1991, p. 9.
115. Rolf Peter Sieferle, *Epochenwechsel. Die Deutschen an der Schwelle zum 21. Jahrhundert*, Frankfurt-on-Main, 1994, p. 103.
116. Gregor Schöllgen, 'Ängstlicher Riese im Vakuum', *Die Welt*, 20 Feb. 1993, p. G1; idem, 'Keine Angst vor der Macht', *Die Zeit*, 25 Febr. 1994, p. 14. See also Michael Stürmer, 'Deutsche Interessen', in: Karl Kaiser and Hanns W. Maull (eds), *Deutschlands neue Außenpolitik*, vol. 1: *Grundlagen*, Munich, 1994.
117. Baring, *Deutschland*, pp. 209 f.
118. Schwarz, *Zentralmacht*, pp. 23, 170-9.
119. Schwarz, *Zentralmacht*, p. 125.
120. Arnulf Baring, 'Schluß mit der Behaglichkeit', *Rheinischer Merkur*, 27 Sept. 1991. For his older views compare idem, *Unser neuer Größenwahn*, Berlin, 1988.
121. Baring, *Deutschland*, p. 63.
122. Ibid., p. 40.
123. Ibid., p. 104.
124. Ibid., p. 166 f.
125. Erdmann, 'Vierzig Jahre Bundesrepublik', pp. 270 f.
126. Michael Salewski, 'Der deutsche Osten und die deutsche Geschichte', *GWU*, vol. 42, 1991, pp. 220-31.
127. Peter Moraw, 'Jüngste deutsche Geschichte und ältere deutsche Geschichte', *GWU*, vol. 41, 1990, p. 395.
128. Hellmut Diwald (ed.), *Handbuch zur deutschen Nation*, vol. 4: *Deutschlands Einigung und Europas Zukunft*, Tübingen, 1992, p. 8.
129. Wehler, *Gegenwart*, pp. 257, 261. Also highly critical of the alleged 'normalisation' of German foreign policy is Wolfram Wette, 'Sonderweg oder Normalität? Zur Diskussion um die internationale Position der Bundesrepublik', *Blätter*, vol. 41, 1996, pp. 61-70.
130. Eberhard Jäckel, 'Kanzler Kohl hat nicht genügend Sinn für Geschichte', *Berliner Zeitung*, 13/14 Feb. 1993; Wolfgang Mommsen, 'Der künftige deutsche Staat', in: Sternburg (ed.), *Geteilte Ansichten*, pp. 151 f.
131. Dieter Senghaas, 'Was sind der Deutschen Interessen?', in: Unseld (ed.), *Politik*, pp. 463-91.
132. Kocka, *Vereinigungskrise*, pp. 174-5, 177. For introductions to the debates on Germany's new foreign policy see Karl Kaiser and Hans W. Maull (eds), *Deutschlands neue Außenpolitik*, vol. 2: *Herausforderungen*, Munich, 1995; Karl Kaiser and Hans-Peter Schwarz (eds), *Die neue Weltpolitik*, Bonn, 1995.
133. Heinrich Potthoff, *Die 'Koalition der Vernunft'. Deutschlandpolitik in den 80er Jahren*, Munich, 1995.
134. Jens Hacker, 'Die Ostpolitik der konservativ-liberalen Bundesregierung seit dem Regierungsantritt 1982', *aus politik und zeitgeschichte*, 4 April 1994, pp. 16-26.

135. 'Schuld muß jeder mit sich selber ausmachen. Historiker Wolffsohn stellt Fragen nach der Ostpolitik', *Berliner Zeitung*, 19 May 1992.
136. Weißmann, *Rückruf*, pp. 100 f.
137. Hans-Peter Schwarz, 'War die Bundesrepublik ein penetriertes System?', *Rheinischer Merkur*, 4 Feb. 1994. That the SPD and the Protestant church in particular were guilty of wanting to betray the German fatherland by formally accepting a GDR citizenship by the late 1980s, this is also the tenor of church historian Gerhard Besier, '"Was ist des Deutschen Vaterland?"', *Rheinischer Merkur*, 19 March 1993.
138. Wolfgang Leonhard, 'Demokratisierung wird ersetzt durch Vereinigung', *Die Tageszeitung*, 2 Oct. 1990.
139. Löw, ... *bis zum Verrat*; Hacker, *Deutsche Irrtümer*; Zitelmann, *Republik*, pp. 41-63, 164 ff.
140. Peter Brandt, 'Die ostpolitische Position der SPD seit dem zweiten Weltkrieg', in: Faulenbach and Stadelmaier (eds), *Diktatur*, pp. 171-6; Glotz, *Normalisierung*, p. 260.
141. Mathias Zimmer, 'Vorgeschichte der Wiedervereinigung? Die Regierung Kohl und die deutsche Frage vor der Wende', *ZfG*, vol. 43, 1995, p. 256.
142. Peter Bender, 'Der goldene Angelhaken: Entspannungspolitik und Systemwandel', *aus politik und zeitgeschichte*, 8 April 1994, pp. 11-5.
143. Hacker, *Deutsche Irrtümer*, p. 363; Karl Dietrich Erdmann, 'Die Revolution Mitteleuropas – historische Perspektiven', *GWU*, vol. 41, 1991, p. 536.
144. Zitelmann, *Republik*, p. 131.
145. Meier, *Deutsche Einheit*, p. 57; idem, 'Deutschland zwischen der Bonner und der Berliner Demokratie', *ZfP*, vol. 41, 1994, p. 265.
146. Hagen Schulze, *Staat und Nation in der europäischen Geschichte*, Munich, 1994, p. 329.
147. Mommsen, 'Die DDR', p. 20.
148. Jürgen Kocka, 'Revolution und Nation 1989. Zur historischen Einordnung der gegenwärtigen Ereignisse', *TAJB*, vol. 19, 1990, p. 493.
149. Jürgen Kocka, 'Nur keinen neuen Sonderweg', *Die Zeit*, 19 Oct. 1990.
150. Heinrich August Winkler, 'Abschied von einem deutschen Sonderweg: wider die postnationale Nostalgie', *Die neue Gesellschaft/Frankfurter Hefte*, vol. 40, 1993, pp. 633-6; idem, 'Rebuilding of a Nation', p. 119.
151. Hans Mommsen's contribution to the panel discussion 'Sackgasse aus dem deutschen Sonderweg', in: Kocka and Sabrow (eds), *Die DDR als Geschichte*, pp. 214-7.
152. M. Rainer Lepsius, 'Deutschland, ein Staat und zwei Gesellschaften?', in: *Deutschland auf dem Prüfstand*, Heidelberg, 1994, pp. 19-32.
153. Kocka, 'Von der Verantwortung'.
154. Loth, 'Die Deutschen', in: Mommsen (ed.), *Der lange Weg nach Europa*, p. 66.
155. Karl Dietrich Bracher, 'Der deutsche Einheitsstaat – ein Imperativ der Geschichte?', *Basler Zeitung*, 17 Feb. 1990.
156. Zitelmann, *Republik*, p. 7.
157. Winkler, 'Nationalismus', in: idem and Kaelble (eds), *Nationalismus*, p. 27.
158. Bernd Weisbrod, 'Die Wiederkehr der Krisen. Geschichtsbilder in der Wendezeit', *Blätter*, vol. 38, 1993, pp. 1,355-8.
159. Heiko Feldner, 'Politischer Umbruch und Geschichtswissenschaft in Deutschland. Gedanken zur Debatte', *GG*, vol. 22, 1996, p. 94 points out: 'In contemporary German historiography a scholarly critical distance to one's own history, to the history of the FRG is rather rare.'

Chapter 9

THE NATIONAL REVIVAL IN GERMAN HISTORIOGRAPHY

Reunification of Germany in October 1990 convinced some historians that a re-evaluation of the role of the nation in German history was on the cards. They now attributed a new 'normality' to the nation in their writings. This new national rhetoric also found expression in the search for new national symbols. It became prominent in the context of political efforts to whip up national sentiment after November 1989. The national debate in Germany brought, amongst other things, frequent calls for a paradigm change in German historiography from society to nation. All these aspects of the renationalisation of German identity need to be addressed in the following.

In November 1989 many historians still expressed their belief in the continued existence of two German states for some time to come. During 1990 they tended to discover, in the words of Christian Meier the 'strong feeling of togetherness' of Germans east and west.[1] By April 1990 Meier was talking for the first time about the developments in the GDR 'necessarily' leading to German unity.[2] Once the crisis of the GDR had become apparent, even those who had remained dedicated advocates of national unity throughout the 1970s and 1980s, like Schwarz, did not immediately jump to the conclusion that reunification was a distinct possibility. In July 1989 he envisaged the separate existence of a kind of Austrianised GDR.[3] By February 1990, however, Schwarz was vigorously demanding immediate reunification under Article 23 of the Basic Law.[4] Many of those who argued in favour of quick reunification in the spring often did so by stressing that the process leading to the end of the country's division was, in any case, unstoppable. Sieferle wrote with hindsight: 'When the Soviet empire crumbled and out of its ashes the peoples rose to form new political structures, German reunification took place with the force of a natural principle.'[5]

From the moment the nation was back on the agenda, liberal-conservative historians contrasted an allegedly artificial commitment to the old Federal Republic with 'true' and 'normal' national sentiment. Kielmannsegg summed it up rather neatly: 'What Germany needs ... is a perspective of normality. One can understand and welcome reunification as not more than an opportunity for such normality'.[6] The nation was supposedly the prime focus for an individual's identity: Europe, the West, Socialism, Postmodernism, Feminism, Individualism – all these concepts were now pushed to the sidelines and the nation moved centre stage again. Nothing, the argument went, could ultimately replace national identity. Hildebrand warned against 'rashly ignoring the historically powerful notion of the nation'.[7] For the new right Weißmann declared that 'belonging to a nation is of existential importance ... So long as the planet exists as pluriverse, the nation will remain the constitutive form of human existence.'[8] For the more mainstream historians Hagen Schulze pleaded for a return of Germans to 'normal' national identity and even wrote a history of Germany which has been described as 'having good prospects of becoming the favourite history booklet of the Kohl generation ... the *Zeitgeist* which demands soothing identity is served with some tasty nibbles'. Here, even the more unpalatable aspects of German history are portrayed in the 'mild light of a self-satisfied conservatism'.[9]

The rhetoric of 'normality' has often been linked to demands for a renationalisation of German identity.[10] For Geiss, it will be of prime importance to overcome the 'all-German blues' *(gesamtnationale Katzenjammer)* which only leads to 'self-paralysis' and 'self-destruction'.[11] Alleged deficits of national identity will have to be overcome at long last. For Christian Meier the nation as the 'historically grown community of solidarity' will redevelop a new national identity 'in the process of getting it all together'.[12] A 'fruitful national debate' will establish the importance of the national idea in Germany again,[13] and 'develop the "mental infrastructure" of the nation'.[14] Germany, Meier argued, is suffering from *dementia transitoria* which will only be overcome by the renationalisation of German historical consciousness which, in turn, will provide 'the basis for German self-confidence'.[15] A 'country without traditions', Gunther Mai argued, cannot fill the national vacuum which allegedly contributes to the prolonged reunification crisis.[16] The absence of national pride, according to Wolffsohn, has made Germany a 'confused' and 'insecure nation'.[17] What is needed, according to Gruner, is 'a feeling of community', a 'common identity'.[18] Karl-Heinz Ruffmann has called it the 'great patriotic task' of the future to develop 'a self-confident national feeling, as is normal amongst our neighbours'.[19] For Nipperdey, those lacking such feelings suffer from a clinical condition: 'Anyone who does not naturally possess national identity has an identity problem, suffers from a loss of identity or a defect.'[20]

Calls to renationalise German identity encompass very different notions. The ongoing debate about the content of national identity will be an important focus of the public discourse for some time to come. Liberal conservatives like Hildebrand or Meier clearly have very different ideas from representatives of the new right like Zitelmann or Weißmann. The new right set out their agenda for a 'self-confident nation' in a programmatic book published in 1994. Here, as far as historians are concerned, Seebacher-Brandt conjures up the love of the fatherland as the return to European normality and the solution to the unification crisis.[21] Klaus Rainer Röhl identifies the roots of German self-hatred and 'national masochism' in the anti-fascist tradition of the left and the brainwashing effect of Allied re-education programmes.[22] Nolte's critique of Western liberalism[23] goes hand-in-hand with Zitelmann's plea for the development of a new democratic right in Germany which would, in his view, fill the vacuum left by the liberal centre parties.[24] Wolffsohn reiterates his belief that only a return to an unaggressive 'inward nationalism' will allow the Germans to face the difficult domestic and foreign policy tasks of the future.[25] Weißmann portrays the concept of the 'civil society' as the last refuge of the left. According to him, only the concept of the nation in conjunction with a strong state and the recognition of the occasional necessity of warfare will solve the unification crisis.[26] What is most striking in this programmatic statement of the new right is the messianic undertone. The events of 1989/1990 are perceived as a major opportunity to end the alleged hegemony of the 1968 generation in Germany. The renationalisation of German historical consciousness is closely linked to an almost complete redefinition of the self-understanding of the old Federal Republic. It is precisely at this point that many liberal conservatives part company with the new right. Their demands for a renationalisation of German identity remain, on the whole, more committed to the ethos of the old FRG, and they usually insist that any return to national 'normality' will have to include the continued preoccupation with the Third Reich and in particular the Holocaust. A renaissance of the autonomous nineteenth century nation-state is, by and large, rejected. The federal as well as the European perspectives of reunification are stressed. Alleged deficits of national historical consciousness have to be overcome but in line with a continued intra-German regionalism and in line with a continued commitment to ever closer union in Europe. The common discourse of national identity should not be allowed to blur important differences between liberal conservatives and the new right.

Those who have directly called for a revival of Prussian values in the reunified Germany remain on the margins of the profession. In place of the alleged prevailing hedonism which will supposedly make Germans lead a life of 'fellahs' *(Fellachendasein)*,[27] Baring, for example, recommended as a foundation for the new Germany 'a sense of duty' and 'the willingness to serve'. 'Are we not lacking in all areas a feeling for the appropriate and congruent self-portrayal of our community such as was characteristic of Prussia in her best times'.[28] Prussia, Stürmer has argued, once gave Germany 'form and composure' and it might serve as a model for the reunified country in its demonstration of 'the need for the state and a sense of the *bonum commune*'.[29] Adopting Prussian values to overcome an allegedly fatal distance from the state and even enmity towards it (described as another evil legacy of the 1968 generation) has also been one of Weißmann's arguments.[30] Another call to look to Prussia for lessons for the reunified Germany has been provided by Joachim Fest, and eulogies on Prussia and Prussian achievements have been legion since 1990.[31] Prussia itself will not be resurrected, but there have been notable efforts to revive its corpse. In 1991 the coffins of Friedrich Wilhelm and Friedrich were taken to Potsdam with great pomp to be reburied in a midnight ceremony attended by, amongst others, Chancellor Helmut Kohl. The same year saw the restoration of the Quadriga on top of the Brandenburg gate, and still in the same year, politicians had to decide on the future capital of the reunified Germany. They opted, with a small majority (brought about only by the PDS), for Berlin. German historians were prominent participants in the public debate on the future capital. They quarrelled in particular over the question of whether Germany was in need of a new 'centre' to allow for the revival of national traditions. The debate at times cut across political lines, as, for example, when Gall favoured Frankfurt as the new capital, warning that the creation of a new national centre might foster political illusions.[32] On the other hand, Peter von Oertzen, close to the SPD, argued that a new national centre was needed precisely not to evade but to confront the problematic German past.[33] Other arguments by more right-wing historians favoured Berlin and attacked Bonn as the very symbol of the FRG's provinciality. Berlin, they insisted, would be the fitting symbol of Germany's return to power politics and to super-power status. Yet others argued that Berlin would be a symbol of Germany's special commitment to the GDR and the whole of Eastern Europe. Finally, by arguing that Berlin had been the capital of the German nation-state since 1871, historians linked the post-1990 Germany directly with Bismarck's creation. National history, the argument went, in its dreadful abberations and its glorious moments, would be best represented in Berlin.[34] After the decision had been taken, the lead article in the *FAZ* on 21 June 1991 underlined its symbolical significance: 'the new Germany has signalled its readiness to shed its semi-sovereign past and take on a new role which will be more adequate to its changed position in the world. It is no longer possible to have the lowest possible profile internationally, only to whisper the word nation and to let others in this tension-ridden world pull the chestnuts out of the fire – as has happened most recently in the Gulf.'

As the debate on the capital demonstrated, some historians fulfilled a useful role within an 'official nationalism' which surfaced after 1990. As the national enthusiasm about reunification quickly evaporated on the streets and gave way to increasing tensions between Easterners and Westerners, the propagation of national sentiment from above was perceived by some as the means to overcome the much-talked about 'wall in the heads' of many Germans. The more it became apparent that mentalities and outlook in the two Germanies remained far more different than Willy Brandt's famous dictum of 'now grows together that which belongs together' suggested, the more the national discourse was needed to get that famous 'train' rolling in the direction of unity.[35] Prominent members of the *Zunft*, such as Nipperdey, Wolffsohn and Nolte have published national rallying cries in right-wing journals such as *MUT* and *Junge Freiheit*. Seibt has indirectly called for 'speeches about sweat and tears' to overcome the reunification crisis. Weißmann has urged politicians to adopt 'true feeling' *(das echte Pathos)* in their rhetoric on the nation.[36]

Facing a prolonged reunification crisis, sections of Germany's political class have continued to play the national tune. It held out the promise of winning back those protest voters who had opted for the extreme right-wing republicans. For the left, conversion to the national idea also seemed to follow almost logically from the devastating defeat of the SPD's allegedly anti-national Oskar Lafontaine in the 1990 general elections. Thus the remilitarisation of German foreign policy, the increased emphasis on the strong state in the fight

against organised crime, and the change in the liberal asylum laws of
the FRG all indicate the renewed national self-confidence in German
politics.[37] Wolfgang Schäuble, who, to all intents and purposes, will be
the next leader of the CDU and potential chancellor, devoted a
whole book to spelling out the new national agenda.[38] In October
1992 right wingers within the CDU founded the Deutschland-Forum
with the explicit aim of emphasising the national theme. In line with
conservative politicians, representatives of the refugees' associations
have shown how difficult they still find it to come to terms with the
fact that the 'German east' will have to remain 'lost' if peace and
stability in Europe are to be maintained. The conflict between Germany and the Czech Republic over the question of compensation
payments to the Sudeten Germans is a prime example, as are efforts
by extreme right-wingers to 're-Germanise' Kaliningrad. Some
activists of the Verein für das Deutschtum im Ausland (VDA) have
been responsible for raising the spectre of German nationalism in
Eastern Europe – at times with financial support from the German
foreign office.[39] National liberal circles in the FDP like the Dresden
'Stresemann club' or the Berlin wing associated with Alexander von
Stahl have already been dreaming of a new conservative revolution.
The new basic programme of the FDP which was adopted at its 1996
party conference is a clear rejection of the party's social-liberal past.
The refounded 'Hofgeismarkreis' in the SPD has vigorously demanded
a closer orientation of the left to the idea of the nation.[40] Helmut
Schmidt, the former Social Democratic chancellor, founded a German National Foundation (Deutsche Nationalstiftung) in Weimar in
April 1994 to overcome the alleged lack of national identity in the
reunified country.[41] Prominent industrialists, publishers and other
notables have founded the association 'We for Germany' (Wir für
Deutschland e.V.) which started a massive advertising campaign
aimed at strengthening national self-confidence.[42] Alfred Mechtersheimer, a former Green member of parliament, has demanded a
'national revolution' in Germany which would make the country a
powerful advocate of international pacifism.[43] It should, however,
equally be noted that the debate about what will constitute the new
national identity remains a highly contentious issue amongst the parties, organisations and individuals mentioned above. It is, for example, characteristic that the ministers of culture of the German Länder
could not agree on a paper which tried to outline ways and means to
deal with the 'German problem', German history and identity within
the school curriculas.[44] So far, an 'official nationalism' has manifested
itself rather modestly, especially if compared with the rise of nationalism in Eastern Europe after 1989. Nevertheless, as the prolongation

of the reunification crisis coincides with economic difficulties, cuts in social welfare and a crisis of confidence in the party-political system of the country, the chances are that Germany's political elites will continue to act like the pied piper of Hamlin. There is an unmistakeable new national rhetoric which also finds expression in the importance attached to national symbols.

Historians have participated in the discussions about the importance of national symbols for the development of an alleged 'healthy' patriotism.[45] The debates on the national anthem and on the dates which should be important to national remembrance signalled a renewed attention to ways and forms in which the nation should celebrate. At best such renewed interest in national symbols has led to demands that a revived national festival culture should 'not contribute to the renaissance of a narrow nationalism' but should instead encourage 'critical historical remembrance and connect it to the will for freedom and reform'.[46] The project of rebuilding the Berlin palace was supported in 1993 by many important public figures from different political spectres. Part and parcel of the renationalisation of German architecture, historians like Wolffsohn and Christoph Stölzl have both argued in favour of the restoration of the palace as a national symbol. In the words of Stölzl: 'The reunification of the Germans has so far lacked the image which would replace all words. Here it is …'[47] Others have mentioned the Berlin Reichstag as the symbol for the refound unity of the nation, thereby brushing aside the problematic history of that building.[48] And the dubious renaming of streets in East Berlin also aims at the reconstitution of an allegedly lost national history. Reinhart Koselleck described the positioning of an enlarged Pieta by Käthe Kollwitz in the centre of the Neue Wache in Berlin, which serves as the national memorial to Germany since 1993, as an example of the hypocritical identity-building that is going on in Germany today.[49] Quite apart from a variety of valid criticisms about the location, the artistic and aesthetic arrangements and the inscription which simply reads 'To the victims of war and tyranny', the main scandal, he argued, lies in the monument's tendency to blur the division between victims and perpetrators. It harks back to the suffering of the mother as victim bemoaning the death of the son as soldier. Being in the Christian tradition it completely ignores anti-Semitism, the Holocaust, German responsibility for two world wars and unprecedented crimes against humanity. For this reason, the monument can truly be described as a 'levelling gesture' *(Nivellierungsgeste).*[50]

As far as national monuments and symbols are concerned, other embarrassments should be noted. The restored monument of Kaiser

Wilhelm at the Deutsches Eck was re-erected on Sedan Day – the day of national memorial in Imperial Germany on which the nation glorified its victory over France in 1870/1871 and commemorated the realisation of national unity. The debates about a central Holocaust memorial in Berlin and a day of remembrance for the victims of National Socialism, can be seen as attempts to nationalise the collective memory of Germans. The construction of a central memorial goes hand-in-hand with the reconstruction of Berlin as the 'centre' of a reunified Germany and thus becomes part of the renationalisation process.[51] Quite apart from the many problematic aspects of such a central memorial which have to do with the location near Hitler's bunker (which might lead to a revival of the idea that the Holocaust had been Hitler's and not a German crime) and the insurmountable aporias of aesthetically depicting the horrors of Auschwitz, the central problem is to prevent the creation of affirmative symbols of national identity which hinder rather than encourage individual cultures of remembrance.[52] The nation cannot constitute a community which shares the same kind of memories. The construction of such a homogeneous national memory – in itself an attempt at nation-building – is inherently anti-pluralist. It produces a false consensus which ignores the segmentation, disparity and incompatibility of personal memories.[53] If the plan for a central Holocaust memorial in Berlin is ultimately mistaken, the good intentions of the plan's organisers, Lea Rosh and Eberhard Jäckel, should not be doubted, and the often personalised attacks on Rosh in particular are evidence of the fact that some in the new Germany do not want to grant prominent public space at all to the memory of the Holocaust.

The depiction of German history in museums can also constitute an important aspect of the renationalisation of German identity since museums tend to fix national images and thus influence historical consciousness by presenting millions of visitors with particular visions and symbols of the national past. Plans for historical museums in Bonn and Berlin preceded reunification, and they had been the centre of controversy in the mid-1980s.[54] On the left there were suspicions about a history arranged from above. History, it was argued, was becoming the new religion of the nation-state. On the right, there were cries of indignation about proposals for a museum dedicated to the history of the Federal Republic because it would deepen the division of the nation. The focus on the achievements of the FRG would lead to increased forgetfulness about the GDR. Reunification finished off plans for a Berlin museum. Instead, the old East Berlin historical museum in the Zeughaus, Unter den Linden, is going to be renovated and redesigned at a cost of DM 450 million to become the German national history museum with an annual budget of around DM 33 million and a permanent exhibition planned to open not before 1998. Such lavish spending plans for a national museum should be juxtaposed with the apparent lack of public funds for a planned permanent National Socialist Documentation Centre or a museum depicting the history of Jewish life in Berlin.[55] The Bonn museum, financially dwarfed by its Berlin rival, was opened in June 1994. Liberal-conservative historians, such as Lothar Gall, Klaus Hildebrand and Horst Möller called the shots in drafting concepts for the museums, with the left-liberal Jürgen Kocka trying to guarantee a plurality of opinions. That conservatives dominated the planning stages is hardly surprising when one considers that the whole idea was launched by the historian-cum-Chancellor Helmut Kohl in his first major speech as Chancellor in October 1982. Despite such imbalances and despite initially widespread criticisms, the reception by fellow historians in 1994 was overwhelmingly positive. Thus Hermann Schäfer, head of the Bonn museum, could rightly state that 'misrepresentations ... which alleged that the House of History [Haus der Geschichte] would disseminate a quasi-governmental view of history, are no longer repeated today.'[56]

The directors of the Haus der Deutschen Geschichte and the German Historical Museum (Deutsches Historisches Museum) have both rejected any exhibition concepts which would consciously contribute to the renationalisation of historical consciousness. For Schäfer, the aim of the museum is 'to encourage people to have a close look at their history'.[57] Critical questioning of the past, he has argued, should be combined with an exhibition concept which would emphasise the Western roots of the Federal Republic. The preliminary museum catalogue leaves the visitor in no doubt as to the central task of the museum: to increase the positive identification of the citizens of the FRG with their nation and to strengthen the democratic traditions of the FRG by portraying the 'first stable liberal state in Germany' as a success story.[58] Stölzl, the head of the Berlin museum, has adopted a concept which involves the integration of German history within a European framework to avoid 'getting bound up in "small-German" views of history' *(kleindeutsche Nabelschau)*.[59] So far, so good, although one might wonder what Stölzl means when he talks about the nation 'having found its true identity' in 1990.[60] It seems, however, that the motivation which was crucial for the founding fathers of the Germanic National Museum in Nuremberg in 1852, namely the strengthening of national consciousness amongst Germans, is absent – at least in the minds of the historians who head the new national museums. Yet there are still two pertinent objections to be made against the general tendency amongst historians to sound the all-clear. First, even without conscious nationalist intentions, the ever-increasing aestheticisation of historical events in museums tends to encourage the irrationalisation and depoliticisation of historical consciousness.[61] Thus several reviews of the Bonn museum's permanent exhibition have emphasised its character as an 'adventure playground', 'flea market', 'great fuss' which fosters and satisfies the 'sentimental consciousness' of its visitors.[62] Such an aesthetical creation of (almost) perfect dream worlds ends by paralysing the critical faculties of visitors. They either go down memory lane (if they belong to an older generation) or they find themselves enthraled by a kind of time machine which allows them the illusion of participating in past events. Schäfer's comment that he was fascinated by the sight of a school class and its teacher spontaneously dancing next to a 1950s music box and ice-cream parlour reveals both the attractiveness of historical hyper-reality shows to the museum creators and their problems for a distanced critical analysis of the past.[63]

The second objection is related to the much-emphasised multi-perspectivity of the museum, as it essentially still leaves one with a problematic functionalisation for national purposes. As Patrick Bahners pointed out, the museum will contribute to the 'renaissance of national history' which 'marks a return to normality'. As the stability of the state cannot be guaranteed by economic success alone, historical museums, in Bahners' perception, should be viewed as the possibility for creating feelings of loyalty within large sections of the population. For him, it is the alleged weakness of the institutions of political democracy which make such identity-building necessary.[64] The museum's contribution to the emergence of positive national identity and hence its homogenising tendency become visible if one contemplates what has been left out. So, for example, there is no notion of political breaks in the history of the Federal Republic. The question of if and how the students' movement of the late 1960s and the ecology movement of the 1970s have shaped the surface of the FRG are not adequately considered. What is intended instead is the smooth image of an increasing success story which knows no ruptures or breaks. Rather fittingly the visitors move upwards via ramps until they reach the present day. Yet this raises the question of just how smooth that history actually was. National Socialism here becomes a dreadful pre-history of the success story, divided from it by the gulf of 1945. In fact, the first part of the exhibition with its overwhelming emphasis on ruins, the misery of German refugees, the black market, and the work of the post-war services to trace missing persons has strengthened the perception of Germany as a victim of war. The history of the displaced persons after 1945, the history of de-Nazification, the history of the foreign workers in Germany, the history of racism, the history of left-wing terrorism and in particular the state's overreaction in the German Autumn (Deutscher Herbst) of 1977 – all these aspects just do not fit into the conceptual framework praised by liberal conservatives like Bahners. And, of course, predictably, the GDR only makes an appearance as a gigantic prison, a gruesome dictatorship characterised by simplistic propaganda efforts and brutal repression. Very little is said about the everyday experience of people in the GDR, how they perceived and lived their everyday lives.

The fact that criticism of the national museums was so muted in 1994 was certainly related to the fact that it could have been much worse, but it may well also be connected to the widespread acceptance of the 'normal' nation-state after 1990. Immediately before the wall came down, many left-liberal historians were quick to dismiss any hope of reunification, arguing instead for the continued existence of a reformed GDR. Any talk of reunification, they insisted, would threaten the Westernisation of the FRG by reinvigorating nationalism. Furthermore, the international situation would, it was widely believed, prevent reunification from happening in any case. Those who saw a chance for reunification were described as 'unimaginative advocates of a past which has done itself out of a future'.[65] At a conference of the SPD's Friedrich-Ebert-Stiftung in Bonn, Wilhelm Bruns argued in June 1989: 'One thing is certain: the eschatological dream of a reunified country in peace and freedom, i.e., following the model of the FRG, cannot be an orientation for any realistic policy'.[66] In October 1989 Wehler maintained categorically: 'The unity of the state is a highly dubious aim.'[67] Some left-liberal historians gave up such sceptical views during the extraordinary events which followed in 1990, and a few have subsequently even subscribed to the idea of national renewal. By February 1990 Winkler could already write of unification as 'the only perspective' in the current situation.[68] Six years later, re-evaluating the *Historikerstreit* of the mid-1980s, Winkler saw only left-wing taboos which are standing in the way of Germany developing a normal 'post-classical' national identity.[69] Kocka came to the conclusion in 1990: 'Any country would be asking too much of itself, if it wanted to build its political existence on the principle of distrusting itself and, for this very reason, abstained from what still is the normal political existence of modern societies, i.e., the nation-state.'[70] Thadden pleaded for a renewed national self-confidence: 'I cannot envisage any community remaining permanently stable if it did not provide its citizens with any reference points for their identity.'[71] Even for Wehler the solidarity with East Germany should be a national one which would be based on a common history, a common language and a common culture.[72] Left-liberal historians have certainly not been unwilling to take up the threads of the national identity debate. According to Wehler, 'it is worth debating the content of identity'.[73] Kocka has found that 'there is a great need for a new debate about German identity'.[74]

It should be noted, however, that left-liberal historians have developed ideas of the nation which are very different from and directly opposed to calls for the renationalisation of historical consciousness by conservative and new-right historians. The nation, Kocka, for example, has argued, was once a left-wing idea; it was only captured by the political right in the last third of the nineteenth century. For the first time since 1848, the revolution of 1989, in this view, marked the coincidence of demands for freedom with demands for national unity. This, the argument goes, presents the left with a unique opportunity to recapture the concept of the nation-state and strengthen the democratic political culture of the old FRG.[75] However, against such views, it needs to be pointed out that, strictly speaking, the revolution in the GDR was not at the same time a national and a liberal revolution. Until the fall of the wall, the GDR saw an almost exclusively liberal-democratic revolution. Most of the early critics of the GDR who organised the vigils and the Leipzig Monday demonstrations wanted to reform the GDR, not abandon it. The national question remained very much on the back burner. It was only in the second phase of the revolution, after the fall of the wall, that the national element was introduced – initially by the ever-growing number of protesters on the streets of the GDR. Encouraged by the 'official nationalism' of the Kohl government, this movement soon drowned the voices of those demanding a reform of the GDR. Most of the protesters of the first hour soon faded into the background.[76] The gulf separating the democratic from the national rhetoric in Germany was thus confirmed rather than overcome by the 1989 revolution in the GDR.

Amongst left-liberal historians, who also stressed the national theme, Peter Brandt reiterated his view, first put forward in the 1980s, that only a democratic and national left could become a leading force in the new Europe. Denouncing constitutional patriotism as bloodless, having no roots in the culture of the nation, Brandt stressed that a left-wing nationalism should indicate the genuine libertarian traditions in German history. He gave historians the task of providing people with 'possibilities for identifying positively' with Germany.[77] The neat distinction made between good left-wing patriotism and bad right-wing nationalism is also present in a number of other texts. Thus Iring Fetscher has pinned his hopes on the 'growth of a legitimate democratic patriotism' grounded in the regional and ecological movements so popular amongst the younger generation of Germans.[78] The notion of a 'democratic patriotism' has also been strong in the case of Tilman Fichter, for whom it has been of central importance 'to link the idea of the nation firmly to the idea of democracy based on human and social rights'.[79] The distinction between good patriotism and bad nationalism is also maintained by Helmut Bleiber who has argued against what he calls 'widespread national nihilism' in the reunified Germany amongst left-liberal historians and intellectuals.[80] Winkler has spoken of the desperate 'need for national solidarity', and the urgent task of strengthening the feeling of national togetherness.[81] Rüsen has been looking for 'new, freer and more open forms of national identity.'[82] In Thadden's view, whereas the concept of constitutional patriotism remains unrealistic and tied to illusory postnationalism, the national idea in the sense of the French nation of citizens *(Staatsbürgernation)* offers the best prospects of weathering the storms of reunification which lie ahead.[83] 'Braudel's ability to identify with France' is recommended to German historians as a model.[84] For Uwe Uffelmann, the newly acquired unity has brought home the message that ' one has finally to begin looking for positive ways in which to develop the concept of the nation'.[85] According to Uffelmann, the whole discipline has to comprehend the topic of the collective identity of the reunified Germans as its prime challenge.[86] Therefore, it is necessary, according to Dagmar Klose, to end 'tabooing the national' and recognise that 'national consciousness' is 'an integral part of historical consciousness'.[87]

A number of historians have called for a renationalisation of German identity within the framework of a political definition of the *Staatsbürgernation.* They tend to emphasise the continued commitment to Western values and Western integration. They are adamant that the history of National Socialism will have to remain a focal point of German identity after 1990. They look disapprovingly on efforts by the new right to re-interpret the history of the FRG discussed in the last chapter. Have we got, then, a sensible, modest left-wing patriotism which recognises that the events of 1989/1990 will alter the historical consciousness in Germany and which hence attempts to fill the emerging national identity with democratic content? Certainly, to stand on the sidelines, distrust the new Germany and indulge in national nihilism would leave the field wide open for the political Right. Therefore, efforts on the Left to present more progressive concepts for liberal national identity should not be misunderstood as a return to the destructive German nationalism of the first half of the twentieth century. It is indeed helpful to distinguish in this respect between the 'old national paradigm' of the nineteenth century and the 'new national paradigm' which emerged in the FRG after 1945. Whereas the former rested on Romantic notions of renewal and salvation, attempting to bridge the deep cleavages in German society, the latter has come to rest on economic success, Westernisation and postnationalism. Amongst left-liberal historians, the search for a new national identity since 1990 can build on the 'new national paradigm'.[88] Ideas of constitutional patriotism, of democratic rights and freedoms, of an enlarged and democratised European Union and of social justice are well developed, left-liberal historians have argued, to serve as pillars for a self-critical national identity. However, one also has to consider that in Germany, a left-wing patriotism has, at several critical junctures in the twentieth century, moved close to the right-wing discourse on nationalism, sometimes becoming almost inseparable from it.[89] The very concept of 'national identity' remains a fudged one, a construct with inherent homogenising tendencies which tends to exist in conflict with the values of tolerance and pluralism. Hence it cannot be the historians' task to propagate national identity, left or right wing. The danger is not an alleged lack of national identity, it is that democratisation may be replaced by renationalisation.[90] It is not the 'self-confident nation' that needs to be dug up – it is a self-confident democratic political culture which needs to be strengthened in the West and developed in the East.

The national principle brings with it a number of irrational and inhumane implications (such as the seemingly unavoidable rivalry amongst nations, or the often violent exclusion of those who are not perceived as part of the nation) which should best not be revived. The national discourse, whether of the left or of the right, has included both participatory and aggressive elements which make a neat dichotomy between good patriotism and bad nationalism untenable.[91] In Germany the anti-democratic connotations of the nation-state far outweigh its democratic ones. A renationalised German identity might well re-invigorate new waves of xenophobic hatred. On a positive note, Wilfried Loth has argued that the Westernisation of the old FRG 'does not allow any simple return to concepts of the nation prevalent in Imperial Germany.'[92] Hence, for Loth, it is 'unlikely that the nation-state will again become the prime reference point' for identity.[93] Alternatively, any such return might, from a pessimist viewpoint, spell the return of political ideas and emotions which preceded the Federal Republic's political culture.[94]

In an age of increasing globalisation of markets and communication, the nation-state will increasingly be unable to solve some of the most pressing problems. It is either too small or too large.[95] 'The nation', Niklas Luhmann found, 'may well prove relevant for football matches, but in a political sense it could rather be counterproductive.'[96] For Hans Mommsen 'the principle of the nation-state is not on the agenda of European policy. It remains a phenomenon of the past.'[97] As Wehler put it: 'Any talk of normality [in terms of nation-states] leads straight into a cul-de-sac'.[98] For Bracher, to perceive the nation as the only form of identity would be an 'impoverishment', and would lead Germany onto its old *Sonderweg* again.[99] The current identity debate starts by posing the wrong questions if it does not take into account social and regional as well as individual life-histories. Such a 'national narrowing of horizons' might well prove reunification to have been, as Helga Grebing feared, 'a national disaster'.[100] National identity is not a necessary ingredient of personal identity. On the contrary, it should best be perceived as the projection of a collective, employed to push through very particularist interests in the name of all. The 'need for a collective identity' remains what it always has been: a romantic invention which can easily be instrumentalised for a return to German power politics. In resisting efforts to rehabilitate national values, Habermas has argued that one cannot extrapolate any sense from Germany's twentieth-century history 'except that every form of sacrifice demanded by the state must be abolished.'[101]

Despite all of its negative characteristics and serious shortcomings, the revival of the national concept has been *the* most important intellectual idea uniting historical revisionism in post-reunification Germany. Despite such a renaissance, which combined with the considerable 'reservoir for "catching-up nationalism"' in the new *Länder*,[102] historians played down any dangers of a revitalised nationalism. For Meier, German nationalism 'to any significant extent only exists as ghosts in the thoughts of those who see in the German present above all the shadows of the past and want to cling to them.'[103] Some, like Otto Dann, have simply turned the accusation of nationalism on its head by arguing that the 'emotionally charged voices of an antinational ressentiment' constitute the real danger.[104] For the new right Weißmann has dismissed any talk of nationalism as a 'defective perception of reality'.[105] Zitelmann has demanded that 'those who were against reunification, should speak or write about different topics for the next couple of years'.[106] The more historians maintain that there is no danger of nationalism, the easier it is for them to demand a thorough renationalisation of the allegedly depraved German identity.

Belittling the dangers of harking back to the national traditions seems thoughtless if one considers that an admittedly small number of German historians and social scientists on the margins of the profession seem willing to uphold the unholy ethnic definition of Germanness prevalent before 1945 and still recognisable in the country's current citizenship laws (article 116 of the Basic Law). Many historians have publicly called for the law to be changed, bringing it into line with the territorial concept of citizenship in France.[107] There has been an increasing emphasis on the importance of the concept of citizenship for historical processes of nation-building.[108] Yet, faced with proposals for a Westernisation of the country's citizenship laws, Schwarz, for example, has been haunted by nightmares of 'armies of permanently emotionally homeless people'.[109] In line with the existing German law, Mayer has argued that a country should aim to be 'an ethnically homogeneous nation'. Its 'natural right of self-preservation ... makes the decision about whom to absorb in its community ... wholly legitimate'.[110] Having painted wild scenarios of floods of foreigners streaming into the German 'boat' and causing it to sink, Baring concluded: 'Of course Germany to the Germans – to whom else? If this country wants to remain identical with itself, it has to build barriers.'[111]

Ethnic nationalism rests on the assumption that a people, like an individual, has certain hereditary characteristics which separate one nation from another. It uses the term 'people' in an ethnocentric, nationalist context, not along the lines of social coalitions against political injustice and social disadvantage.[112] Ethnicity, in this view, is indivisible from the concept of the nation: 'Nations always ... rest on a consciousness of ethnic identity'.[113] Steeped in German Romantic thought, Weißmann has written that 'peoples and nations are collective personalities which have an "identity" and a "character".'[114] Weißmann has managed to combine an amazing number of platitudes in his search for the German national character. Germans, he asserted, are characterised by 'boundless energy', 'constant self-reflectiveness' and 'spiritual depth'. And yet, alas, they also reveal 'a fatal tendency' to 'be vague and shapeless'.[115] The division of Germany, in this view, could not last because it violated the alleged ethnic imperative of nations.

Assuming the existence of a homogeneous people with one common identity, Brigitte Seebacher-Brandt, the widow of the late Chancellor and herself a distinguished labour historian, has written about the necessity of a homogeneous people with one common identity. Intellectuals on the political left are castigated for not being able to understand the 'imponderables of the people's soul'. They will never

be in a position to heal the 'emotional fractures in the life of a people'.[116] Nationality, according to Seebacher, is constituted by birth,
i.e., it is not a conscious choice of the citizen: 'The nation remains the
natural and normal, the obvious frame of reference for the people.
They do not acquire any commitment to the nation, except by being
born into it.'[117] The German people, ethnic nationalists often argue,
had retained a natural feeling of togetherness, where the decadent
anti-German intellectuals had developed artificial ideas like constitutional patriotism and multi-culturalism. Thus anti-intellectualism
goes hand-in-hand with an admiration for the alleged positive primitive naturalism of the people.[118]

    In this view the history of the nation-state becomes the homoge-
neous national history of the people. The nation writ large as collective personality cannot be ambivalent, broken or ruptured depending
on different ethnic, religious, political and social groups with different
interests. This is all in line with Nolte's explicit rejection of a 'population with mixed nationalities'.[119] Knütter has demonstrated how one
can mix xenophobia with denunciation of cosmopolitanism and
arrive at the ideal of a nation defending its borders against threatening hordes of foreigners.[120] If one returns to an understanding of the
nation as *ethnos*, it is only logical to rewrite the German national history from Karl the Great to Kohl the Great,[121] as the centuries-old
fight of the German 'tribes' for self-preservation.[122] If one claims that
the German nation started in the ninth or tenth century, then the
national principle becomes one of the basic foundations of European
society.[123] Such a 'longue duree' might well contribute to the revival
of the medieval myths about German nationhood so prevalent in the
nineteenth century.

    National thinking in Germany has been radicalising itself after
reunification. Warnings have ranged from Peter Glotz's 'normalisa-
tion-nationalism' which, he argued, might easily turn into ethnic
nationalism,[124] to Habermas' warning of 'DM nationalism', which
might lead to the colonisation of Eastern Europe,[125] to Niethammer's
warning of a possible revival of the *völkisch* Sonderweg in central
Europe.[126] For Diner, one of the central questions of the future will
be whether the Germans will turn to the West and define themselves
politically, or whether 'the tendency of a growing return to the memory of a predominantly ethnically defined nation' will become
stronger.[127] Amongst a population which still shows high levels of
ethnocentric and racist attitudes, the neo-nationalist rhetoric, according to Schwan, might be readily picked up.[128] Jost Dülffer has warned
fellow historians not to hark back to an understanding of the nation
as *Volk*, which had been central to the National Socialist path of

destruction and genocide.[129] Wehler has argued against any return to potent national myths demanded by the new German right: 'At present and in the long term the Germans would be badly advised to return to a new nationalism and to revive its old myths.'[130] For Kocka, the compatibility of the reunified country with liberal democracy and European integration is not a foregone conclusion: scepticism about the consequences of reunification remains justifiable.[131] The strong resistance to any renationalisation of German historiography amongst left-liberal historians was most visible when they successfully protested against an invitation of the 'historian' Helmut Kohl to address the *Historikertag* in Leipzig in September 1994, just before the country's general election, on the topic of 'the nation-state in Europe'.

The nation, left-liberal historians have been arguing, may become more important in future, but liberty, prosperity, the welfare state, the social market economy, civil society, increasing equality of opportunities between the sexes and classes, and constitutional loyalty are, they maintain, the values on which the nation should be built. Universal values of a democratic political culture are perceived as superior to the egotistical national values. Regional and cultural diversity of mentalities in a multicultural Europe – these are key ingredients of a historical identity which would not once again tie Germany primarily to the concept of the nation.[132] Kaschuba has reminded his fellow historians that it was a society lacking strong national consciousness which successfully established democratic ideals in the hearts and minds of West-Germans after the Second World War.[133] Furthermore Kühnl has outlined a vision of a 'culture of social and natural peace' as an alternative to the many national visions of the future. He has developed a political agenda in which the notion of progress is uncoupled from productivity growth, and in which the welfare state and the world society replace notions of *Volk* and nation.[134]

However, it has not only been the vision of the future German society that has been contested in the aftermath of reunification. The vision of the past has also been challenged. Demands for a general revision of the methodologies and paradigms in German historiography have gone hand-in-hand with efforts to demolish historical social science. Hacker has accused a range of left-liberal historians of having displayed a 'high degree of unimaginativeness, inflexibility and ignorance' in their writings on the national question.[135] Nolte has argued that historians for four and half decades had been writing a history of self-humiliation in the interest of the victors in the Second World War.[136] For Baring there has been too much feminism and pacifism underpinning German historiography, and too little 'glori-fication of heroic death' and 'manhood'.[137] Critical historians had been, according to Hacke, absorbed by their 'hounding of bourgeois scholars' and by their 'care lavished on a perverse pride in the sin-gularity of the home-made evil'.[138] Zitelmann similarly accused them of fostering 'hypermoralism, anti-anti-Communism and anti-nation-alism' in Germany and thereby contributing to a 'fatal politicisation of scholarship'.[139] Seibt has accused the analytical structural history of the 'Bielefeld school' of having produced 'unreadable' bloodless histories which inadequately mirror the unpredictable contingency of the past.[140] Their failure had become most apparent in 1989 which in turn, according to Gustav Seibt in the *Frankfurter Allgemeine Zeitung*, produced no intellectual reorientation of the profession.[141] Contingency has also been the keyword in Bahners' attacks on the rationality of critical historiography. Having fallen prey to the 'ratio-nalist temptation', they have become 'blind to reality'. Instead of 'abstract structural history' and 'Bielefeld myths', Bahners advocated a 'happy ecclecticism'.[142]

Instead of clinging to an outdated structural history which was responsible for the derision of German national history, Schwarz has pleaded for a return to 'historical reason and political morality'. These virtues, according to Schwarz, ruled supreme in the traditions of German historiography before the 1960s. After 1990 German his-torians should return to the 'enthusiasm of the generation of Sybel and Treitschke'.[143] Schwarz's call to stop playing the 'reunification melody with mute trumpets' has been reminiscent of Ritter's call in 1946 not to stop playing the 'patriotic trumpets' in the face of the Nazi past.[144] Meier urged historians 'to see our history once again with the eyes of identity'.[145] Gall stressed the need to write history which will centre around questions of identity.[146] He maintained that historical myths matter. In his view, they are comparable to religion in that they 'help to make sense of the world'. Much of the problems of German identity, in this perception, derive from the fact that Germany lacked a proper foundational myth, yet there are still the myths of the nine-teenth century many of which still 'touch living roots' amongst Ger-mans and hence are only waiting to be revived.[147] For Nipperdey, the historians' task will be to create 'a picture of the fate of those people whom we call Germans'.[148] Weißmann has called on historians to contribute to the necessary 'basic intellectual and moral renewal' of the nation by returning to Schlegel's concept of the historian as the 'backwards-oriented prophet'.[149] According to Schöllgen, historians will have to come to terms with the renaissance of the national idea if they want to take up the challenge awaiting them: 'who would be in a better position to answer the question about the new Germany's place in the world more competently than the historians.'[150]

Those whose minds have centred on a more powerful role for Germany in the world have demanded a return to the concept of the 'primacy of foreign policy' and a renewed concentration on diplomatic, political and military history. 'Historians', according to Schöllgen, 'are above all called upon to pay more attention to the history of Germany's foreign policy and to international relations in the twentieth century.'[151] Historical social science, in this view, has contributed to the alienation of Germans from power politics.[152] Only by turning their backs on 'fashionable' American models of the 1960s and returning to the allegedly great traditions of German political and diplomatic historiography, can historians in the reunified Germany adequately come to terms with the FRG's new superpower status.[153] Whereas Stürmer praised Gerhard Ritter's *Staatskunst und Kriegshandwerk* for its preoccupation with questions of international politics, he has denounced critical social history as deadening new dogma 'which did not want to know about the drama of history: It was buried under socio-historical statistics and trends'.[154] If the 'drama' or the 'tragedy' of German history in the nineteenth and twentieth centuries has indeed arisen from Germany's geographic position and the power politics of European states, then domestic politics can indeed be neglected for the study of foreign politics. The *Mitte* ideology is part and parcel of renewed attempts to anchor such a tragic emplotment of German history in historical consciousness.[155]

Faced with such criticisms, representatives of historical social science have been arguing for a plurality of methods and viewpoints in German historiography. Any monolithic historical consciousness has been portrayed as alien to pluralist democratic societies. Thus it cannot be the task of historians to achieve consensus on the forms and content of national identity. On the contrary, any exclusively national perspectives would soon reveal their limits.[156] As Wolfgang Mommsen has reminded fellow historians, history in the singular is an artificial construct. Added to the many histories are a multitude of different perspectives. For Mommsen, the criteria of the historical discourse prevents the historian from arbitrariness, but at the same time any genuine historical debate depends on the plurality of possible histories.[157] The task of the historian is still perceived as that of destroying, not creating myths and legends.[158] Comparative history and the further internationalisation and Europeanisation of German historiography have been portrayed as the best safeguards against once again getting bound up in one's own national history: 'it would be completely wrong ... to paint one's own history in black, red and

gold colours and define it even more in the sense of national history
than is almost always done in any case.'[159]

At the same time as left-liberal historians have maintained their
distance from attempts to renationalise German historical consciousness, one has to ask whether a certain degree of renationalisation has been accepted as inevitable? For Sabrow, 1989 'will
strengthen the all-German viewpoint of historiography. The renewal
of the German nation-state ... will now encourage national views of
history in the same way that the previous division of the country
directed one's gaze on the German traditions of particularism.'[160]
Kleßmann has predicted that 'a society which aims at overcoming
the much-quoted "wall in the heads" ... will try to seek out and
emphasise the common aspects of the past ...' [161] And for Kocka, the
national paradigm will become even more 'natural' than it had
already been before 1989, as it will be the 'duty of the historians' to
contribute to 'the inner unification of Germany'.[162] According to
Diner, the change from society to nation will be a necessary one for
Germany to make, and therewith the definition of national identity
becomes of prime importance.[163]

Wolfgang Mommsen seems equally determined not to leave the
renationalisation process to the new right. Shortly before official
reunification he was still writing of the task of the historian as that of
'doing away with the remnants of an old-fashioned national thinking'.[164] At the *Historikertag* in Bochum in 1990, he was in the van-
guard of those who argued that the last thing historians should do is
to contribute to the creation of national myths.[165] For him, there was
no stepping back behind what he perceived as the productive merger
of history with the social sciences from the 1960s onwards.[166] But –
and I think that this has to be seen as crucial for Mommsen's subsequent development – at the time of reunification he thought that the
Historikerstreit had been made redundant by events. A new national
identity had been created in the making of the reunified country.
The prolonged reunification crisis demonstrated that in 1989/1990
this task had been far from accomplished. Hence, thereafter, Mommsen missed few opportunities to endorse the new nation-state and
stress the lack of alternatives to it. According to him, it will be the
duty of the historians to hammer this message home, and thereby
allow the Germans 'to come to terms with their deeply divided historical consciousness'. By writing national history, historians will
make Germans 'comprehend the history of both German part states
in the long-term perspective as part of a common national history'.[167]
By doing this, historians will contribute 'to completing the internal
unity of the two German states'.[168] The writing of political and diplo-

matic history moves to the fore, whilst, according to Mommsen, the times are not rosy for social and structural history: 'the current *Zeitgeist* is not exactly favourable. The wind has turned'.[169]

In the face of the continued onslaught against historical social science, it is notable that some of its representatives critically re-examined some of their key concepts. In many cases such re-examination had already begun before 1989 in response to its many critics. It is easy to overestimate the impact of the national turn, and it is certainly also the case that the rethinking of one's methodological categories is in itself not only legitimate but valuable. It is, above all, a sign of intellectual honesty and development. Yet at times it has been difficult to avoid the impression that there is also a link between such willingness to rethink and the national turn. Apart from the more sceptical evaluation of the *Sonderweg* idea after 1989, discussed above, the importance of the concept of 'class' in social history has been, according to Kocka, substantially reduced.[170] Faulenbach argued that 'class' as an analytical category will become less important whilst at the same time the national paradigm has won a new attractiveness.[171] The primacy of domestic over foreign policy idea has been ditched.[172] However, the interdependency of foreign and domestic policies is often acknowledged.[173] Characteristically, the reviews of Hildebrand's study of Germany's foreign policy between 1871 and 1945 were taken to task in *Geschichte und Gesellschaft* primarily for ignoring this interdependency.[174] In the context of the breakdown of Communism in Eastern Europe, it is argued, the dimension of foreign policy was crucial. Without Gorbachev's willingness to let the Eastern European states go, there would have been no 'velvet revolutions'. One of the lessons of 1989 for historiography was, in Kocka's view, the marked determination by, even dependency on, the high politics of international relations of the social relations of everyday life.[175] Similarly Wolfgang Mommsen has pleaded for a renaissance of classical diplomatic history, and a return to 'the fatal dimensions of international politics'.[176] There has been a greater emphasis on contingency and unpredictable factors in history.[177] Yet the core of structural social history, according to Kocka, has on the whole, been confirmed rather than rejected by the events of 1989 since they demonstrated the strength of historical continuities and the persistence of historical structures.[178] Kocka has also insisted that reunification should free German historians to turn away from narrow national history and instead towards a comparative history of civilisation. As he pointed out, it was the division of the country and the functionalisation of the discipline for legitimating the two German states which had contributed to the continued strength of the national paradigm in German historiography.[179] Wehler has insisted that research on social inequality will remain the 'major task of modern social history' *(Königsweg)*.[180] For his reading of German national history, he is still looking towards the 'unsurpassed modernization theory of Max Weber'.[181] However, Wehler's former attempt to synthesise Marxist and Weberian ideas is gone.[182]

Apart from the renaissance of political and international history after 1989, for some years now there has also been increased attention on 'culture' and cultural history.[183] Kocka for one, has emphasised that political social history has been enriched in recent years by a cultural dimension.[184] Even Wehler has shown a remarkable willingness to admit the shortcomings of his mode of history writing and accept that cultural history might be both rewarding and enriching historical practice. With uncharacteristic humour he declared his intention to try his hand at cultural history and produce, at some unspecified point in the future, 'a very slim, wonderful and almost erotically seductive volume on a cultural history topic ... spiced with a comparative dimension.'[185] Such ironic acceptance of the new cultural historians stands in marked contrast to Wehler's stern refusal to acknowledge the merits of a history of everyday life in the 1980s. This might have something to do with the fact that cultural historians also tend to oppose a conservative renationalisation of German historical consciousness.[186] At its very best, both the new cultural history and a more traditional social history contribute to the deconstruction of nationalist myths in German historiography.[187] However, the flight into cultural history might yet display its own difficulties, since 'culture' can easily be instrumentalised for identity building. The picture of an 'embattled culture' might furthermore lead to the creation of a view of the self and other which will encourage racism and fundamentalism in German society. In this sense, 'culture' will be in line with the renationalisation of German identity.[188]

However, at the same time, it should be admitted that German historiography is characterised at present by a very healthy pluralism of methodologies and research interests.[189] There is no dramatic reorientation, but, as I hope I have demonstrated, there have been a whole number of corrections to research paradigms, methodologies, and, more generally, to historical views on Germany, and these have, overall, strengthened tendencies towards a renationalisation of German historical consciousness. The most consistent efforts to return Germany to the alleged 'normality' of the 'self-confident nation' have been made by a small band of new-right historians associated with Rainer Zitelmann. However, even amongst more mainstream conservative historians there have been clear signals of a national turn. And some left-liberal historians have indeed become 'rational adherents to the national principle' *(Vernunftnational-staatler).*[190] That their idea of the nation is very different from the one espoused by conservatives and the new right has been established in this and the last four chapters as has been their reluctance and opposition to attempts to push German historiography back onto the national track. Yet they clearly have been on the defensive since 1990. Institutionally, this is also reflected in the fact that in appointments of chairs in the new Länder, the conservatives have clearly won out.[191] Some historians on the left, like Roth, have observed 'a worrying abandonment of critical historical analyses' in the rush not to be left behind by renationalisation.[192] However, at the moment the future development of German historiography is far from clear. Alongside the many worrying signs of renationalisation stand some positive ones. So, for example, the new chairman of the Historians' Association, Johannes Fried, emphasised at the 1996 *Historikertag* in Munich the 'gesellschaftskritische Wächterfunktion' of the historical profession. At the same meeting, the president of the FRG, Roman Herzog, declared the nation-state to be a phenomenon of the past, and the joint Czech-German historians' commission (which has existed since 1990) presented a hopeful declaration which was meant to pave the way for genuine reconciliation between these two nations. It seems that the 'search for normality' is at the very least a contested one. In the next chapter I shall consider how historians in Britain and the United States have reacted to the attempts to renationalise German historiography.

NOTES

1. Meier, *Deutsche Einheit,* p. 36.
2. Ibid., p. 46.
3. Schwarz, 'Auf dem Weg', pp. 326-30.
4. Hans-Peter Schwarz, 'Bestandsaufnahme in Deutschland', *Die Welt,* 28 Feb. 1990.
5. Sieferle, *Epochenwechsel,* p. 89.
6. Peter Graf Kielmannsegg, 'Vereinigung ohne Legitimität?', *Merkur,* vol. 47, 1993, p. 575. See also Wolfgang Schuller, 'Alle Deutschen stehen vor einem Neuanfang', *FAZ,* 16 Dec. 1989.
7. Hildebrand, *Das vergangene Reich,* p. 897.
8. Weißmann, *Rückruf,* p. 135; idem, Die Wiederkehr eines Totgesagten: Der Nationalstaat am Ende des 20. Jahrhunderts', *aus politik und zeitgeschichte,* 2 April

1993, p. 5; idem, 'Die Nation denken', *FAZ*, 22 April 1994; also Wolfgang Venohr, 'Argumente gegen zwei Staaten', *Rheinischer Merkur*, 15 Dec. 1989.

9. Hagen Schulze, 'Deutsche fanden ihre Identität', *Berliner Morgenpost*, 7 May 1995 for the new-found 'normality' of the German nation-state. For the assessment of Schulze's *Kleine deutsche Geschichte*, Munich, 1996 see Volker Ullrich, 'Die neue Normalität. Das historische Hausbüchlein für die Kohl-Generation', *Die Zeit*, no. 41, 4 Oct. 1996, p. 29.

10. One of the earliest was the programmatic article by Karl Heinz Bohrer, 'Warum wir keine Nation sind. Warum wir eine werden sollten', *FAZ*, 13 Jan. 1990.

11. Geiss, *Deutsche Frage*, pp. 106, 111.

12. Meier, *Deutsche Einheit*, p. 19.

13. Ibid., pp. 54-86.

14. Christian Meier, *Die Nation, die keine sein will*, Munich, 1991, p. 10.

15. Meier, 'Deutschland', pp. 261-79. A new identity debate has also been demanded by Lothar Gall, 'Die Geschichte ist nicht das Waffenlager der Politik', *Die Welt*, 26 Sept. 1994.

16. Mai, 'Vom Obrigkeitsstaat', in: Knoblich, Peter and Natter (eds), *Auf dem Weg*, p. 80.

17. Michael Wolffsohn, 'Zerrissenheit als Erbe', *Rheinischer Merkur*, 22 March 1991; also idem, 'Wachsam sein und Flagge zeigen', *Die Welt*, 14 Nov. 1992, p. G1.

18. Gruner, *Deutsche Frage*, p. 357.

19. Karl-Heinz Ruffmann, 'Vaterland woher, wohin? Die Deutschen auf der Suche nach einem neuen Selbstverständnis', in: Schönhoven and Staritz (eds), *Sozialismus*, p. 500. A similar clarion call for the 'reconstruction of national identity' can be found in Ansgar Graw, '(Historiker-) Streit', in: Zitelmann, Weißmann and Großheim (eds), *Westbindung*, p. 379.

20. Thomas Nipperdey, 'Die Deutschen wollen und dürfen eine Nation sein', *FAZ*, 13 July 1990.

21. Brigitte Seebacher-Brandt, 'Norm und Normalität. Über die Liebe zum eigenen Land', in: Schwilk and Schacht (eds), *Die selbstbewußte Nation*, pp. 43-56.

22. Klaus Rainer Röhl, 'Morgenthau und Antifa. Über den Selbsthaß der Deutschen', in: ibid., pp. 85-100.

23. Ernst Nolte, 'Links und rechts. Über Geschichte und Aktualität einer politischen Alternative', in ibid., p. 160 f.

24. Rainer Zitelmann, 'Position und Begriff. Über eine neue demokratische Rechte', in ibid., pp. 163-81.

25. Michael Wolffsohn, 'Nationalstaat und Multikultur. Über den deutschen Zivilisationsbruch und seine Folgen', in: ibid., pp. 267-80.

26. Karlheinz Weißmann, 'Herausforderung und Entscheidung. Über einen politischen Verismus für Deutschland', in: ibid., pp. 309-26.

27. Baring, *Deutschland*, p. 206.

28. Ibid., p. 205; see also calls for a return to Prussian values in Wolffsohn, *Deutschland*, pp. 58-70.

29. Michael Stürmer, 'Wenig Staat. Deutschland ohne Preußen', *FAZ*, 30 March 1991.

30. Weißmann, *Rückruf*, pp. 159 f.

31. Joachim Fest, 'Preußen – Abschied und Dauer', *FAZ*, 3 May 1993. See also on the occasion of the 'return' of Frederick the Great to Potsdam Eberhard Straub, 'Vom Hort der Freiheit zum bösen Geist', *Rheinischer Merkur*, 16 Aug. 1991, pp. 4,7.

32. Lothar Gall, 'Brauchen wir eine Mitte?', in: Helmut Engel and Wolfgang Ribbe (eds), *Hauptstadt Berlin – wohin mit der Mitte? Historische, städtebauliche und architektonische Wurzeln des Stadtzentrums*, Berlin, 1993, p. 236.

33. Peter von Oertzen, 'Braucht Deutschland eine Hauptstadt?', in: Udo Wengst (ed.), *Historiker betrachten Deutschland. Beiträge zum Vereinigungsprozeß und zur Hauptstadtdiskussion*, Bonn, 1992, pp. 224-34.

34. Meier, *Die Nation*, pp. 86-99. Also: Joachim Fest, 'Was für Berlin spricht', *FAZ*, 12 April 1990; Patrick Bahners, 'Streit der Symbole', *FAZ*, 16 Feb. 1990.

35. On the renationalisation of German politics see: Ulrike Liebert, 'Kein neuer deutscher Nationalismus?' Vereinigungsdebatte und Nationalbewußtsein auf dem "Durchmarsch" zur Einheit', in: Ulrike Liebert and Wolfgang Merkel (eds), *Die Politik zur deutschen Einheit. Probleme – Strategien – Kontroversen*, Opladen, 1991, pp. 51-91. Evidence of 'official nationalism' and its consequences is also collected in Hajo Funke, *"Jetzt sind wir dran". Nationalismus im geeinten Deutschland. Aspekte der Einigungspolitik und nationalistische Potentiale in Deutschland*, Berlin, 1991; Peter Glotz, *Die deutsche Rechte. Eine Streitschrift*, Munich, 1992.

36. Gustav Seibt, 'Ein Drama ohne Helden: Historische Wissenschaft und gegenwärtige Erfahrung', *FAZ*, 5 June 1990; Weißmann, *Rückruf*, p. 49; Baring, *Deutschland*, pp. 46-8.

37. Wolfram Wette, 'Der Wunsch nach Weltmacht', *Die Zeit*, 30 July 1993, p. 4.

38. Wolfgang Schäuble, *Und der Zukunft zugewandt*, Berlin, 1994.

39. Walter von Goldendach and Hans-Rüdiger Minow, *'Deutschtum erwache!' Aus dem Innenleben des staatlichen Pangermanismus*, Bonn, 1995. Critical of the Sudeten Germans' attempts to torpedo German-Czeck reconciliation is Rudolf von Thadden, 'Die Grenzen der Restauration', *Die Zeit*, no. 52, 20 Dec. 1996, p. 6

40. Michael Rudloff (ed.), *Sozialdemokratie und Nation. Der Hofgeismarkreis in der Weimarer Republik und seine Nachwirkungen. Eine Dokumentation*, Leipzig, 1995, esp. pp. 127-65, 176-210, 328-34.

41. Thomas Assheuer, 'Kein Sonderweg. Niemals', *FR*, 23 April 1994; Micha Brumlik, 'Stifter der Nation. Deutsche Staatsmänner in Weimar', *Blätter*, 1994, pp. 783-5.

42. Otto Köhler, '"Wir sind das Land". Dr. Oetkers neues Volksbindungsmittel', *Blätter*, 1994, pp. 910 f.

43. Alfred Mechtersheimer, *Friedensmacht Deutschland. Plädoyer für einen neuen Patriotismus*, Berlin, 1993, esp. p. 360.

44. 'Was Schüler in Ost und West aus der deutschen Geschichte lernen sollen', *FR*, 9 Oct. 1995.

45. Michael Wolffsohn, 'Deutsche Symbole. Staatsname, Nationalhymne und Nationalfeiertag – und der 9. November', *Die politische Meinung*, vol. 35, Nov./Dec. 1990, pp. 23-8; Patrick Bahners, 'Streit der Symbole', *FAZ*, 16 Feb. 1990; Wolf Jobst Siedler, 'Wo Preußen am preußischsten war', *Die Zeit*, 26 Nov. 1993, p. 63; Rüdiger Voigt, 'Allmählicher Abschied vom Nationalstaat?', *Das Parlament*, 16/23 June 1995, p. 7; Herfried Münkler, 'Trotz aller Widersprüche ist der Wallot-Bau das politische Symbol Deutschlands', *Das Parlament*, 16/23 June 1995, p. 6.

46. Wehler, *Gegenwart*, p. 232.

47. 'Das Schloß der Republik: Menschen brauchen Visionen', *Die Welt*, 15 May 1993, p. G2. On the renationalisation of architecture more generally see Philipp Oswalt, 'Der Mythos der Vergangenheit dient als Vision für die Zukunft', *FR*, 9 July 1994.

48. Jürgen Schmädeke, 'Und doch ein Symbol der Hoffnung', *Das Parlament*, 16/23 June 1995, p. 12.

49. Reinhart Koselleck, 'Mies, medioker und provinziell', *Die Tageszeitung*, 13 Nov. 1993. Also idem, 'Stellen die Toten den Termin?', *Berliner Zeitung*, 11 Nov. 1993, and Rudolf Walther, 'Normalisierung als nationale Verlogenheit', *FR*, 27 Nov. 1993. On both the renaming of streets in East Berlin and on the controversy surrounding the national memorial see Ulla Spittler and Gerd Knischewski, 'Redefining German Identity: Case Studies in Berlin', *Journal of Area Studies*, no. 7, 1995, pp. 100-13.

50. Peter Reichel, 'Die Spuren der Opfer und der Täter', *Das Parlament*, 2/9 Sept. 1994, p. 7.

51. Silke Wenk, 'Ein Ort wie kein anderer', *FR*, 14 Oct. 1995; see also Thomas Assheuer, 'Die Aufgabe der Erinnerung', *Die Zeit*, no. 4, 17 Jan. 1997, pg. 43.
52. Hanno Loewy, 'Wo keiner einsteigt und keiner aussteigt ...', *FR*, 14 Aug. 1995. For useful introductions to the politics of Holocaust memorials see James E. Young, *The Texture of Memory. Holocaust Memorials and Meaning*, New Haven, 1993; Peter Reichel, *Politik mit der Erinnerung. Gedächtnisorte im Streit um die national-sozialistische Vergangenheit*, Munich, 1995.
53. Klaus Naumann, 'Opfer, Täter, Tote. 50 Jahre danach: Erinnerungskultur in der Konsensfalle', *FR*, 19 March 1996.
54. For the initial debate see the contributions by Hartmut Boockmann, Jürgen Kocka, Gottfried Korff and Wolfgang Ruppert in *GG*, vol. 11, 1985 and vol. 12, 1986; also, from different perspectives Geschichtswerkstatt Berlin (ed.), *Die Nation als Ausstellungsstück*, Berlin, 1987. The debate is also documented in Christoph Stölzl (ed.), *Deutsches Historisches Museum. Ideen – Kontroversen – Perspektiven*, Berlin, 1988.
55. For plans to postpone the building of a permanent NS documentation centre see Benedikt Erenz, 'Bubenstück', *Die Zeit*, 8 Nov. 1996, p. 47; for the controversy surrounding the Berlin Jewish museum see Ute Frings, 'Maulkorb – als ginge es um die nationale Verteidigung', *FR*, 13 Jan. 1996. However, it should be noted that money is not the only reason for the deadlock. There is also a prolonged struggle over the museum's remit and concept between the designated head of the museum, Amnon Barzel and the Berlin city administration in the person of Rainer Güntzer. See Ute Frings, 'Braucht Berlin ein jüdisches Museum oder nicht?', *FR*, 28 June 1996.
56. Hermann Schäfer, 'Begegnungen mit unserer eigenen Geschichte', *aus politik und zeitgeschichte*, 10 June 1994, p. 13.
57. Hermann Schäfer, 'Was wir zeigen, ist die Entstehungsgeschichte der Gegenwart', *Das Parlament*, 2/9 Sept. 1994, p. 2.
58. *Zeiträume. Konzept, Architektur, Ausstellungen*, ed. by the Haus der Geschichte der Bundesrepublik Deutschland, Bonn, s.d.
59. Christoph Stölzl, 'Geschichte kann man nicht ausstellen, nur ihre Zeugnisse und Bilder', *Das Parlament*, 2/9 Sept. 1994, p. 2.
60. Christoph Stölzl, 'Zur Situation des Deutschen Historischen Museums Berlin', in: Füßmann, Grütter and Rüsen (eds), *Historische Faszination*, p. 155.
61. Jörn Rüsen, 'Für eine Didaktik historischer Museen', in: idem, Wolfgang Ernst, Heinrich Theodor Grütter (eds), *Geschichte sehen. Beiträge zur Ästhetik historischer Museen*, Pfaffenweiler, 1988, pp. 12 f.
62. Benedict Erenz, 'BRD ab 6', *Die Zeit*, 24 June 1994, p. 47; Christian Thomas, 'Ein zumeist angenehmer Spaziergang', *FR*, 16 June 1994.
63. Hermann Schäfer, 'Was wir zeigen, ist die Entstehungsgeschichte der Gegenwart', *Das Parlament*, 2/9 Sept. 1994, p. 2. For the general problem of providing critical historical consciousness via museums Heiner Treinen, 'Ist Geschichte im Museum lehrbar?', *aus politik und zeitgeschichte*, 10 June 1994, pp. 31-8.
64. Patrick Bahners, 'Glück unter Glas', *FAZ*, 16 June 1994.
65. Heinrich August Winkler, 'Die Mauer wegdenken', *Die Zeit*, 11 August 1989, p. 7.
66. Cited in *Die politische Meinung*, May/June 1990, p. 50.
67. Hans-Ulrich Wehler, 'Deutsche Frage und europäische Antwort', *FR*, 14 Oct. 1989.
68. Heinrich August Winkler, 'Der Staatenbund als Bewährungsprobe', *Süddeutsche Zeitung*, 16 Feb. 1990.
69. Heinrich August Winkler, 'Kehrseitenbesichtigung', *FR*, 29 Oct. 1996, p. 10.
70. Kocka, 'Revolution und Nation, p. 495.
71. Rudolf von Thadden, 'Ohne Möglichkeiten der Identifikation kann kein Gemein-wesen stabil sein', *Der Tagesspiegel*, 16 August 1991.

72. Hans-Ulrich Wehler, 'Aufforderung zum Irrweg', *Der Spiegel*, 24 Sept. 1990.
73. Wehler, *Gegenwart*, p. 201; see also 'Brauchen wir ein normales Nationalgefühl, Herr Wehler?', *Der Tagesspiegel*, 15 Feb. 1996, p. 22.
74. Kocka, *Vereinigungskrise*, p. 149.
75. Jürgen Kocka, 'Der neue Nationalstaat. Suche nach neuer Identität', *Wirtschaftswoche*, 12 Feb. 1991, pp. 28 f.
76. Hartmut Zwahr, *Ende einer Selbstzerstörung*. Leipzig und die Revolution in der DDR, Göttingen, 1993; Konrad Jarausch, *Die unverhoffte Einheit 1989/90*, Frankfurt-on-Main, 1995.
77. Peter Brandt, 'German Identity', *Debatte*, vol. 1, 1993, pp. 30-41; idem, 'Die Linke und ihre nationale Frage', *Vorwärts/SM*, vol. 1, 1990; for his efforts to reconstruct a genuine social democratic patriotism in the nineteenth and twentieth centuries compare also idem and Dieter Groh, *'Vaterlandslose Gesellen'. SPD und Nation*, Munich, 1992.
78. Iring Fetscher, 'BRD ade!', in: Otthein Rammstedt and Gert Schmidt (eds), *BRD ade! Vierzig Jahre in Rück-Ansichten*, Frankfurt-on-Main, 1992, p. 35.
79. Tilman Fichter, *Die SPD und die Nation*, Frankfurt-on-Main, 1993, p. 250; for another call for 'democratic patriotism' also by Iring Fetscher, '... daß nur Freie das Vaterland lieben können', *FR*, 8 Jan. 1994.
80. Helmut Bleiber, 'Neun Anmerkungen zum Problem des Nationalen', *BZG*, vol. 38, 1996, pp. 48-67.
81. Winkler, 'Abschied', pp. 633-6; idem, 'Rebuilding of a Nation', p. 121.
82. Jörn Rüsen, 'Continuity, Innovation and Self-Reflection in Late Historicism: Theodor Schieder (1908-1984)', in: Hartmut Lehmann and James van Horn Melton (eds), *Paths of Continuity: Central European Historiography from the 1930s to the 1950s*, Cambridge, 1994, p. 353.
83. Rudolf von Thadden, 'Nation muß sein – aber wozu?', *GWU*, vol. 45, 1994, pp. 341-6; idem, 'Ein 80-Millionen-Staat ohne klare Konturen?', *Tagesspiegel*, 3 Oct. 1993 (Beilage). See also Kocka, *Vereinigungskrise*, p. 161: 'Constitutional patriotism alone never is sufficient [for national identity].'
84. Rudolf von Thadden, 'Umgang mit der Geschichte. Gedanken zu Braudels "L'identité de la France"', in: Jarausch, Rüsen and Schleier (eds), *Geschichtswissenschaft*, pp. 277-83.
85. Uwe Uffelmann, 'Spielräume für Identitätsbildung im historisch-politischen Lernen?', in: idem (ed.), *Identitätsbildung und Geschichtsbewußtsein nach der Vereinigung Deutschlands*, Weinheim, 1993, p. 250.
86. Uwe Uffelmann, 'Identitätsbildung und Geschichtsdidaktik', *aus politik und zeitgeschichte*, 14 Oct. 1994, p. 12. Bernd Mütter, 'Geschichte der deutschen Geschichtsdidaktik in der Epoche der Teilung 1945-1990. Perspektiven einer gesamtdeutschen Geschichtsdidaktik', in: Uwe Uffelmann (ed.), *Historisches Lernen im vereinten Deutschland. Nation – Europa – Welt*, Weinheim, 1995, p. 99 has similarly called on historical didactics to contribute towards overcoming the unification crisis by providing the basis for a consensual view on the past.
87. Dagmar Klose, 'Prägungen und Wandlungen ostdeutscher Identitäten', *aus politik und zeitgeschichte*, 14 Oct. 1994, p. 9 f.
88. Bernd Weisbrod, 'German Unification and the National Paradigm', *German History*, vol. 14, 1996, pp. 193-203.
89. Stefan Berger, 'Nationalism and the Left', *NLR*, no. 206, 1994, pp. 55-70.
90. Wolfgang Leonhard, 'Demokratisierung wird ersetzt durch Vereinigung', *Die Tageszeitung*, 2 Oct. 1990.
91. Langewiesche, *Nationalismus*.
92. Loth (ed.), *Die deutsche Frage*, p. 227.
93. Loth, 'Die Deutschen', in: Mommsen (ed.), *Europa*, p. 66.

94. Arno Klönne, *Rechts-Nachfolge. Risiken des deutschen Wesens nach 1945,* Cologne, 1990.
95. Klaus Naumann, 'Geschichte als Politik', *Blätter,* vol. 36, 1991, p. 1,396.
96. Niklas Luhmann, 'Immer noch Bundesrepublik: Das Erbe und die Zukunft', in: Rammstedt and Schmidt (eds), *BRD ade!,* p. 100.
97. Hans Mommsen, 'Die Sozialdemokratie und die Nation: Nationale Loyalität und internationale Solidarität in der deutschen Arbeiterbewegung', in: Rudloff (ed.), *Sozialdemokratie und Nation,* p. 25.
98. Wehler, *Gegenwart,* p. 133.
99. Karl Dietrich Bracher, 'Erschreckend ist die Hilflosigkeit der Demokratie', *Die Welt,* 26 April 1993.
100. Helga Grebing, 'Ein Pakt der Vernünftigen', in: *Neues Deutschland,* pp. 54-7.
101. Jürgen Habermas, 'Die Last der doppelten Vergangenheit', *Die Zeit,* 13 May 1994, p. 54.
102. Winkler, 'Nationalismus', in: idem and Hartmut Kaelble, *Nationalismus,* p. 31. The term 'catching-up nationalism' is used in analogy to Habermas's characterisation of the 1989 revolutions in Eastern Europe as 'catching-up revolutions'. In his view, Eastern Europe was trying to catch up with the modernisation processes which had occurred in Western Europe since the end of the Second World War and which had been prevented by Communism in Eastern Europe. Similarly, nationalism was not overcome in Eastern Europe, it was just kept under the lid. With Communism gone, it came out in the open again.
103. Christian Meier, 'Wir sind ja keine normale Nation', *Die Zeit,* 21 Sept. 1990, p. 7. Similarly Kielmannsegg, 'Vereinigung', p. 573; Hans-Peter Schwarz, 'Bestandsaufnahme in Deutschland', *Die Welt,* 28 Feb. 1990; idem, *Zentralmacht,* p. 208.
104. Otto Dann, *Nation und Nationalismus in Deutschland 1770-1990,* Munich, 1993, p. 318.
105. Weißmann, *Rückruf,* p. 124.
106. Rainer Zitelmann, 'Randnotizen eines Diskurs-Agenten – Antwort auf Alfred Schobert', *Deutschland-Archiv,* vol. 25, 1992, p. 1,201.
107. On the two contrasting concepts of citizenship see Roger Brubaker, *Citizenship and Nationhood in France and Germany,* New York, 1992.
108. Dieter Gosewinkel, 'Staatsbürgerschaft und Staatsangehörigkeit', *GG,* vol. 21, 1995, pp. 533-56.
109. Hans-Peter Schwarz, 'Bürger oder Mitbürger?', *Die Welt,* 10 June 1993.
110. Tilman Mayer, 'Fragmente zur Bestimmung der deutschen Nationalstaatlichkeit', in: Zitelmann, Weißmann and Grossheim (eds), *Westbindung,* pp. 501-21.
111. Arnulf Baring, 'Am Ende liegen sich alle in den Armen', *Berliner Zeitung,* 4/5 April 1992.
112. For those different concepts of 'people' (*Volk*) see Wolfgang Kaschuba, '"Wir sind das Volk!". Neue Sichtweisen der Volkskultur in Geschichte und Gegenwart', in: Jarausch, Rüsen and Schleier (eds), *Geschichtswissenschaft,* p. 417.
113. Weißmann, *Rückruf,* p. 95; idem, 'Wiederkehr', p. 9; idem, 'Die Nation denken', *FAZ,* 22 April 1994.
114. Karlheinz Weißmann, 'Trauerarbeiter und Schönfärber', *Die Welt,* 12 Feb. 1994, p. G1.
115. Weißmann, *Rückruf,* pp. 138-43.
116. Brigitte Seebacher-Brandt, 'Die Linke und die Einheit. Unwägbarkeiten der deutschen Geschichte', *FAZ,* 21 Nov. 1989.
117. Brigitte Seebacher-Brandt, 'Nation im vereinigten Deutschland', *aus politik und zeitgeschichte,* 21 Oct. 1994, p. 8.
118. Weißmann, *Rückruf,* p. 10; Zitelmann, 'Wiedervereinigung und deutscher Selbsthaß', pp. 235-48.
119. Nolte, *Streitpunkte,* p. 431.

120. Hans-Helmuth Knütter, *Wanderungsbewegungen – ein Faktum. Multikulturelle Gesellschaft – eine Fiktion*, St. Augustin, 1993.

121. Kohl's portrayal as 'second Bismarck', his characterisation as 'sovereign', 'cool' and endowed 'with conscious instinct for power' has been both shallow and aimed at reminding Germans of the alleged continuity of the nation-state. Compare Geiss, *Deutsche Frage*, pp. 103-6; Korte, *Die verpaßte Chance*, p. 216, and *Welt am Sonntag*, 7 Nov. 1993 which printed a picture of Kohl next to one of Bismarck.

122. Wolfgang Venohr, 'Argumente gegen zwei Staaten', *Rheinischer Merkur*, 15 Dec. 1989, p. 3.

123. Moraw, 'Jüngste deutsche Gegenwart', p. 391.

124. Glotz, *Irrweg*, pp. 130 f., 144. See also idem, *Die falsche Normalisierung*.

125. Jürgen Habermas, 'Der DM Nationalismus', *Die Zeit*, 30 March 1990, p. 62.

126. Lutz Niethammer, 'Geht der deutsche Sonderweg weiter?', in: Grunenberg (ed.), *Welche Geschichte*, p. 51.

127. Dan Diner, 'Gedächtnis und Institution', *Merkur*, vol. 48, 1994, pp. 943-6.

128. Gesine Schwan, 'Die Last zweier Vergangenheiten', *Rheinischer Merkur*, 24 Jan. 1992, p. 3.

129. Jost Dülffer, 'Hitler, Nation und Volksgemeinschaft', in: Dann (ed.), *Die deutsche Nation*, p. 114.

130. Hans-Ulrich Wehler, 'Aufforderung zum Irrweg', *Der Spiegel*, 24 Sept. 1990, p. 29; idem, 'Wider die falschen Apostel', *Die Zeit*, 9 Nov. 1990, p. 54; most comprehensively idem, *Angst vor der Macht? Die Machtlust der Neuen Rechten*, Bonn, 1995. See also Hans Mommsen, 'Das deutsche Amalgam aus Macht und Geist', *FR*, 17 Jan. 1994.

131. Kocka, 'Überraschung und Erklärung', p. 15; idem, 'Revolution und Nation', pp. 494 f.

132. Wehler, *Gegenwart*, pp. 135, 153 f.; idem, 'Wider die falschen Apostel', *Die Zeit*, 9 Nov. 1990, p. 54; Rainer M. Lepsius, 'Nation und Nationalismus in Deutschland', in: Michael Jeismann and Henning Ritter (eds), *Grenzfälle. Über alten und neuen Nationalismus*, Leipzig, 1993, pp. 193-214; Jürgen Habermas, *Staatsbürgerschaft und nationale Identität*, St. Gallen, 1991; Manfred Hettling and Paul Nolte (eds), *Nation und Gesellschaft in Deutschland. Historische Essays*, Munich, 1996.

133. Wolfgang Kaschuba, 'Kulturalismus: Kultur statt Gesellschaft?', *GG*, vol. 21, 1995, p. 95.

134. Reinhard Kühnl, 'Gesellschaft im Umbruch. Versuch, einen Überblick zu gewinnen', *Blätter*, vol. 39, 1994, pp. 747-54.

135. Hacker, *Deutsche Irrtümer*, pp. 352-82.

136. Nolte, *Lehrstück*, p. 100.

137. Baring, *Deutschland*, pp. 197, 204 f.

138. Hacke, *Weltmacht*, pp. 542 f.

139. Zitelmann, *Republik*, pp. 116-8.

140. Gustav Seibt, 'Ein Drama ohne Helden. Historische Wissenschaft und gegenwärtige Erfahrung', *FAZ*, 5 June 1990.

141. Gustav Seibt, 'War da was? Die Historiker und 1989', *FAZ*, 8 Nov. 1994.

142. Patrick Bahners, 'Persönliches Regiment', *Merkur*, vol. 48, 1994, pp. 1,007-13; idem, 'Wissenschaft als Beruf', *Merkur*, vol. 49, 1995, p. 531.

143. Schwarz, 'Mit gestopften Trompeten', p. 703.

144. Ritter, *Geschichte als Bildungsmacht*, p. 40.

145. Christian Meier, 'Wir brauchen Vertrauen', *Der Spiegel*, 30 Jan. 1995, p. 152.

146. Lothar Gall, 'Die Botschaft von 1789', in: von Sternburg (ed.), *Geteilte Ansichten*, p. 77.

147. Lothar Gall, *Confronting Clio: Myth-Makers and Other Historians*, London, 1992, pp. 8, 10, 12.

148. Cited in Adelbert Reif, 'Sinn für Vergangenheit', *Die Welt*, 23 March 1992. Also Thomas Nipperdey, 'Der Abschied von der Utopie wird unsere Zeit bestimmen', *Die Welt*, 3 Dec. 1990.
149. Weißmann, *Rückruf*, pp. 51, 191.
150. Schöllgen, *Angst vor der Macht*, pp. 117 f; idem, 'Die Macht der Nation und die Hilflosigkeit deutscher Intellektueller', *Merkur*, vol. 48, 1994, p. 933.
151. Schöllgen, *Angst*, p. 118. For a similar call for more political history see Lothar Gall, 'Interview', *ZfG*, vol. 42, 1994, p. 1,059.
152. Schöllgen, *Angst*, p. 99.
153. Gregor Schöllgen, 'Herausforderung. Die Prioritäten historischer Forschung in Deutschland und die neue Lage', *Neue Hefte für Philosophie*, vol. 34, 1993, pp. 66-84.
154. Stürmer, *Die Grenzen der Macht*, p. 147.
155. For an explicit defence of *Mitte* ideology which combines with an outright attack on historical social science see Imanuel Geiss, 'Geographie und Mitte als historische Kategorien. Anmerkungen zu einem Aspekt des Historikerstreits', *ZfG*, vol. 39, 1991, pp. 979-94.
156. Ralph Jessen, 'Geschichtsschreibung in der Möglichkeitsform', *FR*, 31 May 1994.
157. Wolfgang J. Mommsen, 'Perspektivengebundenheit und Objektivität historischer Forschung', *ZfG*, vol. 40, 1992, pp. 341-9.
158. Hans-Joachim Gehrke, 'Mythos, Geschichte, Politik – antik und modern', *Saeculum*, vol. 45, 1994, pp. 263 f. See for a similar argument about the task of historiography Wehler, *Gegenwart*, pp. 189-201.
159. Jürgen Kocka, 'Überraschung und Erklärung. Was die Umbrüche von 1989/90 für die Gesellschaftsgeschichte bedeuten könnten', in: Hettling, Huerkamp, Nolte and Schmuhl (eds), *Was ist Gesellschaftsgeschichte?*, pp. 18-20; similar emphasis on the importance of developing a European historical consciousness in Wolf D. Gruner, *Deutschland mitten in Europa. Aspekte und Perspektiven der deutschen Frage in Geschichte und Gegenwart*, Hamburg, 1992, pp. 418, 421.
160. Martin Sabrow, 'DDR-Bild im Perspektivenwandel', in: idem and Kocka (eds), *Die DDR als Geschichte*, pp. 241-5.
161. Kleßmann, 'Verflechtung', p. 30.
162. Kocka, *Vereinigungskrise*, pp. 63, 128 f.
163. Dan Diner, 'Geprägt von fünfzig Jahren Frieden', *Das Parlament*, 16/23 June 1995, p. 7.
164. Wolfgang J. Mommsen, 'Die Deutschen haben einiges dazugelernt', *Die Welt*, 25 Sept. 1990.
165. Wolfgang J. Mommsen, 'Eröffnung des 38. Historikertages in Bochum', in: Eckert et al., *Krise*, pp. 236-41.
166. Wolfgang J. Mommsen, 'Schlußbetrachtung', in: Schulin (ed.), *Deutsche Geschichtswissenschaft*, p. 295.
167. Wolfgang Mommsen, 'Fata Morgana aus Plattenbauten', *Die Welt*, 27 March 1993.
168. Mommsen, 'Die DDR', p. 29.
169. Mommsen, 'Geschichtswissenschaft', p. 81. For a completely different assessment of the prospects of social history in medieval studies after reunification compare M. Borgolte, 'Der mißlungene Aufbruch. Über Sozialgeschichte des Mittelalters in der Zeit der deutschen Teilung', *HZ*, vol. 260, 1995, pp. 365-94.
170. Kocka, 'Überraschung und Erklärung', pp. 16 f.
171. Bernd Faulenbach, 'Zur Bedeutung der Umwälzungen in Mittel- und Osteuropa für das Geschichtsverständnis der deutschen Arbeiterbewegung', *BZG*, vol. 34, 1992, p. 40.
172. Jürgen Kocka, 'Überraschung und Erklärung', pp. 16 f.; Wolfgang J. Mommsen, 'Die Geschichtswissenschaft nach der "demokratischen Revolution" in Ostmitteleuropa', *Neue Rundschau*, vol. 105, 1994, pp. 75-88.

173. Wehler, *Gegenwart*, pp. 259-61.
174. Ernst-Otto Czempiel, 'Deutsche Außenpolitik von 1871 bis 1945' and Hans-Ulrich Wehler, '"Moderne" Politikgeschichte? Oder: Willkommen im Kreis der Neorankeaner vor 1914', both in *GG*, vol. 22, 1996, pp. 243-66, see esp. pp. 247, 250, 252, 262. For a similar, albeit less scathing critique see Wolfgang Mommsen, 'Die Außenpolitik des Reiches', *Merkur*, vol. 50, 1996, pp. 1,064-70.
175. Jürgen Kocka, 'Sozialgeschichte der neunziger Jahre', *Die neue Gesellschaft/Frankfurter Hefte*, Dec. 1993, p. 1,125.
176. Mommsen, 'Geschichtswissenschaft', p. 86.
177. Jürgen Kocka, 'Es droht die Zementierung der alten Verhältnisse', *Die Welt*, 19 Dec. 1990; Hans-Ulrich Wehler, 'Einleitung', in: idem (ed.), *Scheidewege der deutschen Geschichte. Von der Reformation bis zur Wende 1517-1989*, Munich, 1995, p. 8 f.
178. Kocka, *Die Auswirkungen*, p. 20.
179. Jürgen Kocka, 'La Reunification et la Recherche Historique Allemande', *Vingtième Siècle*, vol. 34, 1992, pp. 32-6.
180. Hans-Ulrich Wehler, 'Selbstverständnis und Zukunft der westdeutschen Geschichtswissenschaft', in: Jarausch, Rüsen and Schleier (eds), *Geschichtswissenschaft*, p. 77.
181. Wehler, *Gegenwart*, p. 169. For an explicit endorsement of modernisation theory see ibid., pp. 13-59.
182. Nick Stargardt, 'Hans-Ulrich Wehler and the Destiny of Charisma', *Bulletin of the GHIL*, vol. 28, no. 2, 1996, pp. 27-34.
183. Rudolf Vierhaus, 'Die Rekonstruktion historischer Lebenswelten', *FR*, 28 Sept. 1994; Ute Daniel, '"Kultur" und "Gesellschaft". Überlegungen zum Gegenstandsbereich der Sozialgeschichte', *GG*, vol. 19, 1993, pp. 69-99.
184. Kocka, *Vereinigungskrise*, p. 60.
185. Hans-Ulrich Wehler, 'Von der Herrschaft zum Habitus', *Die Zeit*, no. 44, 25 Oct. 1996, p. 46. Compare, however, the much more sceptical evaluation of cultural history in the *GG* special volume 16, 1996.
186. Andreas Helle, 'Neue Geschichte, alte Probleme', *FR*, 15 Oct. 1996.
187. So, for example, Johannes Fried, *Der Weg in die Geschichte. Die Ursprünge Deutschlands bis 1024*, Berlin, 1994, pp. 9-24 and with very different methodological preoccupations Helga Schultz, 'Mythos und Aufklärung. Frühformen des Nationalismus in Deutschland', *HZ*, vol. 263, 1996, pp. 31-67.
188. Kaschuba, 'Kulturalismus', pp. 80-95.
189. This is the impression, one gets, for example from reading Winfried Schulze (ed.), *Sozialgeschichte, Alltagsgeschichte, Mikrohistorie*, Göttingen, 1994.
190. Schwarz, 'Mit gestopften Trompeten', p. 704.
191. Jarausch, 'Kritische Perspektiven', in: idem and Middell (eds), *Erdbeben*, p. 28.
192. Karl Heinz Roth, 'Der historische Revisionismus in Deutschland – Zwischenbilanz und Perspektiven', *1999*, vol. 9, 1994, p. 11.

Chapter 10

———

THE REACTIONS OF BRITISH AND AMERICAN HISTORIANS TO CHANGES IN GERMAN HISTORIOGRAPHY AFTER REUNIFICATION

German historiography has often been so absorbed by its own vitriolic debates that it finds it difficult at times to look beyond national boundaries. Yet after 1945 there have also been important moves in the direction of greater Europeanisation and internationalisation. Never before have there been more exchange programmes, more opportunities for conducting research across national boundaries, more attention in scholarly journals to research published in other countries. Such developments have to be set against the way history departments at German universities are organised, with their great emphasis on German history, and their long *cursus honorum* for younger scholars who have, on the whole, far fewer opportunities for international exchanges than their superiors. Nevertheless, the increased internationalisation of historiography means that national debates and controversies are noted abroad and also discussed there. Hence I would like to end this review of contemporary changes in German historiography by looking briefly at the reactions those changes have produced in Britain and the United States. Of course, it would be interesting to take into account other European countries, particularly France, Italy and some of Germany's 'smaller'

neighbours, such as the Netherlands and Poland. Yet, as I live and
work in a British environment, I only really feel fit to comment on
my adopted home country. I decided to include some U.S. historians
because the flow of academics between Britain and the United States
(and, alas, it is mainly from here to there) is such that one can justifiably speak of an 'Anglo-American' scholarly community.[1]

Ever since the nineteenth century German historiography has created a considerable amount of interest amongst British and U.S. historians.[2] Arnold, Ashley, Seeley and a number of others had been
influenced by German Romanticism, the German school of historical economics, and Ranke in particular.[3] In the first volume of the
English Historical Review Lord Acton eulogised the various 'German
schools of history', singling out the Prussian historians in particular.[4]
At the foundation of the American Historical Association in 1884
Ranke became the only foreign honourary member. As the AHA's
president George Bancroft wrote to Ranke, it was meant to be 'a special homage to yourself as the greatest living historian'.[5] In both
Britain and the United States the organisational and methodological
innovations in the academic historiography of Germany became a
model which many sought to emulate. This was much less the case,
however, with the political and ideological orientation of German
historians. Their illiberal tendencies were noted with a great deal of
critical comment by representatives of American 'New History'. In
Britain many academics distinguished carefully between two Germanies – a 'good Germany' which they identified with culture, economic modernity as well as efficient social provisions and a 'bad
Germany', widely connected to militarism, illiberalism and the lack
of civic courage.[6] The image of the 'bad Germany' clearly prevailed
during the First World War, when British historiography was as
engaged in whipping up national sentiment as its German counterpart. The anti-British tracts of German university professors found
their equivalent amongst John Bull's academic elite and contributed
to a devaluation of German idealist thought in Britain.[7] In the 1920s
and 1930s British historians, however, belonged to the most effective
propagandists against the alleged harshness of the Treaty of Versailles. The most eloquent representatives of appeasement found
themselves bitterly disappointed in 1939.[8] In the United States widespread pro-German sentiments amongst leading academics between
1933 and 1938 were equally disappointed.[9]

After 1945 British and U.S. historians – under the influence of
German emigrée historiography – often critically reinterpreted German national history and 'national character' in a way that underlined
the need for a thorough re-education programme to be implemented

in occupied Germany.[10] In a famous exchange between Geoffrey Barraclough and Gerhard Ritter in the 1950s, the British fear of any revival of historiographic nationalism in Germany was all too clear. Lewis Namier, John Wheeler-Bennett, and E.L. Woodward were amongst a number of British historians who, throughout the 1950s, opposed returning the archives of the German foreign ministry and the Prussian ministry of foreign affairs to West Germany because they feared that the archives would be used for exercises in national apologetics.[11] A.J.P. Taylor's belief in ethnic characteristics was certainly not too favourable for the Germans. In his account of 'the course of German history' he came to the conclusion that Hitler was the result of the extreme national character of the Germans: 'German has meant at one moment a being so sentimental, so trusting, so pious, as to be too good for this world; and at another a being so brutal, so unprincipled, so degraded, as to be not fit to live ... Only the normal person ... has never set his stamp on German history.'[12] The popularity of William Shirer's accounts of Nazi Germany in the United States further points to the endorsement of perceptions of an almost evil German national character. And yet there was also a much more sympathetic view of German history. Berghahn's research on less well-known textbooks of the post-war era suggests a considerable positive influence of those German academics who had been exiled, like Carsten in Britain and Holborn and Rosenberg in the United States.[13]

Despite such well-meaning interpretations of German national history, an intensive, constructive dialogue between German and British historians only really got going from the 1960s onwards. A new generation of German historians were in the process of doing away with the pretensions of Prussianism whilst a new generation of British historians had fewer of the deep-seated reservations against Germany and its historians that characterised those who had experienced the first half of the twentieth century. It also certainly helped that a truly international renewal of historiography in the 1960s meant that historians of different countries faced similar historiographical agendas and worked towards the solution of comparable methodological problems.[14] The role of the London and Washington-based German Historical Institutes in fostering contacts between German and Anglo-American historians surely deserves particular attention. Major works on German history were now being produced in Britain and the United States. The *Sonderweg* debate of the 1980s was instigated, from very different perspectives, by the British historians David Blackbourn and Geoff Eley and the American David Calleo. Anglo-American historians contributed widely in the *Historikerstreit* of the mid-1980s which found enormous repercussions in book and article publications. In the context of this controversy Richard Evans already wrote of a renaissance of nationalism in German historiography.[15] Similar sentiments were present in the analysis of Roderick Stackelberg who distinguished between an 'official historiography' engaged upon creating a national identity in the name of the ruling neo-conservatism on the one hand, and a beleaguered 'critical historiography' with its commitment to democratisation derived from the student revolt of the late 1960s on the other.[16] Many Anglo-American historians came to develop their own interpretations of German history in a fruitful dialogue with the critical historiography of West Germany. Blackbourn and Eley argued that the critical historians' views 'command the most serious attention… We do take the view that if Hans-Ulrich Wehler had not existed, it would have been necessary to invent him … If historians have to be assigned to camps, we are therefore … in the camp of those whose views we have considered critically.'[17] Critical historiography, historians such as Sheehan, Blackbourn, Eley and Kershaw argued, had, in the course of the 1970s, become the new orthodoxy with which one had to engage in debate.[18] In the light of the *Tendenzwende* after 1982 and certainly in the light of events after reunification in 1990, one could ask whether British and U.S. historians did not tend to overestimate what was, after all, a vigorous and lively minority amongst German historians. The sea change of the 1960s had not so much produced a new orthodoxy as it had contributed to a genuine methodological and ideological pluralisation of German historiography.

On the national question, British and U.S. historians tended to share in the widespread belief prior to 1989 that the division of the country might well be irreversible. In 1975 William Paterson predicted the development of a separate national identity in West Germany.[19] In the early 1980s Gordon Craig found himself endorsing Schiller in his rejection of German nation building efforts in the nineteenth century.[20] Michael Balfour could at best envisage a confederation of the two Germanies in the future.[21] In the mid-1980s Walter Laqueur predicted the growing alienation and estrangement of the two Germanies in the light of the manifest differences between the two states.[22] In his speech before the German parliament in 1987, on the occasion of the commemoration of 17 June 1953, Fritz Stern stressed that the rising in the GDR should not necessarily be seen as an outcry for national reunification but as a cry for liberty. He thus argued by implication that 17 June did not lend itself to the renationalisation of German identity.[23] Michael Hughes wrote in 1988: 'The German nation now seems to be irreversibly divided into separate states and there is no evidence of any great desire among the majority of Germans to change this ... The longer the partition lasts, the less it will mean and there must be doubts about the importance of the issue [reunification] to future generations of Germans.'[24] As far as historiography was concerned, James Sheehan in an influential article, pleaded for understanding German national history as an invention by the Prussian school of historiography. He argued convincingly that the limits and shortcomings of the national perception far outweighed its benefits. The politics of German historiography, he concluded, should at long last take into account those 'dimensions of life which do not conform to the politically-imposed boundaries of the nation-state'.[25]

However, in 1989, when the wall came down, and in 1990 when German reunification was achieved, it was precisely the renewed construction of German national identity that was on the cards. In the light of the widespread acceptance of division before 1989, and in stark contrast to both a significant strand of public opinion and a considerable number of politicians and journalists,[26] many historians reacted positively to reunification. Already by July 1989 John Gray was arguing that 'legitimate German aspirations for reunification' would soon be realised.[27] Tim Garton Ash in December 1989 wisely foresaw that 'the logic of events ... may begin to pull both halves together at remarkable speed.'[28] A few months later, in a commentary on the East German elections of 18 March 1990, he pronounced: 'Nobody knows exactly what has begun. All that is certain is what has ended. This has a name. It is called the German Democratic Republic.'[29] Less than a year later his uncertainty had gone, and there was nothing left but admiration: 'there is something truly remarkable in the matter-of-fact normality with which Germany has settled down to being a united democratic state.'[30] Julian Bullard, former British ambassador to the Federal Republic, turned historian, wholeheartedly welcomed reunification and emphasised that Germanophobia was of very little significance in Britain at large.[31] Harold James found little that worried him about reunification,[32] and Gordon Craig argued before a German audience that no-one in the United States would lose any sleep over German reunification.[33] Richard Evans wrote somewhat contemptuously of Chancellor Kohl scrambling 'with almost indecent haste to write his name into the history books as the second Bismarck', but on the whole he dismissed talk of a 'Fourth Reich' as nonsense: 'The way ahead may be fraught with difficulties and dangers but it scarcely seems likely to lead to another Königgrätz or Sedan, let alone another Verdun or another Auschwitz'.[34] Instead, as Fritz Stern has argued, the renewed ascendancy of Germany, based on its economic, technological and human capabilities, might mean a 'second chance' for the country to use its strengths, this time for the good of Europe and the wider world.[35] Similarly Martin Gilbert wrote: 'I always thought the division of Germany after 1945 was unnatural ... In the next decade, a united Germany could be a lifesaver, a source of economic strength and political stability for all the countries of central Europe.'[36] In his account of the unification process, Jarausch provides a cautiously optimistic assessment of the prospects for a peaceful, democratic and European Germany in the twenty-first century.[37]

Of course, there was apprehension at first, and some of the statements in the autumn of 1989 sounded cautious indeed, but on the whole Anglo-American historiography can certainly not be accused of any degree of anti-Germanism. In so far as there was scepticism about reunification, it was often connected to the perception that the Soviet Union would never agree to reunification on purely Western terms.[38] Thus, in September 1989, Alan Bullock could see 'no realistic chance of reunification', and Donald Cameron Watt in a letter to the *Daily Telegraph* sounded confident that 'there will still be two Germanies fifty years from now.'[39]

In Germany there was much justified criticism of the Chequers meeting of then Prime Minister Margaret Thatcher with selected U.S. and British historians of Germany in March 1990. Gordon Craig, Timothy Garton Ash, Fritz Stern, Norman Stone, George Urban and Hugh Trevor-Roper discussed the elusive German national character in less than flattering terms, at least if one follows the leaked memorandum of the meeting. Alleged German characteristics included 'insensitivity to the feelings of others ... obsession with themselves, strong inclination to self-pity, and a longing to be liked' as well as '*Angst*, aggressiveness, assertiveness, bullying, egotism, inferiority complex, sentimentality'.[40] The 'fudgy' concept of 'a national character'[41] can certainly be found in the writings of British historians. Peter Pulzer, for one, argued that 'envy and self pity' as well as 'disdain for the incompetence of other peoples' characterised Germans.[42] Yet, ultimately, what many outraged German observers failed to realise was how positive the assessment of contemporary Germany actually was. Clearly, the participants in the meeting all have very different political and historical backgrounds and their views on Germany are impossible to distil into one. Yet, it seems fair to say that the memorandum adequately reflects that they were not unduly worried by the prospects of German reunification: 'The weight of the evidence and the argument favoured those who were optimistic about life with a united Germany.'[43] Ash's views have already been commented about above. Norman Stone had written in

February 1990 about reunification: '... our Prime Minister should at once have said how great was the moment, and how strongly the British government would support unification, without reserve. ... Have we in the West anything to fear? Resoundingly, no.'[44]

One of the reasons for the overall positive reaction of Anglo-American historians to reunification has been the widespread recognition that the Federal Republic after 1945 achieved a significant turn away from its militaristic and undemocratic traditions. The old *Sonderweg* had finally come to an end. The endorsement of the 'success story' of the FRG forms the background to the endorsement of reunification. When Richard Evans argued in June 1989 that no-one should be worried about the possibility of reunification, he asserted that the materialist identity of the Germans was part and parcel of a wider Western European identity. The Federal Republic's political institutions and economy, he concluded, were stable and the political culture of the country had been soundly westernised after 1945.[45] Garton Ash emphasised 'the fantastic distance that Germany has travelled over the last half-century: the distance to civility, legality, modernity, democracy.'[46] Germany, Garton Ash has argued, far from once again becoming a menace to Europe, could play the role of the saviour of Eastern Europe, helping out economically and providing the best constitutional model for the new democracies in Eastern Europe.[47] For Stone 'the Federal Republic has changed character utterly since 1945, ... She has been a great success economically, and de-Nazification has been total.'[48] Whereas on the left the admiration for economic success and the postnational democracy of the FRG is connected with the hope that the reunified country will become a liberal, tolerant multicultural society,[49] those on the political right, like Dennis Bark and David Gress, combined their admiration of the FRG with a violent denunciation of its critics.[50]

Of course, the overall benign reaction does not mean that Anglo-American historians have not voiced certain worries about the future Germany and, more specifically, about historians in the future Germany. The worries practically all stem from concerns 'that in tone and content, the substance of the old FRG is crumbling away'.[51] There have been sceptical comments on the revival of nationalist overtones in historical writings. For Garton Ash '3 October is not so much the day of German unity. It is the day of German liberty.'[52] Sheehan has warned his German readers not to fall back in the ensuing process of nation-building on the old temptations of nationalism.[53] As Craig has argued: 'We are clearly confronted with *les incertitudes allemandes.* ... The lost eastern lands have, after all, not been forgotten. .... Is it possible that the present wave of national enthusiasm could ... give way to the kind of expansive German nationalism that caused so much devastation and tragedy in the past?'[54] Craig reacted angrily to Wolffsohn's calls for a new 'inner nationalism': 'If the Germans start talking a lot about nation and nationalism again, then they have to be reminded that these terms will always make a bad impression when uttered by a German ... Why are they constantly so bound up in themselves?'[55] Peter O'Brien has drawn a direct link between the signs of xenophobia and racism in the reunited country and the racist definition of citizenship in the Basic Law. For O'Brien the latest round of German xenophobia is only the most recent example of how difficult Germany finds it to elaborate an acceptable means of coming to terms with large non-German minorities in their midst.[56] In the light of the debates on immigrants and asylum seekers in Germany in the early 1990s Michael Burleigh argued: 'How this essentially provincial and none too tolerant society will cope with open frontiers and migration will be *the* German question of the 1990s.'[57]

If there have been worries, the new national identity debate in Germany has been perceived with overall calmness. Peter Pulzer, for example, has been optimistic that a continued sense of economic pride combined with successful Westernisation will prevail and allow Germany to become 'the first normal state in German history', which, in his assessment, is both stable and liberal. The national sentiments of the new right 'are not the stuff from which the Fourth Reich can arise'.[58] In particular the commitment of the Federal Republic to the West and, more specifically, to the EU has been seen by many British and U.S. historians as the ultimate sign that Germany has changed. Their endorsement of reunification was often combined with the express hope that the reunified country would become the motor of further European integration. Thus Craig pleaded for 're-invigorating the vision of Adenauer and Monnet' as counterweight against 'a new provincial patriotism and reawakened dreams of hegemony'.[59] Stern worried that after reunification Germany's commitment to the United States might be endangered by the talk of a 'return of Europe'.[60] Out of fear that a de-Westernisation of Germany might be on the cards, many historians have been arguing for a stronger international and even military role of the reunified Germany within the Western alliance. Otherwise, the argument goes, Germany might turn inward and become absorbed by its unification crisis.[61] For many, a return to geopolitical concepts of *Mitteleuropa* and *Mittellage* would be worse even than isolationism. According to Jill Stephenson, Prussia/Germany had for a long time been an Eastern European country rather than a

Western European one. Its hybrid nature meant that it often acted as a destabilising force in Europe. After 1945, according to Stephenson, it looked as though at least the FRG had become a thoroughly Westernised country. After 1990 she has found it more likely that Germany will return to its muddled identity between East and West.[62] Already some have stressed that German ambitions in central Europe might well lead to efforts to set up German satellite states.[63] Thus it will become a prime concern of the international community to contain not only Russia but also Germany.[64] And yet, even here, more optimistic assessments have pointed to the changed context of German foreign policy, in which the nationalism and expansionism connected with the concept of *Mitteleuropa* in the past, have largely gone.[65]

Those historians who have explicitly endorsed renationalisation form a small but distinct minority. From the vantage point of 1990, Bark and Gress have, in a deeply misleading interpretation, stressed 'the national theme' as 'the single most important topic in postwar German history'.[66] James has been arguing that renationalisation of German identity is necessary to overcome the unification crisis.[67] He has identified the 'self-declared critical historians' as the major stumbling block on the road to a more positive national identity. Due to the dominance of this 'intellectually and politically small-minded orthodoxy', concepts of the nation and the nation-state have been banned from historical discussion and illusions about a post-national German identity have been nurtured. The historical principle of change was ignored and instead replaced by a de-humanising emphasis on structures and processes. In James' view, 1989 revealed that 'their historical imagination had failed critical historiography, totally.'[68] Economic success alone, he had already argued before 1989, would not be sufficient to steer Germany through crises: 'The course of German history has already shown time and again how vulnerable political institutions are when they are guided not by long lasting loyalties but by short-term expediency and economic rationale.'[69] Identification with political institutions in the form of constitutional patriotism thus cannot be enough. Historians are called upon to produce 'national myths, which will be necessary to come to terms with the facts of change'.[70] Hansjoachim Koch, for one, has already provided us with such myths reclaiming a thousand years of German national history with the explicit aim of providing national identity.[71]

However, such calls for a renationalisation of German identity have not been widespread amongst British and U.S. historians. John Gillingham, for one, has reminded his fellow medievalists in Germany that their nationally-tinted glasses have for a long time clouded their views on medieval Germany. Assessing everything on the grounds of whether it hindered or furthered German unity, they missed important aspects of medieval Germany.[72] Sheehan's account of pre-1866 Germany reminded everyone of the contingencies and uncertainties of the nation-building process in the nineteenth century.[73] It has almost become a standard argument in the commentaries of British and U.S. historians that Bismarck's Germany was dead once and for all and should under no circumstances be revived: 'A re-erected Bismarckian empire would have the same effect as the return of Frankenstein.'[74] John Röhl has repeatedly reminded his readers that distinct links connected the history of Imperial Germany with Nazism.[75] Richard Evans and John Breuilly have both criticised Nipperdey's account of Imperial Germany because its underlying rationale was to save the latter from taking responsibility for what came after.[76] Geoff Eley noticed that Wolfgang Mommsen's history of Imperial Germany 'does tend to entrench the *kleindeutsch* or "Prussian" view of German unification'.[77] British and U.S. historians have stressed that the way ahead does not lie with re-interpretations of old terrain (this time with a new national gloss imposed over it), but with the emergence of new directions and new agendas for research.[78]

If there is little love for the new national overtones in the historiography of Imperial Germany, there is understandably even less enthusiasm for the revisionism apparent in the historical work on National Socialism. Although some Anglo-American historians, like Ronald Smelser and Christopher Duffy, have been in the forefront of fostering such revisionism, the response of the majority of historians seems to remain one of strong apprehensiveness. Smelser has worked alongside Zitelmann in a combined effort to demonstrate the modernity of the Nazi regime, concentrating in particular on the DAF and its leader Robert Ley, and attributing far too much importance to the obscure ideas of this relatively unimportant drunkard in the Third Reich.[79] According to Smelser 'Ley did leave a legacy behind, as did in a sense, the Nazi regime itself. The Weimar regime was light years away from being a welfare state. In its propaganda, the Nazi regime posed a vision of what government should do for the little people which ... took it a step beyond Weimar and built a bridge to the Federal Republic today. ... what the Nazi regime offered ... the German people formed much of the agenda of postwar planning. And Robert Ley's frustrated dreams were an important part of that agenda.'[80] Duffy probably did more than anyone in the English language to underpin the extremely one-sided notion, put forward, amongst others, by Hillgruber in the 1980s, that the German army in 1944/1945

was engaged upon a heroic struggle of defending the German territories from the Asian hordes of the Soviet army.[81]

In contrast, Fulbrook as well as Burleigh have shown a healthy
scepticism towards the thesis of National Socialism as a modernising
dictatorship.[82] David Crew, whose position is close to Peukert's, has
accepted the partial modernity of National Socialism but emphasised its destructive pathological side, in particular its close relationship to genocide.[83] Deborah Lippstadt in her impressive account of
the history of attempts to deny the Holocaust has reserved a few
pages for the *Historikerstreit*, where she has argued compellingly that
relativising the Holocaust might well be far more dangerous than
denying it.[84] In the most recent controversy surrounding Daniel
Goldhagen's book about 'ordinary Germans', British and U.S. historians have, on the whole, reacted much less hysterically, revealing
both the substantial conceptual shortcomings of the book and its
many merits. In one of the most informed and to the point reviews
of Goldhagen's book, Jeremy Noakes refutes Goldhagen's central
theses about the 'eliminationist mind-set' of the Germans and the
Holocaust as their long-term 'national project'. Calling the book
both 'deeply flawed' and 'reductionist', he also concedes that in his
case studies in particular, Goldhagen provides much new and
thought-provoking material.[85] Andrei Markovits was especially sur-
prised to discover anti-Semitic overtones in the German debate
about Goldhagen's book. In Germany, he concluded, Goldhagen's
book, which had, after all, won one of the most prestigious prices of
the American Political Science Association, was only reviewed positively by Jewish scholars. The rest had been busy trying to push
Goldhagen's theses to the sidelines of historical discourse ignoring
much of the originality of his cultural-institutional approach towards
the study of the Holocaust.[86]

David Welch, predicting that Germany's search for a 'bearable
past' would intensify after 1990, has been insisting on the centrality
of the National Socialist experience for any future national identity
of Germans.[87] Evans has criticised efforts to depict the conservative
resistance of the generals to Hitler as a model for post-war German
society. Their moral stance against Hitler on 20 July 1944 should not,
according to Evans, hide the fact that 'their political ideas had no
future' – one way or the other.[88] Kershaw showed himself aghast in
the face of the massive inroads revisionism has recently made into
his own field of study: 'Confining Hitler to history – drawing a line
under the Nazi past – which had still not been possible at the time of
the *Historikerstreit*, has become ... more imaginable as a consequence
of unification.'[89] According to Kershaw, the alleged 'normality' of the

nation-state has been increasingly reducing the importance of the Holocaust for the self-understanding of Germans. 'There is', in the words of Peter Pulzer, 'the risk that unification will be a great act of self-forgiveness. The division of Germany ... was at least a permanent reminder that something had gone terribly wrong in recent German history. With the reminder gone, will the memory vanish?'[90]

British and U.S. historians have also reacted cautiously towards the revival of the totalitarian paradigm in German historiography. Bullock, author of a parallel biography of Hitler and Stalin, has rejected any revival of totalitarianism as a valid explanatory concept for historians, as it tends to blur the distinctiveness of the two regimes and to over-emphasise the similarities.[91] Fulbrook has warned of a 'return to any simple equation of the Nazi and communist dictatorships'.[92] For Kershaw, comparison 'is of greatest value in illustrating the differences between the two systems' and 'highlighting the singularity of each system', but his conclusion was that the limitations of the totalitarian paradigm remain such that it should continue to be confined to the dustbin of Cold War rhetoric.[93] Michael Burleigh has stressed that there is no 'intellectually serious comparison to be made between the regimes of Hitler and Honecker or between the Stasi and the Gestapo.'[94] Such rejection goes hand-in-hand with a far more sober assessment of the historical phenomenon of the GDR. For sure, we can find historians who are all too willing to attribute all the difficulties in the reunited Germany to the dreadful 'legacy of the SED state', which is described in terms such as 'forty-four years of police state tyranny'. Hence, 'as the comparable Nazi legacy', the GDR legacy will 'trouble German democracy for many years to come'.[95] However, more characteristic have been analyses which have described the 'anatomy' of the GDR in an extremely differentiated way – explicitly avoiding a blanket demonisation. Fulbrook, for example, without euphemising the very real dictatorial aspects of the regime, has demonstrated that the GDR was not built on terror and repression alone. The functional elites of the GDR were organised and disciplined by the regime in such a way as not to allow any challenge to the regime. The homogeneity, consistency and conformity of the country's elites ensured the stability of the regime. Amongst the population at large there existed various forms of protest and resistance as well as a whole range of attitudes which lay between the two extremes of Stasi and citizens' rights movements. It is not just the political history and the history of state power which need to be written to understand the phenomenon GDR, but also social history, a history of everyday life and structural history.[96] Maier has pointed out that the new Federal Republic will prove itself

in the way it deals with the history of the GDR. Victorious Westerners putting it into the straitjacket of hindsight will contribute little to
the understanding of the GDR. He has argued that it will be crucial
to see whether the 'rich ambiguities of GDR history' are accepted in
the new Federal Republic. The GDR, Maier has insisted, was neither
a second German dictatorship nor a mere fifth column of the Sovi-
ets. Instead, he has suggested analysing the GDR in the best traditions of structural historiography as a 'corrupting "contagious state"'
(korrumpierender 'Ansteckungsstaat').[97]

Maier has also combined his call for a differentiated picture of the
GDR's history with a warning not to make GDR historians academic pariahs. Those who had no personal responsibility for the persecution of students and colleagues should be generously integrated
into the profession in the reunited country.[98] In a similar vein Iggers
has argued against a blanket denunciation of GDR historiography as
'legitimation science'. In the light of former GDR historians' overwhelming acceptance of a democratic, pluralist society, they, according to Iggers, should have been integrated as far as possible into the
academic institutions of the reunited Germany.[99] In striking contrast
to their West German colleagues, Anglo-American historians always
had less difficulty in assessing not only the shortcomings but also the
strengths and challenges of GDR historiography. Kershaw, for one,
has refused to share in the new consensus amongst German historians that Marxist analyses should be confined to the dustbin of history. Singling out Bonapartist and Gramscian approaches to history,
he has insisted that these approaches 'have been intellectually fertile
and heuristically stimulating.'[100] Similarly Iggers has insisted that an
undogmatic Marxism shall and will have an important role to play in
any future historiography.[101] Thus it is perhaps little surprising that
many British and U.S. historians have shown rather less enthusiasm
than their West German colleagues about the 'survival crisis' facing
GDR historiography. Renate Bridenthal criticised the 'juggernaut of
West Germany' which 'had flattened the East German intellectual
landscape'.[102] Jarausch argued that the history of GDR historiography has yet to be written and that the last word has not been said by
the West German evaluating commissions.[103]

There have also been few signs, with the exception of James'
utterances, that the legacy of critical historiography has come under
attack from British and U.S. historians. Garton Ash, for example,
showed himself all the more encouraged to endorse reunification by
the thorough self-criticism of 'an exemplary critical historiography'
in West Germany.[104] Yet he would do well to recognise that 'the
renaissance of the nation-state has considerably weakened critical

perspectives on the German past.'[105] The link between historiography and renationalisation has also been perceived by Dick Geary: 'reunification may also have brought with it a resurgence of a specifically nationalist historiography, which until recently at least, was scarcely to be found in the circles of professional historians'.[106] Bartov has deplored the 'strong pressure' on German historians to create a harmonised picture of the national past to which Germans could look back with pride.[107] For Maier, all efforts to create national identity via historiography are marred by the results of previous attempts: 'The Germans always demand an identity from their historians ... This is not the most fruitful historical approach ...'[108] For Breuilly there has been so little 'normality' in a German nation-state that any construction of such 'normality' would be highly problematic. There simply cannot be any essential Germanness, he argued, because ideas of German nationality historically were 'changeable and contingent'.[109] Similarly Mary Fulbrook has argued: 'The historian's role is *not*, as many German historians have recently seen it, to define an identity in which Germans can take pride ... Rather, it is the role of the historian to explain why some views of identity have historically been more successful than others ... .'[110]

Michael Geyer reminded us at the very moment when the national reconstruction of Germany had been on the cards that 'the true theme of central European history is not the rise of the German nation-state, but rather the very fragility and permeability of all national constructions ... The main challenge for all national histories of central Europe on their way to a European history consists in breaking through their fictions of autonomy...'[111] Borrowing heavily from postmodernist discourse on historiography, Geyer and Jarausch have emphasised the multiplicity and diversity of national stories in order to prevent any narrow renationalisation of German historiography after 1990. Thus, in their view, the methodological challenge of poststructuralism which preceded 1989 may well serve as a welcome antidote to a new national straitjacket which otherwise awaits German historians.[112] It is somewhat difficult to understand how, against the background of those insights, Jarausch can come to the suggestion that a 'normalisation' of German national consciousness in the direction of the development of a 'democratic patriotism' may suggest a way forward which avoids the 'opposite dangers of ethnic nationalism and postnationalism'.[113] Instead, Geyer's ingenious plea for a 'historiography of *Rück-Sicht* [which in German means both 'looking back' and 'being considerate'] with an emancipatory purpose' is a far more promising methodological stance for overcoming the predominant national perspective with its homogenising tendencies.[114] To explore a 'genealogy of ruptures' would act as an effective antidote to the renationalisation of German historiography.

The British and U.S. reactions to reunification on the whole do not serve to corroborate the negative impression which the widely commented-on Chequers meeting in 1990 left in Germany. Although the division of the country was widely accepted before 1989, the overall reaction in 1989/1990 was remarkably positive. It reflected a very wide consensus – even amongst those whose politics vary considerably – that the Federal Republic had successfully buried the demons of the German past. The Federal Republic has not only been successful economically; it has also been successful in political terms. It managed to create stable institutions, mentally adopted Western political culture and institutionally tied itself firmly to the West. The frequent calls for the reunified country to play a greater international role have to be understood within this context of trust and admiration. The bottom line of many statements is that this time the power of the new Germany will be used for the good of Europe, and Eastern Europe in particular. Thus, William Paterson perceived a trend amongst some German academics to return to a 'national interest discourse' but at the same time he remains optimistic that Germany will continue to be multilateralist.[115] However, with the exception of a small minority, British and U.S. historians of Germany have remained unspectacularly but firmly opposed to the historiography of national identity which has raised its head again in post-reunification Germany.

NOTES

1. Historians of German origin who work in Britain or the United States have been counted amongst British and American historians, although such classification inadequately reflects their middling position between the two academic communities.
2. See Manfred Messerschmidt, *Deutschland in englischer Sicht. Die Wandlungen des Deutschlandbildes in der englischen Geschichtsschreibung*, Düsseldorf, 1955; Fritz Stern, 'German History in America, 1884-1984', *CEH*, vol. 19, 1986, pp. 131-63.
3. Parker, *Tradition*, pp. 2, 33, 63, 66.
4. Lord Acton, 'German Schools of History', *EHR*, vol. 1, 1886, pp. 7-42.
5. Cited in Stern, 'German History', p. 137.
6. Thomas Kleinknecht, 'Die Gründung des Deutschen Reiches 1870/71 aus der Sicht des britischen Gelehrtenliberalismus', in: Bernd Jürgen Wendt (ed.), *Das britische Deutschlandbild im Wandel des 19. und 20. Jahrhunderts*, Bochum, 1984, pp. 81-102.
7. Stuart Wallace, *War and the Image of Germany: British Academics 1914-1918*, Edinburgh, 1989.
8. Catherine Ann Cline, 'British Historians and the Treaty of Versailles', *Albion*, vol. 20, 1988, pp. 43-58.
9. Karen J. Greenberg, 'The Search for Silver Lining: The American Academic Establishment and the "Aryanization of German Scholarship"', *Annual Bulletin of the Simon Wiesenthal Centre*, New York, no. 2, 1985, pp. 115-37.
10. Donald Cameron Watt, 'Perceptions of German History among the British Policy-Making Elite, 1930-1965, and the Role of British and German Emigré Historiography in its Formation', in: Henning Köhler (ed.), *Deutschland und der Westen*, Berlin, 1984, pp. 140-58 is unduly critical of those emigré historians' alleged distortions of German history. Their critical perspective which paved the way for the fruitful *Sonderweg* debate in the 1960s contributed to the thorough Westernisation of German historical consciousness after 1945. The success of liberal democracy in West-Germany rests to a far greater degree on this turn to the West than on 'German conservatism in education and elsewhere' (p. 157), as suggested by Cameron Watt. For British perceptions of Germany immediately after 1945 compare also Vera and Ansgar Nünning, 'Autoritätshörig, unpolitisch und opportunistisch. Englische Vorstellungen vom deutschen Nationalcharakter am Ende des Zweiten Weltkriegs', *GWU*, vol. 45, 1994, pp. 224-39.
11. Donald Cameron Watt, 'British Historians, the War Guilt Issue, and Post-War Germanophobia: a Documentary Note', *Historical Journal*, vol. 36, 1993, pp. 179-85.
12. A.J.P. Taylor, *The Course of German History*, London, 1988 (first published in 1945), pp. vii, 1.
13. Volker Berghahn, 'Deutschlandbilder 1945-1965. Angloamerikanische Historiker und moderne deutsche Geschichte', in: Schulin (ed.), *Deutsche Geschichtswissenschaft*, pp. 239-72.
14. Iggers, *Geschichtswissenschaft*, p. 7.
15. Richard J. Evans, 'The New Nationalism and the old History: Perspectives on the West German Historikerstreit', *Journal of Modern History*, vol. 59, 1987, pp. 761-97.
16. Roderick Stackelberg, '1986 vs. 1968: The Turn to the Right in German Historiography', *Radical History Review*, vol. 40, 1988, pp. 50-63.
17. David Blackbourn and Geoff Eley, *The Peculiarities of German History. Bourgeois Society and Politics in Nineteenth-Century Germany*, Oxford, 1984, p. 32.
18. Review by James Sheehan, *Journal of Modern History*, vol. 54, 1982, p. 178; Blackbourn and Eley, *Peculiarities*, p. 12; Kershaw, *The Nazi Dictatorship*, p. 199.
19. William Paterson, 'The *Ostpolitik* and Régime Stability in West Germany', in: R. Tilford (ed.), *The Ostpolitik and Political Change in Germany*, London, 1975, p. 41.

20. Gordon A. Craig, *Über die Deutschen*, Munich, 1982, p. 319 f.
21. Michael Balfour, *West Germany. A Contemporary History*, London, 1982.
22. Walter Laqueur, *Germany Today: A Personal Report*, London, 1985.
23. Fritz Stern, 'Opfer, die weder vergessen noch mißbraucht werden dürfen', *FR*, 24 June 1987.
24. Michael Hughes, *Nationalism and Society: Germany 1800-1945*, London, 1988, pp. 7, 221.
25. James J. Sheehan, 'The Problem of the Nation in German History', in: idem and Büsch (eds), *Die Rolle der Nation*, p. 15.
26. Some of the more alarmist commentaries are summarised in David Rieff, 'United States', *TLS*, 2 Nov. 1990, pp. 1,178, 1,189; Richard Davy, 'Großbritannien und die deutsche Frage', *Europa-Archiv*, vol. 4, 1990, pp. 139-44; Günther Heydemann, 'Partner oder Konkurrent? Das britische Deutschlandbild während des Wiedervereinigungsprozesses 1989-1991', in: Franz Bosbach (ed.), *Feindbilder: die Darstellung des Gegners in der politischen Publizistik des Mittelalters und der Neuzeit*, Cologne, 1992, pp. 201-34. Singling out the British government and in particular Margaret Thatcher for criticism and maintaining that the British public and the majority of academics and experts were pro-reunification is Yvonne Klein, 'Obstructive or Promoting? British Views on German Unification 1989/90', *German Politics*, vol. 5, 1996, pp. 404-31.
27. John Gray, 'Glasnostications', *TLS*, 21 July 1989, p. 798.
28. Timothy Garton Ash, 'The German Revolution', *New York Review of Books*, 21 Dec. 1989, p. 19.
29. Timothy Garton Ash, 'East Germany: The Solution', *The New York Review of Books*, 26 April 1990, p. 20.
30. Timothy Garton Ash, 'Germany at the Frontier', *The New York Review of Books*, 17 Jan. 1991, p. 21.
31. Julian Bullard, 'Die britische Haltung zur deutschen Wiedervereinigung', in: Becker (ed.), *Wiedervereinigung*, pp. 27-42.
32. Harold James, 'Germans and their Nation', *German History*, vol. 9, 1991, p. 148.
33. Gordon A. Craig, 'Kein Grund zur Panik', *SZ*, 27/28 March 1993 (Beilage).
34. Richard Evans, 'Towards unification', *TLS*, 4 May 1990, p. 463.
35. Fritz Stern, 'Deutschland um 1900 – und eine zweite Chance', in: Wolfgang Hardtwig and Harm-Hinrich Brandt (eds), *Deutschlands Weg in die Moderne. Politik, Gesellschaft und Kultur im 19. Jahrhundert*, Munich, 1993, pp. 32-44.
36. Martin Gilbert, 'Finding a New Weak Link', *New York Times*, 27 Sept. 1990.
37. Jarausch, *Die unverhoffte Einheit.*
38. George Kennan, 'Wiedervereinigung – noch nicht', *Die Tageszeitung*, 14 Nov. 1989 (transl. from the *Guardian*, 13 Nov. 1989); Gordon A. Craig, 'Zu groß für Europa', *Der Spiegel*, 13 Nov. 1989.
39. Alan Bullock, 'Bei dem Wort "zwangsläufig" höre ich auf zu lesen', *Die Welt*, 2 Sept. 1989; Donald Cameron Watt, Letter, *Daily Telegraph*, 6 Sept. 1989.
40. The document written by Charles Powell, Thatcher's foreign policy secretary, who was present at the meeting, is reprinted in Konrad H. Jarausch and Volker Gransow (eds), *Uniting Germany. Documents and Debates 1944-1993*, Oxford, 1994, pp. 128-31.
41. Thus the criticism of the LSE's Gordon Smith of the Chequers meeting in a letter to *The Times*, 19 July 1990.
42. Peter Pulzer, 'After the Wall', *London Review of Books*, 23 May 1991, p. 5.
43. Jarausch and Gransow (eds), *Uniting Germany*, p. 131.
44. Norman Stone, 'No Threat from a new Germany', *Sunday Times*, 18 Feb. 1990.
45. Richard J. Evans, 'Shifting the Blame', *TLS*, 23 June 1989, p. 685.
46. Timothy Garton Ash, 'Kohl's Germany: The Beginning of the End?', *The New York Review of Books*, 1 Dec. 1994, p. 20.

47. Timothy Garton Ash, 'Eastern Europe: Après Le Déluge', *The New York Review of Books*, 16 Aug. 1990, p. 53; idem, 'Germany Unbound', *The New York Review of Books*, 22 Nov. 1990, pp. 11-15.
48. Norman Stone, 'No threat from a new Germany', *Sunday Times*, 18 Feb. 1990. The rather problematic notion of *Vergangenheitsbewältigung* as a success story is also underlined comparatively by Ian Buruma, *The Wages of Guilt. Memories of War in Germany and Japan*, London, 1994.
49. Most clearly in Norman Naimark, 'Über das Wunder nicht nur in der Wirtschaft', *FR*, 13 May 1995. For an explicit endorsement of Bracher's concept of the FRG as a postnational democracy see Peter Pulzer, 'The End of the Post-War Era', *TLS*, 2 Feb. 1990, p. 109.
50. Dennis L. Bark and David R. Gress, *A History of West Germany*, 2nd edn, Oxford, 1993.
51. Andrei Markovits, 'Ein Glückwunsch und eine Warnung', *Die Tageszeitung*, 2 Oct. 1993.
52. Timothy Garton Ash, in: *Reden über Deutschland*, Munich, 1990, p. 107. See also idem, 'Das Jahr, in dem die Freiheit kam', *Die Zeit*, 7 Dec. 1990, p. 12, and Richard Evans, 'One nation, two states', *London Review of Books*, 21 Dec. 1989, p. 5-6.
53. James J. Sheehan, 'Die immer gleiche Geschichte von Verstimmung und Enttäuschung', *FR*, 13 March 1990. See also idem, 'Back to Potsdam', *TLS*, 2 Dec. 1994, p. 26 for a sceptical view on efforts to return to the Prussian past.
54. Gordon A. Craig, 'A New, New Reich?', *The New York Review of Books*, 18 Jan. 1990, p. 33. See also the extremely worried comments about a possible revival of German expansionism in idem, 'Zu groß für Europa?', *Der Spiegel*, 13 Nov. 1989, pp. 183-7.
55. Gordon A. Craig, 'Wozu diese ewige Nabelschau?', *SZ*, 25 March 1993.
56. Peter O'Brien, 'Identity Crisis in the New Germany', *Debatte*, vol. 2, 1994, pp. 64-81; also idem, 'German-Polish Migration: The Elusive Search for a German Nation-State', *International Migration Review*, vol. 26, 1992, pp. 373-87.
57. Michael Burleigh, 'Inspecting the Fossils', *TLS*, 24 May 1991, p. 12.
58. Peter Pulzer, 'Unified Germany: A Normal State?', *German Politics*, vol. 3, 1994, pp. 1-17; idem, 'Nation-State and National Sovereignty', *Bulletin of the GHIL*, vol. 17, no. 3, 1995, pp. 5-14. Note, however, how the rather dubious notion of 'normality' has affected his own argument.
59. Gordon A. Craig, 'Kein Grund zur Panik', *SZ*, 27/28 March 1993 (Beilage).
60. Fritz Stern, 'The Common House of Europe', *The New York Review of Books*, 7 Dec. 1989, pp. 6-10.
61. Michael Howard, 'Impressions from a Journey in Central Europe', *London Review of Books*, 25 Oct. 1990, p. 3-4. For fears of an inward-looking Germany see also Timothy Garton Ash, 'Germany Unbound', *The New York Review of Books*, 22 Nov. 1990, p. 15; idem, 'Germany at the Frontier', *The New York Review of Books*, 17 Jan. 1991, pp. 21-2; David Walker, 'Friends on both sides', *THES*, 24 July 1993, p. 16; Gordon A. Craig, 'Foreword', in: Hacke, *Weltmacht*, pp. I-VII.
62. Jill Stephenson, 'Anniversaries, Memory and the Neighbours: The "German Question" in Recent History', *German Politics*, vol. 5, 1996, pp. 43-57.
63. Norman Stone, 'What Mrs. Thatcher really thinks', *The Times*, 16 July 1990.
64. Keith Kyle, 'Leap to Unity', *London Review of Books*, 22 March 1990, p. 7-8.
65. Robin Okey, 'Central Europe/Eastern Europe: Behind the Definitions', *PP*, no. 137, 1992, pp. 102-33.
66. Bark and Gress, *West Germany*, vol. 1: *From Shadow*, p. xlvi-xlvii.
67. Harold James, 'Harte Droge ohne Ersatz?', *FAZ*, 18 March 1992; idem, 'Should we fear a German Europe?', *The Times*, 13 July 1995.

68. Harold James, 'Die Nemesis der Einfallslosigkeit', *FAZ*, 17 Sept. 1990. In more detail idem, *Vom Historikerstreit zum Historikerschweigen*, Berlin, 1993. Compare my review in *Bulletin of the GHIL*, vol. 16, no. 3, 1994, pp. 49-53.

69. Harold James, *A German Identity 1770-1990*, rev. edn, London, 1990, p. 234.

70. James, 'Die Nemesis'.

71. Hansjoachim Koch, *Deutsche Nationalgeschichte. Warum?*, Berg, 1990, pp. 9-10, 148.

72. John Gillingham, 'Elective Kingship and the Unity of Medieval Germany', *German History*, vol. 9, 1991, pp. 124-35.

73. James J. Sheehan, *German History 1770-1866*, Oxford, 1990.

74. David Calleo, 'Einheit ja, Frankenstein-Monster nein', *Die Zeit*, 5 Jan. 1990, p. 3. See also James J. Sheehan, 'The Unbending Will', *TLS*, 16 Nov. 1990, p. 1224; Gordon A. Craig, 'The Way to the Wall', *The New York Review of Books*, 28 June 1990, pp. 25-30.

75. John Röhl, 'Monarchical Mentalities and Structures in Imperial Germany', paper given to the AGM of the German History Society, London, 25 Nov. 1994; idem, 'Wilhelm II: "Das Beste wäre Gas!"', *Die Zeit*, 25 Nov. 1994, pp. 13-15 for the continuity of violent anti-Semitism amongst Germany's political elites. In the year of German reunification Röhl also wrote a scathing indictment of the German historians' role in suppressing and manipulating evidence in connection with the question of war guilt during the First World War. What in one sense was a re-affirmation of Fischer could also be read on another level as a warning to German historians not to be tempted into the dodgy area of national apologetics once again. See: John Röhl, 'Imperial Germany', *Modern History Review*, vol. 2, no. 2 and 3, 1990, pp. 8-11 and 9-12.

76. Richard J. Evans, 'Too quick to judge', *TLS*, 5 Oct. 1990; John Breuilly, 'Telling it as it was? Thomas Nipperdey's History of Nineteenth Century Germany', *History*, vol. 80, 1995, pp. 59-69.

77. Geoff Eley, 'Das nationalliberale Zeitalter. Wolfgang J. Mommsens politische Geschichte Deutschlands 1850-1890', *NPL*, vol. 40, 1995, p. 7 f.

78. John Williams, Lora Wildenthal, Jennifer Jenkins and Teresa Sanislo, 'The Kaiserreich in the 1990s: New Research, New Directions, New Agendas', *German History*, vol. 9, 1991, pp. 200-7.

79. Ronald Smelser, *Robert Ley. Hitler's Labor Front Leader*, Oxford, 1988. He has also co-edited with Zitelmann the two volumes of autobiographical portraits of the Nazi elite entitled *Die braune Elite. 22 biographische Skizzen*, 2nd edn, Darmstadt, 1990; *Die braune Elite II*, Darmstadt, 1993.

80. Smelser, *Robert Ley*, p. 5.

81. Christopher Duffy, *Red Storm on the Reich. The Soviet March on Germany 1945*, London, 1991.

82. Mary Fulbrook, *The Fontana History of Germany 1918-1990*, London, 1992; Michael Burleigh and Wolfgang Wippermann, *The Racial State. Germany 1933-1945*, Cambridge, 1992; Michael Burleigh, 'A Political Economy of the Final Solution? Reflections on Modernity, Historians and the Holocaust', *Patterns of Prejudice*, vol. 30, 1996, pp. 29-41.

83. David Crew (ed.), *Nazism and German Society 1933-1945*, London, 1994, pp. 23-5.

84. Deborah Lippstadt, *Denying the Holocaust. The Growing Assault on Truth and Memory*, London, 1993, p. 215 f.

85. Jeremy D. Noakes, 'No Ordinary People', *TLS*, 7 June 1996; see also Michael Burleigh, 'Disregard for eloquence of facts', *Jewish Chronicle*, 12 April 1996.

86. Andrei S. Markovits, 'Störfall im Endlager der Geschichte. Daniel Goldhagen und seine deutschen Kritiker', *Blätter*, vol. 41, 1996, pp. 667-74.

87. David Welch, *The Third Reich. Politics and Propaganda*, London, 1993, p. 133. Similarly Alan Bullock, 'Bei dem Wort "zwangsläufig" höre ich auf zu lesen', *Die*

Welt, 2 Sept. 1989: 'The Germans should always remember the darkest parts of their history rather than playing them down ...'

88. Richard J. Evans, 'The Bomb that Failed', *TLS*, 25 Sept. 1992, p. 33.

89. For Kershaw's perceptive analysis of recent trends see in particular chapter ten of his *The Nazi Dictatorship*, pp. 197-217, and idem, *Germany's Present, Germany's Past. The 1992 Bithell Memorial Lecture*, London, 1992. The quote is from the latter work, p. 12.

90. Peter Pulzer, 'East Berlin Diary', *London Review of Books*, 19 April 1990, p. 21.

91. Alan Bullock, 'Bei dem Wort "zwangsläufig" höre ich auf zu lesen', *Die Welt*, 2 Sept. 1989.

92. Mary Fulbrook's contribution to the panel discussion, 'German history and German nationalism', *Debatte*, vol. 1, 1993, p. 27.

93. Ian Kershaw, 'Totalitarianism Revisited: Nazism and Stalinism in Comparative Perspective', *TAJB*, vol. 23, 1994, pp. 23-40; quotes on p.40.

94. Michael Burleigh (ed.), *Confronting the Nazi Past: New Debates on Modern German History*, London, 1996, p. 1.

95. Bark and Gress, *West Germany*, vol. 2: *Democracy*, pp. 747, 765, 768. See also the denunciation of all but the coldest of Cold War warriors in Melvin J. Lasky, *Wortmeldung zu einer Revolution. Der Zusammenbruch der kommunistischen Herrschaft in Ostdeutschland*, Frankfurt-on-Main, 1991.

96. Mary Fulbrook, *Anatomy of a Dictatorship: Inside the GDR, 1949-1989*, Oxford, 1995.

97. Charles Maier, 'Geschichtswissenschaft und "Ansteckungsstaat"', *GG*, vol. 20, 1994, pp. 616-24. See also idem, 'Gibt es einen Sieger der Geschichte? Geschichtswissenschaft und DDR Vergangenheit', in: Jarausch (ed.), *Zwischen Parteilichkeit*, pp. 213, 215.

98. Maier, 'Geschichtswissenschaft', pp. 616, 618, 624.

99. Georg G. Iggers, 'Geschichtswissenschaft und autoritärer Staat', *Initial. Berliner Debatte*, vol. 2, no. 2, 1991, pp. 125-31.

100. Kershaw, *The Nazi Dictatorship*, p. 198.

101. Georg G. Iggers, 'Die Bedeutung des Marxismus für die Geschichtswissenschaft heute', *ZfG*, vol. 43, 1995, pp. 485-94.

102. Renate Bridenthal, 'The Meaning of Unification for German History and Historiography: an Introduction', *Radical History Review*, vol. 54, 1992, pp. 81-6.

103. Jarausch and Middell, 'Die DDR als Geschichte', in: idem (eds), *Nach dem Erdbeben*, p. 15. See also Jarausch, 'Vom Zusammenbruch', in: idem (ed.), *Zwischen Parteilichkeit*, p. 14.

104. Timothy Garton Ash, 'The Chequers Affair', *The New York Review of Books*, 27 Sept. 1990.

105. Jarausch and Middell, 'Die DDR als Geschichte', in: idem (eds.), *Nach dem Erdbeben*, p. 23.

106. Dick Geary's contribution to the panel discussion 'German history and German nationalism', *Debatte*, vol. 1, 1993, pp. 14, 25.

107. Omer Bartov, 'Wem gehört die Geschichte', in: Heer and Naumann (eds), *Vernichtungskrieg*, p. 615.

108. Charles Maier's contribution to the panel discussion 'Sackgasse aus dem Sonderweg', in: Kocka and Sabrow (eds), *Die DDR als Geschichte*, p. 223.

109. John Breuilly, 'The national idea in modern German history', in: idem (ed.), *The State of Germany. The National Idea in the Making, Unmaking and Remaking of a Modern Nation State*, London, 1992, p. 3. See idem, *Nationalism and the State*, p. 356: 'the signs are that the national idea will intensify'.

110. Mary Fulbrook, *The Presence of the Past: National Identity and German History. An Inaugural Lecture Delivered at University College London 7 May 1996*, London, 1996, p. 28.

111. Michael Geyer, 'Historical Fictions of Autonomy and the Europeanisation of National History', *CEH*, vol. 22, 1989, p. 341. See also on the complex interre-

lationship between national, European and world history J.G.A. Pocock, 'Deconstructing Europe', *London Review of Books*, 19 Dec. 1991, pp. 6-10.

112. Michael Geyer and Konrad H. Jarausch, 'The Future of the German Past. Transatlantic Reflections for the 1990s', *CEH*, vol. 22, 1989, pp. 229-59.

113. Konrad Jarausch, 'Normalisierung oder Re-Nationalisierung? Zur Umdeutung der deutschen Vergangenheit', *GG*, vol. 21, 1995, pp. 571-84. It should be noted that in its attempt to return to a democratic nationalism of the first half of the nineteenth century, Jarausch's position is close to Kocka's and those left-liberal historians who have attempted to use 1989 in order to hark back to a democratic nationalism.

114. Michael Geyer, 'Geschichte als Wissenschaft für eine Zeit der Unübersichtlichkeit', in: Jarausch and Middell (eds), *Nach dem Erdbeben*, pp. 38-65.

115. William E. Paterson, 'Beyond Semi-Sovereignty: The New Germany in the New Europe', *German Politics*, vol. 5, 1996, pp. 167-84.

Chapter 11

———

CONCLUSION

History does not have to repeat itself, in fact, it rarely does. The national turn in historiography which I have depicted in chapters five to nine, leaves vast swathes of German historians unaffected, and the plurality of opinions on the nation-state seems, for the time being at least, guaranteed. The current situation is a far cry from the predicament of nineteenth-century historiography. The rise of historiographic nationalism in Germany happened in a century that has been rightly described as a classical one for nation-building processes all over Europe. Closely connected to the rise of historism and the emergence of a tight-knit community of scholars *(Zunft)*, the commitment to nation-building and the defence of the nation survived a long history of political ruptures from 1848 to 1945. The idea of the Reich and of the Prussian mission to rebuild it, the notion that power, culture and ethnicity underpinned an essential Germanness, and a wide-spread statism bound up with a strong anti-revolutionary consensus, have been the pillars on which historical nation-building came to rest. Later on, other elements like the Bismarck cult, the justification of German imperialism, the defence of the non-democratic German *Sonderweg,* the rejection of parliamentary democracy and the struggle against Versailles were added to the nationalist framework to which most German historians remained tied. Amongst other things, it prevented a more forthright opposition to Nazism between 1933 and 1945. Even the 'German catastrophe' did not mark any immediate break with the national paradigm, the *Geist* of which survived even amidst the rubble of what once had been Germany's cities.

———

Notes for this chapter begin on page 258.

At best 1945 can be described as a 'delayed break' – one which only came into effect, so to speak, in the 1960s. The ground for a more critical assessment of German national history had been prepared after 1945 by a number of authors such as Dehio, Bracher and Martin. Yet it was the inversion of the *Sonderweg* paradigm by a new critical historiography in the aftermath of the Fischer controversy, which marked a real turning point. The more sceptical analysis of the German nation-state after 1870, which was linked closely to the failure of democracy in Weimar Germany, led to the championing of postnationalism and universal Western values by a significant number of German historians in the 1970s and 1980s. At the same time, the turning away from the glorification of the nation allowed for a growing internationalisation of German historical studies and led to the regionalisation, Europeanisation and comparativisation of important sections of German historiography. The wide-spread reception of the French Annales school and the development of an understanding of history as 'historical social science' brought an important methodological renewal. Yet critical historians never achieved what they themselves had at times declared to be their ultimate goal, namely to replace the apologetic national paradigm with a critical one aimed at the emancipation of the human being from, to use a fashionable phrase from the 1960s, 'false consciousness'. In fact the survival of the national paradigm can be traced through the 1960s and 1970s, and from the early 1980s, with the neo-conservative *Wende* of 1982, a renaissance of the national idea came under way.

The interrelated processes of regionalisation, Europeanisation and comparativisation of German historiography did not come to an end in 1989/1990, and the agenda of critical historiography is far from dead. Wehler, in particular, has frequently confirmed his scepticism about any renationalisation of German identity. On an optimistic note Richter has predicted that 'it is possible that the dimension of the nation-state will not be so strongly accentuated but rather that there will be greater research interest in the continuities and changes of regions, of industrial areas, of the historical structures of countries, of milieus and mentalities.'[1] Yet the repercussions of 1989/1990 have clearly been felt amongst historians. A new right emerged which felt Bismarck's 'coat of God' passing by and attempted to grab it. Weißmann, for example, has argued: 'The paradigm change in historiography, which has been in the air ever since the 1980s, has been accelerated by the process of reunification.'[2] Representatives of the new right have declared their intention to facilitate a new cultural revolution which would put the nation-state at its centre. Only here, on the fringes of historical writing in Germany, have we encountered rumourings of a revival of ethnic definitions of nationhood. Only here have we met with a desire to reverse the Westernisation of the Federal Republic. Only here have we encountered arguments against further European integration and for the return to some kind of nineteenth century concept of the autonomous nation-state. Only here is German history from Bismarck to Hitler reinterpreted in such a way as to allow a return to the national tradition whilst, at the same time marginalising both the criminal energies and specifically German roots of National Socialism.

Some of the most vociferous representatives of this 'new right', such as Zitelmann or Weißmann, are not academic historians, i.e., they have no position within the German university system. Others, such as Nolte or Hoffmann, are retired. Without support from more mainstream liberal-conservative historiography, represented by such distinguished academic historians as Gall, Hildebrand or Schwarz, the chances of the new right being able to bring about the renationalisation of German historical consciousness are minute. So far, liberal-conservatives have, by and large, refused to jump onto the bandwagon of the new right. The largely negative reviews of Weißmann's empathic interpretation of National Socialist Germany in late 1995 and 1996, the distancing of conservative publishing houses such as Springer from the new right in 1996 (Springer reasserted its control over Ullstein and ended Fleißner's attempt to make it a forum for new-right publications.), and the outcome of the Goldhagen debate are the most recent indications that they are increasingly becoming a small band of right-wing mavericks without too much influence in German historiography, let alone the public at large. Consequently, representatives of the new right have portrayed themselves as victims of an alleged cultural and political hegemony of left-liberal historians in the FRG. For Zitelmann, writing in 1995, the years 1989 to 1991 had seen a window of opportunity for the project of the 'self-confident nation'. Thereafter, he observed rather gloomily, the hegemony of the centre-left reasserted itself.[3]

The refusal of the liberal-conservative mainstream to side with the new right can be interpreted as a sign that Conservatism in West Germany has been irrevocably Westernised since 1945. Even if we have encountered much scepticism about the actual process of European integration, there has been a clear emphasis here that Germany's foreign policy should be determined alongside and in tandem with its Western European and NATO partners. German national consciousness and identity cannot unproblematically return to Bismarckian traditions. Furthermore, the National Socialist past is very widely perceived as an important and lasting legacy for any German historical consciousness. At times though, the borders between the new right and liberal conservatism have become blurred. The latter have clearly been intent on contributing to a renationalisation of historical consciousness, albeit a less radical one than the new-right vision of the 'self-confident nation'. Many have pointed to the alleged excesses of *Vergangenheitsbewältigung* as being responsible for the construction of 'artificial' concepts such as 'postnationalism' and 'constitutional patriotism'. Like parts of the new right, liberal-conservatives have come to perceive the collapse of Communism in the GDR as a genuine opportunity to correct what they perceive as the substantial imbalances in the assessment of the 'two German dictatorships'. A second coming to terms with the (Stasi) past will, they hope, put the first one into perspective, i.e., show up its undervalued achievements and its unrealistic excesses from the 1960s onwards. The destruction of GDR historiography has been a sad chapter in the reunification process, and one, in which not only conservative national historians participated. Left-liberal historians could be heard condemning GDR historiography in almost as blanket a fashion as their conservative Western colleagues.

Once reunification seemed inevitable and became accepted amongst left-liberal historians in the West, there were notable efforts to recapture the concept of the nation from the right and 'fill' the national historical consciousness of Germans with democratic content. Having argued (correctly, in my view) that national history never ceased to be at the centre of German historians' interests, there has even been a hint of relief in Kocka's résumé: 'The word "Germany" is crossing one's lips more easily these days, the national symbols have lost part of their broken ambivalence, modern German history has acquired a new vanishing point from which to write it'.[4] In future, he has concluded, the reunified historiography will have to be a good deal more national than the old West German one. Some left-liberal historians, including Kocka, Winkler, Wolfgang Mommsen, Diner and others have rediscovered the discourse of national identity. Taken by surprise at first but then impressed by the strength of national collective feeling that manifested itself in 1989, at times they have subsequently slipped into the rhetoric of 'normality'. The year 1989, they have argued, provided the Germans with an ideal opportunity to redefine the concept of the nation in a democratic sense, since the revolution in the GDR allegedly harked back to the 1848 legacy by combining demands for liberal democratic values with national unity.

To simply state that, following reunification in 1990, there has also been a renaissance of the national paradigm amongst left-liberal historians may well obscure more than it illuminates, for there continue to be fundamental qualitative differences between conservative and new right discourses of the nation and left-liberal historians. The latter have argued for a thoroughly Westernised national identity which would exist harmoniously alongside both regional and European sentiments and bring the FRG, if anything, more into line with Britain or France, where, after all, the nation-state has shown few signs of relinquishing its power over people's minds. Left-liberal historians, in their interpretations of the first German nation-state and in particular of National Socialism have refuted attempts to introduce a more benign national gloss to the perspectives on German history between 1866 and 1945. They have vigorously defended the new national paradigm of the old Federal Republic, in particular its democratic political culture and its Western orientation. Finally, they have, despite some notable modification, upheld the tradition of historical social science in the reunified Germany against all efforts to return to a more traditional political national history writing.

In the light of the important differences between left-liberal historians and their conservative, let alone new-right, colleagues, it seems difficult to speak of any consensus – especially if we consider that we discovered important differences within all three of the historiographical 'camps'. Despite the rhetoric of 'normality' on the right and left of the historiographical spectrum, no new national-liberal consensus seems to be in the making. This is a rather reassuring conclusion, for the nation has been, on balance, an unholy paradigm for historians, precisely because it tends to encourage a 'them and us', or a 'friend and foe' attitude. To a certain extent the commitment to one's own nation necessarily encompasses the potential of rejecting others. Their difference all too quickly becomes sanctionable deviance. No concept of national identity can exist without such dissociations and exclusions. Therefore the whole concept of regaining 'good patriotism' whilst condemning 'bad nationalism' remains fatally flawed. Even the alleged 'good patriotism' of the *Vormärz* liberals could still support ultra-nationalist demands in Schleswig-Holstein and Posen and subscribe to the alleged superiority of German culture over that of other nations. National identity, I would argue, already carries the virulent xenophobic virus which continues to scar the face of Europe today. The nation-state has proved to be a dangerous concept; in future it will not be a very useful one either. After all, for most of the pressing problems of the contemporary world, the nation-state has either become too narrow or too broad. It has been in many respects – but by no means all – supplanted by supra- and sub-national structures and institutions. The concept of the autonomous, sovereign state having specific national interests, which are defined and propagated by, amongst others, historians, should best be confined to the history of the nineteenth century. Instead, as Irmline Veit-Brause has argued, we might have to refocus our attention from national identity to civility and citizenship.[5] Democratic values and civic virtues are a more adequate focus for identity than vague concepts of a common national history or culture.

Despite the serious conceptual and moral shortcomings of the national principle, the myths-makers amongst German historians have, since 1989, been engaged in thrashing out what in their eyes should become the foundations for a post-1990 renaissance of the national idea. If we accept Thomas Nipperdey's distinction between three types of nationalism in Imperial Germany, i.e., 'normal patriotism', 'normal nationalism' and 'radical nationalism', can we not say that there are indications that current German historiography is developing strong signs of a 'normal patriotism' whilst some are venturing out into the untested waters of 'normal nationalism'? 'Moments of national glory' may not be conducive to sober criticisms. In 1848 Theodor Mommsen was already scolding 'those who moan and hesitate, those apprehensive sickly souls, the know-all philistines, who mark the great text of history with their question and exclamation marks, all the faint-hearted laggards, who are not satisfied even by the most wonderful victory, those pour souls who have no trust in God's hand in history, in short all the hopeless cowardice, the disapproving cleverness, which wants to drag down the noble enthusiasm of Germany like a leaden heavyweight.'[6] Contemporary calls for historians not to criticise but to nationalise may therefore perhaps not be all that surprising. As in the Bismarckian nation-state after 1870 some historians have been calling for the functionalisation of history after 1990 to compensate for an alleged lack of national identity. The question therefore has to be asked whether 'historism based on embarrassment' *(Verlegenheitshistorismus)* (Helmuth Plessner) will once again triumph in Germany?

The fires allegedly put out by the *Historikerstreit* are still smouldering in the ruins of the Cold War divisions of Germany. If, by 1989, the passion had almost gone out of the controversy and the first scholarly tomes on the debate were being published, the events of that year rekindled interest. Suddenly, a more positive national identity seemed to have become all the more pressing. More than ever the National Socialist past and *Vergangenheitsbewältigung* were perceived as stumbling blocks on the path to reinvigorated national pride. Old agendas, such as the renewed interest in the legacy of Prussia for a reunited Germany and in national symbols more generally as well as the wide-spread abandonment of *Sonderweg* theories, were now given a new lease of life. The contested view that National Socialism provided a legitimate response to Bolshevism has been overtaken and paralleled by an equally contested argument which has portrayed Nazism as a consciously modernising regime. Those who want to use historisation as a means of redressing the balance of judgement on National Socialism hide behind justifiable pleas to historise and not to demonise the National Socialist period. Some revisionist writings on National Socialism have even been geared towards exculpating and marginalising much of its criminal energy. Similarly, calls on the old Federal Republic, since the mid-1980s, to return to the scene of power politics and recognise its status as an important world power, have been given credence by the restoration of a greater Federal Republic. All this has been accompanied by yet another return to the rhetoric of *Mittellage* and the emphasis on geopolitical factors in international relations. There has been much talk about Germany's role as the central power in Europe and one of the central players in world politics.

If some of the historiographical debates of the 1990s sound familiar from the 1980s, others have a relatively fresh look. The more positive assessment of Bismarckian Germany and the wide-spread portrayal of the history of the FRG as a provincial *Sonderweg* were both absent from the debates of the 1980s. The rejection of Westernisation and the virulent anti-Europeanism had no real equivalent in the old Federal Republic. The concepts of constitutional patriotism and postnational democracy have all come under attack as products of a very specific German neurosis about the nation-state. Whilst the dangers of a revamped nationalism in the reunified country have been continuously played down, conservative and new right historians have quickly dusted off the national consciousness and some have explicitly called for a paradigm change in historiography: from society to nation. The relative consensus on *Ostpolitik* has given way to the moral condemnation of its leading practitioners. Apart from the extreme right-wing fringes of the Cold Warrior faction, almost no-one discussed the comparability of National Socialist Germany and the GDR before 1989. Thereafter, however, the renaissance of totalitarianist theory brought a return of such simplistic equations. In fashionable post-reunification speak, the 'second German dictatorship' allegedly calls for a second *Vergangenheitsbewältigung*, which has the handy side-effect of morally discrediting those on the democratic left who dared to have dealings with the Communists.

Should historiographical developments in the first half of the 1990s be interpreted as a belated victory for the revisionists in the

Historikerstreit? Such victory, as our short glimpse of Anglo-American reactions underlined, would threaten German historiography with renewed isolation amongst the international community of historians. There can be little doubt that the national paradigm in German historiography has been strengthened by reunification. What is important, in the face of such a revival, is to preserve the plurality of viewpoints, to prevent the *Zunft* from once again closing its ranks and to frustrate all efforts to turn the attempted renationalisation into a take-over. The degree to which public debate can prevent any such streamlining of historiographical discourse will testify to the strength of a genuine democratic political culture in Germany. Otherwise, to paraphrase Mark Twain's famous words, the German comedy may once more prove to be no laughing matter.

NOTES

1. Rolf Richter's contribution to the panel discussion 'German history and German nationalism', *Debatte*, vol. 1, 1993, p. 28.
2. Karlheinz Weißmann, 'Der "Westen" in der deutschen Historiographie nach 1945', in: Zitelmann, Weißmann and Grossheim (eds), *Westbindung*, p. 358; see also Weißmann, *Rückruf*, p. 117.
3. Zitelmann, *Republik*, p. 7. Also Eckhard Jesse, 'Zur Überschätzung der "Neuen Rechten"', *Die Neue Gesellschaft/Frankfurter Hefte*, vol. 42, 1995, pp. 152-4. For the scenario of a national-conservative renaissance in the reunified Germany more generally see Martin and Sylvia Greiffenhagen, *Ein schwieriges Vaterland. Zur politischen Kultur im vereinigten Deutschland*, Munich, 1993, p. 15, 237-51. For the adoption of an 'instrumental nationalism' of parts of the established conservative mainstream in post-reunification Germany see Franz Oswald, 'Integral and Instrumental Nationalism. National-Conservative Elite Discourse: The "What's Right?" Debate of 1994', *Debatte*, vol. 3, 1995, pp. 24-45.
4. Jürgen Kocka, 'Droht eine neue Nationalgeschichte?', in: Jarausch (ed.), *Zwischen Parteilichkeit und Professionalität*, pp. 185-95.
5. Irmline Veit-Brause, 'Rethinking the State of the Nation', in: Joseph A. Camilleri, Anthony P. Jarvis and Albert P. Jaolini (eds), *The State in Transition. Reimagining Political Space*, Boulder, 1995, p. 72.
6. Cited in Wucher, *Theodor Mommsen*, p. 87.

BIOGRAPHICAL APPENDIX

For an English-speaking audience in particular, some of the historians discussed here may not be all that familiar. To facilitate orientation, I have decided to collect brief biographical data which allow the reader some kind of orientation, as to position and career of the historians discussed above. The list is clearly not complete, but I have tried to include especially those historians who have been central to the debates on historiography and nation building.

Main sources: Winfried Schulze, *Deutsche Geschichtswissenschaft nach 1945*, Munich, 1989; Wolfgang Weber, *Biographisches Lexikon zur Geschichtswissenschaft in Deutschland, Österreich und der Schweiz. Die Lehrstuhlinhaber für Geschichte von den Anfängen des Fachs bis 1970*, Frankfurt-on-Main, 1984; Lexikonredaktion des Bibliographischen Instituts (ed.), *Meyers grosses Taschenlexikon in 24 Bänden*, Mannheim, 1981; *Kürschners Deutscher Gelehrtenkalender. Biobibliographisches Verzeichnis deutschsprachiger Wissenschaftler der Gegenwart*, Berlin, 1976 ff.; *Vademekum der Geschichtswissenschaften 1994/95*, Stuttgart, 1994; *Wer ist wer? Das deutsche Who's Who*, Berlin, 1955 ff.; *Neue deutsche Biographie*, ed. by the Historische Kommission bei der Bayerischen Akademie der Wissenschaften, Berlin, 1953 ff.; *Biographisches Handbuch der deutschsprachigen Emigration nach 1933*, 4 vols, Munich, 1980 ff.

Abendroth, Wolfgang (1906-1985): prominent Marxist historian in West Germany; professor of political science at the University of Marburg, 1951-1973; active in the German labour movement.

Alter, Peter (*1940): deputy-director of the German Historical Institute London until 1994; since then professor for Modern European History, University of Duisburg; research focus on Irish history, the history of science and nationalism.

Aly, Götz (*1947): independent historian in Berlin; co-founder of the Association for Research on National Socialist Health and Social Policies; research focus on the history of National Socialism.

Ammon, Herbert (*1943): studied history, English and sociology at the universities of Munich, Erlangen and New Orleans; since 1971 lecturer in the department for foreign students (Studienkolleg für ausländische Studierende) of the Free University Berlin.

Aretin, Karl Otmar von (*1923): professor of early modern history at the Technical University Darmstadt after 1964; director of the Institute for European history at the University of Mainz after 1968.

Arndt, Hans-Joachim (*1923): professor of political science at the University of Heidelberg since 1968; research focus on economic management; business studies; German national identity.

Aubin, Hermann (1885-1969): professor of medieval and modern history in Bonn, Gießen, Breslau and, since 1936, Hamburg; editor of the *Vierteljahresschrift für Wirtschafts- und Sozialgeschichte*, 1925-1967; chairman of the German historians' association, 1953-1958.

Bahners, Patrick (*1967): studied history, philosophy, English and law at the universities of Bonn and Oxford; journalist with the *Frankfurter Allgemeine Zeitung*, 1989-1993; postgraduate student and junior lecturer at the University of Bonn.

Baring, Arnulf (*1932): professor of contemporary history and political science at the Free University Berlin since 1969; Bundespräsidialamt, 1976-1979; Stiftung Wissen und Politik, 1986-1988.

Below, Georg von (1858-1927): professor of history at the universities of Königsberg (1889-1891), Münster (1891-1897), Marburg (1897-1901), Tübingen (1901-1905) and Freiburg im Breisgau (1905-1924); conservative nationalist historian committed to the Romantic tradition and Rankean historism.

Benz, Wolfgang (*1941): worked for a long time at the Munich-based Institute for Contemporary History; at present head of the Centre for Research on Anti-Semitism at the Technical University Berlin.

Berghahn, Volker (*1938): John P. Birkelund Professor of European History at Brown University, Rhode Island; formerly at Universities of East Anglia and Warwick; research focus on German militarism, employers and Imperial Germany.

Bohrer, Karl Heinz (*1935): professor of literature at the University of Bielefeld since 1983; editor of the monthly journal *Merkur*.

Borkenau, Franz (1900-1957): researcher at the Frankfurt Institute for Social Research, 1929-1933; broke with Communism after his experiences in the Spanish Civil War; lecturer in international politics at the extramural departments of the universities of Cambridge and London, 1938-1943; professor of modern history at the University of Marburg, 1946-1949.

Borsdorf, Ulrich (*1944): studied history and German literature at the universities of Bochum and Freiburg; head of the Ruhrland Museum in Essen.

Bosl, Karl (1908-1993): professor of history at the universities of Würzburg (1953-1960) and Munich (after 1960); director of the Institute for Regional History *(Landesgeschichte)* at Munich University; chairman of the commission for *Landesgeschichte* at the Bavarian Academy of Sciences; first chairman of the Collegium Carolinum (Research Institute for the History of the Bohemian lands).

Bracher, Karl Dietrich (*1922): professor of contemporary history and political science at Bonn University since 1959; chairman of the Commission for the History of Parliamentarism and German Political Parties, 1962-1968; chairman of the Research Council *(Beirat)* of the Institute for Contemporary History, Munich, 1980-1988; one of the key proponents of the totalitarian paradigm in the FRG.

Bramke, Werner (*1938): professor of contemporary German history at the University of Leipzig; member of the Saxon Landtag for the PDS.

Brandt, Peter (*1948): historian at the Technical University Berlin and later professor of history at the Open University in Hagen; son of the late chancellor Willy Brandt.

Bredow, Wilfried Frh. von (*1944): professor of political science at the University of Marburg since 1972; research focus on militarism, the Bundeswehr and East-West relations.

Broszat, Martin (1926-1989): from 1955 historian at, and from 1972 onwards director, of the Munich-based Institute for Contemporary History; head of several massive research projects, amongst others the famous 'Bavaria project'; after 1972 honourary professor at the University of Konstanz.

Buchheim, Hans (*1922): historian at the Institute for Contemporary history, Munich, 1951-1966; after 1966 professor of contemporary history at the University of Mainz.

Burckhardt, Jakob (1818-1897): professor for cultural and art history at the universities of Zurich (1855-1858) and Basel (after 1858).

Bußmann, Walter (*1914): professor of contemporary history at the universities of Göttingen (1954/1955), Berlin (1955-1966), Munich (1966-1970) and Karlsruhe (after 1970); research focus on historiography and nineteenth-century European history.

Conze, Werner (1910-1986): professor of modern history in Posen, Göttingen, Münster and Heidelberg, where he founded the Arbeitskreis für moderne Sozialgeschichte. Hugely influential in establishing social history in German historical writing.

Dahlmann, Friedrich Christoph (1785-1860): professor of history in Kiel, Göttingen, Bonn; leader of the Göttingen Seven in 1842 and of the small-German faction in the Frankfurt Assembly of 1848.

Dann, Otto (*1937): professor of modern history at the University of Cologne since 1976; research focus on nationalism, historiography and the development of bourgeois society in the nineteenth century.

Danyel, Jürgen (*1959): historian at the Zentrum für zeithistorische Forschung, Potsdam.

Dehio, Ludwig (1888-1963): archivist and historian; director of the Marburg state archive between 1946 and 1954; editor of the *Historische Zeitschrift*, 1949-1956.

Delbrück, Hans (1848-1929): pupil of Sybel; professor of modern history at the University of Berlin after 1895; co-editor of the *Preußische Jahrbücher* after 1883; a Free Conservative who publicly fought the ultra-nationalism of the Pan-Germans before 1914.

Diner, Dan (*1946): professor of modern history at the universities of Essen and Tel Aviv; director of the Institute of German History at Tel Aviv University.

Diwald, Helmut (1930-1992): professor of early modern history at
    Erlangen-Nürnberg, 1965-1992.

Droysen, Johann Gustav (1808-1884): professor of history in Kiel and
    Berlin; participated in the Schleswig rising against Denmark; influential
    impact on the constitution of the Frankfurt assembly in 1848.

Dülffer, Jost (*1943): professor of modern history at the University of
    Cologne since 1979; research focus on National Socialism.

Eckert, Rainer (*1950): relegated as history student from Humboldt
    University for political reasons; historian at the Central Institute for
    History at the Academy of Sciences of the GDR; member of the
    Independent Historians' Association of the GDR, founded in 1990;
    assistant director of the Institute for German History at the Academy,
    1990/91; since 1992 junior lecturer *(Assistent)* at the deptartment of
    history at the Humboldt University Berlin.

Eichberg, Henning (*1942): historian at the University of Stuttgart since
    1976; research focus on the history of sport, the military and questions
    of national identity.

Engelberg, Ernst (*1909): persecution and emigration to Geneva and
    Istanbul under National Socialism; after 1949 professor of modern
    history at the universities of Leipzig and Berlin; member of the
    Academy of Sciences of the GDR.

Erdmann, Karl Dietrich (1910-1990): professor of modern history in
    Cologne and Kiel; chairman of the West German historians' association,
    1962-1967; president of the international historians' association,
    1975-1980; editor of *Geschichte in Wissenschaft und Unterricht*, 1951-1990.

Eschenburg, Theodor (*1904): professor of contemporary history and
    political science at the University of Tübingen, 1952-1972.

Eyck, Erich (1878-1964): worked as solicitor and historian; emigrated to
    Britain in 1937; author of an influential biography of Bismarck, which
    was published in three volumes between 1941 and 1944.

Faulenbach, Bernd (*1943): historian at the Institute for Workers' Education
    at Bochum University; chairman of the SPD's Historical Commission.

Feldner, Heiko (*1963): historian (wissenschaftlicher Mitarbeiter) at the
    University of Halle.

Fest, Joachim (*1926): radio and TV journalist in the 1950s and 1960s;
    editor of the *Frankfurter Allgemeine Zeitung*, 1973-1994.

Fetscher, Iring (*1922): professor of political science at the University of
    Frankfurt-on-Main after 1963.

Fichter, Tilman (*1937): member of the Berlin SDS between 1963 and
    1970; since 1987 educational officer at the SPD party executive,
    Friedrich-Ebert-Foundation, Bonn.

Fischer, Alexander (*1933): professor of East European history at the
    universities of Frankfurt-on-Main (1973-85) and Bonn (since 1986).

Fischer, Fritz (*1908): professor of modern history at the University of
    Hamburg, 1942-1973; co-founder of the Commission for the History of
    Parliamentarism and Political Parties, 1951.

Foltin, Hans F. (*1937): professor of cultural sociology and media studies at
    the University of Marburg since 1972.

Förster, Stig (*1951): professor of modern history at the University of Berne.

Fraenkel, Ernst (1891-1971): economic historian, emigration to Britain in 1939; 1947-1957: teacher at the Pädagogisches Institut Jugenheim/ Bergstraße; after 1957 professor of economic and social history at the University of Frankfurt-on-Main.

Frank, Walter (1905-1945): president of the Reich Institute for the History of the New Germany, founded in 1935; leading Nazi historian; committed suicide in 1945.

Frei, Norbert (*1955): historian at the Munich-based Institute for Contemporary History since 1979.

Frühwald, Wolfgang (*1935): professor of modern German literature at the universities of Trier (1970-1974) and Munich (since 1974).

Fülberth, Georg (*1939): professor of political science at the University of Marburg since 1972.

Gall, Lothar (*1936): professor of modern history at the universities of Gießen (1968-1972), Free University Berlin (1972-1975) and Frankfurt-on-Main (since 1975); editor of *Historische Zeitschrift* since 1975.

Geiss, Imanuel (*1931): professor of modern history at the University of Bremen since 1971.

Gervinus, Georg Gottfried (1805-1871): professor of history at the universities of Heidelberg and Göttingen; as one of the Göttingen Seven sacked from the university; member of the Frankfurt national assembly; trial for high treason in 1853 and subsequent withdrawal of the right to teach at universities.

Giesebrecht, Wilhelm (1814-1889): pupil of Ranke; schoolteacher in the 1840s; professor of modern history at the universities of Berlin (1851-1857), Königsberg (1857-1861) and Berlin (after 1861); long-time secretary of the Historical Commission.

Glaser, Hermann (*1928): cultural historian; honourary professor at the Technical University Berlin; head of the cultural and educational department of the city administration of Nuremberg, 1964-1990.

Glotz, Peter (*1939): leading SPD politician; editor of *Die neue Gesellschaft/Frankfurter Hefte.*

Goetz, Walter (1867-1958): professor of medieval and modern history at the universities of Leipzig, Munich, Tübingen and Straßburg; member of parliament for the left-liberal DDP, 1922-1933; president of the historical commission of the Bavarian Academy of Sciences in 1945.

Gregorovius, Ferdinand (1821-1891): German writer; extremely successful with popular cultural history works such as the eight-volume 'History of the City of Rome in the Middle Ages', published between 1859 and 1872.

Groehler, Olaf (1935-1995): professor of modern history at the Institute for German History at the Academy of Sciences in the GDR after 1983; assistant director of the Central Institute for History, 1985-1990; representative of the GDR in the International Committee for the History of the Second World War; historian at the Zentrum für zeithistorische Forschung, Potsdam.

Groh, Dieter (*1932): professor of modern history at the universities of Heidelberg (1973/1974) and Konstanz (since 1974).

Grundmann, Herbert (1902-1970): professor of medieval history at the universities of Leipzig, Königsberg, Münster and Munich; one of the founding members of the Association of German Historians; president of the *Monumenta Germaniae Historica,* 1959-1970.

Gruner, Wolf (*1944): professor of modern European history at the University of Hamburg, 1982-1993; after 1993 professor of modern history at the University of Rostock.

Hacke, Christian (*1943): professor of political science and international politics at the army University in Hamburg.

Hacker, Jens (*1933): professor of political science at the University of Regensburg since 1982.

Haller, Johannes (1865-1947): professor of medieval history at the universities of Gießen and Tübingen.

Heimpel, Hermann (1901-1988): professor of medieval and modern history at the universities of Freiburg, Leipzig, Straßburg and Göttingen; after 1956 director of the Max-Planck-Institute for History in Göttingen.

Helbok, Adolf (1883-1968): professor of history at the universities of Innsbruck (1923-1935; 1941-1945) and Leipzig (1935-1941); key representative of *Volkshistoriker* in 1920s and 1930s; co-editor of *Volk und Rasse* after 1925.

Herre, Paul (1876-1962): historian at the University of Leipzig, 1906-1920 (professor since 1912); senior civil servant in the Foreign Office, 1920; director of the national archives (*Reichsarchiv*), 1921-1934.

Herzfeld, Hans (1892-1982): professor of modern history in Halle-Wittenberg, Potsdam, Freiburg and Berlin; sacked by the Nazis first from his chair in 1938 and subsequently in 1943 from another position at the Research Institute of the Army; chairman of the historical commission in Berlin from 1959-1979.

Heydemann, Günther (*1950): historian at the German Historical Institute, London; since the early 1990s professor of modern and contemporary history at the University of Leipzig; executive member of the Gesellschaft für Deutschlandforschung.

Hildebrand, Klaus (*1941): professor of modern history at the universities of Bielefeld (1972-1974), Frankfurt-on-Main (1974-1977), Münster (1977-1982) and Bonn (since 1982).

Hillgruber, Andreas (1925-1989): historian at the University of Marburg, 1953-1968; professor of modern history at the universities of Freiburg im Breisgau, 1968-1972 and Cologne, after 1972.

Hintze, Otto (1861-1940): professor of medieval and modern history at the University of Berlin; introduced sociological methods into historiography; seminal works on comparative constitutional history.

Hockerts, Hans Günther (*1944): professor of modern history at the universities of Frankfurt-on-Main (1982-1986) and Munich (since 1986).

Hoetzsch, Otto (1876-1946): professor of East-European history at the universities of Posen, 1906-1913, and Berlin, 1913-1935; co-founder in 1913 of the German Society for the Study of Eastern Europe; DNVP member of the Reichstag, 1920-1929.

Hofer, Walter (*1920): lecturer and later professor of modern history at the Free University Berlin, 1950-1960, and the University of Berne after 1960.

Hoffmann, Christa (*1964): studied political science and Romance language and literature at the Catholic University Eichstätt and at the

University of Trier; Ph.D. on a comparison of *Vergangenheitsbewältigung* after 1945 and 1989 with a grant from the CDU's Konrad-Adenauer-Foundation.

Hoffmann, Joachim (*1930): senior historian at the Militärgeschichtliches Forschungsamt, Freiburg.

Holborn, Hajo (1902-1969): pupil of Friedrich Meinecke; professor of history and international relations at the Berlin *Hochschule für Politik*, 1931-1933; emigration, 1933; professor of history at Yale University, 1934-1969; head of the 'research and analysis' department in the Office of Strategic Studies, 1942-1945; president of the American Historical Association, 1967-1969.

Iggers, Georg (*1926): professor of history at the University of Buffalo/SUNY; fled Nazism as a boy; politically active in the U.S. Civil Rights Movement at Little Rock, Arkansas and in the anti-Vietnam campaign.

Jäckel, Eberhard (*1929): historian at the University of Kiel, 1961-1966; professor of modern history at the University of Stuttgart since 1967.

Jakobi, Franz-Josef (*1940): professor of medieval history at the University of Münster since 1984; head of the city archives in Münster since 1986.

Jesse, Eckhard (*1948): professor of political science at the University of Chemnitz since 1994; lecturer in political science at the University of Trier, 1990-1994.

Jessen, Ralph (*1956): junior lecturer at the Free University of Berlin and historian at the Zentrum für zeithistorische Forschung, Potsdam.

Kaehler, Siegfried A. (1885-1963): professor of modern history at the universities of Marburg, Breslau, Halle-Wittenberg, Jena and Göttingen.

Kaelble, Hartmut (*1940): professor of social and economic history at the Free University Berlin since 1971; one of the key proponents of a genuinely comparative European history.

Kaltenbrunner, Gerd-Klaus (*1939): since 1962 the commissioning editor in a publishing house.

Kaschuba, Wolfgang (*1950): lecturer in cultural studies at the University of Tübingen; recently professor of European ethnology at the Humboldt University, Berlin.

Kehr, Eckart (1902-1933): historian in Berlin; one of the staunchest critics of the national tradition in German historiography; died prematurely during a research visit to Washington in 1933.

Kielmannsegg, Peter Graf von (*1937): professor of political science at the universities of Cologne (1971-1985) and Mannheim (since 1985).

Kiesewetter, Hubert (*1939): professor of modern history at the Catholic University of Eichstätt.

Kittel, Manfred (*1962): historian at the Munich-based Institute for Contemporary History; Ph.D. on *Vergangenheitsbewältigung* in the FRG after 1945 with a grant from the CDU's Konrad-Adenauer-Foundation.

Kleßmann, Christoph (*1938): historian at the *Ostkolleg*, Cologne, 1967-1970; junior lecturer *(Assistent)* at the Ruhr University Bochum, 1970-1976; professor of contemporary history at the University of Bielefeld since 1976; currently Director of the Zentrum für Zeithistorische Forschung Potsdam.

Klönne, Arno (*1931): professor of sociology at the University of Paderborn.

Klueting, Harm (*1949): professor of modern history at the University of Cologne since 1989; research focus on the regional history of Westfalen, eighteenth-century foreign policy and early modern history.

Knopp, Guido (*1948): television journalist; producer of the most recent nine-hour documentary on National Socialism shown on German television in 1995.

Knütter, Hans-Helmuth (*1934): since 1972 professor of political science at the University of Bonn.

Kocka, Jürgen (*1941): professor of modern history at the University of Bielefeld (1973-1988) and subsequently professor for the history of the industrial world at the Free University of Berlin; permanent fellow at the *Wissenschaftskolleg*, Berlin; founding member of the Academia Europaea, 1988, and of the Berlin-Brandenburg Academy of Sciences, 1993; acting head of the *Forschungsschwerpunkt Zeithistorische Studien*, Potsdam until the end of 1995.

Korte, Karl-Rudolf (*1958): deputy director of the Research Group Germany at the Institute for Political Science at Mainz University.

Koselleck, Reinhart (*1923): professor of modern history at the universities of Bochum (1966-1968), Heidelberg (1968-1973), and Bielefeld (after 1973); one of the doyens of *Begriffsgeschichte*.

Kossock, Manfred (1930-1993): professor of modern history at the University of Leipzig after 1963; head of the Interdisciplinary Centre for Comparative Research on Revolutions, 1976-1990; member of the Academy of Sciences of the GDR in Berlin and of the Academie Nacional de Historia Venezuela.

Krockow, Christian Graf von (*1927): between 1961 and 1969 professor of political science at the universities of Göttingen, Saarbrücken and Frankfurt-on-Main; after 1969 writer and publisher.

Kuczynski, Jürgen (*1904): doyen of Marxist historiography in the GDR; professor of social and economic history at the University of Berlin; founder of the Berlin Institute of Economic History.

Kühnl, Reinhard (*1936): professor of political science and contemporary history at the University of Marburg since 1971.

Küttler, Wolfgang (*1936): junior lecturer *(Assistent)* in history at the universities of Jena and Leipzig, 1958-1967; historian at the Central Institute for History at the Academy of Sciences of the GDR after 1967; director of the Institute in 1990/1991; after its dissolution he has been working at the Forschungsschwerpunkt Wissenschaftsgeschichte und - theorie in Berlin.

Lamprecht, Karl (1856-1915): professor of modern German history at the universities of Marburg and Leipzig; efforts to introduce social history into German historiography led to so-called *Methodenstreit* which ended in victory for the historist tradition of political history.

Lenz, Max (1850-1932): professor of modern history in Berlin and Hamburg; major representative of the so-called neo-Rankean school.

Lepsius, Mario Rainer (*1928): professor of sociology at the universities of Mannheim (1963-1981) and Heidelberg (since 1981).

Loth, Wilfried (*1948): professor of modern history at the University of Berlin (1984-1985) and Münster (since 1985).

Löw, Konrad (*1931): professor of political science at the universities of Erlangen (1972-1975) and Bayreuth (since 1975).

Lübbe, Hermann (*1926): professor of philosophy at the universities of Bochum (1963-1969), Bielefeld (1969-1973) and Zürich (since 1973).

Luden, Heinrich (1778-1847): after 1806 professor of history at the University of Jena; his national liberal historiography had a strong influence on university students.

Machtan, Lothar: lecturer in history at the universities of Halle and (since 1993) Bremen.

Mann, Golo (1909-1994): emigration under Nazism to Switzerland, France and the United States; military service in the U.S. army; lecturer at various American colleges between 1947-1958; 1958-1964 professor of political science in Münster and Stuttgart.

Marcks, Erich (1861-1938): professor of modern history at the University of Berlin; key representative of the neo-Rankean revival around the turn of the century; conservative enemy of the Weimar Republic.

Markov, Walter (*1909): after 1949 professor of modern history at the University of Leipzig; KPD member in the Weimar Republic; after 1933 member of a resistance group at Bonn University; imprisoned by the Nazis, 1935-1945.

Maser, Werner (*1992): professor of history at the University of Halle.

Mayer, Gustav (1871-1948): journalist with the *Frankfurter Zeitung,* 1896-1906; independent writer and publisher; for political reasons his *Habilitation* was vetoed by nationalist historians at the University of Berlin, 1917; professor for history of democracy, socialism and political parties in Berlin, 1922-1933; exile in Britain after 1933.

Mayer, Tilman (*1953): head of research at the Germany research institute of the Jakob-Kaiser-Foundation in Königswinter and lecturer of political science at the University of Erfurt.

Meier, Christian (*1929): lecturer *(Privatdozent)* in ancient history at the universities of Frankfurt-on-Main and Freiburg, 1963-1966; professor of ancient history at the universities of Basel (1966-1968; 1973-1976), Cologne (1968-1973), Bochum (1976-1981) and Munich (after 1981).

Meinecke, Friedrich (1862-1954): professor of modern history at the University of Berlin; first president of the Free University of Berlin; editor of *Historische Zeitschrift,* 1896-1934; chairman of the Historical Commission of the Reich, 1928-1934.

Meusel, Alfred (1896-1960): economist, sociologist and historian in Aachen and Berlin; exile from Nazi Germany in Denmark and Britain; member of the KPD after 1937; director of the museum for German history in East Berlin, 1952-1960.

Meyer, Georg: military historian at the Militärgeschichtliches Forschungsamt, Freiburg.

Mittenzwei, Ingrid (*1929): historian at the Central Institute for History at the Academy of Sciences of the GDR until 1991.

Mitter, Armin (*1953): until 1990 historian at the Academy of Sciences in the GDR; co-founder of the Independent Historians' Association of the GDR in 1990; 1990/1991: historian at the Gauck Institute for the Stasi files; since 1991 junior lecturer/*Assistent* at the department of history, Humboldt University, Berlin.

Mohler, Armin (*1920): head of the Carl Friedrich von Siemens Foundation, Munich, 1964-1985.

Möller, Horst (*1943): assistant director of the Institute for Contemporary History, Munich, 1972-1982; professor of modern history at the University of Erlangen-Nürnberg, 1982-1989; since 1989 director of the Institute for Contemporary History, Munich and honourary professor at the University of Regensburg.

Mommsen, Hans (*1930): professor of modern history at the University of Bochum since 1968; founder and director (1977-1983) of the Institute for the History of the European Labour Movement at Bochum University.

Mommsen, Theodor (1817-1903): after 1861 professor of Roman history at Berlin University; liberal politician and member of parliament; opponent of Bismarck's political system; Nobel Prize for Literature, 1902.

Mommsen, Wilhelm (1892-1966): professor of modern history at universities of Göttingen and Marburg.

Mommsen, Wolfgang J. (*1930): professor of modern history at the University of Düsseldorf after 1968; director of the German Historical Institute London, 1977-1985; chairman of the historians' association from 1988 to 1993; president of the International Commission for the History of Historiography.

Moraw, Peter (*1935): professor of medieval history at the University of Gießen since 1973; director of the Institute for *Landesgeschichte* at Gießen University.

Müller, Karl Alexander von (1882-1964): professor of modern history at the University of Munich; editor of the *Historische Zeitschrift*, 1935-1944; sacked for his proximity to Nazism for a brief period after 1945.

Niebuhr, Georg Barthold (1776-1831): professor of Roman history at the University of Bonn after 1823; Danish (1806-1810) and Prussian (1813-1823) civil servant; of key importance for the establishment of methodological ground rules for the writing of history.

Niethammer, Lutz (*1939): professor of modern history at the University of Essen (1973-1982), Open University Hagen (1982-1993) and the University of Jena (since 1993); one of the founders and one-time head of the Institute for Cultural Studies at the *Wissenschaftszentrum*, Nordrhein-Westfalen; doyen of Germany's oral history and history of everyday life.

Nipperdey, Thomas (1927-1993): professor of modern history at the universities of Karlsruhe (1963-1967), Berlin (1967-1971) and Munich (since 1971); member of the Bavarian Academy of Sciences and the American Academy of Arts and Sciences.

Nolte, Ernst (*1923): professor of modern history at the University of Marburg, 1963-1973, and the Free University Berlin, 1973-1991.

Pätzold, Kurt (*1930): professor of modern history at Humboldt University Berlin until 1991.

Peukert, Detlev (1950-1990): professor of modern history at the University of Essen; head of the Hamburg-based Research Institute for the History of the Labour Movement and of National Socialism.

Plessner, Helmuth (1892-1985): fled Nazism in 1933; professor of sociology at the University of Göttingen after 1951.

Prinz, Michael (*1952): lecturer in history at the University of Bielefeld since 1984.

Probst, Lothar (*1952): political scientist at the University of Bremen.

Puhle, Hans-Jürgen (*1940): professor of political science at the University of Frankfurt-on-Main since 1990; taught at the University of Bielefeld, 1979-1990.

Quidde, Ludwig (1858-1941): historian in Munich; editor of the *Reichstagsakten Ältere Reihe*; head of the Prussian Historical Institute, Rome, 1890-1892; the publication of a thinly veiled critique of Wilhelm II in 1894 *(Caligula. Eine Studie über römischen Cäsarenwahnsinn)* ended his career as a historian; became a liberal politician; convinced democrat and pacifist activist; Nobel Peace Prize, 1927; fled Nazi Germany in 1933.

Ranke, Leopold von (1795-1886): professor of history at the University of Berlin after 1825; official historiographer of the Prussian state, 1841; first chairman of the Historical Commission of the Bavarian Academy of Sciences, 1858.

Rantzau, Johann Albrecht von (*1900): historian at the University of Hamburg, 1946-1954; professor of modern history at the Technical University Berlin after 1954.

Reichel, Peter (*1942): professor of political science at the University of Hamburg.

Repgen, Konrad (*1923): professor of modern history at the University of Bonn after 1962.

Rhenanus, Beatus (1485-1547): friend of Erasmus of Rotterdam; important works on the German history of the middle ages.

Richter, Rolf (*1945): formerly Director of one of the sections of the Academy of Sciences at the Central Committee of the SED; professor of history and deputy director of the Institute for Applied Research into Youth Aid, Berlin.

Ritter, Gerhard (1888-1967): professor of modern history at the University Freiburg im Breisgau; in the Third Reich member of the resistance group around Carl F. Goerdeler; imprisoned by the Gestapo in 1944; chairman of the Association of German Historians, 1948-1953.

Ritter, Gerhard A. (*1929): professor of modern history at the universities of Berlin (1963-1965), Münster (1965-1974), Munich (after 1974); honourary fellow of St. Antony's College, Oxford.

Röhl, Klaus Rainer (*1928): studied history and German literature in Hamburg and Berlin; since 1954 he works and lives as independent writer and publisher in Cologne; husband of Ulrike Meinhof; one-time editor of the journal *Konkret*.

Rosenberg, Arthur (1889-1943): lectured in ancient history at the Friedrich-Wilhelms University Berlin in the Weimar Republic; member of parliament for the KPD; broke with Communism in the late 1920s; emigrated to Britain; lecturer in ancient history at the University of Liverpool; professor of history at Brooklyn College, New York, 1938-1943.

Rosenberg, Hans (1904-1988): professor of modern history at the universities of Cologne, New York (Brooklyn College) and Berkeley; emigrated to the US in 1936; returned to the FRG in 1970; his blend of political and social history proved hugely influential amongst post-Second World War generations of German historians.

Rosh, Lea (*1936): radio and TV journalist; after 1991 head of NDR Landesfunkhaus Hannover.

Roth, Karl Heinz (*1942): medical doctor and historian; head of the Hamburg Foundation for Social History of the Twentieth Century; editor of *1999. Zeitschrift für Sozialgeschichte und -politik.*

Rothfels, Hans (1891-1976): professor of medieval and modern history at the universities of Königsberg (before 1939) and Tübingen (after 1951); emigrated to the U.S. in 1939 where he taught in Providence and Chicago; returned to the FRG permanently in 1951; founder and co-editor of the *Vierteljahreshefte für Zeitgeschichte.*

Rotteck, Karl von (1775-1840): professor of history at the University of Freiburg im Breisgau; sacked for his endorsement of the principles of the July revolution in 1832; liberal member of the Badenese parliament.

Ruffmann, Karl-Heinz (*1922): professor of East European and contemporary history at the University of Erlangen-Nürnberg after 1962.

Rumberg, Dirk (*1963): after spending some time as assistant to Arnulf Baring at the University of Berlin, member of a research group on contemporary social history at the University of Munich.

Rüsen, Jörn (*1938): professor of history at the universities of Bochum (1974-1989), Bielefeld (1989-1997) and Witten-Herdecke (since 1997); research focus on historiography, the methodology of historical writing and historics.

Sabrow, Martin (*1954): historian at the Zentrum für Zeithistorische Studien, Potsdam.

Salewski, Michael (*1938): professor of medieval and modern history at the University of Kiel since 1971; chairman of the Ranke Society since 1984.

Schäfer, Hermann: (*1942) director of the Bonn history museum of the Federal Republic of Germany (Haus der Geschichte) since 1987.

Schieder, Theodor (1908-1984): professor of modern history at the universities of Königsberg and Cologne; editor of the *Historische Zeitschrift*, 1957-1984; chairman of the Association of German Historians, 1967-1972; president of the Historical Commission at the Bavarian Academy of Sciences, 1964-1984.

Schlögel, Karl (*1948): since 1990 professor of Eastern European history at the University of Konstanz.

Schmidt, Walter (*1930): professor for the history of the German labour movement at the Institute (later Academy) for Social Science at the Central Committee of the SED, 1965-1984; director of the Central Institute for History at the Academy of Sciences of the GDR in Berlin, 1984-1990.

Schmoller, Gustav von (1838-1917): founder of the so-called younger historical school of economics; professor at the universities of Halle, Straßburg and Berlin; member of the Prussian *Staatsrat* after 1884 and representative of Berlin University in the Prussian *Herrenhaus* after

1899; co-founder (in 1872) and head (after 1890) of the *Verein für Socialpolitik.*

Schnabel, Franz (1887-1966): professor of modern history at the universities of Karlsruhe and Munich; sacked for political reasons by the Nazis in 1936; president of the Historical Commission at the Bavarian Academy of Sciences, 1951-1959.

Schneider, Michael (*1944): historian at the research institute of the Friedrich-Ebert-Foundation since 1971.

Schoeps, Hans-Joachim (1909-1980): professor of history at the University of Erlangen after 1950; emigrated to Sweden in 1938; returned to Germany in 1946; publicly favoured a return to the monarchy after 1945.

Schöllgen, Gregor (*1952): professor of modern history at the universities of Münster, 1983-1985 and Erlangen-Nürnberg since 1985.

Schulin, Ernst (*1929): professor of history at the Technical University Berlin, 1967-1974 and the University of Freiburg im Breisgau since 1974.

Schuller, Wolfgang (*1935): professor of ancient history at the PH Berlin, 1972-1976, and at the University of Konstanz since 1976; research focus on Greek history and the political criminal law of the GDR.

Schultz, Helga (*1941): historian at the University of Rostock, 1966-1977, and at the Central Institute for History at the Academy of Sciences of the GDR in Berlin, 1983-1990; head of the research section on regional history; professor since 1986; at present at the University of Frankfurt/Oder.

Schulz, Eberhard (*1926): assistant director of the research institute of the Deutsche Gesellschaft für Auswärtige Politik, Bonn since 1966; honourary professor at the University of Bonn since 1980.

Schulze, Hagen (*1943): editor of the *Akten der Reichskanzlei,* 1968-1971; historian at the *Geheimes Staatsarchiv,* Berlin, 1971-1976; professor of modern history at the Free University Berlin since 1979.

Schulze, Winfried (*1942): professor of early modern European history at the universities of Kassel (1974-1976), Berlin (1976-1978), Bochum (1978-1994) and Berlin (since 1994).

Schwan, Alexander (1931-1989): professor of political science at the Free University Berlin since 1966; under the impact of the events in 1968 he changed party cards from the SPD to the CDU.

Schwan, Gesine (*1943): professor of political science at the Free University Berlin since 1977.

Schwarz, Hans-Peter (*1934): professor of political science and contemporary history at the PH Osnabrück (1963-1966) and at the universities of Hamburg (1966-1973), Cologne (1973-1987) and Bonn (from 1987); head of the CDU's Konrad Adenauer Foundation.

Schweigler, Gebhard (*1943): political scientist; B.A. (Harvard), 1967; M.A. University of California, Berkeley, 1968; Ph.D. (Harvard), 1972; since 1972 research fellow at the Research Institute of the German Society for Foreign Affairs in Bonn.

Seebacher-Brandt, Brigitte (*1946): studied history and German literature in Bonn, Cologne and Berlin; Ph.D. about a biography of Erich Ollenhauer, 1984; has worked as freelance journalist and publisher ever since; second wife of the late chancellor Willy Brandt.

Seibt, Gustav (*1959): journalist with the *Frankfurter Allgemeine Zeitung*, head of its *Feuilleton*; moved to *Berliner Zeitung* in 1997.

Seiffert, Wolfgang (*1926): professor at the Academy for State and Legal Sciences of the GDR, 1967-1978; vice-president of the Society for International Law of the GDR; after moving to the FRG professor of law at the University of Kiel since 1978; head of the Institute for Law, Politics and History of the Socialist States at the University of Kiel since 1989.

Siedler, Wolf-Jobst (*1926): head of the Siedler publishing house in Berlin.

Sontheimer, Kurt (*1928): professor of political science at the Free University Berlin, 1962-1969, and at the University of Munich after 1969.

Staritz, Dietrich (*1934): professor of contemporary history and political science at the universities of Berlin and Mannheim; director of the section on 'history and politics of the GDR' at the Mannheim-based Institute of Social Sciences until 1996.

Steinbach, Peter (*1948): historian at the Free University Berlin, 1973-81; professor of modern history at the University of Passau since 1982; head of the research team on the Permanent Exhibition 'Resistance against National Socialism', Berlin, 1983-1989; since 1989 head of the Gedenkstätte Deutscher Widerstand, Berlin.

Sternberger, Dolf (1907-1989): journalist with the *Frankfurter Zeitung*, 1934-1943; co-editor of the journals *Die Wandlung*, 1945-1949, and *Die Gegenwart*, 1950-1958; co-founder of the *Politische Vierteljahresschrift*; after 1955 professor of political science at the University of Heidelberg; president of the FRG's P.E.N., 1964-1970.

Stölzl, Christoph (*1944): director of the Museum for German History, Berlin since 1987.

Streit, Christian: teacher at a grammar school in Mannheim; author of a seminal study on the German army in the Second World War and Soviet prisoners of war.

Striefler, Christian (*1962): Ph.D. about the final years of the Weimar Republic with a grant from the Friedrich Naumann Foundation (close to the FDP); civil servant in Saxony.

Stürmer, Michael (*1938): historian at the universities of Mannheim and Darmstadt, 1965-1970; professor of modern history at the University of Erlangen since 1973; director of the Research Institute for International Politics and Security: Foundation Science and Politics, Ebenhausen; close political advisor to Helmut Kohl in the 1980s.

Sybel, Heinrich von (1817-1895): professor of history at the universities of Bonn, Marburg and Munich; pupil of Leopold von Ranke; founder of the *Historische Zeitschrift*, 1859; national liberal member of the Prussian parliament, 1862-1864 and 1874-1880.

Syring, Enrico (*1960): studied history and geography at the University of Göttingen; graduate student at the universities of Bonn and Bremen.

Thadden, Rudolf von (*1932): professor of modern history at the University of Göttingen since 1967; Directeur d'Etudes associé at the Ecole des Hautes Etudes, Paris since 1983; president of the German-French Institute, Ludwigsburg since 1985.

Thamer, Hans-Ulrich (*1943): professor of modern history at the University of Münster since 1983.

Thies, Jochen (*1944): journalist, since 1993 with *Die Welt (Ressortleiter Außenpolitik)*.

Treitschke, Heinrich von (1834-1896): professor of history at the universities of Kiel (1866/1867), Heidelberg (1867-1874) and Berlin (after 1874); successor of Ranke as official historiographer of the Prussian state after 1886; member of the Prussian Academy of Science after 1895; one of the editors of the *Preußische Jahrbücher*, member of parliament, 1871-1884.

Uffelmann, Uwe (*1937): professor of historical didactics at PH Heidelberg since 1973; chairman of the Conference for Historical Didactics.

Valentin, Veit (1885-1947): his academic career at the University was destroyed for political reasons in the First World War – he had criticised the German attack on Belgium; after 1923 archivist in Potsdam; sacked in 1933 for political reasons; fled to Britain and the United States.

Veit-Brause, Irmline (*1937): Associate Professor of History of Ideas at Deakin University, Geelong, Victoria, Australia.

Vierhaus, Rudolf (*1922): historian at the University of Münster, 1961-1964; professor of modern history at the University of Bochum, 1964-1971; director of the Max Planck Institute for History in Göttingen from 1971 to 1990.

Weber, Hermann (*1928): 1947-1949 student at the SED party University 'Karl Marx'; since 1975 professor of contemporary history and political science at the University of Mannheim; head of the section on GDR history at the Mannheim Centre for European Social Research at the University of Mannheim since 1981; member of the SPD Historical Commission.

Weber, Max (1864-1920): professor of economics at the universities of Freiburg im Breisgau (1894-1897) and Heidelberg (1897-1903); professor of sociology in Vienna (1918) and again for economics in Munich (1919/1920); prominent member of the *Verein für Socialpolitik*; co-founder of the German Society for Sociology and the German Democratic Party; member of the commission for the Weimar constitution.

Wehler, Hans-Ulrich (*1931): professor of modern history at the universities of Berlin and Bielefeld since 1971.

Weidenfeld, Werner (*1947): professor of political science at the University of Mainz since 1975; since 1988 co-ordinator for German-American Cultural Co-operation in the German Foreign Office.

Weißbecker, Manfred (*1935): professor of modern history at the University of Jena, 1970-1993; chairman of the *Jenaer Forum* with close ties to the PDS.

Weisbrod, Bernd (*1946): historian at the German Historical Institute, London; professor of modern history at the University of Göttingen since 1990.

Weißmann, Karlheinz (*1959): studied history and Protestant theology in Göttingen; schoolteacher in Lower Saxony since 1993.

Wendt, Bernd-Jürgen (*1934): since 1976 professor of medieval and modern history at the University of Hamburg.

Wengst, Udo (*1947): historian *(wissenschaftlicher Mitarbeiter)* at the Kommission für Geschichte des Parlamentarismus und der politischen Parteien in Bonn.

Westphal, Otto (1891-1950): historian at the universities of Göttingen, Hamburg and Königsberg; council member of the Nazi 'Reichsinstitut'.

Wette, Wolfram (*1940): since 1971 historian at the *Militärgeschichtliches Forschungsamt* and lecturer *(Privatdozent)* at the University of Freiburg.

Willms, Bernard (1931-1990): professor of political science at the Ruhr University of Bochum after 1970.

Wimpfeling, Jakob (1450-1528): lectured at the universities of Heidelberg, 1469-1501, and Straßburg, 1501-1515; 'praeceptor Germaniae'; his historical works are characterised by patriotism for Emperor and Reich.

Winkler, Heinrich August (*1938): professor of modern history at the universities of Freiburg (1972-1991) and Berlin (since 1991).

Wippermann, Wolfgang (*1945): professor of modern history at Free University Berlin since 1984.

Wolffsohn, Michael (*1947): historian at the University of the Saarland, 1975-1980; professor of modern history at the army University Munich since 1981.

Wolle, Stefan (*1950): relegated as a history student from Humboldt University Berlin for political reasons; historian at the Academy of Sciences of the GDR in Berlin; co-founder of the Independent Historians' Association, 1990; 1990/1991: historian at the Gauck Institute for the Stasi files; since 1991 junior lecturer *(Assistent)* at the dept. of history of the Humboldt University Berlin.

Ziekursch, Johannes (1876-1945): professor of modern history at the universities of Breslau and Cologne; left-liberal and pro-republican views; member of the DDP; kept his chair in 1933 but did not publish anything until his death in 1945.

Zitelmann, Rainer (*1957): studied history at the Technical University Darmstadt; junior lecturer *(Assistent)* at the institute for social science research of the Free University Berlin, 1987-1992; commissioning editor-in-chief of the Ullstein publishing house, 1992-1994; after 1994 journalist with *Die Welt*; politically active in the FDP.

Zmarzlik, Hans-Günther (*1922): professor of modern history at the University of Freiburg im Breisgau since 1961.

Zwahr, Hartmut (*1936): professor of German social and economic history at the University of Leipzig.

Select Bibliography

Newspaper archives:

NOTE: None of the many daily and weekly newspaper and magazine articles have been included in the bibliography. I am indebted to four newspaper archives for their help in locating many of the articles on which this study is based. They are:

1) Zeitungsausschnittssammlung der Bibliotheken der Stadt Dortmund, Nordrhein-Westfälisches Hauptstaatsarchiv, Düsseldorf,
2) Medienstelle, Universität Duisburg,
3) Archiv, Otto-Suhr-Institut, Freie Universität Berlin
4) Abteilung Geschichte der Publizistik, Universität Köln

Books and articles:

Alter, Peter, *Nationalism*, 2nd edn, London, 1994
Aly, Götz, *Macht, Geist, Wahn. Kontinuitäten deutschen Denkens*, Berlin, 1997
Anderson, Benedict, *Imagined Communities: Reflections on the Origin and Spread of Nationalism*, rev. edn, London, 1991
Asendorf, Manfred (ed.), *Aus der Aufklärung in die permanente Restauration. Geschichtswissenschaft in Deutschland*, Hamburg, 1974
_____ , 'Was weiter wirkt. Die "Ranke-Gesellschaft – Vereinigung für Geschichte im öffentlichen Leben', *1999*, vol. 4, 1989, pp. 29-61

Bahners, Patrick, 'Persönliches Regiment', *Merkur*, vol. 48, 1994, pp. 1,007-13
_____ , 'Wissenschaft als Beruf', *Merkur*, vol. 49, 1995, pp. 531-9
Baring, Arnulf, 'Patriotische Fragezeichen', *Der Monat*, vol. 14, 1962, pp. 7-13
_____ , *Unser neuer Größenwahn*, Berlin, 1988
_____ , *Deutschland, was nun?*, Berlin, 1991
_____ (ed.), *Germany's New Position in Europe. Problems and Perspectives*, Oxford, 1994
Becker, Josef (ed.), *Wiedervereinigung in Mitteleuropa. Außen- und Innenansichten zur staatlichen Einheit Deutschlands*, Munich, 1992

Becker, Ulrich, *Zwischen Angst und Aufbruch: das Lebensgefühl der Deutschen in Ost und West nach der Wiedervereinigung*, Düsseldorf, 1992

Beier, Rosmarie, 'Deutsch-deutsche Befindlichkeiten', *GWU*, vol. 46, 1995, pp. 206-22

Below, Georg von, *Die deutsche Geschichtsschreibung von den Befreiungskriegen bis zu unsern Tagen*, 2nd rev. edn, Munich, 1924

Bender, Peter, 'Ansätze zu einer deutschen Nachkriegsgeschichte', *Merkur*, vol. 47, 1993, pp. 197-206

_____, 'Der goldene Angelhaken: Entspannungspolitik und Systemwende', *aus politik und zeitgeschichte*, 8 April 1994, pp. 11-5

_____, 'Ganz und gar am Ende. Über die Notwendigkeit der deutschen Niederlage 1945', *Merkur*, vol. 49, 1995, pp. 450-6

Bennhold, Martin, 'Mitteleuropa – eine deutsche Politiktradition. Zu Friedrich Naumanns Konzeption und ihren Folgen', *Blätter*, vol. 37, 1992, pp. 977-89

Berger, Stefan, 'Nationalism and the Left in Germany', *NLR*, no. 206, 1994, pp. 55-70

_____, 'Anticommunism after the Fall of Communism? The Anti-Left Syndrome of the SPD and its Impact on Contemporary German Politics', *Debatte*, vol. 3, 1995, pp. 66-97

_____, 'Historians and Nation-Building in Germany after Reunification', *Past and Present*, no. 148, 1995, pp. 187-222

_____, 'Challenge By Reunification: The "Historical Social Science at Era's End', *TAJB*, vol. 25, 1996, pp. 259-80

_____, 'The Rise and Fall of "Critical Historiography"? Some Reflections on the Historiographical Agenda of the Left in Britain, France and Germany at the End of the Twentieth-Century', *European Review of History*, vol. 3, no. 2, 1996, pp. 213-32

Berghahn, Volker, 'Die Fischer-Kontroverse: 15 Jahre danach', *GG*, vol. 6, 1980, pp. 403-19

_____ and Schissler, Hanna (eds), *Perceptions of History. An Analysis of School Textbooks*, Oxford, 1987

Biefang, Andreas, 'Der Streit um Treitschkes "Deutsche Geschichte" 1882/3. Zur Spaltung des Nationalliberalismus und der Etablierung eines national-konservativen Geschichtsbildes', *HZ*, vol. 262, 1996, pp. 391-422

Birtsch, Günter, *Die Nation als sittliche Idee. Der Nationalstaatsbegriff in Geschichtsschreibung und politischer Gedankenwelt Johann Gustav Droysens*, Cologne, 1964

Blanke, Horst Walter, *Historiographiegeschichte als Historik*, Stuttgart, 1991

Blänsdorf, Agnes, 'Die deutsche Geschichte in der Sicht der DDR. Ein Vergleich mit der Entwicklung in der Bundesrepublik Deutschland und in Österreich seit 1945', *GWU*, vol. 39, 1988, pp. 263-90

Bleiber, Helmut, 'Neun Anmerkungen zum Problem des Nationalen', *BZG*, vol. 38, 1996, pp. 48-67

Bohrer, Karl-Heinz, 'Provinzialismus', *Merkur*, vol. 44, 1990, pp. 1,096-1,102, vol. 45, 1991, pp. 255-66, 348-56, 719-27, vol. 46, 1992, pp. 88-90

Borries, Bodo von, *Geschichtsbewußtsein als Identitätsgewinn? Fachdidaktische Programmatik und Tatsachenforschung*, Hagen, 1990

Brandt, Peter, 'German Identity', *Debatte*, vol. 1, 1993, pp. 30-41
Breuilly, John (ed.), *The State of Germany. The National Idea in the Making, Unmaking and Remaking of a Modern Nation State*, London, 1992
———, *Nationalism and the State*, 2nd rev. edn, Manchester, 1993
Brinks, Jan Herman, *Die DDR-Geschichtswissenschaft auf dem Weg zur deutschen Einheit. Luther, Friedrich II. und Bismarck als Paradigmen politischen Wandels*, Frankfurt-on-Main, 1992
Brubaker, Roger, *Citizenship and Nationhood in France and Germany*, New York, 1992
Burleigh, Michael, *Germany Turns Eastwards. A Study of 'Ostforschung' in the Third Reich*, Cambridge, 1989
Büsch, Otto and Sheehan, James (eds), *Die Rolle der Nation in der deutschen Geschichte und Gegenwart*, Berlin, 1985

Chickering, Roger, *Karl Lamprecht. A German Academic Life (1856-1915)*, Atlantic Highlands, N.Y., 1993
Conze, Werner, *Deutsche Einheit – Erbe und Aufgabe*, Munich, 1956
———, 'Deutsche Geschichtswissenschaft nach 1945. Bedingungen und Ergebnisse', *HZ*, vol. 225, 1977, pp. 1-28
———, *The Shaping of the German Nation. A Historical Analysis*, London, 1979

Dahlmann, Friedrich Christoph, *Kleinere Schriften und Reden*, Stuttgart, 1886
Dahrendorf, Ralf, 'Die Sache mit der Nation', *Merkur*, vol. 44, 1990, pp. 823-34
———, 'Die Zukunft des Nationalstaats', *Merkur*, vol. 48, 1994, pp. 751-61
Dann, Otto, *Nation und Nationalstaat in Deutschland 1770-1990*, Munich, 1993
——— (ed.), *Die deutsche Nation. Geschichte – Probleme – Perspektiven*, Greifswald, 1994
Danyel, Jürgen, 'Wandlitz auf dem Ettersberg? Zur Debatte um die roten Kapos von Buchenwald', *ZfG*, vol. 43, 1995, pp. 159-66
——— (ed.), *Die geteilte Vergangenheit. Zum Umgang mit Nationalsozialismus und Widerstand in beiden deutschen Staaten*, Berlin, 1995
———, 'Die Historiker und die Moral. Anmerkungen zur Debatte über die Autorenrechte an der DDR-Geschichte', *GG*, vol. 21, 1995, pp. 290-303
Dehio, Ludwig, *Gleichgewicht oder Hegemonie. Betrachtungen über ein Grundproblem der neueren Staatengeschichte*, Krefeld, 1948
———, *Deutschland und die Weltpolitik im 20. Jahrhundert*, Munich, 1955
Deletant, Dennis and Hanak, Harry (eds), *Historians as Nation-Builders: Central and South-East Europe*, London, 1988
Diner, Dan, 'Deutschland im Epochenwechsel', *Blätter*, vol. 38, 1993, pp. 1,111-18
———, 'Gedächtnis und Institution', *Merkur*, vol. 48, 1994, pp. 943-6
Diwald, Hellmut (ed.), *Handbuch zur deutschen Nation*, vol. 4: *Deutschlands Einigung und Europas Zukunft*, Tübingen, 1992
Donat, Helmuth and Wieland, Lothar (eds), *Auschwitz erst möglich gemacht? Überlegungen zur jüngsten konservativen Geschichtsbewältigung*, Bremen, 1991

Dotterweich, Volker, *Heinrich von Sybel. Geschichtswissenschaft in politischer Absicht (1817-1861)*, Göttingen, 1978

Dudek, Peter, '"Vergangenheitsbewältigung". Zur Problematik eines umstrittenen Begriffs', *aus politik und zeitgeschichte*, 3 Jan. 1992, pp. 44-52

Ebbinghaus, Angelika and Roth, Karl Heinz, 'Deutsche Historiker und der Holocaust', *1999*, vol. 6, 1991, pp. 7-10

Eckert, Rainer, 'Geschichtswissenschaft in der ehemaligen DDR: eine ostdeutsche Sicht', *Deutschland-Archiv*, vol. 25, 1992, pp. 175-80

——, 'Vergangenheitsbewältigung oder überwältigt uns die Vergangenheit? oder: Auf einem Sumpf ist schlecht bauen', *IWK*, vol. 28, 1992, pp. 228-32

——, Küttler, Wolfgang, Seeber, Gustav (eds), *Krise – Umbruch – Neubeginn. Eine kritische und selbstkritische Dokumentation der DDR-Geschichtswissenschaft 1989/90*, Stuttgart, 1992

——, 'Ein gescheiterter Neuanfang?', *GG*, vol. 20, 1994, pp. 609-15

——, Kowalczuk, Ilko-Sascha, Stark, Isolde (eds), *Hure oder Muse? Klio in der DDR. Dokumente und Materialien des Unabhängigen Historiker-Verbandes*, Berlin, 1994

——, 'Die Geschichtswissenschaft der DDR im Deutschland-Archiv', *Deutschland-Archiv*, vol. 28, 1995, pp. 948-63

Ehlers, Joachim (ed.), *Ansätze und Diskontinuität deutscher Nationsbildung im Mittelalter*, Sigmaringen, 1989

Erdmann, Karl Dietrich, 'Die falsche Alternative', *GWU*, vol. 23, 1972, pp. 357-60

——, 'Drei Staaten – zwei Nationen – ein Volk? Überlegungen zu einer deutschen Geschichte seit der Teilung', *GWU*, vol. 36, 1985, pp 671-83

——, 'Vierzig Jahre Bundesrepublik – geteilte Nation im geteilten Europa', *GWU*, vol. 41, 1990, pp. 257-71

——, 'Die Revolution Mitteleuropas – historische Perspektiven', *GWU*, vol. 41, 1991, pp. 523-45

Esch, Arnold and Petersen, Jens (eds), *Geschichte und Geschichtswissenschaft in der Kultur Italiens und Deutschlands*, Tübingen, 1989

Evans, Richard J., *In Hitler's Shadow. West German Historians and the Attempt to Escape from the Nazi Past*, London, 1989

Faulenbach, Bernd (ed.), *Geschichtswissenschaft in Deutschland*, Munich, 1974

——, *Ideologie des deutschen Weges. Die deutsche Geschichte in der Historiographie zwischen Kaiserreich und Nationalsozialismus*, Munich, 1980

——, 'Eine Variante europäischer Normalität? Zur neuesten Diskussion über den "deutschen Weg" im 19. und 20. Jahrhundert', *TAJB*, vol. 16, 1987, pp. 285-309

——, 'Zur Bedeutung der Umwälzungen in Mittel- und Osteuropa für das Geschichtsverständnis der deutschen Arbeiterbewegung', *BZG*, vol. 34, 1992, pp. 35-42

——, 'Eine neue Sicht der Geschichte? Zur Diskussion über die deutschen Vergangenheiten', *Blätter*, vol. 37, 1992, pp. 809-17

—— and Stadelmaier, Martin (eds), *Diktatur und Emanzipation. Zur russischen und deutschen Entwicklung 1917-1991*, Essen, 1993

_____ , 'Auf dem Weg zu einer gemeinsamen Erinnerung? Das Bild vom deutschen Widerstand gegen den Nationalsozialismus nach den Erfahrungen von Teilung und Umbruch', *ZfG*, vol. 42, 1994, pp. 589-97

_____ , Meckel, Markus and Weber, Hermann (eds), *Die Partei hatte immer recht. Aufarbeitung von Geschichte und Folgen der SED-Diktatur*, Essen, 1994

Feldner, Heiko, 'Politischer Umbruch und Geschichtswissenschaft in Deutschland. Gedanken zur Debatte', *GG*, vol. 22, 1996, pp. 90-6

Fest, Joachim, *Die schwierige Freiheit. Über die offene Flanke der offenen Gesellschaft*, Berlin, 1994

Fichter, Tilman, *Die SPD und die Nation*, Frankfurt-on-Main, 1993

Filbinger, Hans, and Karst, Heinz (eds), *Identität und Zukunft der Deutschen. Klaus Hornung zum 65. Geburtstag*, Frankfurt-on-Main, 1992

Fischer, Alexander and Heydemann, Günther (eds), *Geschichtswissenschaft in der DDR*, vol. 1: *Historische Entwicklung, Theoriediskussion und Geschichtsdidaktik*, Berlin, 1988, vol. 2: *Vor- und Frühgeschichte bis neueste Geschichte*, Berlin, 1990

Fischer, Fritz, *Griff nach der Weltmacht: Die Kriegszielpolitik des Kaiserlichen Deutschland 1914-1918*, Düsseldorf, 1961

_____ , *Krieg der Illusionen: Die deutsche Politik von 1911 bis 1914*, Düsseldorf, 1969

_____ , *Hitler war kein Betriebsunfall*, Munich, 1992

Fletcher, Roger, 'Recent Developments in West German Historiography: The Bielefeld School and its Critics', *German Studies Review*, vol. 7, 1984, pp. 451-80

Forster, Karl (ed.), *Gibt es ein deutsches Geschichtsbild?*, Würzburg, 1961

Francois, Etienne, Siegrist, Hannes, Vogel, Jakob (eds), *Nation und Emotion. Deutschland und Frankreich im Vergleich, 19. und 20. Jahrhundert*, Göttingen, 1995

Frank, Walter, 'Zunft und Nation', *HZ*, vol. 153, 1936, pp. 6-23

Frei, Norbert, 'Wie modern war der Nationalsozialismus?', *GG*, vol. 19, 1993, pp. 367-87

_____ , *Vergangenheitspolitik. Die Anfänge der Bundesrepublik und die NS-Vergangenheit*, Munich, 1996

Fulbrook, Mary, *Anatomy of a Dictatorship: Inside the GDR, 1949-1989*, Oxford, 1995

_____ , *The Presence of the Past: National Identity and German History. An Inaugural Lecture Delivered at University College London, 7 May 1996*, London, 1996

Funke, Hajo, *'Jetzt sind wir dran'. Nationalismus im geeinten Deutschland. Aspekte der Einigungspolitik und nationalistische Potentiale in Deutschland*, Berlin, 1991

Füssmann, Klaus, et al. (ed.), *Geschichtskultur heute*, Cologne, 1994

Gall, Lothar, *Confronting Clio: Myth-Makers and Other Historians*, London, 1992

_____ , 'Interview', *ZfG*, vol. 42, 1994, pp. 1,059-65

Geiss, Imanuel, *Studien über Geschichte und Geschichtswissenschaft*, Frankfurt-on-Main, 1972

_____ , 'Die westdeutsche Geschichtsschreibung seit 1945', *TAJB*, vol. 3, 1974

_____ , 'Zwischen Auschwitz und Weimar. Nationale Identität als deutsche Frage', *Evangelische Kommentare*, vol. 12, 1984, pp. 673-6

_____ , *Die Habermas-Kontroverse. Ein deutscher Streit*, Berlin, 1988

_____ , 'Europäische Perspektiven nach der deutschen Einigung', *aus politik und zeitgeschichte*, 21 Dec. 1990, pp. 41-7

_____ , '"Wende" und Ende im "Historikerstreit"', *Historische Mitteilungen*, vol. 4, 1991, pp. 101-42

_____ , 'Geographie und Mitte als historische Kategorien', *ZfG*, vol. 39, 1991, pp. 979-94

_____ , *Der Hysterikerstreit: ein unpolemischer Essay*, Bonn, 1992

_____ , *Die deutsche Frage 1806-1990*, Munich, 1992

Gellner, Ernest, *Nationalism*, Oxford, 1983

_____ , *Encounters with Nationalism*, Oxford, 1994

'German History and German Nationalism. Seven historians give their views', *Debatte*, vol. 1, 1993, pp. 5-29

Geschichtswerkstatt Berlin (ed.), *Die Nation als Ausstellungsstück*, Berlin, 1987

Geyer, Michael, 'Historical Fictions of Autonomy and the Europeanization of National History', *CEH*, vol. 22, 1989, pp. 316-42

_____ and Jarausch, Konrad, 'The Future of the German Past. Transatlantic Reflections for the 1990s', *CEH*, vol. 22, 1989, pp. 229-59

_____ , 'Why Cultural History? What Future? Which Germany?', *New German Critique*, 1995

Giesen, Bernhard, *Die Intellektuellen und die Nation. Eine deutsche Achsenzeit*, Frankfurt-on-Main, 1993

Gillingham, John, 'Elective Kingship and the Unity of Medieval Germany', *German History*, vol. 9, 1991, pp. 124-35

Glaser, Hermann, 'Von einigen meiner deutschen Augenblicke', *aus politik und zeitgeschichte*, 10 June 1994

Glotz, Peter, *Der Irrweg des Nationalstaats*, Stuttgart, 1990

_____ , *Die deutsche Rechte. Eine Streitschrift*, Munich, 1992

_____ , *Die falsche Normalisierung. Essays*, Frankfurt-on-Main, 1994

Goetz, Walter, *Historiker meiner Zeit*, Cologne, 1957

Goldendach, Walter von and Minow, Hans-Rüdiger, *'Deutschtum erwache!' Aus dem Innenleben des staatlichen Pangermanismus*, Bonn, 1995

Grebing, Helga, *Der 'deutsche Sonderweg' in Europa 1806-1945. Eine Kritik*, Stuttgart, 1986

Greenfield, Liah, *Nationalism. Five Roads to Modernity*, Boston/Mass., 1993

Greiffenhagen, Martin and Sylvia, *Ein schwieriges Vaterland. Zur politischen Kultur im vereinigten Deutschland*, Munich, 1993

Groh, Dieter, *Geschichtswissenschaft in emanzipatorischer Absicht*, Stuttgart, 1973

Grunenberg, Antonia (ed.), *Welche Geschichte wählen wir?*, Hamburg, 1992

Gruner, Wolf D., *Die deutsche Frage. Ein Problem der europäischen Frage seit 1800*, Munich, 1985

_____ , *Deutschland mitten in Europa. Aspekte und Perspektiven der deutschen Frage in Geschichte und Gegenwart*, Hamburg, 1992

_____ , *Die deutsche Frage in Europa 1800 – 1990*, Munich, 1993

Habermas, Jürgen (ed.), *Stichworte zur geistigen Situation der Zeit*, 2 vols, Frankfurt-on-Main, 1979
_____ , *Eine Art Schadensabwicklung*, Frankfurt-on-Main, 1987
_____ , *Die nachholende Revolution*. *Kleine politische Schriften* vii, Frankfurt-on-Main, 1990
_____ , *Staatsbürgerschaft und nationale Identität*, St. Gallen, 1991
Hacke, Christian, *Weltmacht wider Willen, Die Außenpolitik der Bundesrepublik Deutschland*, 2nd rev. edn, Frankfurt-on-Main, 1993
Hacker, Jens, *Deutsche Irrtümer: Schönfärber und Helfershelfer der SED Diktatur im Westen*, Frankfurt-on-Main, 1992
Haffner, Sebastian, 'Die Deutschen und ihre Nation', *Politik und Kultur*, vol. 10, 1983, pp. 60-7
Hahn, Roland, 'Die Idee der Nation und die Lösung der deutschen Frage', *aus politik und zeitgeschichte*, 13 July 1990, pp. 3-12
Haller, Johannes, *Epochen der deutschen Geschichte*, Berlin, 1923
Hammerstein, Notger (ed.), *Deutsche Geschichtswissenschaft um 1900*, Stuttgart, 1988
Hardtwig, Wolfgang (ed.), *Über das Studium der Geschichte*, Munich, 1990
_____ , *Geschichtskultur und Wissenschaft*, Munich, 1990
_____ , *Nationalismus und Bürgerkultur in Deutschland 1500-1914*, Göttingen, 1994
Hättich, Manfred, *Deutschland – eine zu späte Nation*, Mainz, 1990
Heer, Hannes and Naumann, Klaus (eds), *Vernichtungskrieg. Verbrechen der Wehrmacht 1941-44*, Hamburg, 1995
Heimpel, Hermann, *Der Mensch in seiner Gegenwart*, Göttingen, 1954
_____ , *Kapitulation vor der Geschichte*, Göttingen, 1956
_____ , 'Über Organisationsformen historischer Forschung in Deutschland', *HZ*, vol. 189, 1959, pp. 139-222
Heinemann, Ulrich, 'Arbeit am Mythos. Neuere Literatur zum bürgerlich-aristokratischen Widerstand gegen Hitler und zum 20. Juli 1944 (Teil 1)', *GG*, vol. 21, 1995, pp. 111-39
Heinrich, Arthur, and Neumann, Klaus (eds), *Alles Banane – Ausblicke auf das endgültige Deutschland*, Cologne, 1990
Helbok, Adolf, *Was ist deutsche Volksgeschichte? Ziele, Aufgaben, Wege*, Berlin, 1935
Hellfeld, Mathias von, *Die Nation erwacht. Zur Trendwende der deutschen politischen Kultur*, Cologne, 1993
Henke, Klaus-Dietmar and Natoli, Claudio (eds), *Mit dem Pathos der Nüchternheit: Martin Broszat, das Institut für Zeitgeschichte und die Erforschung des Nationalsozialismus*, Frankfurt-on-Main, 1991
Hennigsen, Manfred, 'Der deutsche Sonderweg – am Ende?' *Merkur*, vol. 49, 1995, pp. 379-89
Henrich, Dieter, *Nach dem Ende der Teilung: Über Identitäten und Intellektualität in Deutschland*, Frankfurt-on-Main, 1993
Herbert, Ulrich and Groehler, Olaf, *Zweierlei Bewältigung. Vier Beiträge über den Umgang mit NS-Vergangenheit in den beiden deutschen Staaten*, Hamburg, 1992
Hettling, Manfred, Huerkamp, Claudia, Nolte, Paul and Schmuhl, H.W. (eds), *Was ist Gesellschaftsgeschichte? Positionen, Themen, Analysen*, Munich, 1991

_____ , Nolte, Paul (eds), *Nation und Gesellschaft in Deutschland. Historische Essays*, Munich, 1996

Hildebrand, Klaus, 'Geschichte oder "Gesellschaftsgeschichte"? Die Notwendigkeit einer politschen Geschichtsschreibung von den internationalen Beziehungen', *HZ*, vol. 223, 1976, pp. 328-57

_____ (ed.), *Wem gehört die deutsche Geschichte? Deutschlands Weg vom Alten Europa in die europäische Moderne*, Cologne, 1987

_____ , *Das vergangene Reich. Deutsche Außenpolitik von Bismarck bis Hitler*, Stuttgart, 1995

Hillgruber, Andreas, 'Politische Geschichte in moderner Sicht', *HZ*, vol. 216, 1973, pp. 529-52

_____ , 'Deutsches Nationalbewußtsein heute – in zeitgeschichtlicher Perspektive', *Geschichte, Politik und ihre Didaktik*, vol. 4, 1976, pp. 55-65

Hobsbawm, Eric and Ranger, Terence (eds), *The Invention of Tradition*, Cambridge, 1983

Hobsbawm, Eric, *Nations and Nationalism Since 1780. Programme, Myth, Reality*, 2nd edn, Cambridge, 1992

Hockerts, Hans Günther, 'Zeitgeschichte in Deutschland. Begriff, Methoden, Themenfelder', *aus politik und zeitgeschichte*, 16 July 1993, pp. 3-19

Hoffmann, Christa, *Stunden Null? Vergangenheitsbewältigung in Deutschland 1945 und 1989*, Bonn, 1992

Hoffmann, Christhard, 'Der Berliner Antisemitismusstreit 1879/80', *GWU*, vol. 46, 1995, pp. 167-78

Hübinger, Gangolf, *Georg Gottfried Gervinus. Historisches Urteil und politische Kritik*, Göttingen, 1984

Hughes, Michael, *Nationalism and Society: Germany 1800-1945*, London, 1988

Hutchinson, John, *Modern Nationalism*, London, 1994

_____ and Smith, A.D. (eds), *Nationalism*, Oxford, 1994

Iggers, Georg G., *Neue Geschichtswissenschaft. Vom Historismus zur Historischen Sozialwissenschaft*, Munich, 1978

_____ , *The German Conception of History. The National Tradition of Historical Thought from Herder to the Present*, 2nd rev. edn, Middletown/Ct., 1983

_____ (ed.), *The Social History of Politics: Critical Perspectives in West German Historical Writing Since 1945*, Leamington Spa, 1985

_____ , 'Social History, the Social Sciences and Political Culture, 1890-1914. An International Perspective', *TAJB*, vol. 16, 1987, pp. 117-34

_____ , 'New Directions in Historical Studies in the German Democratic Republic', *History and Theory*, vol. 28, 1989, pp. 59-77

_____ , 'Geschichtswissenschaft und autoritärer Staat', *Initial. Berliner Debatte*, vol. 2, 1991, pp. 125-31

_____ , *Geschichtswissenschaft im 20. Jahrhundert*, Göttingen, 1993

_____ , 'Die Bedeutung des Marxismus für die Geschichtswissenschaft heute. Fritz Klein zum 70. Geburtstag', *ZfG*, vol. 43, 1995, pp. 485-94

Jäckel, Eberhard, *Umgang mit Vergangenheit*, Stuttgart, 1989

_____ , *Die zweifache Vergangenheit. Zum Vergleich politischer Systeme*, Bonn, 1992

Jacobmeyer, Wolfgang (ed.), *Deutschlandbild und deutsche Frage in den historischen, geographischen und sozialwissenschaftlichen Unterrichtswerken der Bundesrepublik Deutschland und der Deutschen Demokratischen Republik von 1949 bis in die achtziger Jahre*, Brunswick, 1986

Jaeger, Friedrich and Rüsen, Jörn, *Geschichte des Historismus. Eine Einführung*, Munich, 1992

Jäger, Wolfgang, *Historische Forschung und politische Kultur in Deutschland. Die Debatte 1914-1980 über den Ausbruch des ersten Weltkrieges*, Göttingen, 1984

James, Harold, *A German Identity 1770-1990*, rev. edn, London, 1990

_____, 'Germans and their Nation', *German History*, vol. 9, 1991, pp. 136-52

_____, *Vom Historikerstreit zum Historikerschweigen*, Berlin, 1993

Jarausch, Konrad (ed.), *Zwischen Parteilichkeit und Provinzialität. Bilanz der Geschichtswissenschaft der DDR*, Berlin, 1991

_____, Rüsen, Jörn and Schleier, Hans (eds), *Geschichtswissenschaft vor 2000. Perspektiven der Historiographiegeschichte, Geschichtstheorie, Sozial- und Kulturgeschichte. Festschrift für Georg G. Iggers*, Hagen, 1991

_____ and Gransow, Volker (eds), *Uniting Germany. Documents and Debates 1944-1993*, Oxford, 1994

_____ and Middell, Mathias (eds), *Nach dem Erdbeben. (Re-)konstruktionen ostdeutscher Geschichte und Geschichtswissenschaft*, Leipzig, 1994

_____, *Die unverhoffte Einheit 1989/90*, Frankfurt-on-Main, 1995

_____, 'Normalisierung oder Re-Nationalisierung? Zur Umdeutung der deutschen Vergangenheit', *GG*, vol. 21, 1995, pp. 571-84

Jaspers, Karl, *Hoffnung und Sorge. Schriften zur deutschen Politik, 1945-65*, Munich, 1965

Jeismann, Karl-Ernst (eds), *Geschichte als Legitimation? Internationale Schulbuchrevision unter den Ansprüchen von Politik, Geschichtswissenschaft und Geschichtsbedürfnis*, Brunswick, 1984

_____, '"Identität" statt "Emanzipation"? Zum Geschichtsbewußtsein in der Bundesrepublik', *aus politik und zeitgeschichte*, 1986, pp. 3-16

_____ (ed.), *Einheit – Freiheit – Selbstbestimmung. Die Deutsche Frage im historisch-politischen Bewußtsein*, Bonn, 1987

Jeismann, Michael and Ritter, Henning (eds), *Grenzfälle. Über alten und neuen Nationalismus*, Leipzig, 1993

Jerzykiewicz-Jagemann, F.E.O., 'Geschichtsbilder. Anmerkungen zur Ranke-Gesellschaft', *Historische Mitteilungen*, vol. 5, 1992, pp. 130-49

Jesse, Eckhard, '"Vergangenheitsbewältigung" und politische Kultur', *Politische Bildung*, vol. 23, 1990, pp. 53-66

_____, 'Der Totalitarismus-Ansatz nach dem Zusammenbruch des realexistierenden Sozialismus', *Die neue Gesellschaft/Frankfurter Hefte*, vol. 38, 1991, pp. 983-92

_____, 'War die DDR totalitär?', *aus politik und zeitgeschichte*, 7 Oct. 1994

_____ (ed.), *Totalitarismus im 20. Jahrhundert. Eine Bilanz der internationalen Forschung*, Bonn, 1996

Jessen, Ralph, 'Die Gesellschaft im Staatssozialismus. Probleme einer Sozialgeschichte der DDR', *GG*, vol. 21, 1995, pp. 96-110

Johnston, Otto W., *Der deutsche Nationalmythos. Ursprung eines politischen Programms*, Stuttgart, 1990

Joll, James, *National Histories and National Historians: Some German and English Views of the Past*, London, 1985
Judt, Tony, 'The Past is Another Country: Myth and Memory in Post-War Europe', *Daedalus*, vol. 121, 1992, pp. 83-118

Kaehler, S.A., *Studien zur deutschen Geschichte des 19. und 20. Jahrhunderts*, Göttingen, 1961
Kaelble, Hartmut, Kocka, Jürgen and Zwahr, Hartmut (eds), *Sozialgeschichte der DDR*, Stuttgart, 1994
Kaschuba, Wolfgang, 'Kulturalismus: Kultur statt Gesellschaft?', *GG*, vol. 21, 1995
Kearney, Richard, 'Postmodernity and Nationalism: a European Perspective', *Modern Fiction Studies*, vol. 38, 1992, pp. 581-93
Kedourie, Elie, *Nationalism*, 4th edn, London, 1993
Kehr, Eckart, *Der Primat der Innenpolitik*, Berlin, 1965
Kershaw, Ian, *Germany's Present, Germany's Past. The 1992 Bithell Memorial Lecture*, London, 1992
_____ , *The Nazi Dictatorship. Problems and Perspectives of Interpretation*, 3rd edn, London, 1993, pp. 197-217
_____ , 'Totalitarianism Revisited: Nazism and Stalinism in Comparative Perspective', *TAJB*, vol. 23, 1994, pp. 23-40
Kielmannsegg, Peter Graf, 'Vereinigung ohne Legitimät', *Merkur*, vol. 47, 1993
Kiesewetter, Hubert, 'Die offene Gesellschaft ohne ihre Feinde', *Historische Mitteilungen*, vol. 6, 1993, pp. 225-34
Kittel, Manfred, *Die Legende von der "Zweiten Schuld". Vergangenheitsbewältigung in der Ära Adenauer*, Frankfurt-on-Main, 1993
Klein, Fritz, 'Historiker und Politik. Erfahrungen in einem schwierigen Verhältnis', in: Christian Jansen, Lutz Niethammer and Bernd Weisbrod (eds), *Von der Aufgabe der Freiheit. Politische Verantwortung und bürgerliche Gesellschaft im 19. und 20. Jahrhundert. Festschrift für Hans Mommsen*, Berlin, 1995, pp. 51-68
Kleßmann, Christoph, 'Zwei Diktaturen in Deutschland – Was kann die künftige DDR-Forschung aus der Geschichtsschreibung zum Nationalsozialismus lernen?', *Deutschland-Archiv*, vol. 25, 1992, pp. 601-6
_____ , 'Zweierlei Vergangenheit – Über den Umgang der Deutschen mit ihrer jüngsten Geschichte nach 1945 und nach 1989', *Deutsche Studien*, vol. 116, 1992, pp. 390-6
_____ , 'Verflechtung und Abgrenzung. Aspekte der geteilten und zusammengehörigen deutschen Nachkriegsgeschichte', *aus politik und zeitgeschichte*, 16 July 1993, pp. 30-41
_____ , Sabrow, Martin, 'Zeitgeschichte in Deutschland nach 1989', *aus politik und zeitgeschichte*, 20 September 1996, pp. 3-14
Klönne, Arno, *Zurück zur Nation? Kontroversen zu deutschen Fragen*, Cologne, 1984
_____ , *Rechts-Nachfolge. Risiken des deutschen Wesens nach 1945*, Cologne, 1990
Klose, Dagmar, 'Prägungen und Wandlungen ostdeutscher Identitäten', *aus politik und zeitgeschichte*, 14 Oct. 1994, pp. 3-11

Knoblich, Axel, Peter, Antonio and Natter, Erik (eds), *Auf dem Weg zu einer gesamtdeutschen Identität?*, Cologne, 1993

Knopp, Guido (ed.), *Die deutsche Einheit – Hoffnung, Alptraum, Illusion?*, Aschaffenburg, 1981

_____ and Kuhn, Ekkehard, *Die deutsche Einheit. Traum und Wirklichkeit*, Erlangen, 1990

Knütter, Hans-Helmuth, 'Vergangenheitsbewältigung nach der Wende im Herbst 1989', *Deutsche Ostkunde*, vol. 36, 1990, pp. 122-36

_____ , *Deutschfeindlichkeit gestern, heute und morgen ...?*, Asendorf, 1991

_____ , *Wanderungsbewegungen – ein Faktum. Multikulturelle Gesellschaft – eine Fiktion*, St. Augustin, 1993

_____ , *Die Faschismus Keule. Das letzte Aufgebot der Linken*, 2nd edn, Frankfurt-on-Main, 1994

Kocka, Jürgen, 'Nation und Gesellschaft. Historische Überlegungen zur "deutschen" Frage', *Politik und Kultur*, vol. 8, 1981, pp. 3-25

_____ , *Geschichte und Aufklärung*, Göttingen, 1989

_____ , 'Revolution und Nation 1989. Zur historischen Einordung der gegenwärtigen Ereignisse', *TAJB*, vol. 19, 1990, pp. 479-99

_____ , *Die Auswirkungen der deutschen Einigung auf die Geschichts- und Sozialwissenschaften*, Bonn, 1992

_____ , 'La Reunification et la Recherche Historique Allemande', *Vingtième Siècle*, vol. 34, 1992, pp. 32-6

_____ (ed.), *Historische DDR-Forschung. Aufsätze und Studien*, Berlin, 1993

_____ , 'Sozialgeschichte der neunziger Jahre', *Die neue Gesellschaft/ Frankfurter Hefte*, vol. 40, Dec. 1993, pp. 1,125-9

––- , 'Crisis of Unification: How Germany Changes', *Daedalus*, vol. 123, 1994, pp. 173-92

_____ , 'Ein deutscher Sonderweg. Überlegungen zur Sozialgeschichte der DDR', *aus politik und zeitgeschichte*, 7 Oct. 1994, pp. 34-45

_____ and Sabrow, Martin (eds), *Die DDR als Geschichte. Fragen – Hypothesen – Perspektiven*, Berlin, 1994

_____ , Puhle, Hans-Jürgen and Tenfelde, Klaus (eds), *Von der Arbeiterbewegung zum modernen Sozialstaat. Festschrift für G.A. Ritter*, Munich, 1994

_____ , *Vereinigungskrise. Zur Geschichte der Gegenwart*, Göttingen, 1995

Kogel, J., Schütte, W. and Zimmermann, H. (eds), *Neues Deutschland. Innenansichten einer wiedervereinigten Nation*, Frankfurt-on-Main, 1993

Korte, Karl Rudolf, *Die Chance genutzt? Die Politik zur Einheit Deutschlands*, Frankfurt-on-Main, 1994

Koselleck, Reinhart, 'Wozu noch Historie?', *HZ*, vol. 212, 1970, pp. 1-18

Kossock, Manfred, 'Im Gehäuse selbstverschuldeter Unmündigkeit oder Umgang mit Geschichte', *BZG*, vol. 35, 1993, pp. 24-36

Kowalczuk, Ilko-Sascha, '"Wo gehobelt wird, da fallen Späne." Zur Entwicklung der DDR-Geschichtswissenschaft bis in die späten fünfziger Jahre', *ZfG*, vol. 42, 1994, pp. 302-18

Krill, Hans-Heinrich, *Die Ranke-Renaissance. Max Lenz und Erich Marcks. Ein Beitrag zum historisch-politischen Denken in Deutschland 1880-1935*, Berlin, 1962

Krockow, Christian von, 'Nationalbewußtsein und Gesellschaftsbewußtsein', *Politische Vierteljahresschrift*, vol. 1, 1960, pp. 141-52
_____ , *Von deutschen Mythen. Rückblick und Ausblick*, Stuttgart, 1995
Krüger, Peter (ed.), *Deutschland, deutscher Staat, deutsche Nation. Historische Erkundungen eines Spannungsverhältnisses*, Marburg, 1993
Kühnl, Reinhard, 'Anmerkungen zur politischen Funktion der deutschen Geschichtswissenschaft seit der Reichsgründung', *Das Argument*, no. 70, 1972, pp. 5-21
_____ , 'Gesellschaft im Umbruch. Versuch, einen Überblick zu gewinnen', *Blätter*, vol. 39, 1994, pp. 747-54
Kuss, Horst, 'Geschichtsdidaktik und Geschichtsunterricht in der Bundesrepublik Deutschland (1945/49-1990)', *GWU*, vol. 45, 1994, pp. 735-58 and vol. 46, 1995, pp. 3-15
Küttler, Wolfgang, 'Nach dem Umbruch: Historischer Systemvergleich und marxistische Ansätze heute', *GG*, vol. 19, 1993, pp. 54-68
_____ , Rüsen, Jörn and Schulin, Ernst (eds), *Geschichtsdiskurs*, vol. 1: *Grundlagen und Methoden der Historiographiegeschichte*, Frankfurt-on-Main, 1993

Lambert, Peter, 'German Historians and Nazi Ideology. The Parameters of the Volksgemeinschaft and the Problem of Historical Legitimation, 1930-45', *EHQ*, vol. 25, 1995, pp. 555-82
Langewiesche, Dieter, *Nationalismus im 19. und 20. Jahrhundert zwischen Partizipation und Aggression*, Bonn, 1994
Lehmann, Hartmut and Melton, James van Horn (eds), *Paths of Continuity: Central European Historiography from the 1930s to the 1950s*, Cambridge, 1994
Lenz, Max, *Die großen Mächte. Ein Rückblick auf unser Jahrhundert*, Berlin, 1900
_____ , *Wille, Macht und Schicksal*, Munich, 1922
Liebert, Ulrike and Merkel, Wolfgang (eds), *Die Politik zur deutschen Einheit. Probleme – Strategien – Kontroversen*, Opladen, 1991
Lipp, Carola, 'Writing History as Political Culture. Social History versus "Alltagsgeschichte". A German Debate', *Storia della Storiografia*, vol. 17, 1990, pp. 66-100
Lippstadt, Deborah, Denying the Holocaust. *The Growing Assault on Truth and Memory*, London, 1993
Lohmann, Hans-Martin, *Extremismus der Mitte*, Frankfurt-on-Main, 1994
Loth, Wilfried, *Ost-West Konflikt und deutsche Frage – Historische Ortsbestimmungen*, Munich, 1989
_____ , 'Das Ende der Nachkriegsordnung', *aus politik und zeitgeschichte*, 26 April 1991, pp. 3-10
_____ , 'Epochenjahr 1945: Zäsuren und Optionen', *Blätter*, vol. 40, 1995, pp. 31-6
Löw, Konrad, ... *bis zum Verrat der Freiheit. Die Gesellschaft der Bundesrepublik und die 'DDR'*, 2nd edn, Munich, 1994
Luden, Heinrich, *Einige Worte über das Studium der vaterländischen Geschichte*, Jena, 1810
_____ , *Geschichte des teutschen Volkes*, vol. 1, Gotha, 1825

Lüdtke, Alf (ed.), *Alltagsgeschichte. Zur Rekonstruktion historischer Erfahrungen und Lebensweisen*, Frankfurt-on-Main, 1989

Machtan, Lothar (ed.), *Bismarck und der deutsche National-Mythos*, Bremen, 1994

Maier, Charles, *The Unmasterable Past. History, Holocaust and German National Identity*, Cambridge/Mass., 1988

_____, 'Geschichtswissenschaft und "Ansteckungsstaat"', *GG*, vol. 20, 1994, pp. 616-24

Maser, Werner, *Der Wortbruch. Hitler, Stalin und der Zweite Weltkrieg*, Munich, 1994

Matthiesen, Michael, *Gerhard Ritter. Studien zu Leben und Werk bis 1933*, 2 vols, Cologne, 1993

Mayer, Tilman, *Prinzip Nation: Dimensionen der nationalen Frage, dargestellt am Beispiel Deutschlands*, Opladen, 1986

_____, 'Die nationalstaatliche Herausforderung in Europa', *aus politik und zeitgeschichte*, 2 April 1993, pp. 11-20

Meier, Christian, *Deutsche Einheit als Herausforderung. Welche Fundamente für welche Republik?*, Munich, 1990

_____, *Die Nation, die keine sein will*, Munich, 1991

_____, 'Am Ende der alten Bundesrepublik', *Merkur*, vol. 48, 1994, pp. 561-72

_____, 'Deutschland zwischen der Bonner und der Berliner Demokratie', *ZfP*, vol. 41, 1994, pp. 261-79

Meier, H. and Schmidt, W. (eds), *Erbe und Tradition in der DDR. Die Debatte der Historiker*, Berlin, 1988

Meinecke, Friedrich, *Die deutsche Katastrophe. Betrachtungen und Erinnerungen*, 6th edn, Wiesbaden, 1965

Meineke, Stefan, *Ein Liberaler in postliberaler Zeit. Persönlichkeit und politisches Denken Friedrich Meineckes bis zum Ende des Ersten Weltkrieges*, Berlin, 1995

Messerschmidt, Manfred, *Deutschland in englischer Sicht. Die Wandlungen des Deutschlandbildes in der englischen Geschichtsschreibung*, Düsseldorf, 1955

Meuschel, Sigrid, 'Überlegungen zu einer Herrschafts- und Gesellschaftsgeschichte der DDR', *GG*, vol. 19, 1993, pp. 5-14

Mohler, Armin, *Der Nasenring: die Vergangenheitsbewältigung vor und nach dem Fall der Mauer*, Munich, 1991

Mommsen, Hans, 'Historical Scholarship in Transition: The Situation in the Federal Republic of Germany', *Daedalus*, vol. 100, 1971, pp. 485-508

_____, 'Zum Problem des deutschen Nationalbewußtseins in der Gegenwart', *Der Monat*, vol. 31, 1979, pp. 75-83

_____, 'Noch einmal: Nationalsozialismus und Modernisierung', *GG*, vol. 21, 1995, pp. 391-402

Mommsen, Wolfgang J., *Die Geschichtswissenschaft jenseits des Historismus*, 2nd edn, Düsseldorf, 1972

_____, 'Gegenwärtige Tendenzen in der Geschichtsschreibung der Bundesrepublik', *GG*, vol. 7, 1981, pp. 149-88

_____, *Nation und Geschichte. Über die Deutschen und die deutsche Frage*, Munich, 1990

————, *Der autoritäre Nationalstaat. Verfassung, Gesellschaft und Kultur im deutschen Kaiserreich*, Frankfurt-on-Main, 1990
————, *Das Ringen um den nationalen Staat. Die Gründung und der innere Ausbau des Deutschen Reiches unter Otto von Bismarck 1850-1890*, Berlin, 1992
———— (ed.), *Der lange Weg nach Europa. Historische Betrachtungen aus gegenwärtiger Sicht*, Berlin, 1992
————, 'Die DDR in der deutschen Geschichte', *aus politik und zeitgeschichte*, 16 July 1993, pp. 20-9
————, 'Die Geschichtswissenschaft nach der "demokratischen Revolution" in Ostmitteleuropa', *Neue Rundschau*, vol. 105, 1994, pp. 75-88
Moraw, Peter, 'Jüngste deutsche Geschichte und ältere deutsche Geschichte', *GWU*, vol. 41, 1990, pp. 389-95
Moses, John A., *The Politics of Illusion. The Fischer Controversy in German Historiography*, London, 1975
Muhlack, Ulrich, *Geschichtswissenschaft im Humanismus und in der Aufklärung. Die Vorgeschichte des Historismus*, Munich, 1991
Müller, Karl Alexander von, *Vom alten zum neuen Deutschland*, Munich, 1935
Mütter, Bernd and Quandt, Siegfried (eds), *Historie, Didaktik, Kommunikation. Wissenschaftsgeschichte und aktuelle Herausforderung*, Marburg, 1988

Naumann, Klaus, 'Geschichte als Politik', *Blätter*, vol. 36, 1991
————, '"Neuanfang ohne Tabus". Deutscher Sonderweg und politische Semantik', *Blätter*, vol. 39, 1994, pp. 435-46
Niethammer, Lutz (ed.), *Der "gesäuberte" Antifaschismus. Die SED und die roten Kapos von Buchenwald. Dokumente*, Berlin, 1994
Nipperdey, Thomas, 'Kann Geschichte objektiv sein?', *GWU*, vol. 30, 1979, pp. 329-42
————, *Nachdenken über die deutsche Geschichte. Essays*, Munich, 1986
————, *Deutsche Geschichte 1866 – 1918*, 2 vols, vol. 1: *Arbeitswelt und Bürgergeist*, vol. 2: *Machtstaat vor der Demokratie*, Munich, 1990 and 1992
————, Doering-Manteuffel, Anselm and Thamer, Hans-Ulrich (eds), *Weltbürgerkrieg der Ideologien. Antworten an Ernst Nolte*, Berlin, 1993
Nolte, Ernst, 'Zur Konzeption der Nationalgeschichte heute', *HZ*, vol. 202, 1966, pp. 603-21
————, *Lehrstück oder Tragödie? Beiträge zur Interpretation der Geschichte des 20. Jahrhunderts*, Cologne, 1991
————, *Streitpunkte: heutige und künftige Kontroversen um den Nationalsozialismus*, Frankfurt-on-Main, 1993

O'Brien, Peter, 'Identity Crisis in the New Germany', *Debatte*, vol. 2, 1994, pp. 64-81
Oberkrome, Willi, *Volksgeschichte. Methodische Innovation und völkische Ideologisierung in der deutschen Geschichtswissenschaft 1918-1945*, Göttingen, 1993
Oncken, Hermann, *Nation und Geschichte. Reden und Aufsätze*, Berlin, 1935
Overesch, Manfred, *Buchenwald und die DDR oder die Suche nach Selbstlegitimation*, Göttingen, 1995

Pampel, Bernt, 'Was bedeutet "Aufarbeitung der Vergangenheit"'? Kann man aus der "Vergangenheitsbewältigung" nach 1945 für die "Aufarbeitung" nach 1989 Lehren ziehen?', *aus politik und zeitgeschichte*, 6 Jan. 1995, pp. 27-38

Papcke, Sven, 'Nationalismus – ein Alptraum?', *aus politik und zeitgeschichte*, 21 Oct. 1994, pp. 10-7

Parker, Christopher, *The English Historical Tradition Since 1850*, Edinburgh, 1990

Pätzold, Kurt, 'Research on Fascism and Antifascism in the German Democratic Republic. A Critical Retrospective', *Radical History Review*, vol. 54, 1992, pp. 87-109

———, 'What New Start? The End of Historical Study in the GDR', *German History*, vol. 10, 1992, pp. 392-404

Pehle, Walter H. (ed.), *Der historische Ort des Nationalsozialismus*, Frankfurt-on-Main, 1990

———, and Sillem, Peter (eds), *Wissenschaft im geteilten Deutschland. Restauration und Neubeginn nach 1945*, Frankfurt-on-Main, 1992

Plessner, Helmuth, *Das Schicksal des deutschen Geistes im Ausgang seiner bürgerlichen Epoche*, Zürich, 1935

Podewils, Clemens Graf (ed.), *Tendenzwende? Zur geistigen Situation der Bundesrepublik*, Stuttgart, 1975

Prinz, Wolfgang and Weingart, Peter (eds), *Die sogenannten Geisteswissenschaften: Innenansichten*, Frankfurt-on-Main, 1990

Probst, Lothar, 'Deutsche Vergangenheiten – Deutschlands Zukunft', *Deutschland-Archiv*, vol. 27, 1994, pp. 173-80

Pulzer, Peter, 'Unified Germany: A Normal State?', *German Politics*, vol. 3, 1994, pp. 1-17

———, 'Nation State and National Sovereignty', *Bulletin of the GHIL*, vol. 17, no. 3, 1995, pp. 5-14

Rammstedt, Otthein and Schmidt, Gert (eds), *BRD ade! Vierzig Jahre in Rück-Ansichten*, Frankfurt-on-Main, 1992

Rantzau, Johann Albrecht von, 'Geschichte und Politik im deutschen Denken', *Die Sammlung*, vol. 1, 1945/46, pp. 544-54

———, 'Individualitätsprinzip, Staatsverherrlichung und deutsche Geschichtsschreibung', *Die Sammlung*, vol. 5, 1950, pp. 284-99

———, 'Das deutsche Geschichtsdenken der Gegenwart und die Nachwirkungen Rankes', *GWU*, vol. 1, 1950, pp. 514-24

Reichel, Peter, '"Vergangenheitstraum", "Fortgeschrittenheit" und Völkermord. Zur Diskussion um Modernität und Modernisierung im NS-Staat', *Historicum*, vol. 27, 1991, pp. 18-26

Repgen, Konrad, 'Methoden- und Richtungskämpfe in der deutschen Geschichtswissenschaft seit 1945', *GWU*, vol. 30, 1979, pp. 591-610

Reulecke, Jürgen, 'Von der Landesgeschichte zur Regionalgeschichte', *Geschichte im Westen*, vol. 6, 1992, pp. 202-8

Ritter, Gerhard, *Geschichte als Bildungsmacht. Ein Beitrag zur historisch-politischen Neubesinnung*, Stuttgart, 1946

———, *Europa und die deutsche Frage*, Munich, 1948

_____, 'Gegenwärtige Lage und Zukunftsaussichten deutscher Geschichtswissenschaft', *HZ*, vol. 170, 1950, pp. 1-22
_____, *Das deutsche Problem*, Munich, 1962
_____, 'Wissenschaftliche Historie einst und jetzt. Betrachtungen und Erinnerungen', *HZ*, vol. 202, 1966, pp. 574-602
Ritter, Gerhard A., *The New Social History of the Federal Republic of Germany*, London, 1991
Röhl, Klaus Rainer, *Linke Lebenslügen. Eine überfällige Abrechnung*, Frankfurt-on-Main, 1994
Rohlfes, Joachim, 'Geschichtsdidaktik in der Zwangsjacke. Kritische Gedanken zum Geschichtsunterricht im SED-Staat', *GWU*, vol. 41, 1990, pp. 705-19
Roth, Karl Heinz, 'Anschlußhistoriker – Historikeranschluß', *1999*, vol. 6, 1991, pp. 8-12
_____, 'Verklärung des Abgrunds. Zur nachträglichen "Revolutionierung" der NS-Diktatur durch die Gruppe um Rainer Zitelmann', *1999*, vol. 7, 1992, pp. 7-11
_____, 'Der historische Revisionismus in Deutschland – Zwischenbilanz und Perspektiven', *1999*, vol. 9, 1994, pp. 7-11
_____, 'Revisionist Tendencies in Historical Research into German Fascism', *IRSH*, vol. 39, 1994, pp. 429-55
Rothfels, Hans, 'Grundsätzliches zum Problem der Nationalität', *HZ*, vol. 175, 1952, pp. 339-58
_____, 'Zeitgeschichte als Aufgabe', *VfZ*, vol. 1, 1953, pp. 1-8
_____, 'Zur Krise des Nationalstaats', *VfZ*, vol. 1, 1953, pp. 138-52
Ruppert, Wolfgang (ed.), *'Deutschland, bleiche Mutter' oder eine neue Lust an der nationalen Identität?*, Berlin, 1992
Rüsen, Jörn, *Für eine erneuerte Historik. Studien zur Theorie der Geschichtswissenschaft*, Münster, 1976
_____, 'Geschichte als Aufklärung', *GG*, vol. 7, 1981, pp. 189-218

Salewski, Michael, 'Der deutsche Osten und die deutsche Geschichte', *GWU*, vol. 42, 1991, pp. 220-31
Sander, Hans-Dietrich, *Die Rückkehr des nationalen Elements in die Politik*, Göttingen, 1983
Sarkowicz, Hans, *Rechte Geschäfte. Der unaufhaltsame Aufstieg des deutschen Verlegers Herbert Fleißner*, Frankfurt-on-Main, 1994
Schäfer, Hermann, 'Begegnungen mit unserer eigenen Geschichte', *aus politik und zeitgeschichte*, 10 June 1994
Schieder, Theodor, 'Die deutsche Geschichtswissenschaft im Spiegel der HZ', *HZ*, vol. 189, 1959, pp. 1-104
_____, *Nationalismus und Nationalstaat: Studien zum nationalen Problem im modernen Europa*, 2nd edn, Göttingen, 1992
_____, *Das deutsche Kaiserreich von 1871 als Nationalstaat*, 2nd edn, Göttingen, 1992
Schildt, Axel, 'NS-Regime, Modernisierung und Moderne. Anmerkungen zur Hochkonjunktur einer andauernden Diskussion', *TAJB*, vol. 23, 1994, pp. 3-22

Schleier, Hans, *Sybel und Treitschke. Antidemokratismus und Militarismus im historisch-politischen Denken großbourgeoiser Geschichtsideologen*, Berlin, 1965
_____, *Die bürgerliche deutsche Geschichtsschreibung der Weimarer Republik*, 2 vols, Berlin, 1975
_____ (ed.), *J.G. Herder und progressive bürgerliche Geschichts- und Gesellschaftstheorien zwischen 1720 und 1850*, Berlin, 1979
Schlögel, Karl, *Die Mitte liegt ostwärts. Die Deutschen, der verlorene Osten und Mitteleuropa*, Munich, 1986
Schmidt, Gustav, *Deutscher Historismus und der Übergang zur parlamentarischen Demokratie*, Lübeck, 1964
Schnabel, Franz, 'Der Ursprung der vaterländischen Studien', *Blätter für deutsche Landesgeschichte*, vol. 88, 1951, pp. 4-27
Schneider, Michael, 'Nationalsozialismus und Modernisierung? Probleme einer Neubewertung des 'Dritten Reiches', *AfS*, vol. 32, 1992, pp. 541-5
_____, *'Volkspädagogik' von rechts. Ernst Nolte, die Bemühungen um die 'Historisierung' des Nationalsozialismus und die 'selbstbewußte Nation'*, Bonn, 1995
Schöllgen, Gregor, *Die Macht in der Mitte Europas. Stationen deutscher Außenpolitik von Friedrich dem Großen bis zur Gegenwart*, Munich, 1992
_____, 'Herausforderung. Die Prioritäten historischer Forschung in Deutschland und die neue Lage', *Neue Hefte für Philosophie*, vol. 34, 1993, pp. 66-84
_____, *Angst vor der Macht. Die Deutschen und ihre Außenpolitik*, Berlin, 1993
_____, 'Die Macht der Nation und die Hilflosigkeit deutscher Intellektueller', *Merkur*, vol. 48, 1994, pp. 932-7
Schönhoven, Klaus and Staritz, Dietrich (eds), *Sozialismus und Kommunismus im Wandel*, Cologne, 1993
Schönwälder, Karen, *Historiker und Politik. Geschichtswissenschaft im Nationalsozialismus*, Frankfurt-on-Main, 1992
Schroeder, Klaus (ed.), *Geschichte und Transformation des SED-Staates*, Berlin, 1994
Schulin, Ernst, *Traditionskritik und Rekonstruktionsversuch. Studien zur Entwicklung von Geschichtswissenschaft und historischem Denken*, Göttingen, 1979
_____ (ed.), *Deutsche Geschichtswissenschaft nach dem Zweiten Weltkrieg: (1945-1965)*, Munich, 1989
Schultz, Helga, 'Das Fiasko der historischen Gerechtigkeit – Ostdeutsche Geisteswissenschaften im Umbruch', *GG*, vol. 21, 1995, pp. 430-9
_____, 'Mythos und Aufklärung. Frühformen des Nationalismus in Deutschland', *HZ*, vol. 263, 1996, pp. 31-67
Schulze, Hagen, *Gibt es überhaupt eine deutsche Geschichte?*, Berlin, 1989
_____, 'German Unification in the Context of European History', *German Studies Review*, special issue on 'German Identity', winter 1992, pp. 7-20
_____, *Staat und Nation in der europäischen Geschichte*, Munich, 1994
_____, *Kleine deutsche Geschichte*, Munich, 1996
Schulze, Winfried, '"Das traurigste Los aber traf die Geschichtswissenschaft". Die DDR-Geschichtswissenschaft nach der deutschen Revolution', *GWU*, vol. 41, 1990, pp. 683-96
_____, *Deutsche Geschichtswissenschaft nach 1945*, Munich, 1993

_____, 'Von München über Leipzig nach Berlin? Zur Entstehung des Historikertages vor 100 Jahren', *GWU*, vol. 45, 1994, pp. 551-7

Schwarz, Hans-Peter, 'Einheit der Nation?!', *Jahrbuch der Albertus Universität zu Königsberg/Preußen*, vol. 25, 1975, pp. 41-68

_____, *Die gezähmten Deutschen. Von der Machtbesessenheit zur Machtvergessenheit*, Stuttgart, 1985

_____, 'Auf dem Weg zum post-kommunistischen Europa', *Europa Archiv*, vol. 44, 1989, pp. 319-30

_____, 'Mit gestopften Trompeten. Die Wiedervereinigung Deutschlands aus der Sicht westdeutscher Historiker', *GWU*, vol. 44, 1993, pp. 683-704

_____, *Die Zentralmacht Europas. Deutschlands Rückkehr auf die Weltbühne*, Berlin, 1994

Schwilk, Heimo and Schacht, Ulrich (eds), *Die selbstbewußte Nation: 'Anschwellender Bocksgesang' und weitere Beiträge zu einer deutschen Debatte*, Frankfurt-on-Main, 1994

Seebacher-Brandt, Brigitte, 'Nation im vereinigten Deutschland', *aus politik und zeitgeschichte*, 21 Oct. 1994, pp. 3-9

Seiffert, Wolfgang, *Das ganze Deutschland. Perspektiven der Wiedervereinigung*, Munich, 1986

Sheehan, James J., 'What is German History? Reflections on the Role of the Nation in German History and Historiography', *Journal of Modern History*, vol. 53, 1981, pp. 1-23

Sieferle, Rolf Peter, *Epochenwechsel. Die Deutschen an der Schwelle zum 21. Jahrhundert*, Frankfurt-on-Main, 1994

Simon, Christian, *Staat und Geschichtswissenschaft in Deutschland und Frankreich 1871-1914. Situation und Werk von Geschichtsprofessoren an den Universitäten Berlin, München und Paris*, 2 vols, Bern, 1988

Smith, A.D., *The Ethnic Origins of Nations*, London, 1986

_____, *National Identity*, London, 1991

Srbik, Heinrich von, *Deutsche Einheit. Idee und Wirklichkeit vom Heiligen Römischen Reich bis Königgrätz*, Vienna, 1935

_____, *Geist und Geschichte vom deutschen Humanismus bis zur Gegenwart*, 2 vols, Munich, 1950-51

Steinbach, Peter, 'Teufel Hitler – Beelzebub Stalin? Zur Kontroverse um die Darstellung des Nationalkomitees Freies Deutschland in der Gedenkstätte Deutscher Widerstand', *ZfG*, vol. 42, 1994, pp. 651-62

Steinle, Jürgen, 'Hitler als "Betriebsunfall in der Geschichte". Eine historische Metapher und ihre Hintergründe', *GWU*, vol. 45, 1994, pp. 288-302

Stern, Frank, 'Wolfsschanze versus Auschwitz. Widerstand als deutsches Alibi', *ZfG*, vol. 42, 1994, pp. 645-50

Stern, Fritz, 'German History in America 1884-1984', *CEH*, vol. 19, 1986, pp. 131-63

Sternburg, Wilhelm von (ed.), *Geteilte Ansichten über eine vereinigte Nation: ein Buch über Deutschland*, Frankfurt-on-Main, 1990

_____, *Fall und Aufstieg der deutschen Nation. Nachdenken über einen Massenrausch*, Frankfurt-on-Main, 1993

Stölzl, Christoph (ed.), *Deutsches Historisches Museum. Ideen – Kontroversen – Perspektiven*, Berlin, 1988

Streisand, Joachim (ed.), *Studien über die deutsche Geschichtswissenschaft*, 2 vols, Berlin, 1963-65

Striefler, Christian, *Kampf um die Macht. Kommunisten und Nationalsozialisten am Ende der Weimarer Republik*, Berlin, 1993

Stürmer, Michael, *Die Grenzen der Macht. Begegnung der Deutschen mit der Geschichte*, Berlin, 1990

Sühl, Klaus (ed.), *Vergangenheitsbewältigung 1945 und 1989: Ein unmöglicher Vergleich?*, Berlin, 1994

Sybel, Heinrich von, *Kleinere historische Schriften*, vol. 1, 3rd edn, Stuttgart, 1880

Thadden, Rudolf von, 'Nation muß sein – aber wozu?', *GWU*, vol. 45, 1994, pp. 341-6

Theisen, Alfred, 'Die Vertreibung der Deutschen – ein unbewältigtes Kapitel europäischer Zeitgeschichte', *aus politik und zeitgeschichte*, 10 Feb. 1995, pp. 20-33

Thimme, Anneliese, *Hans Delbrück als Kritiker der Wilhelminischen Epoche*, Düsseldorf, 1955

Timmermann, Heiner (ed.), *Geschichtsschreibung zwischen Wissenschaft und Politik. Deutschland-Frankreich-Polen im 19. und 20. Jahrhundert*, Saarbrücken, 1987

Uffelmann, Uwe (ed.), *Identitätsbildung und Geschichtsbewußtsein nach der Vereinigung Deutschlands*, Weinheim, 1993

——— , 'Identitätsbildung und Geschichtsdidaktik', *aus politik und zeitgeschichte*, 14 Oct. 1994, pp. 12-20

——— (ed.), *Historisches Lernen im vereinten Deutschland. Nation – Europa – Welt*, Marburg, 1995

Unseld, Siegfried (ed.), *Politik ohne Projekt? Nachdenken über Deutschland*, Frankfurt-on-Main, 1993

Veit-Brause, Irmline, 'Zur Kritik an der "Kritischen Geschichtswissenschaft": Tendenzwende oder Paradigmawechsel?', *GWU*, vol. 35, 1984, pp. 1-24

——— , 'Rethinking the State of the Nation', in: Joseph A. Camilleri, Anthony P. Jarvis and Albert J. Paolini (eds), *The State in Transition. Reimagining Political Space*, Boulder, 1995, pp. 59-76

Venohr, Wolfgang (ed.), *Die deutsche Einheit kommt bestimmt*, Bergisch-Gladbach, 1982

Wagner, Helmut, Schwan, Alexander and Hahn, Roland (eds), *Fragen und Antworten zur deutschen Identität*, Berlin, 1987

Weber, Hermann, 'Die DDR-Geschichtswissenschaft im Umbruch? Aufgaben der Historiker bei der Bewältigung der stalinistischen Vergangenheit', *Deutschland-Archiv*, vol. 23, 1990, pp. 1,058-70

_____ , 'Weiße Flecken in der DDR Geschichtsschreibung', *aus politik und zeitgeschichte*, 9 March 1990, pp. 3-15

Weber, Wolfgang, *Priester der Klio. Historisch-sozialwissenschaftliche Studien zur Herkunft und Karriere deutscher Historiker und zur Geschichte der Geschichtswissenschaft 1800-1970*, 2nd edn, Frankfurt-on-Main, 1987

_____ , 'The Long Reign and the Final Fall of the German Conception of History: A Historical-Sociological View', *CEH*, vol. 21, 1988, pp. 379-95

Wehler, Hans-Ulrich (ed.), *Deutsche Historiker*, 9 vols, Göttingen, 1971-82

_____ , *Preußen ist wieder chic. Politik und Polemik in zwanzig Essays*, Frankfurt-on-Main, 1983

_____ , *Deutsche Gesellschaftsgeschichte*, Munich, 1987 ff

_____ , *Aus der Geschichte lernen?*, Munich, 1988

_____ , *Die Gegenwart als Geschichte*, Munich, 1995

_____ , *Angst vor der Macht? Die Machtlust der Neuen Rechten*, Bonn, 1995

_____ (ed.), *Scheidewege der deutschen Geschichte. Von der Reformation bis zur Wende 1517-1989*, Munich, 1995

Weidenfeld, Werner (ed.), *Die Identität der Deutschen*, Bonn, 1983

_____ (ed.), *Politische Kultur und deutsche Frage. Materialien zum Staats- und Nationalbewußtsein in der BRD*, Cologne, 1989

_____ (ed.), *Deutschland. Eine Nation – doppelte Geschichte. Materialien zum deutschen Selbstverständnis*, Cologne, 1993

Weigand, Wolf Volker, *Walter Wilhelm Goetz 1867-1958. Eine biographische Studie über den Historiker, Politiker und Publizisten*, Boppard am Rhein, 1992

Weisbrod, Bernd, 'Die Wiederkehr der Krisen. Geschichtsbilder in der Wendezeit', *Blätter*, vol. 38, 1993, pp. 1,347-58

_____ , 'German Unification and the National Paradigm', *German History*, vol. 14, 1996, pp. 193-203

Weißbecker, Manfred, *Der Ort des 30. Januar 1933 – alte Schwierigkeiten und neue Hemmnisse im Umgang mit der Geschichte des Nationalsozialismus*, Jena, 1993

_____ , 'Zwischen Beharrung und neuen Grenzen. Problematisches im heutigen deutschen Zeitgeschichtsdenken', in: Ekkehard Wagner and Hannes Kaschkat (eds), *Daß Deutschland eins werde*, Lauf an der Pegnitz, 1994, pp. 133-54

Weißmann, Karlheinz, 'Die Wiederkehr eines Totgesagten: Der Nationalstaat am Ende des 20. Jahrhunderts', *aus politik und zeitgeschichte*, 2 April 1993, pp. 3-10

_____ , *Rückruf in die Geschichte. Die deutsche Herausforderung. Alte Gefahren – Neue Chancen*, 2nd rev. edn, Frankfurt-on-Main, 1993

_____ , *Der Weg in den Abgrund. Deutschland unter Hitler, 1933-1945*, Berlin, 1995

Welzer, Harald (ed.), *Nationalsozialismus und Moderne*, Tübingen, 1993

Wendt, Bernd Jürgen (ed.), *Vom schwierigen Zusammenwachsen der Deutschen. Nationale Identität und Nationalismus im 19. und 20. Jahrhundert*, Frankfurt-on-Main, 1992

Wengst, Udo (ed.), *Historiker betrachten Deutschland. Beiträge zum Vereinigungsprozeß und zur Hauptstadtdiskussion*, Bonn, 1992

_____ , 'Geschichtswissenschaft und "Vergangenheitsbewältigung" in Deutschland nach 1945 und nach 1989/90', *GWU*, vol. 46, 1995, pp. 189-205

Werner, Karl Ferdinand, *Das NS-Geschichtsbild und die deutsche Geschichtswissenschaft*, Stuttgart, 1967

Wette, Wolfram, 'Rückkehr zu "Normalität" und Weltmachtdenken. Die Renaissance des Militärischen im neuen Deutschland', *Blätter*, vol. 39, 1994, pp. 981-90

_____ , 'Sonderweg oder Normalität? Zur Diskussion um die internationale Position der Bundesrepublik', *Blätter*, vol. 41, 1996, pp. 61-70

White, Hayden, *Tropics of Discourse. Essays in Cultural Criticism*, London, 1978

Wieland, Lothar, 'Der deutsche Griff nach der Weltmacht. Die Fischer-Kontroverse in historischer Perspektive', *Blätter*, vol. 37, 1992, pp. 742-52

Willms, Bernard, *Idealismus und Nation. Zur Rekonstruktion des politischen Selbstbewußtseins der Deutschen*, Paderborn, 1986

Winkler, Heinrich August, 'Der deutsche Sonderweg. Eine Nachlese', *Merkur*, vol. 35, 1981, pp. 793-803

_____ , 'Bismarcks Schatten. Ursachen und Folgen der deutschen Katastrophe', *Die neue Gesellschaft/Frankfurter Hefte*, vol. 35, 1988, pp. 111-21

_____ , 'Ein Erneuerer der Geschichtswissenschaft. Hans Rosenberg 1904-1988', *HZ*, vol. 248, 1989, pp. 529-55

_____ , 'Abschied von einem deutschen Sonderweg. Wider die postnationale Nostalgie', *Die neue Gesellschaft/Frankfurter Hefte*, vol. 40, 1993, pp. 633-6

_____ and Kaelble, Hartmut (eds), *Nationalismus – Nationalitäten – Supranationalität*, Stuttgart, 1993

_____ and Stern, Carola (eds), *Wendepunkte deutscher Geschichte 1848 – 1990*, rev edn, Frankfurt-on-Main, 1994

_____ , 'Rebuilding of a Nation: The Germans before and after Reunification', *Daedalus*, vol. 123, 1994, pp. 107-27

Wolffsohn, Michael, 'Deutsche Symbole. Staatsname, Nationalhymne und Nationalfeiertag – und der 9. November', *Die politische Meinung*, vol. 35, 1990, pp. 23-8

_____ , *Keine Angst vor Deutschland*, rev. edn, Frankfurt-on-Main, 1992

_____ , *Ewige Schuld? 40 Jahre deutsch-jüdisch-israelische Beziehungen*, 5th edn, Munich, 1993

_____ , *Die Deutschland-Akte. Juden und Deutsche in Ost und West. Tatsachen und Legenden*, Munich, 1995

Wolfrum, Edgar, 'Diktaturen im Europa des 20. Jahrhunderts. Ein neuer zeitgeschichtlicher Förderschwerpunkt der Stiftung Volkswagenwerk', *VfZ*, vol. 40, 1992, pp. 155-8

Wucher, Albert, *Theodor Mommsen. Geschichtsschreibung und Politik*, Göttingen, 1956

Zens, Maria, 'Zur Wiederherstellung nationaler Größe im Hause Ullstein', *Blätter*, vol. 38, 1993, pp. 1,364-75

Zimmer, Mathias, 'Vorgeschichte der Wiedervereinigung? Die Regierung Kohl und die deutsche Frage vor der Wende', *ZfG*, vol. 43, 1995, pp. 247-56

Zitelmann, Rainer, Jesse, Eckart and Syring, Enrico (eds), *Die Schatten der Vergangenheit. Impulse zur Historisierung des Nationalsozialismus*, Frankfurt-on-Main, 1990

Zitelmann, Rainer, *Adenauers Gegner – Streiter für die Einheit*, Erlangen, 1991

_____, Weißmann, Karlheinz and Grossheim, Michael (eds), *Westbindung. Chancen und Risiken für Deutschland*, Frankfurt-on-Main, 1993

_____ and Prinz, Michael (ed.), *Nationalsozialismus und Modernisierung*, 2nd edn, Darmstadt, 1994

_____, *Wohin treibt unsere Republik?*, Berlin, 1995

Zmarzlik, Hans-Günter, *Wieviel Zukunft hat unsere Vergangenheit? Aufsätze und Überlegungen eines Historikers vom Jahrgang 1922*, Munich, 1970

INDEX

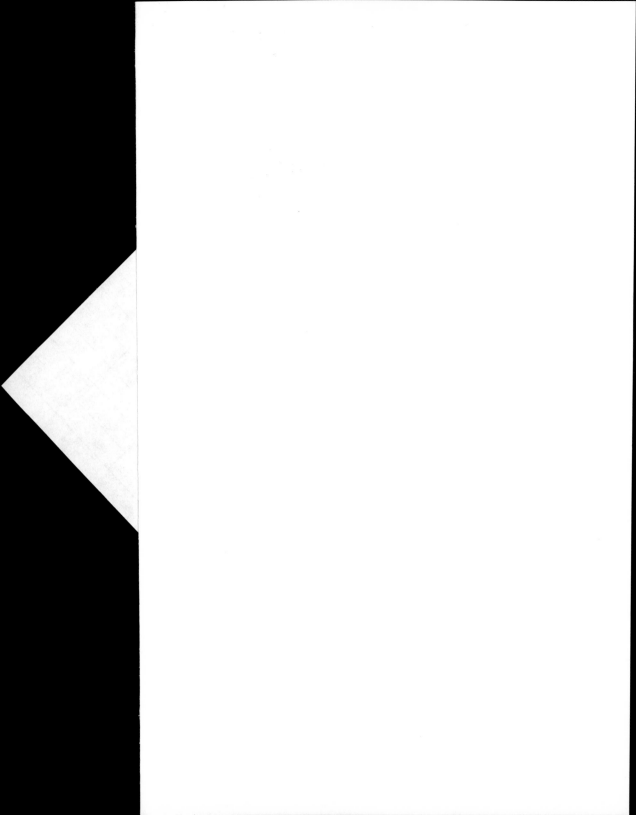

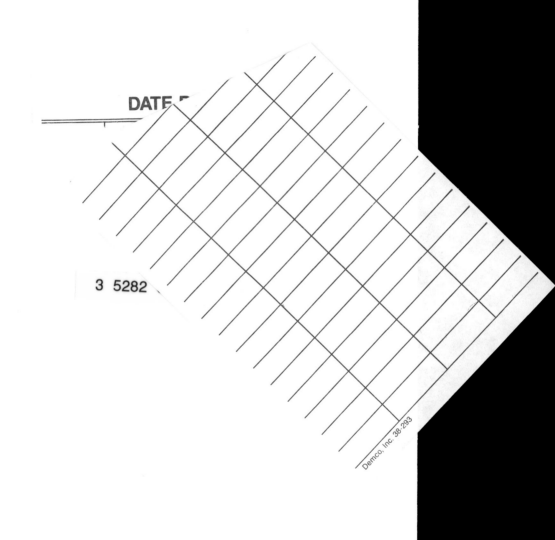

DATE

3 5282

Demco, Inc. 38-293